Introduction to Recreation Services

Sustainability for a Changing World

Introduction to Recreation Services

Sustainability for a Changing World

Karla A. Henderson

Venture Publishing, Inc.
State College, PA

Library of Congress Catalogue Card Number 2013956831
ISBN-10: 1-939476-03-8
ISBN-13: 978-1-939476-03-6

Dedicated to my mom and dad—
They taught me about hard work so I could study
and enjoy leisure

Table of Contents

List of Tables and Figures

Foreword

This textbook, *Introduction to Recreation Services: Sustainability for a Changing World*, explores the meanings of leisure for people and the importance of recreation services in society. The focus is on all sectors of the recreation services field, including public, nonprofit, and private business entities. The emphasis is on introducing students to career opportunities in recreation services and the benefits as well as challenges facing recreation professionals in a changing world. The philosophy that I unabashedly present in this book is that social, economic, and environmental sustainability concerns should underlie all recreation services. Many perspectives could be taken to provide an introduction to recreation services, but this book targets recreation services embodied in specialties such as parks and recreation, sports, tourism, event management, outdoor leadership and management, and therapeutic recreation.

Throughout this book, I refer to leisure experiences to mean primarily the outcomes that individuals receive because of their commitment of time and resources to pursue meaningful recreation activities. Recreation services are used collectively to describe the organizational structures for facilitating people's leisure. I also use the term 'sustainable recreation,' which can be defined as services that are capable of being supported, upheld, enduring, and maintainable. 'Sustainability' means to be responsible for upholding maximum social, economic, and environmental dimensions of leisure experiences and recreation services.

I believe passionately in the value of leisure to optimize human development and the potential of recreation services to facilitate social, economic, and environmental justice in communities. Inclusion and justice must be considered regardless of the sector in which services are offered. Inclusion refers to ensuring that all individuals—regardless of characteristics such as race, class, religion, physical or mental abilities, sexual identity, gender, or any other defining characteristics—have the right to leisure. Justice refers to facilitating equitable and fair recreation services for citizens as well as visitors.

This book is divided into four units, with short chapters within each unit. The first unit focuses on leisure, recreation, and society. We explore the meanings of leisure, recreation, and play and how opportunities for recreation services have evolved. In the second unit, the historical and comparative roots of leisure in society and the growth of professional recreation services are described.

Without an understanding of the past, people cannot move ahead successfully into the future to address emerging opportunities and challenges. In the third unit, a range of career opportunities in recreation services is presented. The final unit addresses issues and challenges regarding the facilitation of recreation services for sustainability.

Whether you are considering a career in some area of recreation services or just want to know more about your opportunities for awesome leisure experiences, I hope the value of leisure experiences and sustainable recreation services becomes apparent. The structured approach to facilitating leisure through recreation services now has over a century of history in the United States and around the world. A critical exploration of the meanings of leisure experiences and recreation services in society is a logical step toward the advancement of this field of study.

I am deeply indebted to many colleagues and friends in the preparation of this work. Although this book is new and not simply another edition of previous books, I have been deeply inspired by the individuals who laid the groundwork from previous books: Harold D. Meyer and Charles K. Brightbill, who I only know through history, and H. Douglas Sessoms, who was my friend, colleague, and mentor for many years. Some of the ideas for this new book came from my writing with previous University of North Carolina-Chapel Hill colleagues: Deb Bialeschki, John Hemingway, Jan Hodges, and Dana Kivel. My current colleagues at North Carolina State University have been highly supportive of this writing endeavor, including especially my Department Head, Dorothy Anderson. I also appreciate the assistance of graduate assistant Kelly McFadden. Linda Oakleaf, a former student of mine and now a faculty member at Benedict College in South Carolina, was invaluable in her assistance with the teaching materials that accompany this book. Further, I am grateful for the support of my family and friends including especially Deb Bialeschki, Leandra Bedini, Sherryl Kleinman, Kelly Myers, and the Sunday Hiking and Eating (SHE) group. Most of all, I am indebted to the professionals in recreation services who will provide the expertise and enthusiasm to promote sustainable recreation services into the future.

Acknowledgments

This book is new. However, my previous involvement in the 7th and 8th editions of earlier introductory books has greatly influenced the content of this new book with its broader focus on the sustainability of all areas of recreation services. Although new chapters have been added and all material has been updated and revised, I want to acknowledge the intellectual input from others in the 7th and 8th editions that guided my thinking for this book:

Leandra Bedini
Deb Bialeschki
Richard Gittleson
John Hemingway
Jan Hodges
Dana Kivel
Doug Sessoms

Thank you!

Chapter 1

Overview
and Contemporary Society

Leisure experiences and recreation activities are important to most people. Some people feel they have too little leisure, while others may have too much. Too little leisure may create stress and anxiety. Too much leisure can create boredom. Having time, money, and opportunities to do what one really wants to do is important and significant. Leisure is associated with an individual's well-being and the quality of life in communities.

Recreation and leisure are major forces in the economic and social life in the United States. Billions of dollars are expended for vacation trips, health club memberships, golf fees, concerts, weekend outings, and other forms of recreation. Statistics suggest that by 2020, over 40% of the jobs in the United States will be in the area of leisure and tourism. This figure is expected to grow to 50% by 2050 (Begun, 2000).

This textbook about sustainable recreation services is focused on the growing and changing roles of recreation services in U.S. society. Leisure and recreation are experienced around the world and many commonalities exist across countries and cultures. However, this book intentionally addresses the United States and the challenges of sustaining recreation services. 'Recreation' connotes all sectors of this field, including public, nonprofit, and private business opportunities. This book affirms that underlying sustainable recreation services is the mandate to tackle the meanings of leisure and to ensure inclusion and justice as vital service components in contributing to the quality of life in communities.

Sustainable recreation services are a means to optimize human development and create communities that can maintain and improve health and well-being for all residents and visitors. Recreation services, however, are not inherently good unless measures are taken to ensure sustainable and inclusive outputs and outcomes. Sustainable recreation includes activities that address social needs and interests by considering economic implications while preserving the environment and respecting people's lives.

Inclusion and social justice must be considered regardless of the sector in which services are offered.

Work and leisure are interrelated activities. The exact nature of this relationship has been the subject of speculation for years among economists, sociologists, and other social and behavioral scientists. Over 30 years ago, a leisure society was predicted where people would work no longer than it took to maintain their desired lifestyle, most workers would be content with subsistence, and most people would stop working when their incomes rose beyond that subsistence level (U.S. Department of Labor, 1980). That expectation has not held true since many workers seem to enjoy the consumption of more goods made possible by more work and higher wages (Schor, 1991). At the same time, Americans today generally *perceive* that they have less leisure than desired regardless of how much they work.

This perceived scarcity of leisure is noteworthy since leisure experiences and recreation activities are valued as desirable opportunities for creative expression and life satisfaction. Most Americans want a quality of life that includes adequate free time and meaningful activities. The economy grows on the assumption that people work for pay and spend their money on subsistence and recreation activities. Therefore, those recreation opportunities need to be diverse, well-managed, and successful in meeting human needs as well as people's free-time desires and interests. In this first unit of the book, we explore the relationships of leisure, recreation, and society, which lead to opportunities for recreation services in the United States.

Contemporary Society

Leisure experiences and recreation services are a product of industrialization as well as the desire that people have to enjoy activities during their free time. The Industrial Age established that because people spent specific time at work (i.e., they worked a particular number of hours each day), they wanted and believed that they had earned time for enjoyable activities during nonwork time or leisure. A system of services and activities in the public, nonprofit, and private business sectors evolved to meet needs, expectations, and desires of workers and their families. This recreation-services system in the United States began as a social movement during the early 1900s, and the evolution of these services continues into the 21st century.

According to the National Recreation and Park Association (NRPA; the largest national organization addressing public parks, recreation, and conservation), nearly every county, city, and/or town in the United States has organized public recreation and parks services available to its citizens.

Four out of five Americans use their local parks or recreation systems and 70% have a park or recreation facility within walking distance of their home. Billions of tax dollars are spent each year for the acquisition, construction, and operation of public recreation and park programs, areas, and facilities in cities and counties across the United States (http://www.nrpa. org/Content.aspx?id=669).

Nonprofit organizations and private commercial business offerings also are common in most communities and comprise numerous additional opportunities within the field of recreation services. Few industries, except maybe technology, have expanded more rapidly in the past century than those organizations and businesses that cater to people's recreation behavior. The demand for recreation equipment, vacation areas, and other recreation products and services sometimes exceeds the supply of goods and opportunities. Ball caps, tech t-shirts, sweatshirts, microfiber vests, and running shoes are standard wearing apparel for millions of youth and adults during their recreation. Millions of people attend sporting events and watch sports on TV.

Although leisure will not likely replace the importance of work in U.S. society, many factors influence leisure behavior and the choices people make about their recreation pursuits. Social, economic, and environmental changes influence how people in the United States think about and value their time and sense of well-being. These values translate into providing recreation services in the public, nonprofit, and private business sectors.

Changing Social Structures

The face of the United States, as well as those of many other countries, is changing. The Baby Boom Generation (i.e., people born 1946–1964) is reaching retirement age and the Millennials (i.e., Generation Y; individuals born between about 1982 and 2002) are redefining the relationship between work and leisure. The definition of family is widening with multiple structures. Unfortunately, the economic gaps between the *haves* and the *have nots* seem to be growing. The changing roles of women and the acknowledgment that traditional minorities will undoubtedly become the majority of the population in the United States during the 21st century are important to note. The ready access to technology and the proliferation of social and digital media is changing the way people communicate. In addition, the recognition that climate change has specific implications for work and leisure cannot be discounted. Some of these changing situations are useful to highlight, since they have implications for people's leisure and the delivery of recreation services.

Family Structure and Income

Society appears to be less stable in many ways and although family structures have changed, some equilibrium has occurred. For example, between 1970 and 1990, the proportion of children in two-parent families decreased from 85% to a little over 70%. In 2004, that percentage remained at about 70%. One in four children lives with a single parent (Roberts, 2008). Although negative associations often exist for children in single-parent families, the great majority of these children do well (Zill, Morrison, & Coiro, 1993). The percentage of children living in two-parent families differs by race and ethnicity with 87% of Asian-Americans, 78% of non-Hispanic Whites, 68% of Latinos, and 38% of African-Americans in traditional two-parent families.

Each year, the Census Bureau calculates a poverty rate based on a family's pretax income compared to poverty thresholds. For example, a single individual under age 65 years has a threshold of $11,344. Two adults with two children have a threshold of $22,113 (http://www.npc. umich.edu/poverty/). In 2010, 15% of all persons in the United States lived in poverty. The poverty rate in 2010 was the highest since records have been kept for over 50 years (http://www.census.gov/newsroom/releases/ archives/income_wealth/cb11-157.html). However, since the late 1960s, the poverty rate for people over 65 years has fallen dramatically. The poverty rate for people in households headed by single women (32%) remains significantly higher than the overall poverty rate.

The poverty rates also differ substantially by race and ethnicity. Poverty rates for African-Americans and Latinos exceed the national average. In 2010, 27% of African Americans and 27% of Latinos were poor, compared to 10% of non-Hispanic Whites and 12% of Asian-Americans. Although children represent only 24% of the population, they comprise 36% of the poor population (http://www.census.gov/newsroom/releases/archives/income _wealth/cb11-157.html).

Median incomes are a good way to assess the social and economic context of society. These statistics enable measuring the ability of a family at the midpoint of the income distribution to purchase goods and services required to raise children and have a desired quality of life. Real median household income was $49,445 in 2010, which represented a 2% decline from 2009. Since 2007, median household income has declined 6% (from $52,823) and is 7% below the median household income peak ($53,252) that occurred in 1999 (http://www.census.gov/newsroom/releases/archives/

income_wealth/cb11-157.html). The economic recession that started in 2008 has had a huge impact on the spending power in many households.

Despite the high unemployment rate in the United States during the late 2000s, women have continued to be employed in greater numbers. Women, in fact, are on the verge of outnumbering men in the workforce for the first time (http://www.usatoday.com/news/nation/2009-09-02-womenwork_N.htm). In 2009, women held half of the nation's jobs. This high represented trends that have been ongoing for decades. Women have tended to be in jobs (e.g., healthcare, education, and government) that have not felt the impact of the recent recession as severely as construction and manufacturing. Women will not likely outnumber men in the workforce, but equality in the workforce is reflecting the culmination of many cultural changes, especially regarding how families operate and how children are raised.

Baby Boomers are continuing to impact society. This generation waited longer to have children than did their parents. When they did start families, they were often smaller than past families. The growth in numbers of school-age children is slowing during the first two decades of the 21st century, but the median age of the population continues to increase. The oldest Baby Boomers are moving into their retirement years and will continue to be a population bulge. These older adults are more active, have more money, and are living longer than previous generations did.

Health Conditions

Even though people are living longer, health issues are of central concern. One major health issue is the prevalence of overweight and obese children and adults. Part of the energy equation (i.e., energy intake = energy output) relates to people being less physically active. This concern has received significant attention as more medical data link being overweight with hypertension, coronary heart disease, diabetes, and some cancers. In 2010, one third of all adults were obese, according to the Centers for Disease Control and Prevention (http://www.cdc.gov/obesity/data/adult.html). Begun (2000) predicted a decade ago that at the current rate, by mid-21st century, over three fourths of all males and females in the United States will be overweight, with over one third classified as obese. Unfortunately, this prediction has come to fruition. Further, in 2008, medical costs associated with obesity were estimated at $147 billion each year. The medical costs paid for people who are obese were $1,429 higher per year than costs for normal-weight individuals.

Children have also become fatter. An alarming study purports that, for the first time in over two centuries, the current generation of children may have shorter life expectancies than their parents. The rapid rise in childhood obesity may shorten children's lifespan by two to five years (http://www.nytimes.com/2005/03/17/health/17obese.html). Almost one third of the children between the ages of 2 and 19 years are overweight, and 17% of those are classified as obese. The number of obese children has at least doubled since 1980, and some studies suggest that the rate has tripled or even quadrupled. The sad aspect is that 85% of obese children are likely to remain obese as adults, unless something changes drastically in their lives.

Overweight and obesity are a function of caloric imbalance. More calories are consumed than are expended through physical activity. The Centers for Disease Control and Prevention has reported that 80% of adults do not achieve the recommended amount of regular physical activity (http://www.healthypeople.gov/2020/topicsobjectives2020/overview.aspx?topicid=33). Inactivity increases with age and is more common among women than men and among those individuals with lower income and less education compared to higher income or greater education. In addition, over half of young people aged 12–21 years are not vigorously active on a regular basis. Physical activity tends to decline dramatically during adolescence, with female adolescents becoming more physically inactive than males.

Attitudes about the Future

Health issues include more than just physical health. They also include mental health and what individuals believe about their social environments. A study conducted in 2009 examined U.S. high school students' views about the future (http://www.voanews.com/content/a-13-2008-08-28-voa41-66759882/563487.html). The study indicated that U.S. teenagers were less hopeful than they were five years ago about society's ability to address critical problems such as the economy and global warming. However, these young people remained optimistic about their own futures and their potential to succeed in life. Almost two thirds said they were confident that they would be able to achieve their life goals.

American teens also indicated in this survey that they knew they needed to prepare for an increasingly competitive global economy. One third said the most important school subjects were science and technology. However, many high school students said they used the Internet more for entertainment and social networking than for researching their homework. Almost one third of the surveyed teens said online bullying was a greater threat than the physical bullying already taking place in many U.S. high schools.

Issues surrounding the social environment for people also related to environmental concerns. The survey showed a rise in American teens' interest in voting and playing a role in issues of national importance including the environment. The survey showed that 72% of American teens believed global warming is an urgent or serious problem.

Environmental Concerns

Both young and old are concerned about the environment. Some people are far more concerned than are others. Most environmental concerns are not new but little progress has been made in addressing some of them. An alarmist concern in the 1970s with environmental degradation led to some changes in federal and state laws. For example, some endangered species facing extinction in the latter half of the twentieth century have now experienced some repopulation as concerns about habitat preservation rose. However, many people remain complacent about environmental issues. Further, in difficult economic times, the tension between economic development and environmental sustainability often rises to the surface.

Climate change is an area that has received increased attention in the early-21st century (http://webecoist.com/2008/08/18/most-important-environmental-issues-of-today/). Global warming has concerned scientists for decades, but Al Gore brought the concern to a wider audience with his controversial film, *An Inconvenient Truth*. The melting polar ice caps, catastrophic weather, and threatened ecosystems suggest that climate change is real and is a result of the production of greenhouse gases, mainly stemming from carbon dioxide and methane.

Clean water is also an environmental commodity that is in short supply. In the United States, many people do not think about this issue but one in five humans across the globe does not have access to safe water (http://webecoist.com/2008/08/18/most-important-environmental-issues-of-today/). Land management is also a concern that may be particularly important to recreation services providers. Little land is left that is undeveloped and all land seems to be threatened by light and noise pollution.

Other environmental issues have also been described, such as renewable energy, energy dependence, fracking, biofuels, and offshore drilling, to mention only a few. Landfill waste is an issue that often is overlooked, since many people have taken for granted the throwaway society in which we live. Unfortunately, people have come to consume resources in a way that is simply not sustainable. This lifestyle is not healthy or maintainable given the earth's resources.

Values as a Basis for Change

These statistics paint a picture of a changing society and the challenges of living sustainable lifestyles. The future is bound to the social and personal values that are expressed. A person's value system gives direction for choosing between alternative forms of behavior and the relative importance of any experience. Every society develops a social value system and socializes young people to honor what is deemed acceptable and essential. As societies evolve, value systems may also change. The questions of how individuals shape society and how society shapes individuals relate to these values. Each person has perceptions and beliefs about how life ought to be lived, which results in specific behaviors. For example, social drinking is acceptable in some groups but not in others. Some groups place a premium on family activity, while others stress individual pursuits and interests. A multitude of personal value structures exist, yet most reflect the dominant values of cultures and the U.S. society.

The United States has become an urban society with an urban value system. The values of conspicuous consumption (e.g., buying products to show how wealthy one is whether needed or not) and conspicuous display (e.g., wearing name-brand clothing), as well as most people's desire for immediate gratification, have had their effects on personal and social behaviors and the concomitant attitudes about recreation and leisure. For example, most people expect as much convenience as possible in what recreation activities they undertake (e.g., Wi-Fi in parks, plenty of available parking).

Time, and the lack of it, has had great impact on values and the changing American lifestyle. Time traditionally has been measured and valued in its economic sense. Labor is paid for by the hour, wages by the week, and pensions according to the number of years worked. Time off is something most workers look forward to, whether as vacations or over weekends. People are time conscious and want to make the most of their time.

Even though time for leisure is valued, and is often considered a right to be enjoyed, the work ethic remains at the heart of the American value system. Most Americans believe that people should earn leisure by working hard, being self-supporting, and taking pride in achievements. Some people in the United States disdain people who are homeless or on welfare because they are not a part of the employment system. Career and economic success is valued. People believe that those who use their skills wisely to advance the economy should be rewarded. Unfortunately, some people lack the physical or mental abilities to develop or use their skills to contribute economically to society.

Many of these values have shaped changes in leisure interests as well as recreation services. Americans have approached the provision of recreation services in much the same way they have handled educational and welfare programs. Nonprofit and private business resources add to what the government can supply. To meet the changing interests and needs of society, recreation services professionals must use the information available about demographic characteristics, values, and behaviors to facilitate sustainable recreation opportunities to promote enjoyment as well as the quality of life in communities.

Challenges for Leisure

Although enjoyment and happiness are important, leisure experiences and recreation services are not always highly valued. The work ethic dominates in the United States. Work is sacred, and most other activities have been second to economic productivity. As noted earlier, when economic times are difficult, leisure may be viewed as a threat to economic growth. For example, George Bernard Shaw said, "a perpetual holiday is a good working definition of hell." In addition, Schor (1991) noted:

> The danger of increasing leisure time voluntarily is that it could replace one inequity with another—as inequality of income creates inequality of time. The poorest third would work just as many hours as ever—or more, as more work became available—while the top two-thirds would gradually become a leisured class. The people who would gain free time would be those who already had the financial resources that make it possible—education, homes, and a bank account. They would be mainly white and mainly upper and middle class.

A *leisure society* has been predicted for many years but has been slow to materialize because most people really do not want such a society. The 40-hour workweek has been accepted as the standard, although some people question whether the workweek is really 40 hours since people now spend more time traveling to and from the job than they did in former years. Some people work more than 40 hours a week in their professional jobs, while other people spend some of their work time socializing with others and using the Internet for personal tasks. Further, with the increase in technology, people are doing more work at home at all times of the day. Technology has also enabled people to be connected to work all the time if they wish and has raised the expectation that if one can work faster, he or she should also get more work done. For many women in the paid workforce, more hours continue to be spent in a *second shift* doing housework after spending the day at work (Hoschild & Machung, 1990). In addition, the number of temporary or part-time workers who may hold two or more jobs has risen. Without benefits, these workers have to work much longer than if they had one full-time job.

Yet other scholars (e.g., Robinson & Godbey, 1999) have argued that people have more leisure today than in the past. A problem arises, however, when people's time diaries show they have more leisure, but they do not feel like they do. Many people feel stressed and under great pressure and do not recognize opportunities for leisure. Further, because of technology like smartphones and tablet computers, many people can be plugged into work 24/7. Scheduling recreation opportunities has become increasingly difficult for many families with two adults working, children in year-round schools, and multigenerational family responsibilities. When people have free time, they are frequently too exhausted to seek out opportunities other than watching TV. Television watching is generally *not* perceived as leisure by a majority of people.

The U.S. Congress enacted legislation in 1968 designating that certain holidays (e.g., Memorial Day, Veterans Day, Martin Luther King, Jr. Day) were to be celebrated on Mondays, thereby giving federal employees several long weekends each year. However, the United States still ranks below almost all industrial nations in the average number of vacation days granted workers. The U.S. average of 20 days of holiday and vacation per year is half the number taken by workers in most European countries. Although movements such as the Take Back Your Time (http://www.timeday.org/) initiative have been instigated to challenge the epidemic of overwork—as well as over-scheduling and time famine that now threaten health, families and relationships, communities, and the environment—progress has been slow.

Nevertheless, changes are occurring in society. These changes have a direct impact on how people use their time and resources, which may influence their perceptions and behaviors around leisure. The changes in society and the way that people choose to use their time and money have many implications for recreation services in all sectors, which are explored in the next chapter.

Reflection Questions

1. What do you think are the significant changes influencing leisure today in U.S. society?

2. What social, economic, and environmental changes are most likely to affect your leisure in the future?

3. As a young adult, what are your positive as well as negative beliefs and attitudes about the future?

4. What would a leisure society look like? Is that something that should be a goal in the United States? What would be its value and limitations?

5. Why do people work? Getting a paycheck is certainly important, but what might be other reasons?

6. How do you value work and leisure in your life? Does your family make these same value distinctions? What relationship do you hope leisure and work will play in your life when you begin your professional career?

Chapter 2

Overview of Recreation Services

Recreation services facilitate a wide range of opportunities for people to meet their leisure interests and needs. Many career opportunities exist within these recreation services. Regardless of the opportunity offered, the sustainability of the services must be considered based on social, economic, and environmental viability.

The purpose of this book is to provide a foundation for appreciating and understanding the field of recreation services. Therefore, several underlying premises are addressed that guide this introduction to recreation services. First, what differentiates the field of recreation services from other fields and the tie that binds the recreation specialties (e.g., resources management, therapeutic recreation, tourism, sports management, outdoor leadership) is the connection to leisure and leisure behavior. Although many of the skills needed to be a successful recreation professional might be similar to what professionals in other fields (e.g., business managers, environmental planners, therapists) do, the core of recreation services addresses the behavioral choices people make regarding their free time and leisure.

Second, recreation services is a broad field of study but the people who are academically educated to lead and manage these services are professionals. Therefore, recreation services is a profession because it meets the basic tenets necessary for a profession: alliance with a social concern, professional associations, a specialized body of knowledge (associated with academic majors and credentialing), and a code of ethics. In this book, 'recreation professionals' refers to the leaders and facilitators of recreation services. These people have many titles relative to the area of application such as event manager, park ranger, community center director, or recreation therapist, and they all can be considered professionals. For continuity in this book, I use 'recreation professionals' to refer to people across the profession, who may have many different job titles.

Third, people in this field sometimes refer to recreation and leisure interchangeably. The definitions and conceptualizations of leisure and recreation are discussed later in this book but in general I refer to leisure as a behavior and to recreation as activities. Recreation professionals facilitate activities that might be associated with sports, parks and natural resources, special events, arts, and other areas that are discussed in more detail in this book. Leisure and recreation certainly overlap. In fact, 'leisure services' was once a term used frequently. However, today I believe that 'recreation services' is the best descriptor when talking about the provision or facilitation of recreation activities regardless of the specialty area. Recreation services enable leisure experiences and outcomes. Recreation professionals do not provide leisure but they provide opportunities that facilitate leisure outcomes. This distinction may seem like a fine line but may be important to consider as you read further and consider a career in a specialty in this field.

Fourth, leisure and recreation services should be a force for positive benefits or outcomes. What is meant by 'positive' and who gets to determine what is positive is a matter of values. Leisure experiences as well as recreation services should be edifying, but they also can be detrimental to personal, social, community, and environmental health. Leisure experiences and recreation services are not inherently good. The recreation experiences offered can be positive, however, if they are intentionally focused on the well-being of individuals and the sustainability of the services, as well as the sustainability of the communities in which the services occur. Students interested in careers in recreation services must be able to advocate for the benefits and goodness that recreation services can provide. However, being reflective and sometimes critical is necessary if recreation services are to be a positive force in society.

Fifth, this book is an overview of leisure behavior and recreation services. Other textbooks address leisure philosophy and theory as well as specialties such as sports management, natural resource management, therapeutic recreation, or outdoor leadership in much greater detail. This book is introductory. I hope it interests you in a way that you will want to explore leisure in greater depth and consider a possible career in recreation services.

Sixth, the sustainability of recreation services in a changing world is the underlying foundation of this book. I define sustainability, as most scholars do, as including social, economic, and environmental aspects. The typical definition of sustainability means that something such as recreation services can be supported, upheld, and enduring. Some people believe sustainability means maintaining the status quo but I do not view sustainability that narrowly. I envision sustainability as a means for continual improvement. Sustainability related to recreation services means that opportunities for leisure experiences will be available for today's generations and generations to come. In essence, sustainable recreation includes activities that address social needs and interests by considering economic implications while preserving the environment and respecting people's lives. Sustainable recreation services also mean that opportunities are inclusive and just (i.e., fair) for individuals.

Finally, I refer to sectors and specialties related to recreation services throughout this book. Recreation services include three basic subsets of providers referred to as sectors: public services, nonprofit agencies, and private businesses. Each type of provider has its own features and mission, although overlap does occur. Specialties include those specific activity areas that are part of recreation services and that offer professional career opportunities. As you will see in this book, these specialties have a broad range but also share similarities. Each of these specialties is described in Unit Three. This chapter focuses on an overview of the three sectors where recreation services occur.

Characteristics of the Sectors

Together, the public, nonprofit, and private business sectors provide the system for meeting the leisure interests of individuals in communities. In the United States, the recreation as well as the parks and conservation movements began at about the same time, over 100 years ago. Many nonprofit organizations and private businesses also began about this same time. Recreation services emanated from a concern for the social and educational needs of people. The ways that services have been facilitated over time has changed, but the focus on the importance related to improving children's and adults' well-being and the quality of life in communities has not changed.

The public sector includes recreation and park opportunities that are available to all individuals and that are financed primarily through revenues obtained from taxation. Nonprofit agencies operate mainly through fees and donations and serve the interests and needs of individuals associated with the organizations. Private businesses aim to offer specific opportunities targeted for people who are willing to pay. Table 2.1 provides a number of comparisons that are discussed further in this book. Please note, however, that while distinctions exist among these sectors, they also overlap in many ways.

Table 2.1 Comparison among Elements of Recreation and Leisure Services

	Public	Nonprofit	Private
Philosophy of Service	Enrichment of the life of the total community by providing opportunities for the meaningful use of leisure.	Enrichment of the life of participating members by offering opportunities for meaningful use of leisure, frequently with emphasis on the group and individual.	Attempt to satisfy public demand for recreation experiences and services in an effort to produce profit.
Objectives of Service	To provide recreation opportunities contributing to the social, physical, educational, cultural, and general well-being of the community.	To provide activities that appeal to members that provide opportunities for close group association with an emphasis on citizenship, behavior, and social values.	To provide activities or services that will appeal to customers and to meet competition and net a profit while serving the public.
Type of Agencies	Governmental units (federal, state, county, and local) such as park and recreation departments, recreation and park districts, and state park departments.	Boy Scouts, Girl Scouts, Camp Fire, "Y" organizations, tennis clubs, swim clubs, environmental groups, neighborhood recreation associations.	Corporations, franchises, partnerships, and private ownership (e.g., resorts, theme parks, and professional sports).
Finance	Primarily by taxes, but also by gifts, grants, trust funds, fees, and charges.	By gifts, grants, endowments, donations, fund-raising drives, and membership fees.	By investment of the owner or promoters with users who pay admission and charges.
Facility Examples	Community buildings, parks (national, state, local), athletic fields, playgrounds, playfields, stadiums, camps, beaches, museums, zoos, and golf courses.	Community centers, youth centers, athletic facilities, play areas, clubs, camps, and aquatic areas.	Theaters, clubs, bars, night clubs, race tracks, bowling lanes, amusement parks, and stadiums.
Leadership	Professionally prepared individuals provide and manage comprehensive recreation programs. Part-time staff and volunteers are also used.	Professionally prepared individuals provide programs, frequently on a social group-work basis. Part-time staff and volunteers are also used.	Professionally prepared business and sales-oriented personnel design and manage services to produce a profit, in compliance with state and local laws.
Membership	Unlimited and open to all.	Limited to some extent by organizational mission and membership requirements.	Limited generally by economics to participants who pay for the service or product.

For clarification, I use the term *nonprofit* in this book, although often *not-for-profit* is used. Some differences exist between the two words, but they are generally used interchangeably. I use nonprofit because it broadly refers to an organization established for purposes other than making money beyond what is needed to support that organization. Any profits made in these organizations are used to further the organization. As discussed in detail later, examples of nonprofit groups include youth-serving organizations (e.g., Girls Scouts), amateur athletic leagues, social clubs, and charitable organizations.

The recreation services that focus on making a profit usually are referred to as *private businesses*. They have been traditionally called *commercial organizations* in the recreation services field. However, I believe the term 'private business' encompasses a broader genre of services, as discussed in Unit Three. Private businesses such as bars, saloons, and pubs, for example, provide recreation and have been around much longer than public or nonprofit services.

The roles of recreation services can be viewed in two ways. One perspective, often associated with a facilities/space (i.e., park) approach, suggests that recreation professionals should be primarily concerned with the management of selected areas or facilities so people can enjoy recreation pursuits. For example, an agency provides an opportunity (e.g., a park) and the participant plans and directs his/her own leisure activity (e.g., goes for a run). The second view, the program/activities (i.e., recreation) approach, acknowledges the responsibility and opportunities within public recreation agencies, nonprofit organizations, and private businesses to develop and administer recreation activity programming. For example, an agency would direct or schedule activities for participants or tourists such as classes, tours, events, or sports leagues. Both of these roles (i.e., facilities/space and program/activities) are evident in the specialties within the field of recreation services.

When you ask people what they do for recreation, they typically answer with some activity. People have accepted certain activities as recreation, especially those activities that are structured for enjoyment during their free time. More often than not, the basic skills for these activities were learned during childhood and are enjoyed on the weekend, after work or school, or on a holiday. Classes to learn recreation skills, sports tournaments, and social occasions such as festivals and performances are typically described as organized or structured recreation services.

The public has generally supported the view that governmental entities should provide facilities and space for recreation activities available to every member of the community. Included in this public mandate is the development and maintenance of natural resources, the provision of programs and services, and the promotion and care of cultural activities and historic sites. However, citizens expect and rely on the nonprofit and private business sectors to meet other remaining recreation interests that exist in communities.

Recreation Services Providers

Great strides were made during the last half century of the 20th century to establish recreation services as an academic area of study and a professional field with distinct characteristics and social responsibilities. Recreation professionals are not physical educators, social workers, or physical therapists, although they may work closely with these other professions. Recreation professionals are, however, knowledgeable about human development, economic and community development, program development, and administration and management. Professional status is enhanced by educational background, expertise in managing organizations, and the public's perceptions and respect for the services that are provided.

Individuals who manage, lead, or facilitate recreation services are generally referred to as recreation professionals. However, many different people with varying educational levels and degrees as well as job duties comprise recreation services. In occupational indices, the government refers to these individuals as recreation workers. The duties and tasks that recreation workers perform are critical in all service sectors, but not all these responsibilities require professional education.

Further, recreation professionals have a plethora of possible titles. Just a few examples might be parks and recreation director, superintendent of parks, facilities manager, sports director, special populations coordinator, recreation therapist, chief executive officer, golf professional, park ranger, aquatics coordinator, fitness director, camp director, outdoor adventure leader, events manager, and convention bureau manager, to mention only a few. All of these titles can be found in every sector. Regardless of the title, a recreation professional is educated and prepared to be employed to further the goals of recreation services related to areas of specialty.

In summary, the facilitation of recreation services occurs in public, nonprofit, and private business organizations that have somewhat different mandates and organizational structures. Specialties are available within each of the sectors. Further, each of these specialties offers numerous career opportunities. In the next chapter, the foundational bases of leisure, recreation, and play is discussed to better understand why the goals and outcomes of recreation services are important and valuable in the United States as well as across the world.

Reflection Questions

1. What recreation services have you used in the past? What differences have you noticed in the ways that different sectors might provide services?

2. Do you believe that recreation services should be called a profession? How would you argue that it should or should not have professional status?

3. Public, nonprofit, and private business sectors have different structures. What characteristics might be common to all of them?

4. Based on what you have read to this point, do you believe that leisure and leisure behavior are the glue that holds specialties within recreation services together? What challenges exist if leisure is the glue? What challenges exist if leisure is not the glue? Do you see another commonality that might also be considered?

5. Leisure may not always be a positive force in people's lives. Why might some people believe leisure is positive while others do not share this belief?

Chapter 3

Conceptualizing Leisure and Recreation

Some Christians might argue that the idea of leisure has existed since Adam and Eve were in the Garden of Eden (the "curse" that God put on them was to toil instead of to leisure). However, the contemporary notion of leisure grew from the modern industrial age, and the definitions and meanings of leisure have continued to expand.

Leisure can be described in many ways, and that variety of descriptions can lead to misunderstandings. People go about their routine lives every day and often do not think about what leisure means. They know when they have it and when they don't have it. What it is might range from simply "doing nothing" to having a peak or life-changing experience on a wilderness trip.

Many *leisures* seem to exist. Saying leisures rather than leisure might be more descriptive of the ubiquity of ideas about what leisure is. In addition, ideas about leisure differ greatly between individuals and within and between cultures. Although the term 'leisure' is used throughout this book, recognize that it has many meanings, as you will see in this chapter. Nevertheless, as "slippery" as defining leisure may seem, the process of considering its meanings is essential to understanding its significance and importance related to recreation services. Scholars have offered several widely varying definitions and conceptualizations of leisure.

Sometimes students who study leisure and recreation services conclude that no one really agrees on how to define leisure. This conclusion can be positive because it underlines how leisure is a highly personal experience that may defy definition. On the other hand, understanding what leisure means can allow recreation professionals to better facilitate opportunities that will be considered leisure by participants. Further, to do research about leisure requires that definitions are operationalized.

Nevertheless, as someone once told me, *finding* leisure is much more important for people than *defining* it. Most people would probably agree.

However, professionals interested in the connections between leisure experiences and recreation services must have some sense of what leisure is, what it means to people, and how recreation professionals can facilitate opportunities to help people find leisure in their experiences. Professionals also should understand what recreation means, although this term is more concrete since most people agree that recreation relates to activities that may be active or sedentary. As noted in the previous chapter, recreation services professionals aim to enable opportunities (e.g., activities, facilities, spaces, programs, tours, tournaments, interventions) for leisure experiences. Thus, the purpose of this chapter is to introduce the definitions, meanings, and conceptualizations of leisure, recreation, and play. Play is discussed in more detail in the next chapter.

Distinctions among Leisure, Recreation, and Play

'Leisure' and 'recreation' are frequently used interchangeably, particularly as they connote activity. If people are asked what they do in their leisure, they will sometimes give you the same response as when you ask what they do for recreation. Yet 'leisure' and 'recreation' are not necessarily synonymous. Some distinctions may be helpful to make since leisure is frequently misunderstood.

As noted in the previous chapter, recreation services have sometimes been called leisure services. The name changed largely because leisure often connoted frivolity, lack of structure, and amorphousness, and these connotations marginalized it, especially compared to other services in a community such as police and fire protection. Recreation generally is associated with activities that are voluntary, organized, socially redeeming, and fun that occur during free time. For these reasons, the term 'recreation services' (rather than 'leisure services') is more contemporary, easily understood, and descriptive of the variety of specialties that it encompasses.

For the most part, however, the distinction between leisure and recreation is seldom an issue for people. However, professionals in this field of recreation services should understand and be able to explain the meanings of the language that is used. Leisure relates to individual behaviors and experiences that usually bring enjoyment and that represent relative freedom of choice and intrinsic motivation. Recreation includes activities pursued for enjoyment as well as for personal and social benefits. Play is pleasurable, spontaneous, self-expressive, and can range from purposeless disorganized activity to complex involvements (e.g., digital games). Play is quite similar to leisure and recreation, but has been more often associated with children. Many adults, however, like to be spontaneous and find "childlike play" a refreshing break from the structure and reality of everyday worlds. More about play is discussed in the next chapter.

Leisure has traditionally been defined in three ways: time, activity, and state of mind. Leisure as free time is contrasted to work time or unobligated time. Leisure described as activity relates to what people do for enjoyment or fun, which is quite synonymous with definitions of recreation. State of being, intrinsic enjoyment, and perceived freedom and choice offer a definition of leisure as a psychological experience or state of mind. Additional approaches can also conceptualize leisure in other ways, as described later in this chapter.

Leisure as Time

Time-based definitions of leisure appeared over a century ago because of the transition to the modern industrial organization of work. The motivation to work was assumed to be the desire for wages received in exchange for spending a specified time in a specified place. Leisure came to be defined as time when people were not paid, away from the workplace, and in control of their own activities.

This definition of leisure as free time separate from work reflects two important elements of paid work: the distinction between work time and nonwork time, and the separation of paid work from other life activities. To define leisure as free time, then, is actually to define it as what it is not (i.e., it is *not* work), rather than as what it is.

Within the notion of time, leisure also has been described as unobligated time. 'Unobligated time' denotes non-paid work but also suggests that obligations in life such as personal care, child care, social support, housekeeping, and other similar activities require time that takes away from the potential for leisure.

Early economists who regarded leisure as a threat to economic stability were among the first to define leisure as non-paid time and the opposite of paid time at work. One problem with this definition was, and continues to be, the unspoken assumption that only paid work away from the home has value. The definition overlooks socially vital activities like childrearing, household management, personal care, and community volunteering. Since women traditionally perform many of these activities, this definition often excludes their contributions and the structures of their time. These economic-based definitions would also connote that anyone who does not do paid work cannot have leisure.

Leisure as free time continues to be an important definition because time is a prerequisite for most activities. However, free time as a simple measurable way to describe leisure raises questions to consider in understanding the meanings of leisure. Some questions relate to the distribution of work and leisure.

How much time is spent working compared to being *at work* is an aspect to consider. Although individuals in some jobs may spend eight hours at work, the amount of time they are actually working sans personal Internet time, breaks, and office interaction may not constitute work. Numerous examples exist today in large companies of work time spent in purposeful "fun" activities among (mainly pink- and white-collar) workers to increase morale (i.e., food functions, birthday parties, and casual Fridays) and make workers more productive. These activities also blend work and leisure.

Sometimes work and leisure also are hard to separate because they may offer some of the same intrinsic outcomes. For example, when an individual really loves his or her job, it may feel like leisure irrespective of time commitments. Changes in the workplace such as flexible work schedules as well as electronic communications also may blur the lines between work time and free time.

Nevertheless, time is a necessary and important conceptualization attached to leisure. Many people feel they never have enough time in their lives. Many people feel time stressed. However, only examining hours attached to leisure leaves out the meanings associated with priorities for time use, opportunities available for leisure, the perceived and actual amount of time available, how an individual feels about the value of his/her time, and social mores (e.g., guilt) that may play into the enjoyment that might be associated with leisure.

Leisure and Recreation as Activity

Leisure is defined as activity that is pursued for its own sake and for enjoyment or fun. Leisure as activity means the same as recreation to many people. Leisure activities or recreation can be categorized into activity sets or clusters of activities sharing important characteristics (Goodale & Godbey, 1988). Examples of activity sets include competitive sports, cooperative games, outdoor endeavors, cultural pursuits, and socializing. Table 3.1 shows a list of activities that adults said they participated in during

Table 3.1 Adult Participation in Selected Leisure Activities by Percentage: 2010

Activity	Percent Participating*
Adult education courses	7.3
Attend auto shows	8.5
Attend art galleries or shows	9.2
Attend classical music/opera performances	4.3
Attend country music performances	4.9
Attend dance performances	4.4
Attend horse races	2.9
Attend rock music performances	11.0
Backgammon	1.9
Baking	25.3
Barbecuing	34.7
Billiards/Pool	8.5
Bird watching	6.1
Board games	16.7
Book clubs	2.5
Chess	3.0
Cooking for fun	22.0
Crossword puzzles	13.2
Dance/go dancing	9.2
Dining out	49.3
Entertain friends or relatives at home	38.3
Fantasy sports league	3.9
Furniture refinishing	2.8
Go to bars/night clubs	19.1
Go to beach	25.7
Go to live theater	13.4
Go to museums	14.5
Home decoration and furnishing	10.0
Karaoke	3.6
Painting, drawing	6.1
Photo album/scrapbook	6.7
Photography	11.5
Picnic	11.5
Play bingo	4.5
Play cards	20.3
Play musical instruments	7.9
Reading books	37.9
Sudoku puzzles	11.6
Woodworking	4.5
Word games	9.7
Zoo attendance	12.3

* Percent is based on total projected population of 228 million adults
Source: http://www.gfkmri.com

2010. Dining out appears to be the most popular. Other activities could probably be added to this list, but when considering leisure as activity the opportunities are clearly broad.

Defining leisure as activity assumes not only that participants, members, customers, or visitors have available time for recreation activity, but also suitable places or environments for involvement. Historical evidence suggests that individuals as well as societies have consistently created both time and opportunities for recreation activities.

Leisure activity is often studied by inventorying the distribution and frequency of participation in specific recreation activities, as shown in Table 3.1. Data on participants in leisure activity and the frequencies of their participation are important to recreation planners, programmers, researchers, and business people. Local, state, and federal recreation agencies compile such information, as does the Bureau of the Census. Trade associations and business groups often offer good sources of information on activity patterns. Knowing what recreation activities people do for leisure helps to plan optimal recreation services.

One of the problems with the conceptualization of leisure as activity, however, is that not all traditionally identified recreation activities are leisure for every person. For example, many people regard bowling as a common leisure activity. Yet, some individuals have tried bowling and found it to be *not* enjoyable for many reasons. Another problem with leisure defined only as activity is that activities are sometimes perceived as mainly physically active. An individual may really enjoy sitting on a park bench watching the sunset, but this activity may not be found on recreation activity checklists. Activity checklists do evolve over time, but some endeavors that might be considered leisure such as sitting quietly may not ever be on a leisure activity inventory.

The scope of leisure as activity has expanded as new activities have been added and meaningful activities have been redefined. For example, the focus on extreme sports has added a new and challenging opportunity within sports and outdoor settings. Further, recognizing that nontraditional recreation activities such as texting, shopping, surfing the Internet, or participating in religious endeavors may be leisure for many people is important.

Leisure as activity can be examined in terms of being an end in itself, or as a means to accomplish other goals. An activity can be undertaken for its own sake and/or it can have intentional, instrumental value. An activity such as a fitness workout can be a means to an end if the goal is better health or perhaps weight reduction. When leisure activities serve as both ends and means simultaneously, they are often perceived as being the most enjoyable. In other words, people want to enjoy doing an activity but they also want to feel that it benefits them or their community in some way. The personal, social, economic, and environmental outcomes of certain types of activities for individuals as well as communities may vary greatly.

Neither time nor activity, however, provides a perfect definition of leisure. Free or non-obligated time and activity participation can be measured, but determining when one is at leisure psychologically is difficult. You may have unobligated time between classes, but is that leisure? If you read a book assigned for your English class that you really enjoy, is that leisure? Therefore, in addition to time or activity, leisure involves a state of mind or a mindset that usually revolves around intrinsic motivations and outcomes such as enjoyment or personal development.

Leisure as Psychological Experience or State of Mind

An individual's subjective assessment of whether he or she is experiencing leisure generally includes a psychological or a state-of-mind influence. In this view, time and type of activity may have little to do with the experience achieved. Neulinger (1981) was one of the first psychologists to study leisure. He contended that the possibility exists for a person to be at leisure even when at work (i.e., engaged in some activity for which one is obligated or paid money) if a sense of perceived freedom and intrinsic motivation exists.

Leisure may come from any experience where motives are of prime importance rather than the activity or the time spent. In this context, a person is at leisure when in harmony with his or her own rhythms, when the experience is chosen in relative freedom, and when a person is intrinsically motivated and experiencing enjoyment. Leisure, then, can be a psychological experience where activity provides enjoyment and satisfaction. It is psychologically associated with free time and enjoyable activities, but not limited to a specific time or activity.

Psychological definitions of leisure distinguish between leisure and non-leisure in at least three ways: a) leisure is freely chosen and not compulsory; b) leisure is done for its own sake (i.e., intrinsic motivation), not as a means to another goal (i.e., extrinsic motivation); and c) leisure allows the participant a sense of control over its outcomes.

Neulinger's (1981) concept of *perceived freedom* suggests that any activity carried out freely may be associated with the experience of leisure.

However, no one has any freedom without also having responsibility. Choice is important, but people should not be free to do activities that are harmful to themselves or to others. People are never completely unobligated or free to do anything anytime they wish.

Therefore, two qualifications must be considered with this psychological approach. First, individuals always perceive degrees of freedom, not complete freedom. Second, the motivation for an individual's activity is associated with perceived freedom. Perceived freedom is more likely if an individual is intrinsically rather than extrinsically motivated.

With the conceptualization that leisure is a state of mind, almost anything could be considered leisure depending how individuals interpret their experiences. Measuring these states of minds, however, is complex. Scales have been developed to try to capture the subjective meanings of leisure as a state of mind, but many of these scales have been inadequate in addressing the agreed-upon objective meanings of leisure. Nevertheless, these quantitative efforts have been useful in understanding the psychological dimensions of leisure as a state of mind.

Another way to understand how individuals experience leisure as a state of mind for themselves has been uncovered in research undertaken using qualitative approaches (i.e., word-based and not statistics-based). When individuals can articulate in their own words what leisure means, they can describe the feelings and satisfactions associated with their psychological experience. For example, in a research project where my colleagues and I asked women about their leisure, they said they had none (Henderson & Rannells, 1988). They also could not always name typical recreation activities that they defined as leisure. Yet, they could describe pausing to watch the beauty of a sunset or the joy they experienced in watching their children play sports. When further probed, many women agreed that these experiences were meaningful and enjoyable in a context of leisure. The subjective feelings that surround leisure are meaning-making for people.

Leisure characterized as a *state of mind* can be associated with spiritual as well as psychological experiences. Pieper (1963) described leisure as "a mental and spiritual attitude" (p. 40) independent of time or work. As the opposite of idleness, Pieper also described leisure as an "inward calm" or "silence," and a "receptive attitude of mind" (p. 41). Psychologically, leisure can provide a sense of peace within oneself and a connection with the bigger world. For example, many people experience leisure in wilderness experiences that allow for connections with nature.

Finally, the illusion or perception of the psychological state-of-mind experience of leisure as freedom may be more important than its reality.

Ellis and Witt suggested "perceiving oneself as 'free' from necessity is more important than actually being free" (1985, p. 106). Neulinger (1981) asserted that whether perceived freedom is true freedom or only the illusion of freedom is irrelevant because even illusions have real consequences. The importance of a state-of-mind definition of leisure is the perception of its value. Psychologically, leisure can afford people an escape from the responsibilities and tasks of daily life, even if just for a few minutes. Most people know when they are in this psychological state of being.

Leisure as a Cultural Construct

Although the three typical perspectives of time, activity, and state of mind are central to leisure, these ideas focus primarily on the individual and how he or she creates or finds meanings. Leisure, however, is greatly impacted by circumstances outside the individual. Leisure cannot be separated from other aspects of life. Human activity is more complex than these definitions suggest and is not solely focused on individuals.

Therefore, another way to define leisure conceptually in a social context is to examine leisure as a cultural construct. The outcomes anticipated through leisure are socially and culturally defined. Further, leisure is not free from the influence of social and moral norms. Social values and peer pressures often limit choices of activity regardless of personal preferences.

The symbolic meanings of leisure generally come from one's culture. In this sense, 'culture' is defined as shared beliefs and values held by a group. Cultures provide characteristic repertoires of behaviors or actions that people use in deciding how to act in different situations. People may or may not think about why they make their leisure or recreation decisions. Whether activities are regarded as work or leisure, what is preferred, and what is expected from the activities depend significantly on customary behaviors within one's culture. Care is needed, however, to be open to the diversity of meanings and values likely to be associated with leisure within different cultures.

The holistic cultural approach to defining leisure focuses attention most directly on leisure's social contexts. These contexts influence both people's expectations about leisure and how they structure their time and activity to fulfill their expectations. Social roles are among the ways that people order their actions. Social roles incorporate cultural values and culturally defined expectations that establish the ranges of behaviors acceptable for individuals related to leisure as well as other life domains.

However, people never occupy only one social role at a time. Role conflict occurs when circumstances arise in which different social roles impose differing expectations. The mediation of role conflict draws on values established by cultural and social contexts, and on individual interpretations of them.

Cultural influences also affect freedom in leisure. For example, Kelly (1978) asked people why they had participated in specific leisure activities based on issues of freedom and social role expectations. He then used the reasons people gave to classify leisure into four types: unconditional (high freedom, low social role), compensatory or recuperative (low freedom, low social role), relational (high freedom, high social role) and role-determined (low freedom, high social role). When the four types of leisure were analyzed for their relations to social role expectations, only unconditional leisure was relatively independent of social role. Compensatory or recuperative leisure activities contrasted deliberately with the demands imposed by social role expectations such as relaxation to recuperate from the stresses of parenthood or work. Relational leisure activities enhanced personal relations as part of expectations associated with social roles like being a friend or neighbor. Respondents did not experience these role expectations as constraints, but said the expectations guided them in making leisure choices.

Thus, leisure often is relative to social roles and the cultural expectations about behavior that shape involvement in activities. People define and organize their leisure activities in response to cultural expectations and in anticipation of the consequences of conforming or not conforming to them. Cultural diversity can lead to ambiguous role expectations, especially in multicultural societies. The freedom that people expect from their leisure and how they structure their leisure varies across cultural contexts. All recreation professionals should be sensitive to cultural diversity and its implications for people's leisure choices.

Places and Spaces

Another conceptualization of leisure that goes beyond examining leisure as solely an individual experience is the physical environment or the places and spaces that give leisure salience. Places and spaces define environments where leisure and recreation can occur. According to Tuan (1977), the concept of space has absolute and relative dimensions with concrete boundaries. Place is perceptually and socially produced by individuals. Thus, spaces become places when they mean something significant. Spaces exist where leisure occurs and these spaces often become special places when associated with something important like leisure. A sense of place involves an emotional and affective bond between an individual and a particular space, and may vary in intensity from immediate sensory awareness to long-lasting, deeply rooted attachment. A sense of place is often a quintessential concept in thinking about nostalgia, memory, and the images that are evoked as a result of leisure experiences.

The physical place may be less important, however, than the meanings that people attach to places in their minds as they participate in leisure. Therefore, people can make interpretations of their psychological states regarding leisure based on physical realities. Space cannot be disassociated from the people who use the space. A sense of placelessness often exists in today's society and a sense of place experienced through leisure can provide meaning whether it refers to a neighborhood Starbucks or a special mountain lake. Therefore, places combined with a sense of time to enjoy, opportunity to participate, and an open state of mind contribute to many people's understanding and appreciation of leisure.

Expanding Leisure Meanings

The three traditional definitions of leisure as time, activity, and state of mind, as well as the two emerging views of cultural context and places and spaces, provide ways of examining leisure conceptualizations and meanings. However, these five areas do not encapsulate all the ways to conceptualize leisure. Since leisure is a dynamic concept, ideas about its conceptualization are always open for new thinking. Clearly many leisures exist.

Some scholars, for example, have argued that leisure has enlarged in ways that emphasize economics. Globalization implies that the most obvious way to promote positive leisure experiences is to provide activities that can be experienced, bought, and consumed. Therefore the commodity of leisure and the way that it is consumed or experienced is a way to think about leisure. If people are not satisfied with their leisure, then perhaps more and better products and services are needed. The recreation services that have evolved in industrialized countries over the past 50–75 years are based on the idea that people's demands for leisure create supplies or opportunities. Regardless, an economic notion of leisure is also bound to time, the nature of activities, state of mind, culture, and place.

Leisure is often associated with aspects of multiple identities, the reflexive self, the breakdown of clear divisions between work and leisure, and the ambiguous and contradictory aspects of rapidly changing societies. Many scholars have been critical of traditional definitions because they are not broad enough. A tension remains between recognition of expanded meanings and the idea of commonality of experience related to leisure. For some researchers, perhaps the concept of tension itself is an important and useful element that mediates leisure. Taking into account the individually defined contexts of leisure as well as the possibility of shared social and cultural experiences continues to be a challenge worth addressing.

The different but related definitions, conceptualizations, and meanings associated with leisure are both strengths and weaknesses. Lack of a *definition* of leisure can be problematic not only for researchers but also for public understanding. On the other hand, an open-ended definition allows interpretations about the meanings of leisure socioculturally as well as in situ. Most leisure perspectives focus on positive meanings. However, leisure is not always ideologically good when it results in some individuals and communities receiving negative outcomes that do not support social, economic, and environmental sustainability and justice. Some activities such as sex tourism, pornography, drug taking, smoking, gambling, and other risky behaviors are problematic. Nevertheless, because leisure has the potential for good, it also has the potential for evil.

Despite the many conceptualizations, leisure and recreation are central to the facilitation of recreation services for adults and children. Play was mentioned briefly in this chapter but the next chapter focuses specifically on play related to both children's and adult's leisure.

Reflection Questions

1. How do you define leisure? Did your definition change any as a result of reading this chapter?

2. How would your parents or your siblings define leisure? What about your grandparents? Do you think definitions of leisure might vary based on an individual's age?

3. Why is time so valuable in people's lives? Time is finite and it is impossible to get more time. How does time for leisure also link to priorities and responsibilities in your life?

4. If leisure is defined as a state of mind, then what (if anything) separates it from a paid job that an individual truly loves?

5. Think about a place where you enjoy recreation. What is it about a particular place that makes your recreation more enjoyable?

6. Can an individual be a successful recreation professional without understanding the conceptualizations of leisure? Justify your response.

7. What leisure activities do you do that are not reflected in Table 3.1? Why do you think these activities are not on the list?

Chapter 4

People and Play

The motto of the city of Durham, North Carolina, Parks and Recreation Department is "Play More." The Boulder, Colorado, Parks and Recreation Department is supported in part by the *PLAY Boulder Foundation* that advocates for parks and recreation programs and services in the Boulder area. The U.S. Play Coalition is a recently formed partnership to promote the value of play throughout life. Organizers of this group argue that given the many problems with obesity and other social ills that have occurred with the erosion of play opportunities (for children and adults), it is time to begin the second great play movement (the first play movement began at the turn of the 20th century). All of these groups believe the time has come to ensure that children and adults enjoy the benefits of play opportunities in communities.

Play and leisure have many similarities. Having a separate chapter on play may seem a bit redundant, but the idea of play linked to leisure is central to recreation services. Usually play has been associated more with children than adults. However, reclaiming the idea of play for all seems to be an important endeavor. Goodale and Godbey (1988) stated, "The surest sign of mature adulthood . . . may be the ability to be a child; to be able, as a child, to play" (p. 165). Pieper (1963) suggested that leisure is the basis of culture, and Goodale and Godbey substantiated that play can also be described as the basis of culture. A classic text by Huizinga (1950) claimed that the fundamental element of human culture is the instinct to play. His book, *Homo Ludens*, translates as "man [sic] the player." He also demonstrated that law, science, poetry, war, philosophy, and the arts are facilitated and enriched by an essence of play.

Leisure is characterized by perceived freedom, enjoyment, and intrinsic outcomes. When play is described as voluntary, spontaneous, joyful, not serious, and necessary, then it has very similar characteristics compared to leisure. Many attempts have been made to explain the meaning and purpose of play as related to leisure and recreation in the past 100 years. Play has interested biologists, physiologists, psychologists, sociologists, and educators, as well as recreation services professionals.

Recreation services exist because people want and need to play. Recreation professionals in all sectors provide the environments and opportunities for selected play, leisure, and recreation expressions. Approaches and theories of play have given direction to recreation services regarding the design and functions of facilities and equipment, and provide a rationale for the importance of leisure experiences for children and adults.

Descriptions of Play

The term 'play' comes from the Anglo-Saxon words *plegian and plegan* and from the German *pfegen*, which all mean taking care of oneself. 'Play' traditionally has been used to describe the free, natural, engaging, spontaneous, and satisfying activities of children and animals. However, people really never cease to play, but play behavior may be refined and described by some other label such as "fooling around" or "chilling out" when adults are involved.

Recreation and play can be characterized in ways that highlight their similarities or their differences. The term 'recreation' emerges from the Latin *recreare*, which meant to re-create, restore, and renew. Recreating can describe the play activities of adults, although this definition of recreation is more purposeful than may be connoted in the previously mentioned definitions of play. However, both are engaging forms of expression freely chosen without concern for external gain or achievement, but for the satisfaction derived from being in the moment. Both are self-contained experiences with intrinsic rewards. Recreation suggests more formal organization compared to play with its implied spontaneity that occurs outside a structure. Playing in a softball league, however, certainly constitutes play as structure.

Because play, leisure, and recreation behaviors are part of the overall pattern of human expression, the theories offered as explanations for them are connected to theories offered to explain behavior in general. Play theories are considered in the context of the history and culture in which they were formed and offered.

Theories of Play Applied to Recreation and Leisure

Prior to scientific research, most explanations for all behaviors were simple and direct. Most explanations were based on philosophy, spirituality, or people's stories. One played "when the spirit moved him or her." This view changed with the coming of scientific methods and the need to have testable hypotheses and theories to describe and predict action accurately and consistently. Theories offer explanations for observed behavior and stimulate further questions about those behaviors.

Many theories of play have been identified. The essential goal is to explain this universal form of expression. These theories have been grouped into four major schools of thought: physiological, psychological, sociological, and contemporary perspectives. These theories are aimed at understanding why people play.

Physiological Explanations

The earliest explanations of play stressed genetic and biological factors. These theories, offered during the latter half of the 19th century, reflected the thinking of the Darwinians who ascribed all human behaviors to genetics. People thought children played because they were genetically programmed for those activities. Play developed the necessary skills for survival, and children ceased to play or modified their forms of play when it was no longer needed. These theories suggested that children had little to say about what they were going to play since those determinations were biologically and genetically set. Some notions of letting children play to drain off their energies relates to this physiological explanation. These physiological explanations also suggested that because males appeared naturally more active than females, they should be encouraged to play sports more so than girls.

As the inadequacies of the biological explanations became apparent, new schools of thought developed. The first of these were the psychological-biological theories that suggested people had certain basic innate needs and drives that had to be met. These needs could be fulfilled in a variety of ways with play being one of them. Play was assumed to be a compensatory and cathartic activity and a way of releasing the energy of children and the emotional tensions of adults. Work was tension producing and play was the opposite. Therefore, play provided an emotional balance. Play was a way to *re-create* oneself and had implications for adults.

Psychological Explanations

With a growing awareness of the role played by the social environment in shaping behavior, new psychological explanations of the origin and function of play were offered in the 20th century. Sigmund Freud (1964) influenced many of the early psychological theorists. Later psychological play theorists embraced the views of developmental psychologists such as Erik Erikson and Jean Piaget. These views cited the relationship of play to growth and development especially for children, and acknowledged the interaction between play motivated by inner drives and urges, and social controls in society.

One of the more interesting Freudian analyses of play suggested that society had legitimized certain forms of play that allowed individuals to deal with internal conflicts and to express basic urges. For example, the death wish might be accommodated and released through automobile racing, whereas exhibitionist tendencies might be handled through acting and dramatic performances. This view also offered that instead of attacking someone when feeling frustrated, one could go hit a baseball. Psychologists also implied that some forms of play were better than others.

Psychologists Erikson (1968) and Piaget (1962) cited the role of play in the developmental process of children. Erikson emphasized that play was essential for the establishment of self and that certain types of play were critical to particular stages of development. He suggested that children's pleasures first came from being physically able to engage in movement. A child also learns to deal with social relationships through play. He contended that the ability to master play satisfies and moves the developmental process forward. For adults, Erikson suggested play provides an escape from work expectations, but also a means of continuing the developmental (i.e., learning) process.

Piaget (1962) also acknowledged the developmental sequence of growth and the role of play. He described how children go from random and symbolic stages of play to more structured games as they move through their own developmental process. According to Piaget, play through games contributed to the intellectual development of the child. Through play, children learn to assimilate behavior and accommodate the world by adjusting to the external order of things (e.g., winning and losing). These lessons can continue to be applied into adulthood.

Sociological Explanations

Although some sociologists wrote about the role of play earlier in the 20th century, most sociologists did not devote much attention to it until George Herbert Mead discussed its role in the socialization of young children in

1932. Sociologists did not attempt to explain why people play, but focused upon the forms of play and the role in maintaining social groups and social organizations. They assumed that play was natural and useful and that it served definite societal functions. According to sociological theory, play helps to maintain the social structure. Consequently, play reflects and perpetuates the values of society.

According to the anthropologist Margaret Mead (1963), play is second only to language in the development of the social self. In play, children explore social roles and learn the ethic and morals of a society. For example, through fantasy play a child can assume and act out various roles such as father, mother, astronaut, or firefighter. Games reinforce social expectations, since the nature of a game requires playing by the rules and recognizing one's role and the role of others playing the same game.

One of the more recent concerns of sociology as it relates to play behavior is the difference in participation among different groups of people based on gender, race and ethnicity, ability, and socioeconomic status. The Civil Rights Act, Americans with Disabilities Act, and the Women's Movement in the United States, for example, have underlined the need to examine whether all individuals have equal opportunities to play and experience leisure and recreation benefits. Sociologists as well as leisure researchers have explored patterns of play and leisure behavior related to the demographic characteristics of groups. Social justice emphasizes play opportunities that are equitable for all.

Contemporary Explanations

The newer concepts of play and its relationships, particularly to recreation, blend the physiological, psychological, and sociological views into multiple explanations. Play continues to be studied by scholars in many disciplines, and research about leisure has expanded greatly in the past 40 years. Today's theories suggest play is necessary for human development throughout the lifespan. People need play (i.e., leisure) for their total functioning and to interact with the environment at an optimum level. Further, play, recreation, and leisure are essential for contributing to the well-being of individuals and the quality of life in communities and societies. Through play, people express who they are, interact socially, and reflect their culture.

Social psychologists identify motives that drive play and leisure behaviors, including satisfactions that come from adventure, being a part of a group, learning something new, expressing creativity, engaging in fantasy, and experiencing solitude. These satisfactions have been associated with the numerous benefits of leisure that have been widely described (Driver, Brown, & Peterson, 1991). Theorists argue that leisure, recreation, and play experiences are satisfying because of the qualities inherent in the experiences. These benefits are described more fully later in this unit.

This brief introduction to play emphasizes the importance of theory to traditional and more recent understandings of play. Although some differences exist among the theories presented in this chapter, several points of agreement exist:

- All of the explanations conceive of play and recreation as action rather than inaction or idleness. Action does not necessarily mean vigorous physical activity, but it does imply the expending of energies in the play pursuit, whether psychological, physical, or mental energy.

- Nearly all of these ideas suggest that play and recreation are pleasurable and most often motivated by the satisfactions derived from the play experiences. Play activities are freely chosen. Neither children nor adults will continue doing activities unless they are satisfying and enjoyable.

- Play allows for the social development of individuals as well as provides learning and exploration opportunities for children and adults.

Through play, leisure, and recreation, an individual can develop and test his or her concepts of self within the world. Regardless of outcomes, children and adults experience enjoyment through play. The importance and excitement of providing recreation services means that professionals enable sustainable opportunities for people, regardless of age or any other identifying characteristic, to play and have fun. Play More!

Reflection Questions

1. What was your favorite thing to play as a child? What is your favorite way to play as an adult?

2. What is the value of play for children's development?

3. What is the value of play in your life?

4. What does it mean for someone to be playful?

5. Do you consider play and leisure synonymous? Justify your answer.

6. How are cultural values conveyed through play?

Chapter 5

Applying Concepts of Leisure

An understanding of people and their leisure behaviors is necessary for facilitating sustainable recreation services regardless of the sector or the specialty. Definitions and descriptions of leisure, recreation, and play are important. The focus of this chapter, however, is about the concepts and frameworks that have been applied specifically to understanding leisure experiences. Among the interesting ideas presented in this chapter are values and leisure, freedom and leisure, the recreation experience spectrum, social psychological frameworks, leisure needs, serious leisure perspective, flow, constraints, and social ecology.

Values and Leisure

Although leisure experiences and recreation services are not inherently good, they can offer numerous benefits. What is deemed beneficial, however, depends on the values that are associated with the experiences and opportunities. The values may be explicit or implicit. Further, values refer to beliefs and behaviors that an individual or society regards as important for social good. A value system gives guidance for choosing among options for behavior. Values shape what people do in leisure. Further, values shape how recreation services are provided and the choices people make. Whether a hierarchy of values should be associated with leisure is debatable, but values have been a concept applied to leisure for many years.

Jensen (1977) described a hierarchy of leisure-time uses arranged similarly to how Maslow built the hierarchy of needs (see Figure 5.1). Jensen suggested that the bottom of the pyramid (valued as 0) includes acts destructive to society or self. At the one (1) level is amusement and time-fillers, under which most TV watching probably falls. At the two (2) level is emotional involvement in someone else's performance such as

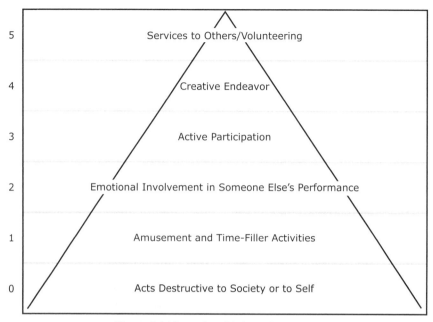

Figure 5.1 Hierarchy of Leisure Time Uses
(Source: Adapted from Jensen, 1977, p. 12)

attending a symphony or being a spectator at a college football game. The next higher valued level is active participation (3), followed by creative endeavors (4), and finally service to others (5). This hierarchy illustrates the social values that traditionally have been associated with leisure and specifically recreation activities. Values change over time and perhaps new systems could be developed today. Generally hierarchies are not widely embraced, but this pyramid provides a visual way of thinking about some of the ways recreation services have been planned.

Freedom, Leisure, and Responsibility

Freedom has long been associated with leisure. Freedom related to leisure can be discussed related to two dimensions including *freedom from* and *freedom to*. Freedom from suggests an individual is not hindered in leisure by external forces. Freedom from might relate to having leisure when an individual is not responsible for paid work (e.g., going on vacation) or family obligations (e.g., a woman might have a "night out" with her friends without children present).

Freedom to means the ability to do or enjoy something (e.g., leisure) considered worth doing or that brings intrinsic rewards. This freedom relates to the rights, privileges, and opportunities that people have related to leisure. Rights also imply entitlements and access to available resources.

However, freedom is never completely free. People cannot just do anything they want without also considering the rights of others. All freedom is relative. In the United States, we believe we are free, but only to the extent that we do not hurt ourselves or others. Therefore, many laws exist that may appear to inhibit personal freedom (e.g., speed limits, fishing catch limits, no smoking areas) for the sake of social good in a civil society. Being free and having freedom to choose leisure also means that one has responsibilities to oneself and others both in the present and for the future. Freedom is a central concept applied to leisure but it also must be critically understood related to the responsibilities that leisure also connotes.

Recreation Experiences Spectrum

Recreation activities and leisure experiences can be planned or spontaneous, social or solitary, and passive or active, with all points in between. When people do something they enjoy or accomplish a goal—such as finishing a 5K race or making a yummy cake to celebrate a friend's birthday—happiness and satisfaction are experienced. However, it is not just the race or just eating the cake that defines the experience. The recreation experience is framed by what precedes the activity as well as what follows it.

Recreation experiences are not constituted by one isolated activity. An experience is more than just the here and now of an activity. On the simplest level an individual might **anticipate or plan** a recreation opportunity, **participate** in the actual activity, and then **recollect or reminisce** about the experience. Although specifically discussing outdoor recreation, Clawson and Knetsch's (1966) explanation of recreation as a multifaceted experience is a useful framework. They noted that several distinct stages or phases are involved and can be summarized in the following way:

- Planning—preparation for the trip, the planning and anticipation of what will occur, and the satisfactions to be derived

- Travel to the site—just going somewhere

- Intense involvement with the recreation activity—the doing stage

- Returning home—pleasure comes from the anticipation of getting home

- Memory of the experience—reminiscing about what happened, thinking about the next trip, showing photographs

All of these stages provide satisfaction and add to the motivation and enjoyment of an actual recreation activity. Involvement in a recreation experience consists of more than just the activity or the actual time spent in leisure. The best activities are often those where a great deal of build-up occurs prior to the event, the logistics such as travelling to and from are well managed, the activity itself is enjoyable, and there are opportunities after the activity to reminisce with fellow participants and to share the experience with others.

Social Psychological Frameworks of Leisure

Prior to the 1980s, most people who studied leisure used either a psychological approach (e.g., Neulinger, 1981) or a sociological perspective (e.g., Dumazdier, 1967). The social psychological approach has addressed how people come to perceive time or behavior as free, how they choose to fill their unobligated time, why they make the choices they do, and the implications of these choices for enjoyment and personal growth. Social psychology is also concerned with how leisure is influenced by other people and in other domains of life including family, work, and the community (Kleiber, Walker, & Mannell, 2011).

Leisure researchers studying leisure have borrowed heavily from social psychology as a framework applied to other areas of behavior. This approach is scientific as a way of systematically collecting data and analyzing it to understand how behavior occurs whether related to leisure or other life endeavors. Theories are used to ascertain to the extent possible the cause and effect of individual behaviors that occur in social situations. Attitudes and behaviors related to motivations, satisfactions, benefits, and constraints are examined within the lives of individuals. Further, an important aspect of social psychology is understanding how age, gender, race, ethnicity, and culture might influence behavior. The purpose of these frameworks is to enable individuals to optimize leisure outcomes and to provide guidance for professionals facilitating recreation services.

Leisure Needs

Talking about leisure needs occurs frequently in textbooks like this one. A need is usually defined as a requirement. This definition raises the question of whether leisure is a requirement of life. If it is, then talking about leisure needs makes sense. However, if leisure is not a requirement to live in the way food or water are, then maybe leisure needs do not exist. According to Maslow, people have needs for food and shelter, safety and security, love and belonging, esteem, and self-actualization. Leisure scholars have argued that leisure is a means to belonging and esteem that leads to self-actualization and is, therefore, a need. However, other people might argue that the needs at the base of Maslow's hierarchy are more important needs. For example, police protection in a community is necessary to address safety and security whereas recreation services are only important when other base needs have been addressed. Therefore, recreation services may not receive the same priority of funding as other public services.

Most recreation professionals agree that leisure is a need and should be facilitated for people's well-being and for a desirable quality of life within communities. Leisure experiences may not be the only way that people's belonging, esteem, and self-actualization needs are met but recreation, leisure, and play are important. In marketing some types of recreation services, participants or consumers are led to believe that they need recreation or the goods associated with it. Felt needs may be different than created needs, but they are both important. When leisure needs are noted in this book they are frequently connected to leisure interests. A fine line may exist between leisure needs and interests, but they are both important and interrelated ways of understanding leisure behavior.

Serious Leisure Perspective

Stebbins (1982) has put forward a perspective called serious leisure. Serious leisure is the systematic pursuit of an amateur role, hobby, or volunteer activity that participants find so substantial and interesting that they often center their lives on the special skills, knowledge, and experience associated with the activity. People involved in serious leisure might be amateur musicians, or volunteers who contribute many hours to social causes. Another aspect of serious leisure has been described as project-based in which an individual focuses on an activity intensely but only for a short period of time, not as a life-long pursuit.

Serious leisure can be contrasted with casual leisure, described as immediately intrinsically rewarding, relatively short-lived pleasurable activity requiring little or no training to enjoy. Casual leisure might include relaxation, passive entertainment such as television or listening to a CD, sociable conversation, or sensory stimulation such as eating or drinking (Stebbins, 1999). Kleiber (2000) has argued that people have often neglected the value of relaxation as a means for appreciation, contemplation, and peacefulness. To do things "at your leisure" speaks to a slower and more relaxed way of doing things.

Stebbins implies that serious leisure is a more valuable and desirable way of experiencing leisure. It has many benefits and can be associated with a variety of pursuits. Not everyone, however, has the means in terms of time and money to engage in serious leisure pursuits.

Serious leisure can also be associated with recreation specialization in which an individual moves beyond the beginner stage to higher levels of commitment and involvement (e.g., buys better equipment, or spends more time pursuing an activity). Similar to serious leisure, participants who specialize in recreation activities may be more likely to seek new challenges in their leisure endeavors. Serious leisure and specialization have both provided solid frameworks for examining how personal values can be associated with leisure and how recreation services providers might address the changing and maturing leisure interests of individuals.

Flow

Csikzentmihalyi's (1975, 1990) work with flow is another example of a social psychological response to understanding play and leisure. Flow occurs when an individual's skills and the environment's challenges can be successfully negotiated. When a situation is no longer challenging (i.e., it's boring) or exceeds the skill level of the individual (i.e., produces anxiety), the response is either to discontinue or not engage in the activity, or possibly to change the activity to become manageable. If a game becomes too complex, for example, an individual develops the skills necessary to play, does not play, or modifies the rules. See Figure 5.2.

If individuals like something that provides a sense of enjoyment and accomplishment, they are more likely to continue to pursue that activity in the future. The more the activity is pursued, the more challenge may be needed to avoid boredom. Sometimes the individual provides challenge for the self, but other times the recreation providers may need to consider how challenge can be facilitated to contribute to the personal benefits desired. A

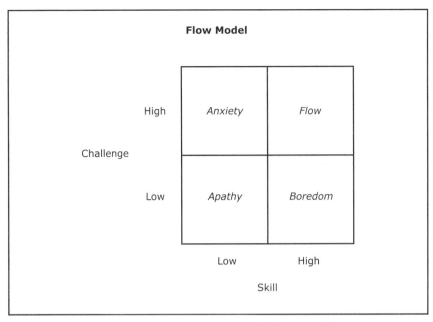

Figure 5.2 Csikzentmihalyi's (1990) Concept of Flow

person who is internally motivated can take responsibility for actions and behaviors, but part of recreation provision may be ascertaining the levels of skill and challenge needed for optimal human development. Flow has been an exciting concept to apply to leisure, although it is important to note that flow is as likely to occur in work as in leisure. Enjoyment must be present as must this sense of appropriate challenge and necessary skills.

Constraints to Recreation and Leisure

The benefits of leisure and recreation services are discussed conceptually in detail in the following chapters. However, a related area that has been widely discussed in leisure research and recreation services is the constraints that may keep people from fully enjoying leisure. Not everyone has the skills, abilities, or opportunities to participate in particular recreation activities. Individuals might be aware of the importance of leisure in their lives as well as their need for leisure, but may be unable to experience leisure fully because of constraints that impede involvement or full satisfaction. Constraints can also influence the preference for a particular recreation activity.

Leisure constraints include any factors that affect leisure participation negatively by not only preventing participation but also by reducing the frequency, intensity, or duration of participation, or reducing the quality of experience or satisfaction gained from the activity (Jackson & Scott, 1999). Therefore, constraints do not only affect what a person does, but also how individuals might psychologically feel about an activity (i.e., how much they enjoy it).

Models have been developed to conceptualize and understand leisure constraints as they primarily apply to individuals. One tested model suggests that leisure constraints can be classified into four categories: intrapersonal, interpersonal, individual structural, and social structural constraints.

- *Intrapersonal constraints* may lead to a lack of personal interest in a particular activity because of attitudes about leisure and/or personality factors that may make involvement less appealing. For example, an individual who has never been exposed to some type of activities like camping may never become interested in participation.

- *Interpersonal constraints* are associated with relationships with others. For example, some activities may require a leisure partner. If a friend or family member is not available, a constraint may exist. Some women in particular, may not feel comfortable going out alone at night, which becomes a constraint to certain types of activities.

- *Individual structural constraints* intervene between the expression of interest in an activity and a person's ability to participate. Lack of money, lack of transportation, or lack of facilities, for example, may influence how an individual participates in a recreation activity. These constraints can also lead to less than optimal participation and a reduced level of enjoyment. Although these structural constraints are influenced by society, they usually focus on what individuals could do to overcome them. If a person is constrained by money and cannot go on a week-long vacation to the beach, he or she might do a "staycation" in his city (e.g., visit parks, museums).

- *Social structural constraints* exist in society and can prevent individuals from experiencing leisure to the fullest. Examples might be stereotyping of activities (e.g., girls don't do boxing) and a lack of funding for activities for some segments of the population. These structural constraints cannot be overcome by the individual alone, but require a social effort or societal change. Another example might be that an individual may want to walk for exercise but cannot because there are no safe trails in the neighborhood for walking.

These constraints, while not mutually exclusive, provide a means for understanding why individuals may not be able to experience the personal benefits of recreation and leisure to the extent they would like. Some people are able to negotiate constraints better than others. Identifying the individual strategies used to negotiate constraints is useful. Further, understanding how people make decisions and how they seek to overcome obstacles they encounter may help recreation professionals better plan and implement recreation services.

Social Ecology

A framework that has been applied extensively to health promotion and physical-activity involvement is the social-ecological model. This model also has implications for recreation services in general. The core assumption of social ecology is that the well-being of people is influenced by multiple facets in both their physical and social environments. The model can be viewed in Figure 5.3. This model has important implications for how leisure experiences might be experienced.

Ecology refers to the interrelations between organisms and their environments. Social-ecological concepts address people's transactions with their physical and sociocultural environments. Social ecology is derived from systems theory with people and environment interactions characterized by their mutual influence (Bronfenbrenner, 1979; Stokols, 1992). The general thesis of ecological models of behavior is that environments restrict the range of behaviors (e.g., related to leisure) by promoting and sometimes demanding certain actions and by discouraging or prohibiting other behaviors (Sallis, Bauman, & Pratt, 1998).

According to McLeroy, Bibeau, Steckler, and Glanz (1988), five classes of factors affect how or why a person might participate or fail to participate in a healthy behavior related to any health behavior such as physical activity: intrapersonal, interpersonal, institutional, community, and public policy. The intrapersonal is the only factor focused on the individual per se. The

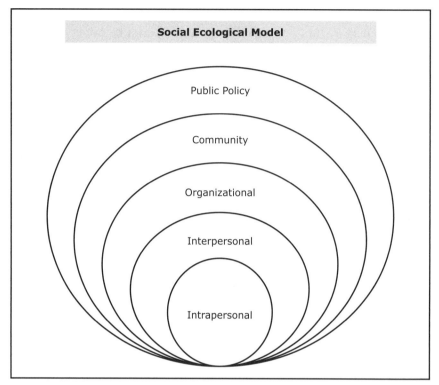

Figure 5.3 Social Ecological Model

other four relate to the context of people's lives relative to supportive others (e.g., family, friends, work colleagues) as well as community opportunities and government policies that enable or constrain opportunities to enjoy parks, sports, and other active leisure activities. Therefore, constraints and motivations for physical activity can be better understood by examining the leisure environments in which people live.

The emphasis on social psychology and educational approaches that has dominated leisure literature research may be inadequate in getting people to undertake enjoyable recreation experiences. A focus on individual behavior is useful, but it may present only part of the picture regarding how people are encouraged to participate in any type of outdoor, sport, or recreation activity. If people do not have places and spaces to be active, they are likely not to be active regardless of how motivated they might be. Ecological efforts can add explanatory value beyond the personal factors that influence people's involvement and participation in any form of recreation.

Other Frameworks and Applied Concepts

The concepts described in this chapter are some of the most popular ones that have influenced a broad understanding of leisure. Each specialty area has frameworks and concepts applied to the specific area. For example, recreation resource management uses frameworks such as place attachment and the recreation opportunity spectrum (ROS). Youth development usually focuses on a positive youth development framework. Sport uses models related to marketing and levels of participation. Each specialty has some specific frameworks that guide an understanding of the services provided. Without frameworks, understanding how the field fits together and how explanations can be developed for behavior related to what participants do as well as how professionals function would be diminished.

An important conceptual area not yet discussed relates to the benefits associated with leisure and recreation services. Benefits are addressed in the next two chapters of this book.

Reflection Questions

1. Describe ways that leisure might relate to *freedom from* as well as *freedom to*. What examples can you give in your life of how you use leisure as freedom from or freedom to?

2. What is the connection between leisure, freedom, and responsibility?

3. How do your values influence what you do in your recreation?

4. According to the recreation experience model, the enjoyment of a recreation activity is more than just the isolated activity. Describe a time when the aspects of anticipation, travel, and recollection made your recreation activity special to you.

5. What are your biggest constraints to your enjoyment of leisure? What strategies do you or could you use to address those constraints?

6. Have you ever experienced flow? What were you doing, who were you with, what did flow mean to you?

7. Are you involved with an activity that you might consider serious leisure? How would you contrast this activity to more casual leisure that you might undertake? Is one better than another?

8. Social ecology has become a popular framework for understanding health behaviors but it also has implications for any type of leisure behavior. Why do you believe the framework has become so useful in a field like recreation services?

Chapter 6

Benefits of Leisure to Individuals

Why do you enjoy having coffee with a friend? Watching your college basketball team play on TV? Going to a rock concert? People seek leisure experiences because of the personal and social benefits associated with these activities. People seek enjoyment and positive outcomes in their leisure.

In a society that values people for what they "do" relative to their gainful employment, there seems to be less tolerance for thinking about people in terms of the activities they engage in outside of paid work. In a casual conversation, most people define themselves by their work, or for students, by their major. For example, individuals are more likely to say they are a teacher or a pilot or an English major rather than to say they are a runner or a band member, even if those activities represent a form of meaningful or even serious leisure for them. If people are really honest with themselves, however, most individuals would acknowledge that the core of who they are is most likely to be found outside the realm of work or study. Leisure is central and vital to most people's lives because it has meanings and individual benefits for them.

Several years ago the National Recreation and Park Association (NRPA), the largest citizen and professional organization in the United States that advocates for the value of recreation in communities, launched a campaign called "Recreation: The Benefits are Endless." This campaign aimed to show the importance of recreation by describing benefits associated with individuals, communities, the environment, and the economy. Although this media campaign is no longer used by NRPA, articulating the individual benefits and community contributions that can be associated with leisure experiences and recreation services is important.

The focus of this chapter is on benefits to individuals. The next chapter focuses on the contributions of recreation services to communities and society. Overlap certainly exists between what is good for individuals and what is good for communities, but for purposes of discussion, these artificial distinctions are made. This chapter emphasizes how people can experience personal growth as well as meaningful social relationships through leisure. It also addresses the research available that documents these benefits.

Overview of Benefits

Regardless of the sector of recreation services or the activity area, people will participate because they expect outcomes like enjoyment and satisfaction. People who choose to pay or to spend their time in recreation have expectations about what they are going to gain from involvement. Parents who enroll their children in particular activities want to know that not only will the children have fun, but that they will also have opportunities to develop life skills such as making new friends and/or cooperation and teamwork. City council members, nonprofit board members, and other decision-makers will want to ensure that the money spent on recreation services is resulting in some type of public good for individual citizens. Therefore, the question of the value of leisure as well as recreation services is on most everyone's mind, whether they specifically articulate it or not.

Recreation professionals need to speak articulately and readily about benefits. Sometimes this opportunity will be like an "elevator speech"—a brief description that can be completed in the time that it might take to ride an elevator a couple of floors. Other times, you may be required to make a presentation about benefits based both on the literature that is available as well as evaluation data and business analyses that you might have from your organization. Regardless, professionals should be able to identify what individuals get from leisure related to their personal and social development as well as what the broader public good is related to recreation services.

Benefits can have different meanings but basically they refer to positive changes that result in an improved condition. The negative aspects of leisure can be called dis-benefits. The negative or dark side of leisure is discussed in the last chapter of this unit. Although not all leisure experiences are positive, people expect that their activities will be advantageous, have value, and be desirable. Some outcomes from leisure and recreation benefit individual growth and social relationships, while other benefits relate to cultural, environmental, and economic aspects influencing communities. Although individuals can anecdotally describe the benefits, research has also confirmed individual and community benefits.

Research about Leisure and Its Value

In the past 40 years, research about leisure and recreation has grown substantially. The research in general has focused on two main areas: understanding leisure behavior, including its value; and how to better manage land, fiscal, and human resources for sustainable recreation services. In talking about benefits, research is extensively used to show empirically the value of leisure and recreation services. Many individuals have personal stories about how leisure experiences have improved their lives, and these accounts are important. However, being aware of the evolution of research may be helpful.

Sociology has been instrumental in understanding play, recreation, and leisure. Early studies of play and leisure were conducted within the discipline of sociology with a focus on collective and group experiences related to leisure. This sociological approach was the dominant paradigm through the 1960s.

The sociological approach, however, fell short in addressing what individuals thought, how leisure made them feel, and how it influenced their identities and their relationships with other people. Because sociological explanations of leisure alone were not satisfactory to many professionals, researchers began to develop and promote a social psychology of leisure starting in the late 1970s. A new generation of researchers and theorists began to question dominant disciplinary theories and develop alternative explanations for leisure behavior through social psychology.

Social psychology focused on the leisure experience and behavior of individuals within various contexts. Psychology concentrates on understanding an individual's behaviors relative to cognitive factors. Social psychology broadens the focal point on individuals to understand their social contexts and environments. Thus, social psychologists study the intersection of the individual with her/his environment. Social psychologists ask what happens to the individual when placed in leisure contexts such as sports, arts, media consumption, and the outdoors. They also ask questions about benefits of participation in leisure and the influence on individuals when they cannot engage in leisure.

Although the social psychological paradigm continues to be the foundation for much of the research in North America, as described in the previous chapter, some researchers have broadened this framework by employing critical theory and cultural studies perspectives. Critical approaches have strengthened the understanding of leisure behavior because they emphasize that individuals may not have control over the social structures that enable and constrain them. For example, a woman could be highly motivated to play golf, but until 2012 some prestigious country clubs did not allow women to become members. From another perspective, a young person living in a low-income family might want to learn to play a musical instrument but may not have access to an instrument or to instructors to teach him or her if a school does not offer a music program. A critical perspective also addresses how leisure has the potential to be detrimental to individuals and groups. Research that has implications for benefits can be approached in many ways, as you will see in the examples shown in this chapter and the next.

Personal Benefits Associated with Leisure

Social psychological research has focused largely on individual benefits. Individual benefits generally include the intrinsic satisfactions received from involvement. They can benefit the psychological self, including such aspects as enhanced self-competence, improved sense of self-worth, self-identity, and a better ability to communicate with others. Some of these personal benefits can also relate to physical health, mental health, stress management, spiritual benefits, and positive moods.

The benefits that individuals seek are often closely related to their motivations for involvement as well as the satisfactions and outcomes they expect to receive from recreation participation. Motivations are those inner urges that prompt one to behave in a certain way, often based on what an individual expects. Satisfactions include the fulfillment of a desire, need, or interest. Enjoyment, pleasure, or contentment is often due to being satisfied from participation in a leisure activity. Outcomes refer to how something turns out related to achievement or results. Outcomes could be changes in knowledge, skills, attitudes, or aspirations.

Benefits, motivations, satisfactions, and outcomes are all slightly different in their meanings, but they all refer to expectations that something positive has or will happen. The term benefits will be used in the context of this book, but other terms also support these personal expectations. Among the categories that might be considered related to personal benefits are intrinsic fulfillment and well-being, identity development, mental health, physical health, and spirituality.

Intrinsic Fulfillment and Well-Being

The number one benefit that most people expect from their leisure experiences is enjoyment. Enjoyment can be the means to enabling other benefits to happen or enjoyment can be the end in and of itself. Life is often stressful and having enjoyable breaks during the day or as an extended vacation is essential to people's well-being. A sense of a positive emotion including being happy, healthy, and secure is referred to as well-being.

Some individuals have downplayed the importance of having fun as an aspect of well-being. Fun does not mean hedonism or that anything goes, but alludes to the inner happiness that leisure can provide. Seldom do professionals talk about enjoyment or fun as the only outcome of recreation activities, yet it is quite central and should not be discounted. As a personal outcome, having fun is usually linked to other satisfactions such as learning something new or making a new friend. "All work and no play makes Jack or Jill a dull person" is true.

These terms 'fun' and 'joy' are admittedly value laden, and people have different ways of finding intrinsic well-being. Yet, if recreation professionals do not acknowledge that people need enjoyment, fun, and opportunities for happiness and joy in their lives, then recreation is not a distinct service. However, I want to emphasize that having fun is also associated with other benefits such as personal identity development, mental health, physical health, and spiritual health. Fun can occur while other important benefits are also evident.

Personal Identities

Leisure has ties to personal identity. How people see themselves, how others see them, and how people see themselves as connected with others defines personal and social identity. In addition to the physiological changes that accompany growing up and growing older, people also experience psychological changes over time. Biological, cognitive, and social roles and factors as well as family, peer, work, recreation, and school contexts influence how people construct themselves and their identities. Leisure experiences obviously play a role in this process.

Developmental theorists assert that individuals become aware of the process of identity formation during adolescence. Although identity is a personal characteristic, it is closely linked to social roles. Young people have opportunities to engage in structured and unstructured recreation and leisure activities (e.g., sports, music, and dramatic arts). Whether the activities contribute to identity development or whether identity influences what an individual chooses to do, both directions of influence are important in determining the relationship of structured and unstructured recreation in a person's life.

Leisure may assist with identity formation in several ways. For example, recreation activities (e.g., sports, drama) can provide developmental outcomes such as cooperation, teamwork, flexibility, negotiation skills, working with diverse people, and enhanced listening skills. According to Haggard and Williams (1991, 1992), the more people engage in recreation activities, the more likely they will embrace the social identities that accompany these activities (e.g., an athlete, musician, dancer, writer, or photographer) and continue in lifelong participation and enjoyment.

Recreation can be a positive developmental context for individual identity formation and change. Leisure opportunities, however, can also reinforce social identities that might not be positive. For example, although change has occurred, girls and boys may still be socialized to play with gender-specific toys (e.g., dolls or trucks) and to engage in gender-appropriate activities. No leisure context is free from values and cultural norms. Regardless, understanding the role that leisure experiences can play in people's lives can be helpful in knowing what activities can support their optimal health and identity development.

Mental Health

Mental health is an important benefit of recreation activities. Measuring mental health is sometimes difficult to do, but good mental health generally connotes a life where individuals experience more positive than negative emotions. In a positive mental health state, individuals are able to adapt to a range of events that might occur in their lives. It is more than just the absence of mental illness. It also relates to what was previously described as well-being. The World Health Organization describes mental health as an individual realizing his or her abilities, being able to cope with the normal stresses of life, experiencing paid and unpaid work productively and fruitfully, and making a contribution to the larger community. One key benefit that recreation can provide is to aid in stress management.

Stress is a normal part of life. Everyone experiences it. Further, not all stress is negative. To feel a bit of stress sometimes makes an individual perform better. Many positive aspects of people's lives may be stressful such as graduating from college, or beginning a new job. Stress, however, becomes negative when it overwhelms or immobilizes an individual. In that sense, an individual will need to develop mechanisms for coping with the stress and managing it. Although leisure is not going to help someone be able to pay the rent that is due, it can help to diminish the anxiety and enable individuals to address the situation more rationally.

One way to cope with stress is to pursue activities that are relaxing. Relaxing enables both physical and psychological rejuvenation. Recreation activities such as taking a hike or going to an art museum can provide calmness and revitalization in individuals so they have more strength to face the stressful issues in their lives.

Nature has always been a place where individuals experience numerous benefits. As society becomes more urbanized, the value of nature for emotional and spiritual reflection has become indispensable for some people's mental health. Research has been conducted on the restorative properties of nature. For example, Attention Restoration Theory (ART) asserts that people can focus and concentrate better after spending time in nature, or even looking at scenes of nature (Kaplan, 1995).

The stress-reducing benefits of leisure, which impact both mental and physical health, can be found in almost any activity. Being physically active enables individuals to address stress as well as offers other benefits for physical health.

Physical Health

People know that physical activity is good for them. Yet, many people do not participate in regular physical activity for many reasons. Unfortunately, the number of obese adults and children has grown to epidemic proportions. Obesity is the result of an energy imbalance. More calories are consumed than are "worked off." Therefore, although eating less is one part of the equation, being more physically active is another part. More about the problems created by inactivity are discussed later in this book. However, a good deal of medical evidence suggests that active leisure has many benefits.

Among the benefits associated with physical activity listed by the CDC are:

- Control weight
- Reduce risk of cardiovascular disease
- Reduce risk for type 2 diabetes and metabolic syndrome
- Reduce risk of some cancers
- Strengthen bones and muscles
- Improve mental health and mood
- Improve ability to do daily activities and prevent falls, if you're an older adult
- Increase chances of living longer (http://www.cdc.gov/physica-lactivity/everyone/health/index.html)

The Centers for Disease Control and Prevention (CDC) recommends that adults should have 150 minutes of moderate to vigorous activity each week. The recommendation for children is 60 minutes each day. In addition to aerobic activity, opportunities to develop strength and flexibility at least twice a week are recommended. Note that the term 'physical activity' is used rather than 'exercise.' Exercise often has a negative connotation and suggests particular routines. Physical activity, on the other hand, can include exercise or a variety of fun activities that can be done without a gym or equipment (e.g., walking, dancing, gardening). Sports offer opportunities for physical activity, but many other options exist.

For people to take advantage of physical health benefits, they must have recreation opportunities. The social ecological model discussed in the previous chapter indicated how even though an individual might be motivated to be active, if he or she does not have social support, opportunities within the community, and/or a skills set, the individual may not have access to opportunities since active recreation must be undertaken on a regular basis to achieve the benefits.

Recreation services can provide a variety of opportunities for physical activity. Payne (2002) suggested that recreation services are a core component of the community health systems. Recreation professionals, regardless of the sector, can facilitate spaces and programs to enable physical activity. Some of these opportunities are structured such as sports leagues, but in other cases a park or a gym is available for individuals to participate.

Spiritual Health

In addition to physical and mental health, the spiritual benefits of leisure experiences should be considered. Although religious organizations contribute to the recreation services system as discussed in Unit Three, spirituality is defined more broadly to include a personal belief in something greater than oneself (Henderson, 1993). Leisure is sometimes described as having spiritual dimensions and benefits (Zuefle, 1999). For example, Pieper (1963) described leisure as a gift from God. The concept of flow also can be connected to a peak or spiritual experience.

The spiritual side of leisure is also associated with moral values, compassion, and respect for other humans and life forms. In reaction to urbanism and technology, a growing number of people are exploring their inner feelings to develop a sense of belonging. They are discovering values that rise from direct contact with the beauty, complexities, and mysteries of nature. An *ecospirituality* stresses a reverence for all living and nonliving things.

Many people feel their mortality and limits when they experience the spiritual in recreation activities. Spiritual benefits have also been noted when people are in the outdoors experiencing quiet reflection and appreciating the vastness of the world. Aesthetic benefits related to spirituality might be an appreciation of beauty or an opportunity to enliven one's senses to not only sights but also sounds, smells, and tactile sensations. People who do wildlife viewing are thrilled with seeing animals in their natural worlds. These aesthetic experiences may be spiritual in some situations with the recognition of a power higher than oneself.

Social Benefits Associated with Leisure

In addition to the benefits that have a direct bearing on one's personal life, social benefits of leisure are numerous. For example, leisure can be a means to bring people together to learn from one another and to share. Family leisure is an important element. Leisure experiences also can provide a way to develop friendships and social capital.

Family Leisure

Family is central to most people's lives. The recognition of a variety of family structures has changed greatly in U.S. society. The tradition of two heterosexual parents and two children is less common, with new family forms such as single parents, same sex couples, and intergenerational living arrangements. Although blood relations define a family, many other forms of commitment can exist. Regardless of the structure, however, family leisure can have many benefits.

One conceptualization of family leisure suggests that activities can be described as core or balance activities (Zabriskie & McCormack, 2001). The core-and-balance model of family leisure premises that family leisure involvement meets ongoing needs for levels of stability and change in the family. Core family leisure activities are easily accessible, common, usually home based, and low in cost (e.g., playing board games or eating together as a family). Balance family leisure activities, in contrast, focus on variety, novelty, and are done less often (e.g., family vacations, picnics, going to a museum).

Both core and balance activities offer potential social benefits. Families that frequently participate in core leisure activities have opportunities to bond and develop cohesion. Conversely, balance family leisure activities can provide novel experiences that allow families to learn flexibility and work together in new contexts. Generally, regardless of whether activities are core or balance, family leisure can lead to better communication in a family.

Family leisure is most often focused on the benefits that the activities provide for children (Shaw, 2008). Many parents feel that their duty as "good" parents is to provide opportunities for family leisure. The focus is not only on enjoyment of the activities by children but also that they will learn from the experiences. Thus, a benefit of family leisure can be the educational opportunity that may be available. Families can also be a means for learning leisure skills. Children can learn by participating with their families in outdoor experiences as well as cultural opportunities. The opportunities for learning and sharing within families generally occur during their leisure.

Friendships

In addition to families, friendships experienced through leisure offer social benefits. Recreation activities provide a way to make friends as well as to nurture friendships. Most people agree that friendships are important. For example, according to the Mayo Clinic (http://www.mayoclinic.com/health/friendships/MH00125), friends are good for your health. Friends can help when celebrating good times and help cope during bad times. Friends give companionship and prevent loneliness. Having friends, both the Facebook type and others, can increase your sense of belonging and facilitate happiness. Further friends can reduce stress in your life and encourage healthy behaviors (e.g., exercising). Friendships are also reciprocal in being able to give to others.

Many friendships (unless they are work-related) are formed through leisure. Getting together with friends to go to a movie or to watch a ballgame are common occurrences. Most people appreciate the deep bonds as well as the enjoyment that can occur through shared friendship activities.

Social Capital

People have expressed concern over the loss of community, weak social ties, and the focus on individualism in U.S. society. How people allocate their time— staying home or participating in clubs or other social forms of leisure—is important. These possibilities can be seen when analyzing social capital as a benefit of leisure.

Social capital is a resource, just like financial capital (e.g., money) and human capital (e.g., knowledge). However, unlike financial and human capital, social capital is not "owned" by anyone. It is created and exists only through participation in social structures and activities. When people interact with people in their communities, the potential for social structure exists. Communities in this case may refer to a geographic area or might be a group of people who have a common background and/or some shared interests.

Social capital enables people to accomplish their goals effectively. Instead of developing independent resources, people in environments rich with social capital have access to resources held by their counterparts. The two basic types of social capital are called bonding and bridging social capital (Gittell & Vidal, 1998; Putnam, 2000). Bonding social capital builds up the social relations between people who were already connected in some fashion. Bridging social capital brings together people who previously had no social relation.

Researchers have documented an association between specific forms of leisure activity and higher levels of social capital (Putnam, 1993). The mutual knowledge and trust required for the formation of social capital has a greater opportunity to develop when people participate in social forms of leisure and recreation services such as active memberships in recreation-related clubs and associations, or participate in creating recreation opportunities (Storrmann, 1996). Putnam (2000) argued that Americans are withdrawing more from recreation activities that facilitate social capital formation. The primary culprit in Putnam's view was the domination of free time by television viewing. Today we might wonder if computers also lead to less interaction, although the prevalence of social media might mitigate that argument. How social media might lead to social capital is an area that requires more research. Nevertheless, a concern exists that Americans are less engaged in their communities and in social capital producing activities than in the past.

Leisure experiences and recreation services can facilitate the generation of social capital (Hemingway, 1999). Individuals can seek these opportunities, but recreation professionals also can contribute by creating opportunities for socially interactive leisure that include a diverse range of people. These opportunities extend beyond just providing programs and facilities to include administering them in a democratic fashion that enables participants to engage in designing possible opportunities.

This chapter discusses a number of personal and social benefits that can occur through leisure, whether recreation activities are done on one's own or in connection with structured recreation services. More benefits could be identified but these examples show the importance of leisure in people's lives. The broader community benefits discussed in the next chapter also reflect on individual experiences.

Reflection Questions

1. Think about a recreation activity you did this past weekend. In retrospect, what were you hoping to gain from the experience. Were those benefits realized? Explain how they were or were not and why that might have been the case.

2. Do different recreation activities result in different benefits to people? Are there some common benefits associated with all leisure experiences?

3. How do identities shape the benefits people receive from their leisure?

4. Have you ever had a spiritual experience while in the outdoors? What was that experience like for you?

5. How would your recreation be different if you did not have family or friends to share the experiences with?

6. What are your memories of family leisure? What benefits did activities like family vacations have for you and your family?

7. What role does physical activity play in your life? Is physical activity a leisure experience for you or is it something you do mostly for extrinsic reasons?

8. Everyone experiences stress in their lives. How does recreation help you deal with the stress that you face as a college student?

Chapter 7

Benefits of Recreation Services to Communities

The previous chapter emphasizes the personal and social benefits that can occur from leisure involvement, which may occur in different settings. This chapter addresses the cultural, environmental, and economic benefits to communities. For recreation services to be sustainable, the benefits in all these areas must be clearly articulated. Community benefits can be described in many ways, but in this chapter, they are grouped into three categories of benefits called cultural, environmental, and economic.

Culture includes the diversity of communities and how leisure can serve as a means to develop community pride as well as cultural understanding. Many recreation activities could not exist without natural and built environments. The natural world is important for outdoor recreation. Recreation services can contribute to the appreciation of and the preservation of the environment, which is necessary for sustainability. In addition, a person does not have to be an economist to appreciate the monetary value of leisure. The economic value of any product or service often relates to the supply and demand for it. Goods and services like recreation services exist because of the demand for them. The public, nonprofit, and private business sectors have responded to demand by providing desired areas, facilities, programs, goods, and services. These categories all contribute to the quality of life in communities.

Overview of Quality of Life

'Quality of life' is a term frequently used in discussing recreation services, as I have mentioned throughout this book. Quality of life is based on the community resources that exist. People have a good quality of life because communities have particular services and amenities that contribute to this quality. How leisure opportunities and recreation services *contribute* to a community's quality of life is important and recreation professionals should be able to articulate these community benefits. In indices of quality of life, leisure or recreation is usually considered.

Table 7.1 is an example of how quality of life was measured in the United States in comparison with the two bordering countries of Canada and Mexico. Quality of life can have a variety of meanings but it generally refers to the degree to which communities (or countries) offer individuals an external framework that will enable them to experience well-being. Well-being is described in a previous chapter as being happy, healthy, and safe. As the table shows, the external factors that can contribute to individual well-being and quality of life in communities include cost of living, leisure culture, economic opportunities, environment, freedom, health, infrastructure, risk and safety, and climate. Leisure culture as one element has implications for health, social support, and social capital related to individual benefits.

The table is not meant to suggest competition with our neighbors, but it does highlight the ratings that have been associated with the United States. The table shows how factors vary across the three countries. Based on all countries in the world that were measured, the U.S. ranked 5th on this particular index. However, the importance of this index is not the ranking but the description of the elements that constituted quality of life. Clearly, leisure culture is an important element as are the economy and environment. Recreation services contribute to each of these areas and thus, can contribute to the quality of life of a community, which connects directly to people's well-being.

Table 7.1 Quality of Life Indicators for United States, Canada, and Mexico
(Source: http://www.il-ireland.com/il/qofl2008/)

	Cost of Living	Leisure Culture	Economy	Environment	Freedom	Health	Infrastructure	Risk & Safety	Climate	Final Score
CAN	67	82	64	83	100	86	51	100	64	76
MEX	84	70	61	75	92	79	41	92	87	75
USA	72	79	90	70	92	85	86	100	85	84

Recreation Services and Culture

When discussing the ways that recreation services contribute to communities, it is important to further describe what culture and leisure culture mean. Some of the individual benefits already discussed play into this understanding, such as the facilitation of social capital. However, culture is most often described as what distinguishes one social group from another based on characteristics such as language, beliefs, customs, and institutions. It connotes a large-scale context. Therefore, culture can relate to race or ethnicity (e.g., Latino culture, primitive cultures) or it might relate to some type of group commonalities (e.g., youth culture, drug culture, consumer culture, organizational culture).

One approach, especially for ethnic groups, has been to acculturate by replacing the traits of one culture with the dominant culture. As described in Unit Two, one of the purposes of early recreation and education programs offered through Settlement Houses in the United States was to acculturate new immigrants into American society. The idea was to make distinct social groups alike. Views are quite different today as people recognize that different cultures can strengthen communities and make them more interesting.

Leisure culture includes how leisure and recreation might be expressed and experienced related to opportunities within a community or country. Particular cultural groups often have their own customs and traditions regarding how they live their lives. They find leisure within those domains. Some cultural groups wish to celebrate their heritage together and share it with the wider community. For example, ethnic festivals such as Greek Fests or American Indian powwows are a means to share culture with others. Many larger cities now have Gay Pride festivals and parades. Chicago offers dozens of ethnic festivals each year, mostly in the summer. Recreation services are often a part of these events as the sponsors of the activities. The emerging area of event management, which is discussed in more detail in Unit Three, is often associated in communities with cultural festivals.

Cultural events as a dimension of recreation services can have a number of benefits. As suggested above, they can give a group a sense of pride in who they are, and in their ability to share with others. People involved in these events can develop deeper cultural bonds and appreciation for their own as well as others' culture. They can serve as a way to help others become more aware and knowledgeable about different groups. Further, the events can contribute to developing social capital. Presumably more knowledge can create positive attitudes about the importance of diversity in towns and cities. Participation in customs related to food, music, and dance can offer a new appreciation of this diversity.

Another benefit of recreation services in communities may relate to cultural and historical preservation. This preservation allows a community to understand its history and culture, and share it with others (Crompton, 2007). In addition, this preservation enables visitors to understand the uniqueness of a community. Recreation services can facilitate richness in communities that can result in greater respect and cooperation among the variety of cultural groups that now exist in most communities.

Environmental Benefits

Environmental benefits also exist as a result of recreation services in communities. Environmental protection related to nature-based recreation services has been an outgrowth of the commitment to saving outdoor recreation resources. The ways that recreation services are conducted may also have implications for mitigating the effects of concerns such as climate change. An interesting juxtaposition exists regarding the consumptive aspects of many recreation activities and the degradation of the natural environment. Some concern has existed that "nature is being loved to death." If leisure experiences and recreation services are sustainably managed, this conflict can be minimized.

Similar to some of the other terms used in this book, 'environment' can have several meanings. One broad way of thinking about environment is as the external factors influencing the activities of people as well as plants and animals. Another, more focused definition relates to the natural world and the relationship of human activity on that world. In this chapter, I focus most on the second definition since environment related to recreation services has most often connoted the natural world. This view of the natural world, however, can include the natural area in a family's backyard as well as huge tracts of land set aside for public enjoyment. These ways of thinking are not mutually exclusive.

The connections between outdoor recreation and the environment have been pronounced in the recreation services arena. Many governmental organizations have been charged with managing the natural environment for its resources and for recreation opportunities as discussed in more detail in Unit 3. Land has been preserved throughout the United States to provide parks, trails, seashores, and forests for the enjoyment of people. A variety of recreation land management practices have been employed to ensure that these public lands are available for generations to come.

The relationship between people and the environment goes two ways. One relates to how the environment can benefit people as discussed in the chapter about individual benefits related to such aspects as spirituality and aesthetics. The second way relates to how recreation services can benefit the environment. The latter idea relates to the community benefits of recreation services. Note that these two aspects are highly intertwined and interdependent. However, land preservation, health and safety, and environmental ethics are important benefits not only to individuals but to communities in general.

Land Preservation

Because people realized over a decade and half ago that the amount of land in the continental United States was finite, land was set aside to be managed by governments (i.e., federal, state, and local) to be available for the public. For example, Yellowstone National Park was set aside in 1872 with the purpose of preserving the natural features within the park into perpetuity. Today the National Park System consists of 84 million acres of land; 4½ million acres of oceans, lakes, and reservoirs; 85,000 miles of rivers and streams; and 43,000 miles of shoreline (http://www.nps.gov/aboutus/index.htm). Millions more acres of land are preserved by other government entities at all levels.

Preserving biological diversity also is a benefit of land preservation. The destruction of habitats has resulted in species extinction, or at the least endangerment of species. Managing land for recreation and other activities is a way to keep habitats available for species. The reduction of any species often has a domino effect on others. Large park areas can sustain more biological diversity. In addition, promoting conservation corridors that link open spaces can facilitate the movement of plants and animals (as well as people).

Health and Safety

Preserving land is important, since every day the United States is losing several thousand acres of land to development. Preserving land also has implications for human health and safety. Studies show that living near parks, woods, and other green spaces can improve mental and physical health. Close proximity to green spaces results in stress reduction and less depression anxiety and has been found to be strongest with children and people with low incomes (http://www.webmd.com/mental-health/news/20091014/parks-green-spaces-protect-your-health). Therefore, the environment preserved as a function of public recreation services can contribute to individual and public health.

Green spaces can also improve air quality, which affects everyone. A study in the United Kingdom found that a 10% increase in urban tree coverage in mid-size cities can absorb about 12% of carbon emissions, contributing to cleaner air (http://thecityfix.com/blog/urban-green-space-key-in-improving-air-quality/). Researchers in Portugal discovered that green spaces in cities not only helped with air quality but also created more pleasant soundscapes and provided better thermal comfort conditions, according to the perspectives of residents (https://bibliotecadigital.ipb.pt/handle/10198/3236). Further, a clear link seems to exist between the quality of water and the amount of parkland, forests, and open land in an area, since these spaces tend to filter water rather than having it run off directly into streams and lakes (Crompton, 2007). Also related to water, natural areas serve as sponges when heavy rains occur. The amount of concrete and pavement that exists, particularly in cities, makes flooding a major concern. The more green space available, the less flooding that may occur.

Another way that environmental resources such as trails and bikeways might benefit health within cities is related to pollution and traffic congestion. If people have alternative ways to get to work (e.g., safe and well-maintained biking and walking paths), they will drive less and thus not only reduce congestion but also reduce greenhouse gases. Also related to pollution and reducing energy, researchers have found that shade trees reduce solar heat when strategically placed, and can serve like air conditioners for homes and other buildings (Crompton, 2007). This fact may also be surmised since temperatures in rural areas are often slightly lower than in cities.

Crime and personal safety are health concerns of almost everyone. More police and longer jail terms are not necessarily the answers to reducing crime. Evidence suggests that crime rates drop when open space and recreation opportunities are expanded and improved in cities. Law enforcement authorities and recreation professionals have argued that a dollar spent on recreation reduces the number of dollars the public has to spend on crime prevention and correctional rehabilitation, although these benefits are difficult to document. Recreation professionals work to address the importance of facilities and programs in lowering the crime rate because they provide alternative options, particularly for young people. Recreation services can contribute to public safety. Collaboration with police departments and other community services are often necessary to ensure that this benefit occurs. The more groups, including recreation services organizations, who address this problem of crime and violence, the safer communities will be for people to recreate. See Table 7.2 for an example of the potential contribution of recreation to community health.

Table 7.2 Did You Know?
(Adapted from NRPA brochure, 2000)

It costs approximately $30,000 to incarcerate a juvenile offender for one year. If that money were available to the local Recreation and Park Department, we could:

Take him [or her] swimming twice a week for 24 weeks, and give him four tours of the zoo plus lunch, and enroll him in 50 community center programs, and visit Oxley Nature Center twice, and let him play league softball for a season, and tour the gardens at Woodward Park twice, and give him two weeks of tennis lessons, and enroll him in two weeks of Day Camp, and let him play three rounds of golf, and act in one play, and participate in one fishing clinic, and take a four-week pottery class, and play basketball eight hours a week for 40 weeks after which we could return to you $29,125 (of taxpayer money) and one much happier kid.

By Bob Jennings, Naturalist III, Oxley Nature Center
From the Tulsa Park and Recreation Department Marketing Plan, 1997–1998

Environmental Ethics

People interested in leisure experiences in the outdoors can also benefit the environment in communities by the ways that the environment is perceived as well as the collective actions that can be undertaken. People who care about the environment embody their environmental ethics. People who love the environment want to protect it and do so by such actions as practicing minimum impact and leave no trace, which helps to assure that outdoor opportunities are of the highest quality. Further, these people will be advocates for the value of public lands.

Leave No Trace (LNT), for example, is founded on the principle that education can reduce the impacts on the environment. It focuses on responsible behavior in the outdoors that does not degrade the natural world. The more a person knows about the environment, the less likely he or she is to make decisions that will hurt it. Realistically, just by going into the outdoors, humans change it. But, by being aware of the ethics that should guide behavior, the impact can be lessened.

Numerous environmental nonprofit groups exist to preserve land, to educate people about the environment, and to lobby governmental decision-makers about the need to consider the environment in all legislation proposed. These organizations serve as a means to make people aware, educate them, and provide opportunities for them to practice environmental ethics. One example is the Sierra Club, which serves several functions, including providing outdoor trips that focus on the environment and minimizing impact.

Many recreation services organizations use the natural environment. Some are more focused on environmental ethics than others. Nevertheless, the practices adopted by these organizations speak to the importance of environmental ethics as adopted by individuals that improve community life.

Economic Benefits

Economic benefits of recreation can occur in communities where dollars are spent in tourism or other recreation activities. The value of recreation services also may result in saving money in businesses and corporations due to lack of absenteeism on the job and reduced healthcare costs.

A market for leisure exists. Further, this dynamic market has changing tastes and forms. A discussion of the economic benefits of recreation services relates to overall expenditures, intangible benefits, and employment.

Expenditures

Examining the amount spent each year on selected activities dramatically illustrates the significance of leisure on the economy. Although comprehensive statistics are difficult to obtain, expenditure studies are periodically conducted. One measure of the health of the economy is what people spend on recreation. For example, in the late 1880s, less than 2% of household expenditures were devoted to recreation. By the 1930s, this recreational budget share had risen to 4% and it reached 6% by 1991, and as can be seen in Table 7.3, it represents about 9% today. Even when income falls, recreation spending usually remains the same at about 5–10% of family living expenses. Recreation has been described as recession and inflation resistant. What this statement likely means, however, is that people participate in leisure regardless of the economic conditions, but they may spend their money in different ways (e.g., go on a vacation closer to home).

The category of arts, entertainment, and recreation is one important category that is examined regularly by the U.S. Department of Census. This category is comprised of establishments that are involved in producing, promoting, or participating in recreational activities and amusement, hobby, and leisure-time interests. Table 7.3 also shows a comparison of the expenditures on various recreation activities in 1990, 2000, and 2009.

In addition to the obvious recreation expenditures, a host of related expenditures exist. For example, what percentage of the billions of dollars spent for telephone services can be attributed to leisurely social conversations? What percentage of the billions of dollars spent for clothing, shoes, and accessories were used primarily in recreation behaviors?

Expenditures, in addition, include not only what individuals buy but also how the government spends money for recreation. The United

Table 7.3 Personal Consumption Expenditures for Recreation: 1990, 2000, 2009
[In billions of dollars (315 represents $315,000,000,000), except percent. Represents market value of purchases of goods and services by individuals and nonprofit institutions.]

Type of Product or Service	1990	2000	2009
Total recreation expenditures (in billions)	**315**	**640**	**897**
Percent of total personal consumptions	8.2	9.4	9.0
Categories			
Video and audio equipment, computers, and related services	81	184	265
Video and audio equipment	44	83	107
Information processing equipment	10	44	65
Services related to video and audio goods and computers	28	57	93
Sports and recreational goods and related services	74	148	197
Sports and recreational vehicles	17	35	42
Other sporting and recreational goods	55	109	150
Maintenance and repair of recreational vehicles and sports equipment	2	4	5
Membership clubs, sports centers, parks, theaters, and museums	50	92	127
Membership clubs and participant sports centers	14	26	33
Amusements parks, campgrounds, and related recreational services	19	31	42
Admissions to specified spectator amusements	14	31	46
Motion picture theaters	5	9	10
Live entertainment, excluding sports	5	10	15
Spectator sports	5	12	21
Museums and libraries	2	4	6
Magazines, newspapers, books, and stationery	47	81	105
Gambling	24	68	109
Pets, pet products, and related services	19	40	67
Photographic goods and services	17	20	18
Package tours[1]	3	8	9

[1] Consists of tour operators' and travel agents' margins. Purchases of travel and accommodations included in tours are accounted for separately in other personal consumption expenditures categories.

Source: U.S. Bureau of Economic Analysis, National Economic Accounts, *National Income and Product Account Tables, Table 2.5.5*, August 2010. See also: http://www.bea.gov/national/nipaweb/Index.asp

States spends 0.3% of the gross domestic product on recreation and culture (http://rankingamerica.wordpress.com/2009/06/19/the-u-s-ranks-24th-in-spending-on-recreation-and-leisure/). This amounts to about $45 billion dollars each year. Each year, over $3 billion is spent by the National Park Service (http://www.nps.gov/aboutus/budget.htm). States as well as local governments together also spend billions each year on public recreation services.

Intangible Benefits

The relationship of recreation services to the economy is more than the number of dollars Americans spend each year. It also includes benefits such as the location of recreation and property values, the economic impact of tourist dollars, and leisure goods and services.

Location and Property Values

Parks and greenways help increase land and property values, especially when the recreation areas are properly constructed, maintained, and operated. Realtors support the contention that the presence of recreation facilities frequently has a favorable influence on land and property values. Real estate developers know that when public improvements such as access to parks and trails are made in a residential area, property value increases. As the market value of the land increases, so does the amount of tax the owner pays. For example, waterfront lake properties generally have a higher value than lots without direct access to water. The presence of a community center, park, or swimming pool will generally enhance the overall property value of a neighborhood.

Economic Impact

Not all communities are as intimately involved in recreation as are Aspen, Colorado, or Myrtle Beach, South Carolina. All communities, however, do have private recreation businesses such as bowling lanes, pool halls, and restaurants, and may be benefited by local participation as well as tourism travel. Citizens recreate at home and tourists spend money in places they visit. Recreation businesses use public utilities, contribute to the tax rolls, and employ workers, just as do public and nonprofit organizations.

Economic impact refers to the influence of a program, project, or event on the economy of an area. The area can be a local community, a state, or a nation. The impact is associated with the amount of money brought into an area as well as associated employment opportunities. The analysis calculates the difference between the level of economic activity before and after a program, project, or event occurs. For example, economic impact analyses have been calculated based on the amount of revenues generated as a result of a weekend sports tournament in a community. Many states calculate the amount of tourism dollars that come to the state each year and how those dollars multiply regarding the need for additional services as well as employment.

Measuring the total economic effects of recreation resources, however, is difficult. For example, a water reservoir may be constructed primarily for reasons such as flood control, irrigation, and electrical power. When fully developed, however, recreation use may become the more obvious generator and sustainer of the local economy. New subdivisions in communities may be developed because of the recreation potential of this lake. Marinas and other businesses that depend upon water activity can be established. Motels and resorts accommodating tourists could be built and the community then depends on the lake as a recreation and economic resource. Because planners now recognize the economic potential of natural resource development, they account for recreation as a part of the justification and cost of many projects.

Goods and Services

Recreation also has intangible benefits on larger economic development scales. For example, one criterion that industries often use to determine where to locate their headquarters is the recreation opportunities that might contribute to employees' well-being and quality of life in communities. Therefore, recreation opportunities often can be an important reason why corporations as well as individuals might move to a community. When more people live in a community, more taxes are generated and more additional services will be necessary.

Realtors selling homes often promote the recreation features of a given neighborhood. Many retirement communities and real estate developments are sold related to opportunities for leisure living. Some of these areas are described as recreational developments with a focus on the amenities such as a boat harbor and/or a golf course. Pictures of sailing, power boating, and sunbathing by the lake are often highlighted in these promotions.

Employment

In some communities, recreation services are a primary employer of the community's residents. Examples are ski resorts and beach communities, which may depend almost entirely on tourists for their financial existence. If the Disney Company terminated its operations in Orlando, Florida, for example, the consequences would be catastrophic. Thousands of employees would be without jobs and many of the industries such as hotels and restaurants depending upon tourists would be without clients. Property values would drop, unemployment would increase, and local government would find difficulty in continuing the level of services as tax revenues and property values fell.

The recreation services sectors employ millions of people. In the public sector alone, hundreds of thousands of individuals are employed as managers and supervisors, clerical workers, maintenance personnel, program specialists, and seasonal and part-time employees. The number of individuals working for the nonprofit sector that includes membership as well as youth serving organizations is equally as large. The tourism industry employs millions of people to provide services. More than one fourth of U.S. jobs are related directly and indirectly to recreation and leisure. Every indicator suggests that recreation services will continue to grow in the future (Begun, 2000).

The implications of recreation services on the quality of life of communities are huge when considering the cultural, environmental, and economic influences. When considered together, the individual benefits combined with community contributions show that leisure experiences and recreation services are an integral part of society that must be maintained and enhanced.

Reflection Questions

1. Although all the elements in the Quality of Life index portrayed in Table 7.1 appear to be weighted the same, are some elements more important than others? Where would you rank the three aspects discussed in this chapter: leisure culture, economy, and environment?

2. Everyone is associated with various cultural groups. Can you identify with particular groups? What implications does that cultural group membership have for your leisure?

3. If recreation services provide such major contributions to the cultural, economic, and environmental aspects of communities, why are recreation services not more highly valued?

4. What do you think are the major environmental issues that will need to be addressed in the future? How can recreation services contribute?

5. Do some sectors of recreation services make a greater contribution than others to the quality of life in communities related to cultural, environmental, and economic aspects?

6. Someday, if not already, you may own a home in a community. What would you consider as important when choosing a place to live? Do recreation opportunities factor at all into your preferences?

Chapter 8

Just Leisure and Recreation Services

The previous chapters have extolled the virtues of leisure experiences and recreation services. I believe that professionals in our field must be "believers" in the value of leisure and recreation. Although recreation professionals believe that leisure experiences and recreation services must be sustainable and ought to be available for all, not everyone in society shares that belief. Because of the valuation of work over leisure, sometimes leisure is viewed as frivolous, a waste of time, and something not deemed worthy of thoughtful consideration. Even when students say they are taking a university course about leisure, recreation, sports, or tourism, parents sometimes wonder if it is a good use of tuition money, and friends wonder if this area is a legitimate course of study. Being able to articulate the benefits as described so far in this book is essential.

Although leisure experiences and recreation services offer the potential for well-being and contributions to the quality of life in communities, they also have the potential to be negative and detrimental to individuals, communities, and environments. The Greek philosopher Socrates indicated that the unexamined life is not worth living. Unless we examine leisure experiences and recreation services critically, the full possibilities may not be realized. Therefore, this chapter highlights how recreation services can be a means to make society better when justice (i.e., just recreation) is an outcome of efforts. On the flip side, however, the negative or downside of leisure experiences and recreation services is also discussed.

Just Recreation

Any professional committed to recreation services should consider the fundamental values of justice, equity, and empowerment. Further, recreation services should be intentionally designed to bring about positive outcomes in individuals, groups, communities, and the environment. Leisure is not inherently good and facilitating recreation services cannot be left to fate. Justice is embodied in demonstrating an interest in the protection, growth, health, and well-being of people as well as of their communities and natural environments.

Just recreation or just leisure relates to the notion that leisure and recreation contribute to social as well as environmental justice. Fain (1991) suggested, "Every act of leisure has moral meaning" (p. 7). Therefore, recreation professionals should examine implications for social and environmental justice in all that is undertaken.

Social justice includes a vision of society with an equitable distribution of resources and where individuals feel physically and psychologically safe. In this society, individuals are both self-determining and interdependent. It involves a sense of one's own agency and a sense of social responsibility toward and with others and for society as a whole (Adams, Bell, & Griffin, 1997). Social justice also refers to an understanding of present and historical social inequities to address positive social change.

Just recreation also encompasses environmental justice. Environmental justice is an outgrowth of social justice with a focus on how the environment influences people's lives and vice versa. It goes beyond environmentalism that emphasizes species and land preservation (Warren, 1996). With its roots in problems resulting from environmental racism (i.e., a concern that people of color tend to be ignored regarding environmental problems), environmental justice proposes that individuals and communities practicing just recreation cannot abdicate their responsibility to examine the impact on the environment from ecological and social perspectives. The goals of both social and environmental justice are reflected in social movements that result in inclusion and empowerment.

Leisure has not always been viewed as something positive or just. Nor has it always been assumed that leisure is for everyone. For example, the Ancient Greeks viewed leisure as a necessary component of becoming a citizen, but becoming a citizen was a privilege reserved only for free men. The Ancient Romans used leisure as a means of social control with "bread and circuses" (i.e., entertainment provided along with food distribution) used as a way to distract the masses from the poverty, despair, and powerlessness in their own lives. Both of these perspectives are discussed in more detail in the next unit.

The ways people think about and use leisure and the ways recreation services have been provided has changed over time. For example, with the transition from an agrarian to an industrial economy, family and neighborhood-based leisure shifted toward consumer activities that could be purchased for the right price. People who may have once relied on their families and/or their neighbors began to look outward to others to assist them to meet their recreation interests and needs. Public recreation services, nonprofit organizations, and private business endeavors emerged somewhat together but aimed at different constituencies (e.g., businesses such as resorts were aimed toward wealthy people, nonprofit activities focused on youth). The laws of supply and demand seemed to be at work as people sought more opportunities and sectors provided activities to meet the demand and also created the demand for new activities. Along with this supply, however, disparities in opportunities emerged that continue today.

Recreation Services for All

Although the rhetoric of recreation services is that they should be available for all, professionals must be reflective and critical about the shortfalls of this philosophy. Some debate has ensued over the years regarding whether leisure is a right or a privilege. The World Leisure Organization states in its International Charter for Leisure (2005) that "All people have a basic human right to leisure activities." The Charter goes on to state that all governments should ensure that citizens have accessible recreation opportunities of high quality. Other people, however, sometimes believe that leisure is a privilege, which might refer to a special advantage that one earns in some way. Unfortunately, not everyone has the same opportunities for leisure because of time, money, ability, and health. Leisure and recreation, then, are not distributed equally and may not be perceived as a right for all.

In the United States, the philosophy of public recreation services has been to make opportunities available for all. However, budget cuts and the lack of priority sometimes have resulted in collecting more fees for services. In the past 20 years, more focus has been placed on trying to ensure diversity in all tax-supported organizations, but that intention is more easily said than done. Nonprofit organizations have also sought to target particular groups that may have been underserved but not undeserved.

The social policy of the U.S. government in the 20th century was to expect that all citizens would accept the ideals of the American way of life (i.e., the "melting pot," their theory based on acculturation and assimilation). Regardless of one's background, the basic program of recreation services was the same for all citizens, although the concept of "separate but equal" also existed. For example, racial segregation was openly accepted within public recreation and park departments in many areas of the South, which essentially operated two systems: one for whites and one for blacks. In communities where few minorities existed, recreation services were generally not available to most citizens of color.

The enactment of the Civil Rights Act (1964) ended the dual approach of providing separate recreation services. With the demise of the segregated system, other social changes occurred. Minority groups and people of color began to proclaim their identity. New criteria were applied to measure program success and effectiveness as various groups demanded more participation in the decision-making process. Americans became aware that its citizens were not alike and did not want to be treated alike.

By 1980, a philosophy of programs for diverse groups (e.g., based on race, (dis)ability, income) had become an accepted part of the public recreation mission. The success in translating the philosophy into action, however, largely depended on the approach taken by local communities.

In the 21st century, a philosophy of inclusion is present in many public and nonprofit recreation services organizations. Although discrimination in various forms continues to exist in U.S. society, often much more implicitly than explicitly, the federal law requires equal opportunity in work and leisure. Recreation providers must ensure that programs provide inclusion for all groups (e.g., racial and ethnic groups, males and females, people with and without disabilities), not just because of the law but because it is the right and fair course to take. Some groups may prefer to participate separately, but all recreation services offered should focus on inclusion and welcoming environments.

The Downside of Leisure and Recreation Services

Recreation services can be detrimental to society if they exclude people from their right to leisure. How leisure can be both beneficial and detrimental is complex. As described in the previous chapters, leisure experiences and recreation services contexts can be beneficial from personal, social, cultural, environmental, and economic perspectives. Leisure experiences and recreation services can facilitate physical and mental well-being resulting in personal empowerment. Personal empowerment, however, does little good if it exists within larger exploitative work and economic systems that render some individuals powerless. Further, talking about constraints that can emerge *within* various leisure experiences is important to consider.

The benefits of leisure and recreation can be viewed within a larger context that compares U.S. society to others. For example, many people in the United States have an average of two and a half weeks of paid vacation each year. Compared to other countries in the world, this amount is small (see Table 8.1). Italians get over 8 weeks of paid vacation each year. Further, although 40 hours per week is usually considered the standard work week, many people work many more than 40 hours. These people may be professionals who cannot do all that needs to be done in 40 hours and also includes individuals who make low wages and must work more than one job to make ends meet. Many people have come to believe that they cannot change their work situations. Their futility is illustrative of a larger sense of powerlessness that some people come to accept as a trade-off for being lucky enough to have a job.

Despite the potential benefits of leisure, many people feel time-stressed. There is never enough time each day to get done what is expected and consequently, leisure may be of low priority and less important. A cycle exists that is difficult to break—some people are stressed because they feel they need to work harder and more, they do not have time for recreation activities, which results in feeling more stressed.

A group of people have formed a coalition called "Take Back Your Time" (http://timeday.org) and are challenging the epidemic of overwork, over-scheduling, and time famine that now threatens Americans' health, families and relationships, communities, and the environment. This group

Table 8.1 Paid Vacation Days per Year around the World
[Source: World Tourism Organization (WTO)]

Italy	42 days
France	37 days
Germany	35 days
Brazil	34 days
United Kingdom	28 days
Canada	26 days
Korea	25 days
Japan	25 days
United States	13 days

is also lobbying for laws that require a greater number of days of paid vacation. The progress of this group has been slow, however, since attitudes about work are carried over in how people think about recreation and leisure.

The message that many people get as they grow up is that one is only entitled to leisure once work has been done. "Get your homework done and then you can play" is not an uncommon phrase. Because work and leisure are inextricably linked, leisure and recreation are affected. Leisure for both adults and children can also be constrained if it overly dependent on organized recreation opportunities.

Dependency on Recreation Services

Concerns about dependency on recreation services may seem a bit unusual given that recreation professionals want people to participate in recreation services and enjoy programs, facilities, and events. Recreation services are central to facilitate many people's leisure. Although recreation services can provide opportunities for enjoyment, entertainment, and learning, finding meaningful leisure ought to be something that every individual can also find on his or her own.

A balance between being able to be self-sufficient in leisure and having opportunities to make use of recreation services is the ideal. Many people experience the benefits of leisure because these structured services are available. For example, National Parks have been set aside so that many people can enjoy the great outdoors. Very few people could ever own their own "park." Nevertheless, having the individual attitudes, skills, and abilities to enjoy a park is necessary. Another issue that has been raised concerns the over-programming of children. Some children are so involved in structured activities that they have little time for creative play.

Recreation services professionals must recognize that advocating for recreation services also means enabling people to increase their activity repertoire so they can find meaningful leisure experiences on their own. If recreation professionals help people try something new, challenge them in positive ways, or provide opportunities for expression, then recreation services can be positive. If, on the other hand, people come to believe that they cannot really have leisure if they do not participate in a structured setting, or that they have to spend money or consume products to have leisure, then a negative type of dependency has been fostered.

One way to counteract undesired dependency is to teach participants how to become critical consumers of leisure. People need to learn how to assess their knowledge, attitudes, and behaviors regarding leisure and recreation opportunities. The role of recreation professionals can then be as supporters of recreation interests. Regardless of the service sector, professionals can work with participants, members, clients, and constituents to plan, implement, and evaluate their personal leisure involvement.

Recreation professionals may want to consider moving away from solely service provision toward becoming facilitators of opportunities for leisure experiences. Most individuals have the skills and abilities to become stewards of their own leisure. If recreation and leisure are valuable to people, recreation professionals may want to support individuals and their communities in self-identifying and meeting their own leisure needs and interests. At the same time, citizens may need to be challenged and empowered to take responsibility for their leisure with the support of recreation services professionals.

Moving Toward Justice

Leisure experiences and recreation services can be unjust if they reinforce inappropriate roles (e.g., gender roles and expectations) and/or the status quo. People may learn to behave in particular ways because of recreation settings such as sports, dramatic arts, and dance. Although these settings can teach positive attributes for personal growth, these same settings can reinforce the status quo as well as norms and behaviors that can limit people in their lives. For example, the types of leisure activities and opportunities provided through structured recreation and leisure contexts sometimes are gendered. Although more girls are engaging in sports, the expectation often exists that they will not or should not participate in aggressive and violent sporting contexts. Similarly, many boys are discouraged from involvement in activities like dancing or cheerleading.

Recreation professionals can have important roles in addressing injustices and considering how both personal and professional ethics are evidenced in recreation services. Recreation professionals may need to examine how they as well as the people they serve make choices that reflect personal ethics of caring about themselves, each other, and the environment. Personal as well as professional ethics provide a way of finding the best course to enable a sense of right and just living in a complex world, and what the relationship between people and the environment should be. For example, when a recreation activity is proposed, professionals need to think how this behavior might affect the environment as well as how inclusive it might be. These concerns are also the basis for ensuring that recreation services are sustainable.

This chapter has aimed to show how leisure experiences and recreation services can be contexts for promoting key contributors to social and environmental justice. For recreation services to be an opportunity for change and social justice requires that individuals ask how they can work toward personal and social change in their own lives as well as in the organizations where they work (Kivel & Kivel, 2000).

Some of the criticism of recreation services as being only "fun and games" may lie in professionals' inability to articulate the social implications of recreation services from a reflective point of view. Reflection focuses not only on critique but also on a movement toward action in addressing social problems. Further, change does not occur if current structures benefit only those people in power. Professionals should always consider how recreation services can enhance the quality of life for all and not just for the elite in communities.

Leisure and recreation services are not inherently good, and the limitations and detriments must be acknowledged along with the strengths. The ideals of just leisure and recreation have direct implications for the sustainability of recreation services. Although leisure and recreation services have much to contribute to people's well-being and the quality of life in communities, they must also be intentionally designed to be inclusive and sustainable into the future.

Reflection Questions

1. Why should social justice be an important outcome of recreation services?

2. Some people in communities are able to access leisure opportunities better than others. Why do these types of disparities exist?

3. Inequities in leisure are often attributed to income levels. Have leisure experiences and recreation services become more of a consumer commodity in society than a public good?

4. What is the relationship between social justice and environmental justice?

5. What will be the greatest challenges to recreation professionals in the future as they strive to offer recreation services for all?

6. Do you believe people in the United States should have more days of vacation? Why do you suppose the United States lags so far behind other countries in mandating that vacation should be a right that workers have?

7. One of the purposes of recreation services is to help people develop skills and find their own opportunities for leisure rather than always relying on structured opportunities. Why would this philosophy be good? Why might it be a problem?

Chapter 9

Overview and Early Histories

Leisure as well as recreation services have a long history. This history serves as a testament to human creativity and inventiveness. No single history of leisure exists, so we can refer to the written *histories* of leisure. Just as many leisures exist, many histories of these leisures also exist. These historical analyses of recreation and leisure provide insight into the forces shaping contemporary society. The better these forces are understood, the better prepared future recreation professionals will be.

John Hemingway (Henderson et al., 2001) used an example about history that I believe is worth repeating. He asks you to imagine hiking up a trail in the mountains. As you walk, you note landmarks like a distant peak that comes into view on your left as you gain elevation and a waterfall deep in a ravine at a bend in the trail. Retracing your path later as you walk back down the same trail, the peak and the waterfall are still there but your relationship to them has changed. The peak is on your right now and disappears as you walk while the bend in the trail now hides the ravine from your view until you are past it. You had two distinct angles of vision on that trail, each shaped by your surroundings, activities, and expectations.

History is a lot like that mountain walk. Landmarks catch people's attention depending on the questions important to them and what they think counts as an answer. Both questions and answers change as the historical angle of vision changes. Each generation writes its own version of history not because of historical fact and truth, but because different dimensions of history become important at different times. How people evaluate leisure's history and the profession's origins and development can influence an understanding of leisure and the potential for sustainable recreation services into the future.

Histories of Leisure

Every known culture reveals some evidence of leisure's presence, from the pictographs left by aboriginal peoples to the theaters and stadia of ancient Greece to the arenas of the Roman Empire. Toys, sports equipment, and game pieces have been found at many archeological sites. Examining ancient leisure reveals more than similarities and differences with contemporary leisure. It also demonstrates the human universality of leisure. This chapter focuses on an overview of early histories of leisure from mostly a dominant Western perspective. This approach does not mean to devalue other perspectives. However, the context of Western history reflects the influence of leisure within U.S. society. We begin with a bit about the earliest people and then move to ancient Egypt and Greece.

Early Ancestors

A case can be made that leisure was clearly important to God when the Judeo-Christian interpretation of creation is explored. God worked for six days to create the world. On the seventh day after the work was done, God rested. The Bible also says that God hallowed the seventh day as rest from his work.

The story of Adam and Eve also has implications for work and leisure. God put Adam and Eve into the Garden of Eden where they could live happily. However, after Eve ate the forbidden fruit, God expelled them from Eden and sent them to toil, which ended their comfortable leisure in the Garden. In many ways, work became necessary and leisure had to be earned. Other religions have other interpretations of creation and evolution, but this example dominates Western religions and is interesting to consider.

Early cultures (e.g., cave people) may or may not have had a language for leisure or recreation. Yet, their culture reflects a holistic view of their lives. People have always played, as is evidenced by artifacts that have been left behind from the early stages of human evolution. These people had to *work* to meet their subsistence needs, but leisure appeared indistinguishable from work, ritual, and spirituality. Their lives were intertwined with one another and with meeting their physical and emotional needs. Idealistically, the "oneness" potentially between the environment and humans, and the lack of compartmentalization of the world, made work and play interconnected and holistic with daily living. The separation of work and leisure became more segmented as civilizations developed.

Egypt

The Egyptian civilization endured for thousands of years from approximately 5000 B.C.E. (Before Common Era) into the Roman era. It was among the most highly developed cultures in the ancient world. Ancient Egyptian society was hierarchical. Citizens regarded the pharaoh as a god, indicating the close ties between religion and government. Wealth, status, and privilege were largely hereditary and concentrated in a small elite group of people. Below this high stratum were people engaged in crafts, trade, and agriculture.

Archeological evidence has allowed historians to develop general ideas about Egyptian leisure. Tomb walls were decorated with intricate images that offer important clues about customary leisure activities. Dancing, singing, and musical performances appear to have been frequent forms of entertainment along with dramatic presentations. Bullfights and gymnastic exhibitions are also depicted. Board games similar to chess and backgammon were common. Hunting preserves, gardens, and even animal parks were created for enjoyment, mostly by the elite (Ceram, 1971). The pharaoh's court travelled according to the season or the pharaoh's mood, seeking relief from the intense Egyptian summers. The Egyptians were aware of the restorative benefits of tourism in pleasant climates and environments.

Little is known about Egyptian attitudes toward leisure and work. Some people had a great deal of free time at their disposal because of their high status. For centuries, the Egyptians were a powerful military as well as cultural force. Some vigorous physical activity was necessary to maintain fitness for warfare. Nonetheless, a sense of pleasure-seeking appears to have prevailed among the elite. As for the vast majority of Egyptians, however, less is known about what leisure they had and how they used it.

Ancient Greece

Ancient Greece was actually a collection of small city-states not too distant from the sea and generally surrounded by small agricultural villages. Although a sense of common Greek identity existed based on a shared language and religious beliefs, people thought of themselves as citizens of their city-state. Ancient Greece was never a single political entity in the modern sense. This discussion focuses on Athens since historians know the most about this city-state.

Athenian Society

Definitions of citizenship varied among the city-states, but all established sharp distinctions between citizens and noncitizens. Simply stated, citizens were full members of the city-state, and noncitizens were excluded. Citizenship was restricted to adult, native-born males legitimately descended from a citizen father and native-born mother (Manville, 1990). Women had an ambiguous place in Athens as members of the community but not citizens. They had important public roles in the community, particularly in religious and civic ceremonies and rites (Patterson, 1994), but they were barred from the political arena.

Slavery was a constant feature in ancient Greece. Martin (1996) estimated that by 600 B.C.E., slaves comprised a third of the population in some city-states. The expense, not the immorality, probably prevented average citizens from owning slaves. To the ancient Greeks, "the freedom of some could not be imagined without the servitude of others and the two extremes were not thought of as contradictory, but as complementary and interdependent" (Austin & Vidal-Naquet, 1977, p. 19).

Athenian Leisure

Social distinctions were obvious in Athenian leisure. Among aristocrats, traditional competitive values emphasized the cultivation and display of excellence. Excellence depended on a careful balance of the virtues of mind, body, and character. Aristocratic leisure consisted of intellectual (e.g., philosophy, mathematics) and cultural (e.g., poetry, music) activities, physical exercise, and politics. For many Athenians, politics was an important arena for demonstrating their virtuous character through action informed by thought and experience (Hemingway, 1988). The wealthiest Athenians were also liable to special tax assessments to finance public cultural or religious events.

Aristocratic leisure took place in the home, the public square, the gymnasium, public buildings, meeting places, and theaters. Food and drink were frequently involved. Plato's great dialogue, *The Symposium*, recounts a supper and drinking party where revelers competed by making speeches on the meanings of love. The latest scandals, cultural trends, and political issues were topics of conversation. Wit was highly valued. Aristocrats engaged in impromptu poetry contests or were called on to compose and sing songs, sometimes while dancing. These friendly competitions had important consequences for individual reputations.

Little is known about the leisure of Athenian common citizens. In the agricultural area surrounding Athens, many poor farmers had small plots of land to support their families. Their public lives focused on local affairs, festivals, and rites. In the city itself, the citizens generally were members of the least wealthy property classes. Most citizens lived simple lives. We could say public recreation services were available at that time since the city of Athens provided entertainment with admission to public theatrical and musical performances free for citizens. Women and noncitizens also attended. Common citizens passed time in public areas, gathered in taverns, and visited the market.

Greek Games and Festivals

Religious dimensions were a part of almost all activity in ancient Greece. Ancient Greek games and festivals illustrated this connection. In Athens during 600 B.C.E., around 60 days were devoted to festivals annually (Snodgrass, 1980).

The most famous games were dedicated to Zeus, chief of the Greek gods, and were held every four years during mid-summer at Zeus's shrine in Olympia (Chamoux, 1965). The Olympic Games began the quadrennial cycle of Panhellenic games known as an Olympiad. Founded in 776 B.C.E., the Games contributed to and were evidence of cultural identity in Greece. Safe passage was guaranteed to all competitors and spectators on their way to and from Olympia. Competitors had to satisfy religious requirements since the games were a religious festival that would be profaned if someone unfit participated.

No team events were in the ancient Olympic Games. Athletes competed as individuals in foot races, wrestling, field events, and boxing. The premier event was a foot race of some two hundred yards. Early competitors were wealthy young men with time and energy to develop their athletic skills. Although a garland of olive leaves from a tree at Zeus's shrine was the only prize awarded at Olympia, an Olympic victory was often lucrative once the winners returned home. Statues and plaques were erected and victory odes written to honor the winners. Some city-states awarded stipends to Olympic winners while others allowed them to dine at public expense for life. Eventually, professional athletes and prize money weakened the games (Martin, 1996).

Spectators came from across Greece. Men were admitted as spectators apparently without fees, but sources differ on whether women were admitted. Martin (1996) stated that unmarried women were allowed entrance as spectators, but married women were barred "under pain of death" (p. 46).

Religious ceremonies and athletic contests were not the only attractions at Olympia. Outside the sacred area people thronged to enjoy dramatic and musical entertainments, listen to orators and debaters, and attend public lectures by scholars who came seeking an audience to gain fame and perhaps a patron. The Olympic Games were much more a cultural festival than an athletic competition. Although the Olympic Games were the most famous, other games also were part of the quadrennial cycle.

Women apparently had their own games at Olympia. The Heraea Games were held every four years to honor Hera who was the consort of Zeus. During the Heraea, unmarried women competed in three age groups in foot races approximately five-sixths the distance of those in the Olympic Games. Victors received the Olympic garland and also part of the cow sacrificed to Hera.

Athenian Attitudes toward Leisure and Work

Aristotle wrote that the right use of leisure is the first principle of human activity. He condemned the hunger for wealth that distracted people from the excellences of character developed only in leisure. The ancient Greeks did not regard work as inherently virtuous or ennobling. They understood it as a distinct category of human activity (Austin & Vidal-Naquet, 1977), not part of a larger economic system. Character was revealed by an occupation and the characteristic conditions associated with it. The ancient Greeks thought dependence on someone else for livelihood was a character flaw. Agriculture, for example, was widely regarded as the occupation most suitable for a citizen. Retail trade, commerce, and manufacturing were at the bottom of the scale. These occupations tempted a worker to lust after excessive wealth, which was a fatal character weakness and distracted them from the potential of leisure.

Athenian citizens considered themselves wealthy if they could live without working. Once the modest financial needs of an average Athenian citizen were met, citizens fulfilled their religious and civic obligations and offered appropriate hospitality to relatives and friends. Citizens were expected to turn their energies to activities more important than work. In Athens, leisure was not a consequence of being financially wealthy, but rather an intrinsic component of wealth itself. Non-monetary wealth was achieved in leisure by participating in the intellectual, cultural, and political life of Athens.

By this definition, the majority of Athenian citizens were poor. Athenians and ancient Greeks generally valued leisure more than work. This ideal was always largely aristocratic in content, and only the aristocrats and a few wealthy citizens ever managed to achieve something like leisure, which was defined mostly as a state of being. The majority of ancient Greeks worked because of necessity. Many, despite being citizens, worked alongside slaves to make a living. Unlike slaves, citizens found relief in the knowledge that they retained their freedom, but their freedom was reduced by their need to work. Although leisure was not available in the Greek sense to all, all cultures have played and recreation activity pursuits were not restricted for anyone.

This early history showed leisure as a phenomenon that influenced people for centuries. An understanding of the histories of different groups of people and different times gives a foundation for understanding leisure and recreation services in the present and for the future. Leisure was highly valued in many cultures and reflected the values of the time.

Reflection Questions

1. Why is it important to study the history of any topic?

2. What is special and distinct about studying leisure compared to other domains of life?

3. The earliest people in the world seemed to have a holistic view of leisure. What is appealing about that view? What problems might be associated with it?

4. The early Greek philosophy about leisure is often referred to as the ideal. Why was this approach valuable in understanding leisure? How was the approach socially exclusive?

5. Much more is known about the elite and their leisure in Egypt and in Greece than is known about the common people. Why do we not know more about common people in these civilizations?

Chapter 10

The Roman Empire
and Medieval Europe

Rome's history as an empire and the medieval period that followed are also part of the early history of Western culture. Similar to the Greek ideal, the events during these times also have influenced thoughts about work and leisure today. The purpose of this chapter is to overview leisure and recreation in the Roman Empire and Medieval Europe.

Roman Empire

Rome's history is one of steady expansion from a small hilltop village, dated to 750 B.C.E., into an immense empire followed by spectacular collapse. The division of the empire into western and eastern parts by the emperor Constantine fatally weakened Rome's central imperial authority. The empire had to be secure at its center in Rome, or whatever happened on its frontiers would be irrelevant. Therefore, the Roman emperors' first priority was to ensure their popularity in Rome.

This focus on popularity led to the famous policy of *bread and circuses* with the monthly distributions of food to feed people and frequent entertainments such as circuses to amuse them. Indulgence spread to private leisure, as the Romans poured their wealth into food, drink, and amusement. Internal rot weakened the empire until it could not stand against its enemies. The Romans suffered a significant defeat by the Goths in 378, who overran the city of Rome itself in 410 C.E. Some people might argue that part of the downfall of Rome was due to the inability of the government or citizens to manage their leisure.

Roman Society

The Roman Empire was at its peak of power and prosperity around the years 100 to 150 C.E. There were two classes of citizens in Rome: the patricians and the plebeians. Social distinctions existed between these classes with additional status distinctions among the patricians. The Romans often extended citizenship status to inhabitants of conquered territories, which resulted in regular infusions of new ideas and personalities into Rome. Ideas circulated easily in Roman society and egalitarianism allowed for merit to be recognized and rewarded.

The gap between the Roman elite and the rest of Roman society, however, grew larger over time. At its height, Rome was the administrative center of the empire and taxes flowed in from provinces to support it. This wealth was concentrated in the hands of wealthy elite. The middle class shrunk to almost nothing in Rome. The majority of the population lived in or on the edge of poverty and at least a third relied on charity. Slave owning became more widespread in Rome during the imperial period. Around 200 B.C.E., households owning more than one slave were unusual, but four hundred years later it was unusual to find a household owning *only* one slave. The wealthy often owned hundreds of slaves.

Roman Leisure

The Romans regarded work as the negation of leisure. To Roman citizens, work was an indignity to be avoided, somewhat similar to how some Ancient Greeks felt. Many people did not work and various doles and allowances of food were available, along with a well-developed system of social patronage (Toner, 1995). Citizens could rely on both public and private support. Work was there for citizens who wanted it, but even they did not spend much time at it. Workers usually had all or most of their afternoons free. Merchants and shopkeepers organized themselves so well that they worked only six or seven hours a day. Business transactions were usually completed by early afternoon. Once business was out of the way, the remainder of the day was devoted to leisure. The Romans clearly preferred leisure to work.

The patricians' first task was attention to personal appearance and wardrobe. Men often visited the barber to have their hair done and to collect the latest news and scandal. The rounds of social visits were a significant practice in Roman society. Depending on social rank, people received callers at home or called on others such as their patrons. Patrons were individuals with generally higher status. Patrons dispensed gifts and put in a good word when and where necessary. Calling on patrons was required not only to keep their favor, but so the patrons could display their status. Patrons assembled their followers before setting off on their own visits to make a grander impression.

Plebeians imitated the wealthy to the extent their own needs and limited means permitted. Those plebeians who worked left home early.

Plebeians who did not work visited the houses of patricians where they might receive food, or perhaps small sums of money. Whether employed or not, by mid-afternoon the plebeians also turned to leisure.

All classes enjoyed Rome's attractions and amusements, but social distinctions were evident. People strolled in public squares or gardens and conversed or watched the many street entertainers. They exercised at gymnasiums, ball courts, or athletic fields. In the theaters Romans preferred comedies to dramas, but the theater popularity waned as the circuses became more elaborate. Scholars and authors gave lectures and readings in public halls hoping to find patrons and a demand for their works. Games of chance were highly popular in the street and taverns, particularly guessing games or dice games. The baths were highly popular among the Romans, with facilities to match all tastes and incomes. Dinner itself was frequently a social occasion. In wealthy patrician households, dinners could be extravagant with entertainment between courses, much talk, and lots of wine.

Games and the Circus

Somewhat similar to the Greeks, the Romans had an extraordinary number of public holidays devoted to festivals and games. By McDaniel's (1924) estimate, there were 175 holidays each year in the fourth century. Some emperors attempted to reduce the number of holidays, but with little success. Carcopino (1940) noted that between 100 and 150 C.E. the citizens of Rome enjoyed approximately one day of holiday for every day they worked.

The circus, including chariot races, was the most glamorous of all Roman games. Large arenas, with the largest one holding 385,000 people, enclosed a large rectangular course rounded at one end. Charioteers often leaped on their horses' backs and even did handstands as they raced. These showmen were celebrities in Rome, particularly among the plebeians. Frequent collisions, however, made the activities highly dangerous. To avoid being dragged by their horses if thrown, charioteers carried a small knife to slash the reins. They might scramble to safety before being trampled by the other chariots if they were lucky.

Animal and gladiator games became more sinister as a response to the strong desire for more sensational entertainment. Wild animal shows were especially popular because exotic species could be sent to Rome from the empire's distant provinces. Lions were a particular favorite and on occasions hundreds were present in the stadium at one time. As this lion novelty wore off, human beings were forced into the arena with the wild animals. Sometimes they were armed to fight for their lives and sometimes they were unarmed just to be mauled. In the gladiatorial games, killing was done for the amusement of the onlookers who bonded in their common bloodlust.

The original meanings of Roman festivals and games were obscured when their political uses became more important than the activities. Games and festivals contributed to social stability in Rome by entertaining (and thus, controlling) the citizens. They also allowed the emperor and other members of the elite to establish a degree of contact with the public. When the emperor appeared in the imperial box at the arena, he was seen as the people's benefactor, the source of bread and circuses, and a symbol of Roman power. Wise emperors used games and circuses to gauge as well as influence the people's moods. All classes of Roman society filled the stands along with visitors from throughout Italy, the empire, and beyond. The Romans submerged themselves in amusements reflected in being at the center of an immense empire. However, as noted earlier, the empire eventually fell.

Medieval Europe

The fall of Rome in 410 C.E. shocked the Mediterranean world. Western Europe was the weakest region of the empire and was cut off from intellectual and commercial centers in the Mediterranean and Near East. The western empire disintegrated.

By 700 C.E., conditions further deteriorated in Western Europe. Agriculture, the dominant occupation, lost ground. Commerce, trade, and industry almost disappeared. Technology remained primitive. Craftspeople produced only for local markets and innovation was stifled. Travel and communication were difficult. Roads were little more than paths. Most people remained close to their manors throughout their relatively short lives. Medieval European society was "dominated by a spirit of resignation, suspicion, and fear of the outside world" (Cipolla, 1994, p. 117). Two of the most powerful elements in medieval Europe emerged: the feudal system and the church (Ferguson, 1940; 1968).

Feudal Society

Feudal society consisted of three basic social orders: the peasantry at the bottom concentrated on and around the manors; the nobility, including land-owning manorial lords and royalty; and the clergy. Once the cities began to grow again, artisans, craftspeople, and merchants achieved social status in medieval society. The manors were the center of early feudal society, with at least 90% of the population living in rural areas (Goetz, 1993). Labor time in Medieval Europe was measured by sunrise and sunset (Le Goff, 1980). The day's work was determined by season and climate.

Tenant peasants and serfs had little free time. Free time occurred when agricultural work was slack, and mostly in the winter months. Little reliable information is available about peasants' leisure and recreation, but it was probably confined within the family or the tiny manorial village. Some festivals were celebrated according to the church calendar such as Lenten holidays. Other festivals were common to rural life, particularly at the end of the harvest, the start of the seasons, and May Day. Entire villages joined in celebrating personal events like weddings.

The most characteristic aspect of the medieval nobility was the growth of the courts consisting of the king, a prince or other nobleman of high rank, family, and members of the nobility. Attendants and servants supported this assembly. Routine duties of the nobility included managing estates and manors, resolving claims of land ownership or rights, and maintaining relations with neighboring courts. Knights engaged in regular training to maintain their fighting skills. The nobility did not live altogether in idleness and ease, but this court life was more pleasant than manor life and offered opportunities for leisure. Festivals occurred on established religious holidays and to celebrate special events. Banqueting and socializing followed religious observances. Food and drink were important aspects of all medieval festivals for both nobility and peasantry. Court banquets were accompanied by music and theatrical performances. Dancing was popular. Tournaments were a grand festival that helped define knighthood as a distinct social and professional status. Only larger courts could accommodate the numbers of participants and spectators attracted to tournaments.

Other courtly leisure included the favorite activity of hunting, which allowed the display of skill, courage, and social status. Only the nobility hunted, however, since they retained exclusive rights to the game animals on their lands. Indoor leisure included board games like chess and backgammon, dice games, music, and dancing.

Substantial differences existed among the clergy. Preparation for eternal salvation motivated the creation of the monasteries as self-sufficient communities. Many monks and lay brothers came from poor families and lived simple lives working in the fields or workshops. In monasteries with collections of ancient scrolls and manuscripts, monks who were able to read and write served as copyists. Their transcriptions of these materials were often magnificently illustrated and bound. A few monks were also active scholars and were allowed to devote themselves to theology, philosophy, and the study of ancient languages. Monastic life was organized around the cycles of religious observances. Work and contemplative leisure had their places in these cycles and both were offered up to God.

Outside the monasteries, the clergy lived different lives. Village priests were figures of local importance and often participated in village and manor festivals. Bishops had courts in larger towns that occasionally rivaled or even surpassed the local nobility. As splendid as any royal court, the papal court (i.e., Vatican) sat amidst the ruins of Rome. Leisure in courts of the Pope and bishops resembled leisure in royal and noble courts more than leisure in the monasteries.

Late Medieval Society

Between 1000 and 1300 C.E., Western Europe changed significantly. The population grew more urban. Medieval cities were small by later standards but had more than 20,000 inhabitants, which was considerably larger than manor villages. Feudal social structures remained, however. People found more opportunities in cities, but late medieval cities were not egalitarian.

Commerce revived and new manufacturing techniques were developed as a money economy emerged. In the growing cities, an increasing demand for goods occurred and supplying them provided an opportunity to become wealthy. A distinct urban social class developed called the burghers who had no place in the traditional feudal social orders. Free by birth, burghers engaged in commerce and manufacturing or worked as craftspeople and artisans. To accommodate this emerging social class, new social structures appeared in the cities including occupational guilds, fraternal organizations, and the commune as a form of civic association among all burghers.

Changes in leisure followed these developments in the economy and social structure. Cities became more diverse as they grew larger. Urban markets and fairs attracted a variety of people and goods that could not be found in any manor village. Taverns and public spaces were lively. The new wealth in the cities slowly began to attract entertainers, artists, and scholars who previously had sought patrons at the noble courts. The burghers acquired interests in the learning and culture that had been the prerogative of the clergy and nobility. Fellowship and mutual support were available in the occupational guilds and fraternal organizations and became new venues for leisure activity. Life in late medieval cities remained difficult, but urban leisure began to reflect new vitality.

A number of differences existed between the eras of the Roman Empire and the medieval period. Leisure was important in the Roman Empire and had mass appeal. The corruption of leisure and the focus on amusements, however, were also elements leading to the downfall of Rome. The medieval societies of Europe defined leisure in relation to the feudal systems. Although the wealthy had access to many leisure opportunities, leisure was simple for most of the people living in European cities and manors during this time. Although work and leisure had been distinct aspects of life up to this time, the diversity of opportunities within work and within leisure began to emerge.

Reflection Questions

1. How did the view of leisure of the Romans differ from the Athenian Greeks?

2. What purposes did holidays serve in Roman culture? Would you like to have half of your year spent in holidays? What would be the advantages and disadvantages of such a situation?

3. In today's world, how is leisure used to maintain social order?

4. Is there any relationship between the Romans' desire for spectacular amusement in their stadiums and what people expect today in their entertainment?

5. Some people suggested that the fall of the Roman Empire might be partially attributed to people being unable to manage their leisure and recreation activities. Why might this statement be true?

6. What relationship existed between social status and leisure in medieval societies? Does a similar relationship exist today?

Chapter 11

Renaissance and Reformation

This chapter focuses on a sketch of Renaissance Europe (about 1300 to 1600 C.E.) and the Reformation (about 1500 to 1700 C.E.). Modern ideas about leisure, work, and wealth were intimately bound up with the political and business system that became known as capitalism. Capitalist business practices were established and refined in Europe during the Renaissance. The Protestant Reformation accelerated the spread of capitalist business practices by providing a moral justification for them. These occurrences had implications for leisure in Europe and the New World.

Renaissance

Although the word *renaissance* means rebirth or renewal, this period was more a time of transition when some regions in Europe changed more dramatically than others. Important continuities existed between the late medieval and early Renaissance periods.

Renaissance Society and Economy

Two major difficulties persisted as the transition from the medieval era to the Renaissance got underway. First, agricultural technology remained inadequate to support the steadily increasing population. Second, existing business practices limited economic expansion. Expansion was dependent on human labor rather than machines. Hiring more workers could increase production, but the additional wage costs for employees with less than reliable work habits often diminished potential returns. The lack of established standardized principles for accounting, finance, and contracts imposed other limits.

Distinctively Western capitalism emerged when entrepreneurs began reinvesting their profits to generate larger future profits. The growth in commerce, finance, and manufacturing stimulated artistic, intellectual, political, and social energies. Renaissance artists and scholars restored classical learning, created new styles in the arts and architecture, and conducted important scientific and technological investigations. In larger cities, advancement through talent and ambition allowed burghers, craftspeople, and even a few artisans to claim status similar to aristocracy.

Peter Burke (1987) warned, however, about romanticizing the Renaissance. Changes began in Italy but spread unevenly through Europe. Life continued in many regions as in the medieval era, with unreliable food supplies and fluctuating economic conditions. Life was difficult for many people even in the most revived cities. Further, the Black Death was a devastating plague. In 1420, the population of Europe was about one third what it had been in 1320.

The plague's human costs were varied. Italy never fully recovered, but in northern Europe, development actually accelerated. Demand for food decreased as the population diminished and over-cultivated land became fallow or was turned into pasture and other uses. Soaring labor costs created interest in less expensive machines and tools to replace workers. Gutenberg's invention of moveable metal type was one example of technological innovation. Other technical advances occurred in shipbuilding, construction, and metallurgy.

The Renaissance and Attitudes toward Leisure and Work

The emergence of capitalism included more than the availability of the necessary business practices. It also influenced the social meanings attached to work, wealth, leisure, and time. Business affairs were a common topic and family relationships and friendships were subject to economic calculations. Pullan (1973) noted that the ethic of worldly success and failure began to replace conventional Christian ethics. Work was celebrated. It enabled human beings to develop their physical and mental faculties (Garin, 1965).

Wealth also allowed entrepreneurs to engage in forms of leisure previously open only to the aristocracy and high clergy. This leisure often involved the display of wealth and status. Sometimes businesspeople simply imitated the tastes of the aristocracy, but often they sought opportunities for their own interests and preferences. They helped create a distinctive Renaissance urban culture throughout Europe (Ferguson, 1940). They also financed public buildings, churches, and squares, and were patrons of the arts and of learning, which helped to further their own creative and intellectual projects. Consumer goods (e.g., home furnishings, clothing, and food) were valued in daily life and also reflected leisure (Jardine, 1996).

The aristocrats and high clergy continued to regard leisure as a privilege of their hereditary social rank. For the merchants and manufacturers, leisure was an opportunity to secure a new social status conferred by wealth.

Meanings of time also changed during the Renaissance. Business-people realized that time had economic value. In many cities, life was structured around the daily hours of work. The change regarding work was gradual and did not occur everywhere. Further, traditional religious and agricultural rhythms continued to be important for many years. As Le Goff (1980) noted, time structured around special events (e.g., festivals, Sabbath days, births and deaths) was replaced by regular daily time measured in intervals such as hours. This emerging notion of time was not welcomed by everyone, with conflict sometimes arising. For example, special bells were sometimes installed in church steeples and public towers and used to ring work hours and curfews, which not all workers liked.

Another example of the economic value of time during the Renaissance was the presence of *time thrift*. Prosperity required knowing how to use one's time. Centuries before Franklin wrote that "time is money," Alberti (1969) described a simple formula for success: "make as good use as possible of time," "avoid sleep," and "never remain idle" (pp. 171–172). These ideas continue to dominate for many people in today's culture.

Reformation

The Reformation was an era of economic, political, social, and religious change. In the decades around 1500 C.E., Europe was not peaceful. Peasant uprisings occurred in the country and workers rioted in many cities. This turmoil seemed to be reflective of three fundamental changes occurring in Europe. First, the power of the Catholic Church weakened. The extravagances of the papal courts alienated many believers. The church compounded this problem by selling indulgences and imposing taxes to raise money. These secular practices troubled many in the clergy, including Martin Luther.

A second change was that political power had become increasingly centralized. Europe's political geography reflected its feudal heritage, made up of an array of fiefdoms and principalities ruled by the nobility. Nobles fought with one another, and eventually kings began to assert their influence to stop the violence.

Third, the nature of economic activity changed. Larger business organizations appeared. The values of property and other fixed business capital increased along with sale prices for goods. The nobility and wage earners were threatened. The nobility depended on fixed payments but purchasing power was decreased by inflation. Many minor nobles and younger sons in noble families were forced to abandon family estates. Without other sources of income, wage earners faced impoverishment because wages failed to keep pace with inflationary prices.

The Protestant Ethic

The Reformation unfolded in the turmoil and uncertainty created by these religious, political, and economic changes. One particular concern was with what Max Weber (1930) called the *Protestant ethic*. Weber asked how work, once limited to satisfying material needs, had become an end in itself. This change in the purpose of work happened mainly in England and later in the United States. Weber surmised that this change was due to the fusion of ideas from two Reformation thinkers, Martin Luther and John Calvin. Both Luther and Calvin believed that a relationship between God and an individual based on faith that needed no mediation by a priesthood or church. Calvin also rejected any relationship between political and religious authority and believed the church was an independent community of believers who oversaw their own affairs. For Calvin, the community of believers was the model for a Reformation of society.

Diligent work is praised as a virtue in several Biblical passages. For example, 2 Thessalonians 3:10 states "If any would not work, neither shall he eat." The moral value of work became a central theme in European history. Most people understood a community of workers better than many other kinds of communities. Since work was necessary as a result of humankind's sinful nature, diligent work was accepted. Work glorified God while allowing believers to trust in their salvation. Success in work, including wealth, could be taken as a sign of God's grace and of faith.

Converting this success associated with work into worldly social or political status, however, was problematic. Neither Luther nor Calvin exalted work as an end in itself. Their contribution to ideas about leisure, work, and wealth was to translate religious ideals into a justification for disciplined work. The internalization of work discipline allowed a person to work in the world, but not be consumed by it. Work was part of the evidence of faith. Leisure was time to restore energy for this work, and leisure was primarily undertaken for this utilitarian outcome.

As the history of the Renaissance and Reformation shows, understandings of work and leisure were bound up with the emergence of capitalism, the importance of a work ethic, and a focus on time use. The Reformation led to the Protestant work ethic that made work a virtue. This period of time contributed to the development of attitudes toward work and leisure that remain prevalent in U.S. society today.

Reflection Questions

1. How did the relationship between work and leisure change during the Renaissance and the Reformation?

2. How has capitalism influenced leisure? In what ways is it positive and in what ways is the influence negative?

3. How did the religious philosophies of the Reformation influence people's views about leisure? How have those views changed over time?

4. The Protestant work ethic is often blamed for leisure and recreation services not being important in today's society. How is that work ethic good for people? What drawbacks does the work ethic have related to how people live their lives and experience leisure?

5. Does today's society need to experience another Renaissance? How could leisure change with a new Renaissance?

Chapter 12

Industrialization

The process of industrialization varied in Europe and North America and did not develop linearly. Some economic sectors industrialized before others. Other industries, particularly those requiring extensive craft or detail work, remained only partially industrialized into the 20th century. Industrialization did not occur everywhere. Further, it occurred episodically and was accelerated or delayed by technology, political events, economic cycles, and social changes. The influence of industrialization, however, had a major impact on leisure experiences and recreation services.

The Reformation stirred religious and political turmoil across Europe until around 1700. Explorations such as those of Christopher Columbus yielded discoveries with significance that intensified competition among European countries. For example, religious refugees such as Puritans from England immigrated to New England during the 1630s and 1640s. In the 18th century, European wars reached across the Atlantic to involve English and French traders and colonists, and their American Indian allies.

The 17th and 18th centuries were also periods of European intellectual discovery. For example, modern scientific inquiry owes much to Galileo's use of experiments and Newton's mathematical reasoning. Francis Bacon developed the experimental method as the basis of scientific research. The theme that tied these thinkers together was the significance of human reason to understand the structure of the world. This conviction broadened during what was called the *Enlightenment*, which lasted from about the last quarter of the 17th century through the end of the 18th century. The Enlightenment was a period of intense intellectual and cultural activity that influenced all of Europe and North America. Benjamin Franklin, Thomas Jefferson, and other Colonial leaders saw themselves as part of this Enlightenment period.

Economic Changes

Whether the new ideas and knowledge penetrated society much beyond the elite class is questionable. Aside from wars and other conflict, daily life in Europe was influenced more by ongoing trends (de Vries, 1994) that began in late medieval Europe and continued through the Renaissance into the early modern period. First, agricultural productivity grew, which increased economic activity in rural areas. Second, the population was dynamic, reflecting factors such as migrations. Third, economic activity included growing manufacturing that led to people relocating to cities, seasonal employment, and child and women laborers.

Historians debate whether industrialization occurred because of technological advances in production resulting in a greater supply of goods, or because of an increase in demand for manufactured goods. The evidence is inconclusive, but both were probably causes. Increases in real wages led to more purchasing power, which led to a greater demand and the need for more production.

Changing economic behavior in households was evident. Families could devote resources either to production of goods for consumption in the household, or to production of goods for sale outside the family. These goods could be the same (e.g., vegetables from gardens, honey, or wool). A family's choice was governed by whether these goods were more useful for family consumption or whether by selling, they could purchase manufactured goods. As tastes and fashions changed, manufactured goods became quite attractive and families were more willing to shift their resources to production of marketable commodities.

Leisure was replaced by work so that goods could be produced to enhance the family's purchasing power. Women and children were increasingly involved in household economic activity because they had more disposable time that could be turned to profit. The increased activity began in the household, but later women and children became employed outside the home. Families were able to acquire material goods because available leisure was reduced in the family.

The supplies of manufactured goods also began to expand and were produced in settings that included workshops of various sizes as well as in highly organized factories. Factories were an economic innovation characteristic of industrialization and were made possible by technology and strict worker discipline. Factory discipline entailed fines, suspensions, or dismissals for even minor infractions such as being a few minutes late, talking or singing at work, socializing, and horseplay. The hours and pace of work were set by employers and were often physically exhausting. In workshops, however, workers were freer to set their own hours and pace or even to skip work altogether. Many workers, despite intense dislike of factory work and discipline, chose to work in factories because of the higher wages.

The structure of factory work had economic and social implications. Factories created new senses of time and place. Time became money in the factories. From the employers' perspectives, workers were hired for a specific period of time (i.e., shift) at a pace specified by the employer. The more a worker could produce during this time, the better the bargain was for employers. For workers, on the other hand, factory work created disruptions to their traditional patterns of life. Workers experienced a separation between time sold to the employer (i.e., work) and time that remained their own (i.e., leisure). They lost control over the hours and pace of their work and the necessity to work arose from the external discipline of the clock and not the tasks performed. The social activity that had accompanied pre-industrial work, and that still existed in the workshops, could now occur only away from the *workplace* during *nonwork time*. With the advent of work under factory discipline, daily life began to separate into distinct spheres—work time and one's own time. Between the workplace and nonwork places lies the heart of today's organization of work and leisure.

Some conflict existed, as workers in factories initially resisted the inflexibility of work hours and pace. The workers were not sure how they benefited from these changes (Thompson, 1967). They knew what they were giving up, but not always what they were getting in return. Further, according to Walvin (1978), the reduction of free time left them with few appealing leisure opportunities. Sunday was the only free day, but social and religious pressures existed to not detract from the day of worship. Public and private business recreation options were closed on Sundays. The unintended side effect was increasing time spent in the pubs and taverns because they were the only establishments likely to be open. Eventually younger workers began to accept factory work because of the money, and the level of conflict over work was reduced. However, attempts to control traditional forms of workers' leisure continued for some time.

Industrialization in the United States

No single model of industrialization existed and the process varied not only by industry but also by country. In the United States, industrialization was affected by several factors including the largely rural nature of early settlements, the extent of the United States' territory and natural resources, the influx of immigrants, and the existence of slavery.

Herbert Gutman (1977) suggested that industrialization in the United States was an ongoing process that could be divided into three periods. From 1815 to 1843, U.S. society was largely preindustrial and the workers in the few existing factories generally came from rural areas and villages. From 1843 to 1893, the United States underwent a major transformation with significant tensions existing between traditional preindustrial patterns of work and the parallel development of modern factory work and capitalist financial practices. After 1893, the United States appeared to have a mature industrial economy.

Each of these periods was characterized by specific conflicts over patterns of work, leisure, and time. Between 1860 and 1900, workers struggled to cope with work weeks of more than 60 hours (Hunnicutt, 1985). U.S. workers experienced sharp declines in free time and growing separation between their work and nonwork lives. As the United States became a mature industrial economy and society, resistance to industrial work patterns became more organized as unions advocated for the reduction of work hours along with wage increases. During the Great Depression (1929–1941) U.S. workers shifted from challenging the industrial organization of work and seeking shorter hours toward concentrating on job and wage security (Hunnicutt, 1988). This emphasis continues today. U.S. workers accommodated to industrial work by learning that time is money.

Although this period of industrialization and the growth of cities provided the foundation for many advances in society, the transitions were not easy. For example, inadequate housing often existed in the cities. Some workers lived in the streets or moved to tenements that were largely substandard. In addition, few people understood the influence industrialization had on pollution. Little concern existed that natural resources might be depleted eventually. Disease was also an issue, as people lived in small spaces and lacked medical care if they became ill. Finally, working in factories was often dangerous. People could work long hours without breaks, and no workers' compensation was available if an accident occurred. Nevertheless, many opportunities existed for recreation activities, as is described in the next chapter.

The factors creating industrialization influenced work dramatically as well as the time and financial resources that people had for leisure. The impact has been felt around the world and also continues today. The changes that occurred from ancient times to industrialization set the stage for activity involvement and the development of the recreation services into the 20th century.

Reflection Questions

1. What were the major implications of industrialization for leisure?

2. What implications did industrialization have for recreation services?

3. How difficult do you think it was for people to move from rural areas to the cities? What were the advantages as well as the disadvantages? How was their leisure influenced?

4. Why did industrialization occur at different rates in different places?

5. Some people say that industrialization created a society where people became more interested in acquiring more material possessions. Do you agree? How did industrialization create a demand for more consumer goods? Did acquiring more consumer goods give people more leisure?

Chapter 13

Leisure and Recreation in the United States through the Mid-20th Century

Leisure and recreation in the United States reflected Western history as well as the social and cultural influences of the times. This Unit on history has shown how such social and cultural influences have persistently influenced leisure. Leisure was not necessarily highly valued because of the emphasis on work. People often associated leisure with idleness leading to evil, loose morals, and personal degeneration. Opportunities for leisure were available when *earned*, but leisure was usually meant for constructive purposes, not just fun and entertainment. Blue laws attempted to control such undesirable practices as gambling and drinking by prohibiting these behaviors during certain hours and certain days of the week.

Nevertheless, people have always recreated and played. Recreation activities in early America became more available as the 20th century unfolded. Social life was important to the aristocracy of the South, the industrialists of the North, workers in factories, farmers in rural areas, and residents of small towns. Workers and slaves had their folk and ethnic games. Free-time expressions were controlled but permitted. This chapter gives an overview of leisure and recreation in the United States during the late 19th and first half of the 20th centuries. How recreation activities emerged and changed over that time is explored.

The Roots of Recreation and Leisure in the United States

With the opening of the frontiers and the rise of urban centers in the United States in the 19th century, recreation activities took many forms. Social dancing was popular in the East while square dancing flourished in the West. The waltz, polka, and quadrille emerged as popular dances. Other forms of leisure included sleigh rides, ice skating, and trips to the beach for the daring experience of public bathing. Travel to Europe and to resorts in Western U.S. wilderness areas, for those who could afford it, increased during this period (Dulles, 1965).

Intellectuals and avant-garde educators in the 19th and early 20th century openly discussed the issue of the *new leisure*. Horace Greeley, for example, spoke of the need for the wise use of leisure. This new or wise use of leisure meant activities that had some specific purpose, whether to recuperate to work harder or to enhance one's social status. Leisure was not meant to be the same as idleness (i.e., the Devil's workshop). The prestigious magazine, *The Atlantic Monthly*, carried articles on leisure's significance in making social connections. Gentlemen's clubs such as the New York Athletic Club were organized in the larger cities. Billiard rooms and pool halls were opened and well patronized by middle- and upper-class males. Workers became freed from long hours of work because of new labor laws. With the shorter workweek came time for recreation pursuits. Private businesses responded to the opportunity by encouraging sports, arts, and entertainment opportunities.

Outdoor sports increased in popularity. Turkey shoots, buffalo hunts, and sport fishing were promoted. Professional sports such as boxing, racing, and baseball were organized. For example, football had its beginning in 1869 when Princeton played Rutgers (Dulles, 1965). Americans enjoyed bicycling, bowling, softball, basketball, and volleyball. The Young Men's Christian Association (YMCA) was involved in the promotion of the latter two sports.

Church leaders had been critical of organized play and entertainment, but began encouraging and supporting specific recreation activities during the latter half of the 19th century. They cited the importance of play for proper growth and development of young people. The healthy body was viewed as a living testament. Popularly known as the Muscular Christian Movement, the trend toward melding church and recreation activities reached its height during the late 19th century. By 1895, there were 1400 YMCA branches in the United States (Knapp & Hartsoe, 1979).

Theatrical and literary activities also increased in popularity during the late 19th century. The newly created theaters in Boston, Philadelphia, and New York competed for popular support. Minstrel and variety shows were small-town favorites. Lecture series were also popular. Band concerts in the park, holiday celebrations, taffy pulls, and quilting bees were found in most towns throughout the nation. Thanks to the railroad industry and P. T. Barnum, the circus came to many cities. By 1872, Barnum's circus train had 61 cars and was touring 16 states annually.

Entertainment went to the people in other ways. The traveling medicine and Wild West shows were secondary in spectator appeal only to circuses. Amusement parks and penny arcades, which were forerunners of theme parks and video game arcades, sprang up across the country. Americans learned to play, relax, and spend money on the pursuit of pleasure. Resort areas such as Saratoga Springs and White Sulphur Springs prospered, as did a fledgling tourist industry.

Parks also enjoyed a similar degree of attention and recognition. Although Boston had established its commons in 1634 and the town of Newton, New Hampshire, had acquired a community forest in 1710, the first major public urban parks did not come into being until the mid-1800s. Central Park (New York City) was the cornerstone for the development of large urban park and parkway systems. The park concept rapidly spread throughout the Eastern seaboard and Great Lakes regions. Fairmount Park (Philadelphia) was established in 1867 and Washington Park (Chicago) was created nine years later. These new parks broke with the tradition of simply providing green areas and forest. These parks accommodated activities such as horseback riding, pleasure walking, concerts, and floral gardens. Frederick Olmsted, who was best known for designing Central Park, provided the genesis for modern landscape architecture and park planning.

Concerns for conservation also paralleled the growth of urban areas in the late 1800s. For example, the potential development of spas as commercial areas prompted the United States government in 1832 to reserve the land around Hot Springs, Arkansas, for public use. This area later became the Hot Springs National Park. In 1864, the U.S. Congress gave land grants within the Yosemite Valley to the state of California to operate a state park. Eight years later, Yellowstone was established as the first national park. In 1885, New York made another significant contribution to the conservation movement by acquiring the lands around the Niagara Falls as a preserve. One year later, the Ontario, Canada, government approved the establishment of a provincial park at Niagara Falls. Both of these purchases of land resulted from an active campaign by leading citizens in the U.S. and Canada for the preservation of these areas.

The Turn into the 20th Century

The 20th century began on an optimistic note in the United States. A feeling existed that the quality of life could be enhanced and the problems in society minimized through social reform. It was an era of philanthropy with dedicated citizens focusing on the future. The provision of appropriate environments for play and the wise use of leisure were high priorities of philanthropists and nonprofit organizations in cities. The activities of wealthy philanthropists and social reformers led to the growth of recreation opportunities especially for urban residents. Liberalism and humanism reflected the philosophy of many individuals. Structured leisure opportunities, however, were not as developed in rural areas where people were isolated, had limited discretionary money, and where the church maintained a powerful influence (Braden, 1988). This early 20th century also marked the beginning of the professionalization of recreation services, which is discussed in greater detail later in this book.

Interest in the outdoors continued to grow in the early part of the 20th century. President Teddy Roosevelt strongly supported the outdoors. Interestingly, when a newspaper published a picture of him on a Rocky Mountain hunting expedition with a brown bear dead at his feet, the Ideal Toy Corporation contacted the president for permission to use his name on a new toy—the Teddy Bear (Fraser, 1966).

Manufactured toys were a luxury of the wealthy class but they also reflected life in America at the time. Rocking horses and tea sets, for example, were popular children's toys. As World War I become imminent, toy manufacturers increased production of war toys including soldiers and toy guns.

The invention of moving pictures, automobiles, and the telegraph laid technological grounds for the future. The Nickelodeon, one of the first theaters for mass showings, spread to cities throughout the country. Movies were cheap and popular diversions. Chase movies involving cowboys, bank-robbers, and villains had the greatest appeal (Dulles, 1965). The automobile initially served as a plaything for the wealthy because only the wealthy could afford to own them. Thanks to the mass production technology introduced by Henry Ford, autos became affordable to many people. The growing profit of mass production allowed people, regardless of their social class, to have new leisure options for goods and services.

World War I brought some slowdown of recreation opportunities with efforts put toward the war. However, goods were needed to support the war effort so employment opportunities abounded. Further, the military realized that soldiers needed diversionary services as part of their welfare and morale. Upon returning from the war, they sought recreation opportunities in their communities for entertainment.

The Jazz Age

The Jazz Age brought an awareness of women's rights, political scandal, and economic upheaval. The years following World War I also resulted in extensive expansion of all types of recreation opportunities. Because of unparalleled prosperity, many Americans sought to enjoy somewhat shorter workweeks (about 60 hours), the benefit of mass production, and the expansion of new technology. Only 5,000 radios existed in 1920, but by 1924 there were over one million (Chubb & Chubb, 1981). The first feature-length movie with synchronized sound sequences, *The Jazz Singer*, boosted the movie industry. MGM, Warner Brothers, Paramount, Columbia, and Universal grew and ruled Hollywood film production. The Motion Picture Academy awarded the first awards in 1929. The first Mickey Mouse film was made by Walt Disney in 1928.

Because many people had larger incomes, more recreation opportunities could be purchased in the 1920s. Private business recreation pursuits grew because people were willing to spend their available discretionary money. In addition, private entrepreneurs reported large profits and sought to promote their activities in many ways.

In 1920, women's skirts were ankle length but by 1922 the hemline had steadily risen to just cover a woman's knee. Female emancipation took off and the Flapper was the heroine of the Jazz Age. Short hair, short skirts, turned down hose, and eyes peering from under a pulled down hat marked the fast and brazen modern woman of the 1920s. *Thin was in* and women who did not conform dieted.

The focus on entertainment of the period also fueled the acceptance of African American art forms. The Harlem Renaissance resulted in the Lindy Hop, literature, art, and social commentary about African American culture. Jazz and ragtime blues were lasting contributions to entertainment and leisure offered by African American performers.

Spectator sports grew during the 1920s as did active participation. During this time, Babe Ruth hit 60 home runs in a single season for the New York Yankees. Further, racing automobiles, horses, and dogs became big spectator activities. Public parks were designed with swimming pools, tennis courts, and baseball diamonds. Some universities built new stadiums to house the growing attendees at intercollegiate athletic events (Braden, 1988).

Crossword puzzles, miniature golf, dance marathons, bathing beauty contests, and contract bridge were activities of the day. Train companies provided dictionaries to riders who passed the time completing crossword puzzles. Free street dances drew young people away from the popular dance halls, which were generally considered disreputable places. Fraternal clubs had existed for many years, but during this period, the Rotary, Kiwanis, and Lion's Clubs were founded for men to maintain business associations and provide service to their communities (Braden, 1988).

Not everything was wonderful during the decade of the 1920s, however. The U.S. government responded to a fear (i.e., the first Red Scare) that Russia was attempting to take over the country. Over 10,000 American citizens were unlawfully arrested and questioned about communist behavior. The government established the Anti-Radical Division led by J. Edgar Hoover to stifle the perceived communist efforts during the second Red Scare after World War II. Government further affected the lives of citizens with the enactment of the 18th Amendment, the National Prohibition Act, leading to crime and an illegal alcohol market. Black Tuesday collapsed the stock market. The period of the Roaring Twenties with its growing leisure and recreation activities gave way quickly to the Great Depression.

The Great Depression into World War II

The Great Depression of the 1930s was a time of unemployment lines, personal tragedies, and economic collapse. The decade also brought changing philosophies of economics and government. The New Deal approach of Franklin Roosevelt was a radical departure from dependence on philanthropy for offering social and recreation services. The New Deal programs also reflected the belief that any work was better than idleness from unemployment, and that it was the duty of the government to furnish work when private enterprise was incapable. Public work projects provided jobs for millions.

Many of those jobs benefited recreation participants in the United States, because public swimming pools, bandstands, and picnic shelters were built in many communities. New Deal money supported unemployed artists through the Federal Arts Project and the Federal Theatre. Artists created museum exhibits, taught art fundamentals, and captured the culture of the country through photographs and paintings. They produced art for government buildings, schools, and hospitals with many paintings highlighting regional and small-town life. Community cultural opportunities such as theatres and orchestras began with funding from the Works Progress Administration (WPA). Over 30 million people attended theatre project productions during this time (Bolino, 1998).

Many Americans took respite from economic worries through baseball. Two professional leagues existed separately, the Major League and the Negro League. The Major League played in public stadiums with large crowds coming to see stars like Joe DiMaggio and Lou Gehrig. The Negro League typically played in small-town fields with small crowds.

Women also began to make a place in sports. In 1932, Babe Didrikson set three world records at the Los Angeles Summer Olympics in the javelin, hurdles, and high jump. Also common during this time was the involvement of women in team sports, particularly through industrial sports programs organized by manufacturing companies. During the 1920s, a *play for all* era had arisen that included girls with many opportunities for physical activity. However, in the 1930s an era of *social control* emerged, emphasizing that girls and women should not be placed under the pressures of sport unless the settings were highly structured (Henderson, 1993b).

Outdoor sports were generally expensive and thus, available only to the wealthy. Skiing was season-limited, so resorts that surrounded the ski areas began to provide other luxury accommodations such as heated swimming pools, lounges, and restaurants to expand the attraction. Car travel became a favored vacation and leisure option as the economy recovered in the late 1930s. Miniature golf and softball were favorite outdoor activities for the lower economic class.

During the Depression, movies provided an escape from economic realities. The neighborhood theater offered solace from the heat or cold of the weather as well as opportunities for Hollywood fantasies. Over 15,000 movie theatres came into existence during the 1930s. *Time* magazine in 1939 named Shirley Temple, Clark Gable, Sonja Henie, Mickey Rooney, and Spencer Tracy among the top movie stars in America (Bolini, 1998).

Music of the period was often different based on geographic region. Kansas City jazz, New Orleans Dixieland, Appalachian country and bluegrass, and New York City Broadway hits were enjoyed by Americans. African Americans had great influence on the development of American musical entertainment with Duke Ellington, Louis Armstrong, and Billie Holiday among the leaders. Young people often drove to *roadhouses* located along highways for entertainment, dining, and socializing (Braden, 1988).

The economy of the Depression rebounded with the start of WWII. After the bombing of Pearl Harbor in December 1941, the concerns of the United States focused on preparation and maintenance of war efforts. Similar to WWI, industrial centers grew. Material goods were rationed to provide the necessary supplies and equipment for the war effort. After the war, huge changes occurred in U.S. society. The implications of these changes related to leisure are discussed in the next chapter.

Reflection Questions

1. What was meant by the idea of *wise leisure*?

2. If you had lived during the latter half of the 19th century or early 20th century, what would have been your recreation activity interests?

3. Why do you believe that such a major change occurred in the way recreation was embodied in the Jazz Age (i.e., the Roaring Twenties) compared to the Depression Era? Was the economic situation the only reason for such changes?

4. What role did the church have in influencing leisure in the United States?

5. How did the role of the government in financing recreation opportunities change from the beginning of the 20th century into WWII?

6. What parallels exist between the Great Depression and the economic recession that began in 2008? Do you see any parallels related to leisure and recreation?

Chapter 14

Leisure and Recreation from Post-World War II to Present

Many social changes resulting after World War II altered the face of the United States. The changes related to consumerism, higher education, increased births, and civil rights. The focus of this chapter is to highlight changes in people's lives and leisure that occurred in the last half of the 20th century and into the first decade of the 21st century. These descriptions are presented as decades but many of the changes overlapped and evolved across time.

The Fifties in the Post-War Era

Returning WWII service members had grown accustomed to the recreation services of the American Red Cross and United Service Organization, which had become available to them during the war. Upon return, they demanded similar services in their communities. Because of the GI Bill, people attended college in greater numbers than ever before. People also had more money and discretion in its use for education and for recreation activities.

Television became a household fixture in the 1950s. Shows like "Howdy Doody," "Candid Camera," and "I Love Lucy" were popular. In 1957, "American Bandstand" broadcasted nationally and "Perry Mason" made its first appearance. "The Nat King Cole Show" was the first variety TV series with an African American star. American war movies featured the heroic efforts of young men. *Citizen Kane* depicted the American dream of being rich and famous.

Baseball remained a national pastime during the 1940s–50s. The largest paid crowd for any single baseball game in Wrigley Field history occurred in 1947. The excitement was for Jackie Robinson, the first baseball appearance of a "Negro" athlete as a big leaguer. Over 30,000 of those fans were women who came for the free Ladies Day (Marasco, n.d.). Football, however, was emerging in the United States as the fastest growing of spectator sports.

By the 1950s, Americans were moving to the suburbs. The suburban culture was turning to convenience as demonstrated by labor-saving appliances such as the electric clothes washers, telephones, and flush toilets. In 1948, McDonald's opened their first fast-food stand, and drive-ins began to proliferate. Eat fast, in your car, and keep going was the subliminal message. Diners also became a common social gathering place where teen-aged boys in jeans, loafers, button down shirts, and manicured hair danced with girls with ponytails and poodle skirts. The Wurlitzer jukebox became prevalent and "bopping" at the diner was popular (Sherlock, 1999).

The modes and purposes of transportation also changed. Cars were a part of everyday society. The emphasis on stylish, not just practical, automobiles flourished. Competition ensued to create the fastest car or the wildest looking car. Gadgets like cigar lighters, clocks, and power windows evolved. Air transportation also changed. Prior to World War II, fewer than 2% of all travelers went by air. By the mid-1950s, air traffic equaled rail passenger traffic. Air travel opened many new options for tourism.

During World War II, children were toy-deprived. As the war ended, manufacturing returned to making new toys with new materials. Lithographed tin, die-cast metal, and plastic toys emerged. Plastic Hula Hoops and Frisbees became popular in the 1950s. In 1959, the first Barbie doll appeared. Toy manufacturers were also attending to the needs of children with disabilities. Magnetized or permanently affixed toys were developed to hold toys within reach of children with visual or orthopedic problems.

Technology became more important daily in U.S. society. Microwave technology increased the radio reception of stations across the country as well as enhanced cooking. Radios had long been popular, but with the faster and more mobile society, the transistor was the first step toward electronic mobility for the mass of society. The invention of the electric guitar gave birth to the rock 'n' roll era. Chuck Berry, Elvis Presley, and Bill Haley and His Comets pushed rock 'n' roll forward. African American artists were supported by the development of the Motown recording label.

Life was good for the dominant white culture in the United States during the 1950s. This time also spurred the efforts of marginalized groups to seek their rights. For example, the 1954 Supreme Court ruling of *Brown v. Board of Education* led to the desegregation of schools. African Americans across the country became active in protests about racial discrimination and demanded increased opportunities for community membership. Access to leisure was one of the issues that emerged indirectly in the emerging equal rights focus for people of color as well as women. People began to demand equal opportunities in their leisure experiences and through recreation services.

Activism in the Sixties

The relative complacency of the 1950s came to a halt with the assassination of President John F. Kennedy in 1963. Kennedy's death, followed by assassinations of Martin Luther King and Robert Kennedy later in the decade, changed social life in numerous ways. Until that time Americans felt safe, except for the outside chance that they would die together in a nuclear war.

The 1960s, nonetheless, were a decade of huge economic expansion. Advances in technology provided air-conditioned homes, home entertainment centers, and a multitude of gadgets to increase people's quality of life.

Gasoline prices were relatively inexpensive in the 1960s so Americans took to the road to *see America*. Car camping was promoted by guidebooks listing camping areas in state and national parks. Boats and camping equipment were widely advertised and sold. Americans were looking beyond the developed cities for escapes to the outdoors. To enhance this outdoor recreation, for example, artificial snowmaking became useful to extend the skiing season.

In the 1960s, however, several negative turns occurred. The Vietnam War and the assassination of Martin Luther King Jr. resulted in serious questions about what was happening in American society. Many people spent their time advocating for issues of social justice. The antiwar movement was significant as were the efforts to expand racial equity. Civil unrest heightened when the National Guard oversaw the integration of the University of Mississippi by the first black student in 1962 and when 43 people died in the 1967 Detroit race riot (Sugrue, 1996). Protestors disrupted the 1968 Democratic nominating convention in Chicago to make their voices heard about the Vietnam War and other issues of social unrest.

The social changes facing the United States led to conflicting lifestyles and aspirations among generations. Environmental concerns related to potential damage done by new outdoor recreation activities such as snowmobiling, dune buggies, and trail bikes increased. Environmentalists made dire predictions that with the present rate of air and water pollution, the earth would not support life by the beginning of the 21st century. Paradoxically, consumer leisure was increasing, as evidenced by buying more goods and services, attendance at athletic events, longer vacations, and international air travel. The 1960s showed, however, that great divisions existed among groups of people in American society.

Transition in the Seventies

The decade of the 1970s was a transitional decade in which liberalism of the 1960s gave way to conservatism in the 1980s. The Watergate scandal and the subsequent resignation of President Nixon resulted in less confidence by Americans in their government. Concerns in the early 1970s such as enforcing civil rights, taking care of the urban poor, rights for women, and concerns for the environment and endangered species gave rise to numerous causes and special interest groups.

Many of these concerns resulted in legislative actions that regulated national political, social, and economic behaviors. Federal bureaucracies grew as the government attempted to enforce regulations that would guarantee the rights of all, protect the environment, and ensure a continued rate of economic growth and prosperity. Outdoor recreation took on a new meaning with the publication of the Outdoor Recreation Resources Review Commission (ORRRC) report, which is discussed in greater detail in the next Unit. To accomplish these projects and reforms, taxes were increased.

In 1974, the Congress passed the Education for All Handicapped Children's Act to guarantee equal educational opportunity for youth with disabilities. Further, legislation reduced architectural barriers to public buildings for access by people with disabilities. The large institutions that had *warehoused* people with disabilities began to downsize and people with disabilities began to move back into the community. Community opportunities like the Special Olympics, that had begun in the 1960s, became commonplace. Leisure for people with disabilities became visible for the first time.

Electronic gaming was on the rise. Pong, a computerized tennis game, became a huge success as a bar game. Hand-held games such as Simon and stand-alone games like Space Invaders soon followed.

The music of the 1970s was varied from psychedelic to disco. Psychedelic music dominated the early part of the decade, followed by disco toward the end. Disco music, represented by John Travolta and *Saturday Night Fever*, was the dominant music fad at the end of the decade. Music became portable with 8-track tape players in cars and eventually even more convenient with cassette tapes. To get the most of the music at home, people bought component stereo systems to get a *big* sound.

Television in the 1970s emphasized sitcoms with shows like "The Mary Tyler Moore Show" and Archie Bunker's "All in the Family." Gender battles were fought vicariously through the televised Billie Jean King/Bobby Riggs tennis match. Popular movies of the decade included *Star Wars*, *The Godfather*, and *Rocky*.

The divisions in American society in the 1960s became recognized as differences in the 1970s. Everyone did not always understand the differences, but the variety of public tastes resulted in recreation becoming more important as reflected in the number of public, nonprofit, and private business providers emerging to meet the growing and diversified recreation interests of the American public. The number of curricula in the United States that offered majors in parks and recreation also grew.

Conservatism in the Eighties

By the end of the 1970s, Americans grew weary of big government, big corporations, and big automobiles. In response to the new conservatism, Ronald Reagan was elected President in 1980 on a platform to downsize and deregulate government. The federal government reduced spending for support of outdoor and other recreational facilities. Entrepreneurialism took the place of large government programs. The deregulation of airlines and banking industries helped to stimulate the growth of business ventures including leisure opportunities such as malls and resorts. Social concerns were passé and making money was in vogue during the 1980s.

World politics and violence continued to infiltrate the Olympics as well as other sports. Sports spectatorship grew and women entered the sports arena as a result of the passage of Title IX in the 1970s. However, this act was not visibly enforced until much later in the century. Concerns began to emerge, further, related to the growing commercialization of sport. Sports were further scrutinized by the British soccer stadium riot in which 95 fans were killed and 2,000 more were injured in the mayhem.

Computers were popular and became commonplace in the workplace. The invention of personal computers made the technology available for work in the home as well as for home-based recreation.

The Last Decade of the 20th Century

The conservatism of the 1980s was modified to some extent into the 1990s. Further, the emphasis on material consumption decreased slightly. New age spirituality and back-to-nature aspects occupied some of the aging Baby Boomers who still continued to be concerned with making money. Social liberalism was popular concerning children, homeless people, and immigrants (Sessoms & Orthner, 1992; Kunstler, 1993). Concerns for health and welfare became more important than national defense.

Women's sports continued to grow and the Women's National Basketball Association took root and provided women a professional culture for participation and support. Tiger Woods was sweeping the athletic industry on the heels of Michael Jordan and Nike. Electronic games, personal fitness equipment, and vacations remained popular expenditures.

The Americans with Disabilities Act in 1990 furthered the rights of people with disabilities and established universal standards for new construction of all facilities. More than ever, people with disabilities had access to freely chosen and appropriate leisure opportunities. The Paralympics established itself as an elite sporting event held every four years at the same site as the Olympics.

Satellite television, personal computers, and the Internet connected ordinary citizens with information and other people. The majority of homes had cable television and many homes were connected to the Internet. Home and handheld video games went to a new height of sophistication.

The last decade of the 20th century brought prosperity for many Americans, but a growing number of people did not have the same options for meaningful work and leisure. Throughout all the decades of the 20th century, social trends influenced people's consumerism, work, family lives, and leisure. Economic prosperity and decline, wars, and rapidly advancing technology influenced popular culture and the ways that leisure was viewed, which continued into the beginning of the 21st century.

The First Decade of the 21st Century

A political defining moment of the beginning of the 21st century was the terrorist attacks on September 11, 2001. Few people reading this book will need to be reminded of that day. This day marked the beginning of the War on Terror and resulted in the United States being at war throughout the first decade of the 21st century. Political events coupled with major changes in technology and human rights, and the worldwide financial crisis in the latter years of the first decade, influenced recreation and leisure in the United States and the way that recreation services were provided.

The events of September 11 led to a war in Afghanistan to eliminate the Taliban and Osama Bin Laden, who had been responsible for the terrorist attacks on the United States. In 2003, the United States invaded Iraq because weapons of mass destruction were believed to exist in that country and would be a threat to the United States. These two wars cost billions of dollars and resulted in many civilian deaths in these countries as well as death and injuries to U.S. service members. Fear of future terrorist attacks fed the consciousness of Americans. For a short time, this fear drastically altered international tourism. It also made any type of air travel more cumbersome with the security systems that were mandated.

Globalization was clearly evident throughout the world in the 21st century. The huge changes in technology and transportation brought the world closer together than it had ever been. In addition, the growth of capitalism and the desire for democracy united people's attitudes and behaviors. An international concern about climate change and its impact on the world's resources emerged as never before. Although an environmental movement had been popular in the United States for several decades, the new threat of climate change raised issues about how recreation resources such as beach-front property and ski seasons might change. The recognition of the impact of natural disasters (e.g., Hurricane Katrina, the Asian tsunami, Midwest floods, the Japanese earthquake and tsunami) also showed how quickly environments and the social systems they sustain can change. Human-made disasters such as the Deepwater Horizon explosion in the Gulf of Mexico also showed how environments could be changed quickly in a highly negative way.

Social changes continued into the 2000s. Barack Obama, the first African American president in the United States, was elected in 2008. This election came only a couple of decades after the time when African Americans were considered second-class citizens. In the world, changes occurred in the influence of capitalism on countries such as China as well as the desire for democracy, as evident in the Arab Spring of 2011. People also became aware of the growing gaps between the *haves* and *havenots,* especially after the worldwide financial crisis that began in 2008. The Occupy Wall Street movement of 2011 also signaled the dissatisfaction that the majority of citizens had with huge corporations with rich executives. The Occupy movement spread throughout the world.

Other social issues that were pronounced in the 2010s were the obesity crisis and gay rights. The number of obese adults in the United States doubled from 1980 up to the mid-2010s. The number of obese children *tripled* during that time. The contributions recreation services made to address this issue were highlighted with research as well as intentional community programs. The obesity epidemic seemed to have plateaued in 2011, but the number of adults and children who may have or may get cardiovascular disease, diabetes, and cancer will continue to stretch the healthcare system.

Discussion about gay rights and same-sex marriage also came to the fore in the early 21st century. The Netherlands, for example, legalized same-sex marriage in 2001 and a handful of other countries followed. This issue remained hotly debated in the United States.

Sports continued with worldwide popularity focused on spectatorship as well as nationalism. Beijing, China, hosted the most expensive Olympics ever. The growth of sports in developing countries was reflected by the selection of South Africa to host the FIFA World Cup in 2010 and Brazil to host the World Cup in 2014 and 2016 Summer Olympics. Sports heroes such as multiple Tour de France winner Lance Armstrong were in the news not only for their accomplishments but also for concerns about the use of performance-enhancing drugs. The popularity of motor sports like NASCAR grew rapidly.

Changes in technology continued to have a profound effect on people's work and leisure. The blurring of work and leisure was omnipresent with people being on call for work 24/7 because of being tethered to technology. In addition, while at work many people used personal technology to keep connected with family and friends. Almost everyone seemed to own a mobile phone in the 2010s. Smartphones, 3G and 4G networks, and Wi-Fi hotspots allowed people to connect and communicate easily on the Internet. Social networking such as Twitter and Facebook enabled immediate sharing of information. Other forms of technology created numerous opportunities during leisure, such as the prevalence of DVRs and high-definition TVs. DVDs and Blu-ray discs replaced VCRs, and CDs were largely replaced by digital downloads. These changes made information about and opportunities for leisure available literally at people's fingertips.

All of the ideas discussed in this chapter show how people's recreation and leisure changed and evolved in the United States. These changes had major implications for what recreation services were available, who they were for, and how they were to be facilitated. The discussion of sustainable recreation services cannot occur without acknowledging the political, economic, technological, and social changes that have and will continue to influence leisure experiences and recreation services.

Reflection Questions

1. Sports have played a greater role in people's everyday lives in the past 60 years. Trace the changes that occurred in sports over this period of time.

2. Social issues have been prominent in U.S. society in the past few decades. Why do you think these issues were more pronounced

than in the past? What implications do social issues have related to leisure opportunities?

3. Technology changes constantly. How does technology influence what people choose to do in their leisure?

4. How necessary is consumer spending power for people to have meaningful leisure experiences?

5. Politics have changed over the decades in the United States. How do politics influence what people choose do in their free time and recreation activities?

6. How is internationalism and globalization influencing the leisure of people in the United States today?

Chapter 15

Roots of Recreation Services

Western history and emerging leisure and recreation patterns have influenced the way recreation services have evolved in the United States. Recreation services include the three primary sectors of public, nonprofit, and private business. Although some form of organized and structured recreation services have existed throughout history (e.g., the symposia of the Greeks, the ancient Olympiad, Rome's gladiator sports, jousting matches, folk festivals), the visibility of these services formally began in the United States well over a century ago.

The growth of recreation services in the United States was the result of developments including the growth of public education, industrial and technological progress, advances in science and medicine, and the changing of social and political attitudes. Recreation services frequently emanated from a concern for the quality of life as well as the social and educational needs of citizens. This chapter builds on understanding people's interests in recreation activities in the United States and explores the roots of recreation services within the context of the cultural, social, and political influences.

The Beginnings
of Recreation Services

Public and nonprofit recreation services in cities, particularly the large metropolitan areas, began to take shape toward the end of the 19th century. The public recreation movement started with the sand gardens (i.e., precursors to playgrounds) as an idea brought to America from Europe in 1885. By 1893, a Boston charity called the Massachusetts Emergency and Hygiene Association was operating ten summer playgrounds using both volunteer and paid leadership. Joseph Lee was one of the pioneers in this effort. Lee believed that every child had a right to play. Playgrounds proliferated in cities because of the settlement house movement (i.e., nonprofit organizations in cities that aimed to acculturate immigrants in to American culture), the social concerns of religious reformers, and uncertainty about the effects of urbanization, especially on youth.

Nonprofit organizations such as the YMCA began to thrive toward the end of the 19th century. The YMCA was founded by George Williams in 1844 as a "refuge of Bible study and prayer for young men seeking escape from the hazards of life on the streets" (http://www.ymca.net/history/founding.html). Youth were the major focus for many nonprofit groups.

The parks movement also emerged in the United States during the latter half of the 19th century. The early American pioneers had viewed the natural environment as a dangerous unknown that needed to be tamed. Outdoor resources were thought to be limitless. These people believed in Manifest Destiny (i.e., lands abounded for use in any way needed) and the God-given right to dominate nature and use it for society's benefit. By the mid-1800s, however, the Transcendentalist movement emerged. Transcendentalists viewed nature as the vehicle to inspire intuitive thought, a way to lift human consciousness to greater spiritual wisdom, and a means to learn about nature rather than to exploit it.

Transcendentalist writers such as Emerson and Thoreau inspired future naturalists as well as the general public to respect and preserve the natural world. Federal lands were set aside. The creation of Yellowstone National Park in 1872 was an example of this. Although the National Park Service did not come into existence until 1916, many lands were designated that were often managed by the U.S. military. States also began to preserve land for environmental and recreation purposes. It was not uncommon to begin to find public parks and open spaces (e.g., town squares) in communities of all sizes.

As the 19th century came to a close, small parks dotted the landscape of many communities, public libraries and community centers were established, and America was entering an era of social consciousness. Concerns for the less fortunate, the young, and for the preservation of the environment were a part of this consciousness. These concerns had a significant effect on recreation services.

20th Century Progressive Era

The first two decades of the 20th century were an era of expansion and growth for recreation services of all types. This progressive era was the foundation for many of these opportunities and services. Progressivism was associated with social activism and political reform that flourished from the 1890s to the 1920s. The goals of progressives were related to eliminating corruption in government and achieving efficiency and effectiveness in addressing social issues. The scientific method was applied to addressing some of the social problems. Progressives sought to find new ways to promote the general welfare of citizens, and recreation was an important part of that plan.

The first playground commission within a municipal government was established in 1904 by the city of Los Angeles. Luther Gulick, an early pioneer in youth activity and the first president of the Camp Fire Girls, organized the first public-school athletic league in New York in 1903. Psychologists such as Carl Groos and G. Stanley Hall were citing the importance of play in the development of children. Several youth-serving nonprofit agencies, including the Boy Scouts (1908) and Girl Scouts (1915), began early in the century.

The year 1906 was an important year for parks and recreation, which were not linked to one another at that time in history. It marked the beginning of the Playground Association of America (PAA), which later was known as the Playground and Recreation Association of America (PRAA) and then the National Recreation Association (NRA), and ultimately the National Recreation and Park Association (NRPA). As a service organization supported by voluntary contributions, the PAA promoted the cause of community recreation for more than half a century (Dickason, 1985). Joseph Lee, Henry Curtis, Luther Gulick, and Jane Addams were the first officers, and the association was comprised largely of volunteers and interested citizens.

PAA served both volunteers and professionals through its field staff and national office. Many of these early volunteers were women. Much of the involvement of women came from their efforts to use their talents in a society that tended to view women's roles narrowly as well as a society that often rendered women *invisible*. Henderson (1992) described how an ethic of caring defined many women's lives and opened the door for these volunteers and professionals to address social justice issues through recreation services. Children and their play spaces (i.e., playgrounds) were important concerns. The contributions of groups of women particularly through club activities in both the white and black communities were significant. Without the tireless efforts of many unheralded women, the quality of national and local recreation services would have been greatly diminished in those early years as well as today.

Another major event occurring in 1906 was the enactment of the Antiquities Act, which gave the federal government a tool for protecting scientific and historic areas. The U.S. President was given the power to designate national monuments and to protect these areas from destruction. Devils Tower and the Lassen Peak (Lassen Volcanic National Park) were among the earliest designated monuments. The growing number of national parks and national monuments made imperative the establishment of the National Park Service ten years later.

The public schools were also involved in the development of early organized recreation services. In 1907, staff in Rochester, New York, embarked on a program of making school facilities available as community facilities. This beginning had far-reaching effects on the general use of schools for community purposes. The National Education Association in 1911 recommended the use of school buildings and grounds for recreation, and community school programs emerged. Perhaps none were as successful in this endeavor as was the Milwaukee School System. For years its recreation program, under the leadership of Dorothy Enderis, was nationally acclaimed for its "lighted school houses."

Without the efforts of wealthy philanthropists and social reformers in the early years of the 20th century, the growth of recreation opportunities for urban poor would have been impeded. The settlement houses, established in the slum sections in large cities in the East and Midwest, were the first nonprofit neighborhood service centers that included social and recreation services. Possibly the most famous of these settlement houses was the Hull House in Chicago. It was built in 1889 and operated by Jane Addams, who felt that recreation could be a powerful force in the prevention of delinquency and antisocial behavior. Settlement houses were also places where immigrants could be acculturated to American society.

Organized camps for children began in the last half of the 19th century. These camps were organized by schools, religious organizations, nonprofit organizations, and private businesses. The first school camp appeared in 1861, and private, religiously-affiliated, and agency camps were founded several years later. Initially these camps were only for boys, but girls' camps started in the last decade of the 19th century. By 1916, the organized camp movement was large enough that camp directors organized the Camp Directors Association, later to become the American Camp Association.

20th Century Outdoor Interests

Governmental interest in outdoor recreation management increased during the early 20th century. The National Park Service was established in 1916 to "promote and regulate the use of the Federal areas known as national parks, monuments and reservations . . . to conserve the scenery and national historic objects of the wildlife therein and to provide for the enjoyment of the same and by such manner and by such means as will leave them unimpaired for the enjoyment of the future generation" (Act of August 25, 1916).

In 1903, the voters of Chicago approved the nation's first five million dollar bond issue to acquire and develop parks for the purpose of recreation. Politicians began to see recreation as more than trivial and advocated for recreation and conservation activities. In 1908, President Theodore Roosevelt convened a White House conference with the governors of various states to kick off his public conservation program.

The conservation movement became a major social and environmental focus. This movement grew from the concern over industrialization and its impact on natural resources. Naturalism emerged as a companion to transcendentalism early in the century. For example, machines were used heavily in the lumbering and mining industries with little concern for conservation. Land erosion, droughts, and floods were the natural consequences of these exploitative patterns. These wanton acts of destruction incensed many citizens who banded together, developed political muscle, and became the first lobbyists for conservation. Conservation groups were created such as the Sierra Club (1892), the Scenic and Historic Preservation Society (1895), and the National Audubon Society (1905). Their efforts spearheaded a preservation (i.e., environmental) movement that gained momentum in the mid-1900s and still exists in the mainstream of today's society.

An emerging concept of parks linked them to recreation activity spaces. To some extent, the ideals of conservation and preservation had to be balanced with people's recreation desires. Distinctions were being made between parks and playgrounds, with the former emphasizing land-use design and the latter stressing places for play. People sought ways to address compatible conservation and use in planning parks, which required professional leadership.

The expansion of recreation services related to the outdoors as well as urban areas required the development of professional leadership. In 1912, the New York State College of Forestry at Syracuse University established the nation's first program to educate for park administration and city forestry (Sessoms, 1993). The first training text for professional directors of play services, later to be known as recreation leaders, was published in

1909 under the title, *The Normal Course in Play*. Several universities, including Harvard, Columbia, Northwestern and the University of California at Berkeley, offered courses and institutes about play and summer playgrounds. Among the earliest educators were Luther Gulick (1905, New York University), Neva Boyd (1911, Chicago Training Institute, later a part of Northwestern) and George E. Johnson (1915, Harvard).

Influence of World War I on Recreation Services

The growth of recreation services was affected by the events preceding and surrounding World War I. Organized recreation services began to take a community focus. With the entrance of the United States into World War I in 1917 and the establishment of a universal draft system, community life underwent upheaval. Communities adjacent to military installations and training centers boomed as *war towns* and were particularly affected. Suddenly, thousands of service members and transient workers found themselves in new settings without the traditional support system of the family and small town. To provide some continuity, communities during this time moved to establish recreation services that would accommodate their new citizens and allow for the wholesome use of leisure. Under the leadership of Playground and Recreation Association of America (PRAA), the War Camp Community Service (WCCS) was organized to aid local communities in developing recreation opportunities for the military and defense workers. Neighborhood organization was its plan of action. In those states where racial segregation was legal, the WCCS operated over 100 clubs specifically for black military personnel (Knapp & Hartsoe, 1979).

In addition to the activities of the war camp program, religious organizations and the YMCA established recreation programs on military posts. These programs were approved by the War and Navy departments and emphasized both religious and social welfare activities including recreation. They were forerunners of the special programs now provided by the military branches for their service personnel. With the coming of peace, these special war effort programs were terminated, but their effects were long-lasting. They stimulated the interest of many communities in organized public recreation services as a means to improve the quality of life for all citizens.

The years following World War I resulted in extensive expansion of all types of recreation services. Private businesses saw recreation as a growth industry. Public recreation services emerged along with the demand for paid leadership. Whereas only 400 communities offered organized public recreation services at the beginning of the 1920s, over a thousand were offering them as the decade came to an end. The PRAA responded to this leadership need by establishing a series of training programs.

Financial Crises and World War II

The Great Depression brought bad times for many people, but it was *not* an era of decline for organized recreation services. The Federal Emergency Relief Administration, the Works Project Administration, and the Civilian Conservation Corps made major contributions to park and recreation services and facilities.

The Federal Emergency Relief Administration assumed two approaches to recreation services. One was to employ workers through the construction of facilities. The other was to employ program and activity leadership. For example, writers, musicians, and actors were given jobs through the federal theater.

The Division of Recreation Projects, as part of the organizational structure of the Work Projects Administration (WPA), also became a major employer of recreation personnel. These WPA leaders worked under the general supervision of local tax-supported units such as recreation departments, park boards, school boards, and welfare departments.

The Civilian Conservation Corps (CCC) was created during the Great Depression to give employment and vocational training to unemployed young men. The CCC helped several states establish their state park systems. Participants built roads, picnic areas, campgrounds, cabins, and hiking and riding trails for local, state, and federal park and recreation areas. The CCC also constructed swimming and boating facilities and upgraded the specialized recreation facilities of the National Park Service and the U.S. Forest Service.

Meyer and Brightbill (1964) estimated that these federal work programs during the Depression advanced recreation services by 25 years. These programs stimulated organized recreation at every level of governmental responsibility. In 1930 there were less than 25,000 volunteers and professionals engaged in the field of recreation, with only 2,500 of these people employed full-time. By 1935, that number had increased to 45,000 full-time workers and the number of communities offering recreation services had doubled.

The United States was slowly recovering from the Depression when war broke out in Europe in 1939. By 1941, it seemed inevitable that the entire world would be at war. Similar to World War I, industrial centers expanded, small towns adjacent to military installations were inundated with new military recruits, and the federal government assumed a greater responsibility for the social behaviors of all U.S. residents. Among those programs that had a direct bearing on the lives of military personnel were the activities of the various branches of the armed forces who were encouraged to establish recreation facilities and programs. Meyer and Brightbill (1964) cited, "Never in the history of the armed forces was so much attention given to recreation as a functional part of the total military operation" (p. 20). Nonprofit and business organizations also combined efforts and formed the United Service Organization (USO) to offer entertainment and provide a range of social and recreation services.

Another nonprofit association that contributed significantly to the war effort was the American Red Cross. It operated approximately 750 clubs and 250 mobile units throughout the world. Through these programs, thousands of service members were able to escape, however briefly, the events of war. Whereas the special service programs stressed athletics and theatrical activities, the American Red Cross effort emphasized social programming. Possibly the most significant contribution to the recreation movement at this point was the Red Cross workers in military hospitals who were concerned about recreation activity with therapeutic value for wounded veterans. These efforts marked the beginning of therapeutic recreation services.

The war years also resulted in more jobs and other opportunities for women in many areas including recreation. For a short time during World War II, more women than men were employed as full-time workers in the field of recreation (Henderson, 1992). Many of the functional roles as volunteers and as paid workers in the profession related to support roles, programming, and advocacy. Nevertheless, women represented a diversity of backgrounds and many continued this involvement as leaders and advocates in local communities into the postwar years.

The Mid-20th Century

Recreation services grew even more in the mid-20th century. Following WWII, hundreds of additional towns and cities began to construct community centers, swimming pools, playgrounds, and athletic facilities. The states gave greater attention to their responsibility for recreation and youth services. Hospitals established therapeutic recreation services, universities created degree programs in parks and recreation, and tourism became a major industry. Americans were mobile, seeking new experiences, and enjoying their newfound leisure. The workday and workweek were shortened somewhat and vacation periods were lengthened for some employees. The disruptive years of the Korean Conflict did not derail these changes.

Examples of some of the events that occurred after World War II that helped establish organizational approaches for recreation services included:

- The White House Conference on Aging in 1951 emphasized the role of recreation for a growing population of older citizens.

- The National Association of Recreation Therapists was created as a separate professional body and joined with the Hospital Section of the American Recreation Society to establish the Council for the Advancement of Hospital Recreation.

- The Supreme Court decision made racial segregation in public schools unconstitutional and thereby opened the system to all citizens, regardless of race. This law also affected many community recreation programs that had previously been segregated.

- The growth of international recreation services resulted in the establishment of the International Recreation Association (now the World Leisure Organization).

- Disneyland was established in 1955 on 150 acres in Anaheim, California. It was the first major theme park and became the model for subsequent theme parks as well as a plethora of other private recreation businesses.

- The public's discovery and use of natural resources for recreation purposes quickly resulted in overcrowding in public parks and outdoor recreation areas. In response the National Park Service and the U.S. Forest Service began to upgrade and expand federal recreation and park areas.

- The U.S. Congress established the Outdoor Recreation Resources Review Commission in 1958. The Commission provided estimates of the need for outdoor recreation areas for the years 1976–2000. This report was the foundation for future budget allocations to outdoor recreation facilities and services at local, state, and federal levels.

- The passing of the Federal Aid Highway Act in 1958 created the interstate highway system. This network of superhighways encouraged travel and stimulated the growth of an already expanding motel/franchise quick food industry. In a sense, the highways became the playgrounds for millions. Vacation travel became synonymous with recreation, and especially outdoor recreation.

- The establishment of the President's Council on Youth Fitness and the authorization of the National Cultural Center for Performing Arts (Kennedy Center) resulted in two programs that furthered the nation's interest in leisure related to physical fitness and the performing arts.

- During the 1960s and 1970s a great expansion of private and outdoor recreation facilities and a mushrooming of youth-serving programs occurred as the Baby Boomers entered their adolescence and young adult years.

- The Bureau of Outdoor Recreation (BOR) was established in 1962. Three years later, Congress established the Land and Water Conservation Fund (LWCF), which provided matching funds to enable local recreation units to acquire and develop land for outdoor recreation purposes. LWCF continues today, although not at the same funding level as during the 1960s.

By 1966, several major recreation and park organizations merged to form the National Recreation and Park Association (NRPA). This organization is described in greater depth in the next chapter. One of NRPA's first undertakings was to assess the recreation and park employment situation. According to the 1967–1968 personnel analysis, about 200 universities and colleges were preparing recreation and park specialists (National Recreation and Park Association, 1968). Enrollments in these programs exceeded 15,000 students. The projected need for annual new personnel in 1980 was twice that figure. Although critics of this report questioned its research methodology and validity, all agreed it did accurately reflect the growing importance of recreation services as an area requiring professional expertise.

The Last Quarter of the 20th Century

During the latter half of the 1970s, several significant governmental actions occurred that affected recreation services. In response to the recreation interests of urban residents, the National Park Service established two urban parks, Golden Gate in San Francisco and Gateway in New York City. The national park system embarked on an urban parks program that was intensified in 1978 when the Congress appropriated 1.2 billion dollars for the improvement of the urban and national park systems. Some conservationists responded with alarm to the establishment of an urban parks program that took money away from traditional national parks. Others believed that urban parks would take the pressure off the overuse of many of the national parks. Today many urban areas are associated with the National Park Service because of the designation of National Battlefields, National Monuments, National Parkways, and National Recreation Areas.

In matters concerning human rights, governmental action was equally pronounced. Congress passed the Education for All Handicapped Act in the mid-1970s, which guaranteed equal educational opportunity for handicapped youth in the *least restrictive environment*. The field of therapeutic recreation services expanded, particularly at the local level where hundreds of recreation departments created special program divisions to serve people with disabilities. The Bureau for the Education of the Handicapped also stimulated the growth of these programs through its financial support of the training of therapeutic recreation personnel.

The focus of recreation and leisure studies in the 1980s and 1990s evolved toward entrepreneurialism. Reflecting the general attitudes towards business and government, the private businesses and nonprofit sectors of the recreation services system prospered. The public sector became more businesslike by developing programs and services that were self-supporting or assured the agency some recovery costs. Pricing and marketing concepts became a part of the leisure studies curricula, as did specializations in commercial recreation/resort and tourism management. Some curricula even changed their names to reflect this trend and became Departments of Parks, Recreation, and Tourism.

One of the concerns of the 1980s was the decline in student interest in public recreation and other human-service fields. Enrollments in university curricula dropped except for those specialties embracing entrepreneurialism (i.e., commercial recreation), tourism, and therapeutic recreation. Therapeutic recreation was aided considerably by the passage of the Americans with Disabilities Act and the creation of the American Therapeutic Recreation Association and the National Council on Therapeutic Recreation Certification. Further, for the first time in the history of the profession, more females than males were choosing parks and recreation as a major. By 1990, the ratio was two females for every male (Bialeschki, 1992).

At the end of the 20th century, the growth in public recreation and nonprofit sectors stabilized. After some decline in university programs in recreation, the numbers of students remained relatively constant. Private and commercial recreation and tourism continued to offer opportunities for a variety of recreation activities. Environmental protection remained important but sometimes conflicted with sustainable economic activities like tourism. Youth coming from high-risk communities were the focus of recreation services efforts as were underserved and disadvantaged populations.

Recreation Services in the 21st Century

As the 21st century began, many recreation services providers celebrated birthdays and anniversaries as some of the organizations and services became a century old. The period of 2000 to the present was a time to reflect on the past and what lies ahead. Many organizations spent considerable effort branding themselves to be contemporary for the new century. For example, the YMCA had broadened itself greatly over the years and changed its name to "the Y" to reflect its diversity and breadth. Re-invention and mission-driven efforts became priorities in recreation service organizations. One area discussed in more detail in Unit Four is the repositioning of public parks and recreation.

Many opportunities for recreation were available in communities through all sectors. The first decade of the 21st century marked recognition of how partnerships are essential to remain relevant and to grow in the future. These partnerships occurred within sectors (e.g., parks and recreation in cities working with county programs) and across sectors (e.g., corporate sponsors enlisted to help finance community sports tournaments). These partnerships are also described in more detail in Unit Four.

The perception of an obesity epidemic underlined the value once again of how recreation services provide many opportunities to be physically active and thus healthier. Research showed the value of parks and open spaces in promoting physical activity leading to better physical and mental health.

The decade was also noted for efforts emphasizing sustainability. All recreation services acknowledged social, economic, and environmental aspects over the years. The beginning of the 21st century, however, underlined the need to consider how these three aspects worked together. Economic sustainability had become an issue, and its importance was even more pronounced as public and nonprofit organizations considered alternative forms of funding beyond taxes and membership fees, respectively. The impact of environmental degradation on recreation resources was widely discussed, especially related to the implications of climate change. If no spaces and places exist for people to play, leisure experiences will change dramatically. Although social issues have been at the heart of the recreation movement since its beginnings, and the latter part of the 20th century focused on diversity and human rights, these issues continued to be important. Legislation and policies made discrimination due to gender, race, age, disability, and religion illegal in the United States and recreation professionals sought concrete ways to ensure their programs were inclusive and did not discriminate.

Reflecting on Over 100 Years of Recreation Services

One of the markers of democracy in the United States is the ability of people to organize when they see a social need. Leisure and recreation are social needs addressed through recreation services systems with goals to improve the well-being of individuals and the quality of life in communities. These recreation services have emerged over the years in developmental stages. Table 15.1 summarizes the stages of development that led to the recreation services that exist today: services to youth, diversionary activity, outdoor recreation and the environment, entrepreneurialism, and sustainability.

The desire to serve underprivileged and underserved (but not undeserved) children characterized the earliest stage of recreation services—service to youth. Nonprofit youth organizations such as the Boy and Girl Scouts, the Playground Association of America (later the National Recreation Association), and the YMCA and YWCA dominated the movement and provided the basic programs. They relied heavily on private and voluntary financial support and used the methods and techniques most frequently associated with today's social group work programs. Leisure experiences were seen as a means to an end for the building of character and the development of better communities.

Table 15.1 Stages of Development of Organized Recreation Services in the U.S.

	Stage One (1890–1916) Services to Youth	Stage Two (1917–1955) Diversionary Activity	Stage Three (1956–1976) Outdoor Recreation and Environment	Stage Four (1977–2000) Entrepreneurialism	Stage Five (2001–present) Sustainability
Program Focus	Conservationist and Youth Services	Parks and Diversionary Activity	Outdoor Recreation and Environmental Concerns	Entrepreneurial Approach to Local Services and Tourism	Integrating Social, Economic, and Environmental Factors
Leadership	Volunteers	Volunteers and Professionals	Professionals	Professionals and Volunteers	Professionals and Volunteers
Major Provider of Services	Nonprofit	Federal and Local Governments	Governments, Nonprofit, and Private Businesses	Public, Nonprofit, and Private Businesses	Public, Nonprofit, and Private Businesses

The second stage of development emerged during the Great Depression and reached its peak in the late 1940s. Recreation services became a governmental responsibility and were seen as an activity needed to break the issues associated with poverty and the tensions of war. During this period, local communities developed park and recreation commissions and charged them with the responsibility of providing diversionary recreation opportunities. The number of community recreation buildings, athletic fields, and other sports facilities increased. Organized recreation took a mass approach, and for many, sports became synonymous with recreation. Private businesses focused on various forms of recreation entertainment.

The third period began with the expansion of outdoor recreation interests in the late 1950s. Private investments coupled with expanding federal and state programs had an impact on recreation opportunities. Camping, water and winter sports, and vacation travel grew significantly. The nurturing and development of natural resources to accommodate these interests, and the need for recreation and park professionals with managerial and planning skills to manage these efforts characterized this era of development. During this stage, federal and state governments assumed greater responsibility in providing opportunities for individual recreation pursuits. Private businesses offered the equipment and clothing necessary to make these experiences pleasurable. During this era, a host of public policy issues began to emerge.

Entrepreneurism emerged as governments were forced to cut back on spending. The affluence of the 1960s and 1970s placed great demands upon natural resource agencies. They were pushed to their limit to accommodate the growing outdoor recreation interests while also trying to protect the environment from overuse. Partially in response to both the demand for opportunities and a growing service economy, private entrepreneurs recognized the potential of recreation services as a market. Entrepreneurship was furthered by the tax revolt of the late 1970s that reduced considerably the ability of the public sector to provide programs without seeking some recovery costs from the participants. Public park and recreation agencies had to become more enterprising, offering more programs that were either self-sustaining or capable of recovering costs. They also began to contract out some of their operations, such as maintenance to private companies.

Political actions and debate also characterized the entrepreneurial era. The policy issue became one of whether private businesses or the government were responsible for providing basic recreation services. Rather than be a direct supplier of opportunity, some governmental agencies assumed a facilitator role. They provided the facility and technical assistance but let nonprofit and private businesses do the programming. Private businesses were expected to become more active as suppliers. This shift influenced programs of professional preparation of recreation services personnel as courses in marketing strategies, economic theory, and management were included in many undergraduate curricula. Some educators feared that recreation curricula had moved away from a humanistic social approach to services to a more businesslike or entrepreneurial approach.

As the 21st century unfolds, sustainability seems to dominate in all sectors of recreation services. "Sustainability" means to be responsible for upholding maximum economic, social, and environmental dimensions of leisure experiences and recreation services.

The recognition that social, economic, and environmental elements all must be considered in providing services has come to the fore. This trio is not new, but its importance is continually emphasized. Although some recreation services organizations focus more on one element than another (e.g., private businesses and economics, nonprofit and public on social or environmental concerns), the stage of sustainability as it integrates all sectors is on the forefront of recreation services in the 21st century. To maximize sustainability, recreation professionals are needed who have the skills and abilities to address the emerging issues of the 21st century. Professionalism in recreation services and its evolution is the topic of the next chapter.

Reflection Questions

1. How have legislation, laws, and government regulations influenced recreation services over the past century?

2. What should be the role of governments in providing recreation services? Should the government only provide services that are not otherwise available through other sectors?

3. How would you explain the evolution of the stages of recreation services over the years?

4. Would you say that wars have been positive for recreation services? To your knowledge, have the wars that the United States has been involved with over the past decade (i.e., Iraq and Afghanistan) benefited recreation services in any way?

5. How have political views such as progressivism, liberalism, and conservatism influenced recreation services?

6. Why did recreation services grow so quickly beginning in the 1950s? Why did they seem to be less supported (or were they?) toward the end of the century?

7. If you were to speculate about the future of recreation services, what do you think will happen in each of the sectors?

Chapter 16

The Recreation Services Profession

In this Unit, the history of leisure and the evolution of recreation services as a social movement in the United States are discussed. The purpose of this chapter is to further explore the evolution of recreation services as evidenced in the development of professional status.

Professional Status

One of the characteristics of a social movement is its evolution toward professional status. Social movements, as was the case with the recreation movement, are often initially directed and administered by volunteers and interested lay persons. These social movements then often evolve into formal organizations with professionally educated personnel. Those individuals employed in the movement seek to establish their identity as professionals and assert their importance as a profession (Sessoms, 1990).

Several terms are associated with this discussion of professions. For example, 'discipline' usually relates to a unified body of knowledge that is accepted with its stated tenets of theory and research. Sociology, political science, psychology, and economics are examples of traditional disciplines. Whether leisure and recreation studies have a distinct set of theories or methods is debatable. Therefore, recreation and leisure studies are more accurately referred to as an area or field of study rather than a discipline (Henderson, 2011).

Fields also serve areas of applied expertise and interest. Leisure studies is a relatively new field that relies on its disciplinary (or interdisciplinary) bases (e.g., sociology, psychology, economics related to recreation services) for foundations of application to practice. The field of practice related to recreation services includes professional specialties such as recreation, parks, event management, tourism, therapeutic recreation, or whatever the focus of the applied professional activity. Study and practice are not hierarchical but parallel in a field such as recreation services. Distinctions between disciplines and fields are somewhat arbitrary but they provide a way to think about this field of recreation services as it relates to professionalism.

Professions differ from trades and other classifications of occupations in several ways. A professional is a person who is paid for his or her work and whose identity is tied to an occupation. Professions tend to be a blend of the trades and disciplines. Professionals apply the techniques of performance of specific trades and the theories of selected disciplines or fields to some specific social problem or concern. Professions also develop their own approaches and strategies to address social concerns (i.e., wise use of leisure).

A family analogy might be useful in thinking about the foundations of recreation services as a profession (Henderson, 2010). The grandparents are the traditional disciplines that have shaped an understanding of leisure and recreation (e.g., sociology, economics). The parents are the broad field of leisure studies and recreation management. The specialties such as outdoor recreation management, therapeutic recreation, sports, or tourism comprise the sub-fields, which might be analogous to the children. Recreation professionals have specialties in particular areas where they apply their education. Specialists working in recreation services are part of the evolving profession.

Components of a Profession

When a social movement becomes established within a culture, at some point a distinction is made regarding its professional status. According to most authorities, six criteria must be met before a field of service can be called a profession:

- An alliance with a social concern

- Professional societies or associations

- A code of ethics

- A specialized body of knowledge and practical skills that lead to professional authority

- Programs of professional education and training

- Professional standards attested by accreditation, certification, and licensing

Many aspects of recreation services have satisfied these criteria. The focus on a social concern has been discussed in previous sections of the book. Recreation services professionals, regardless of the sector or specialty, address well-being for individuals, the benefits of recreation, quality of life in communities and the sustainability of recreation services. Therefore, the first aspect of being a profession has been met. The following sections address the remaining criteria related to the recreation services profession.

Development of Professional Associations

Recreation services professionals have established several organizations and associations dedicated to the advancement and improvement of their profession. These groups have given individuals in the profession a chance to pool their common knowledge and interests for their own professional development and the betterment of society. Mutual interests, concerns, and experiences are shared through professional organizations. They provide a means for establishing and developing standards, for exchanging information and ideas, and for developing and influencing public action. Many associations support the recreation services profession. Some of them are described below.

National Recreation and Park Association

The largest professional organization focused primarily on parks, recreation, and conservation is the National Recreation and Park Association (NRPA). Although recreation services are much larger than the interests of NRPA, it was historically the foundation for public parks and recreation in the latter half of the 20th century. NRPA came into existence in 1966 as the result of a merger of five smaller organizations that were all focused on some aspect of public parks and/or recreation:

- The *American Institute of Park Executives (AIPE)* evolved from the New England Association of Park Superintendents, later known as the American Association of Park Superintendents. The AIPE members were drawn from executive leaders in public parks throughout the United States and Canada.

- The *National Recreation Association (NRA)* was organized in 1906 originally as the Playground Association of America. As the first organization to address recreation in neighborhoods and communities, this group was a major force in the development of the recreation movement for 60 years. The NRA membership included primarily private citizens dedicated to advocating for and promoting recreation opportunities for all people.

- The *National Conference on State Parks (NCSP)* was founded in 1921 as a professional and service organization for workers employed by federal and state natural resource agencies. This organization provided information to the public on the values and functions of state parks, historic sites, monuments, and recreation preserves.

- The *American Association of Zoological Parks and Aquariums (AAZPA)* was established as an affiliate of the AIPE in 1924. The AAZPA provided a professional association for zoo and aquarium directors, curators, and other professionals concerned with the preservation of wildlife and its display for the general public. Of note, however, is that this organization withdrew from NRPA shortly after it merged.

- The *American Recreation Society (ARS)* was established in 1938 as the Society of Recreation Workers of America. The primary objective was to unite all recreation professionals in the United States. The ARS viewed itself as a professional rather than a service or public-advocacy association.

In the middle of the 20th century, leaders in recreation services realized that the United States was on the threshold of a new leisure era that would require the combined efforts of many people. Unity within the field of recreation seemed essential but did not occur for 20 years. The first national meeting of the newly formed NRPA was held in Washington, D.C., in October 1966. As recognition of the significance of merger and the nation's concern for adequate recreation and park resources, President Lyndon B. Johnson along with the Secretary of Interior, the Secretary of Agriculture, and the Secretary of Housing and Urban Development, addressed the first national meeting of NRPA.

Professional branches and special-interest sections were established within NRPA at the beginning and included: American Park and Recreation Society, National Society of Park Resources, Armed Forces Recreation Society, National Therapeutic Recreation Society, Citizen and/or Board Members Branch, and Society of Park and Recreation Educators. These branches were transformed in 2009 into a variety of interest groups designed to encourage primarily online connections. The philosophy behind this change was to emphasize the unity of citizens and professionals in not just promoting a specialty but in advocating for the broad field of public parks, recreation, and conservation.

The mission of NRPA today is to advance parks, recreation, and environmental conservation efforts that enhance the quality of life for all people. The organization is financially supported through membership fees, public contributions, self-generated revenue, endowments, and grants. A monthly magazine called *Parks & Recreation* is published along with biweekly online newsletters. Other publications of NRPA are *Journal of Leisure Research, Therapeutic Recreation Journal*, and *Schole*. A national Congress meets every year in rotating cities around the United States, with up to 10,000 participants attending. The NRPA national headquarters are in Ashburn, Virginia. In 2011, NRPA consisted of over 20,000 members.

Additional Professional Organizations

Other professional organizations are related to recreation services. A few of them are briefly described regarding their purpose and function. Some additional organizations will be discussed in the next Unit, when specific recreation specialty areas are explored.

- *Academy of Leisure Science (ALS)*. The Academy of Leisure Sciences was organized as an honorary group with elected members in 1980. The mission of ALS was dedicated to the advancement of leisure studies. However, the primary function of ALS until 2011 was to recognize members (ALS Fellows) for their exceptional scholarly and intellectual contribution to the growth and development of the understanding of leisure in contemporary society. In 2011, after the dissolution of NRPA's educators branch (i.e., Society of Park and Recreation Educators), the Fellows voted to change the constitution and allow for two types of membership. The election of Fellows to the honorary would continue as in the past, but all individuals who subscribed to the mission and purpose could also become members of ALS. The primary purpose of ALS was redefined to bring together people from diverse backgrounds, academic and otherwise, who share a mutual interest in better understanding the roles of leisure in life including various contexts of recreation, park, tourism, outdoor adventure, health, therapy, and sports.

- *American Academy for Park and Recreation Administration (AAPRA)*. Also established in 1980, AAPRA comprises distinguished practitioners and scholars committed to the advancement of park and recreation administration. The honorary is limited to 120 elected members with 80% mandated to be practitioners and 20% educators. This organization encourages the development and enhancement of excellence in administration practices in the delivery of park, recreation, and leisure services and publishes the *Journal of Park and Recreation Administration*. Recent efforts have included providing technical assistance to park and recreation agencies and encouraging emerging leadership in the field through mentoring and externships.

• *American Association for Physical Activity and Recreation/American Alliance for Health, Physical Education, Recreation and Dance (AAPAR/AAHPERD).* AAPAR is one of the major divisions of AAHPERD. The Alliance states that it is the largest organization in the United States of professionals involved in physical education, recreation, fitness, sport and coaching, dance, health education and promotion, and all specialties related to achieving a healthy and active lifestyle. AAHPERD is an alliance of five national associations, six geographic district associations, and a research consortium. AAPAR supports faculty, students, teachers, fitness trainers, recreation instructors, and community leaders who promote lifelong and inclusive physical activity and recreation. The publications that may be of interest to recreation professionals include the *Journal of Physical Education, Recreation and Dance,* and *Research Quarterly for Exercise and Sport.*

• *American Camp Association (ACA).* This association, incorporated in 1910, is made up of representatives of agencies and institutions interested in the development of organized camps, primarily but not exclusively, for children in the United States. The ACA membership consists of camp directors, members of camp staffs, educators, and others directly associated with the operation of camps or interested in the camping movement. ACA represents day and resident camps of all types: religiously affiliated, schools, public, private independent, and nonprofit. The expressed purpose is to further the interests and welfare of children, youth, and adults through camp experiences. Standards for the improvement of camp practices are implemented through a voluntary accreditation program. The official publication of the Association is *Camping Magazine.*

- *American Therapeutic Recreation Association (ATRA).* ATRA was founded in 1984 and is now the largest national membership organization representing the interests and needs of recreational therapists. Recreational therapists are healthcare providers who use recreational therapy interventions for improved functioning of individuals with illnesses or disabling conditions. This organization publishes the *Annual in Therapeutic Recreation.*

- *North American Society for Sport Management (NASSM).* NASSM is a relatively new organization started in 1986 with a focus on supporting and assisting professionals working in the fields of sport, leisure, and recreation. The purpose of NASSM is to promote, stimulate, and encourage study, research, scholarly writing, and professional development in the area of theoretical and applied sport management. Members of the society are interested in sport marketing, future directions in management, employment perspectives, management competencies, leadership, sport and the law, personnel management, facility management, organizational structures, fund-raising, and conflict resolution. The *Journal of Sport Management* is published by NASSM.

- *Travel and Tourism Research Association (TTRA).* The purpose of TTRA is to improve the travel and tourism industry through education, publications, and networking activities. Research and scholarly activity surround topics such as marketing, emerging trends, methodologies, travel motivators, emerging markets, benchmarking, and using research to make strategic decisions. A national conference has been held every year since 2003.

- *National Intramural Recreation and Sports Association (NIRSA).* The mission of NIRSA is to provide for the education and development of professional and student members and to foster quality recreational programs, facilities, and services for diverse populations, primarily in colleges and universities. NIRSA was founded in 1950 by African Americans in historically black colleges who wanted to promote intramurals. Since that time it has grown into a large organization that influences college campuses across the United States. The organization publishes online the *Recreational Sports Journal.*

- *Association for Experiential Education (AEE).* AEE was founded in the early 1970s with the purpose to connect educators and to expand their capacity to enrich lives through the philosophy and practice of experiential education. Experiential education as a philosophy and methodology focuses on educators purposefully engaging with learners in direct experience and in focused reflection to facilitate knowledge, skills, and values. AEE seeks to contribute to making a more just and compassionate world by transforming education and promoting an educational philosophy that fosters personal growth, leadership, development, teamwork, and environmental stewardship. The association is international in scope and publishes a research journal, *Journal of Experiential Education.*

• *Resort and Commercial Recreation Association (RCRA).* RRCA was formed in 1981 to serve the emerging specialty of resort and commercial recreation by creating a network to exchange programming ideas. RCRA has continued its growth in both membership and services over the years and now represents recreation and amenity managers in resorts, hotels, sports clubs, campgrounds, theme parks, special event companies, cruise lines, community developments and colleges/universities. One of RCRA's major contributions has been the development of internship opportunities for students interested in seeking employment in a commercial recreation setting.

• *World Leisure Organization (WLO).* World Leisure (formerly called the World Leisure and Recreation Association) was founded in 1952 as the International Recreation Association, which was for a short time a part of NRPA. The focus of the organization has always been to promote recreation and leisure interests throughout the world. WLO has worked cooperatively with various organizations such as the United Nations. The organization bases its work on the idea that access to meaningful leisure experiences in nations around the world is just as important as the need for shelter, education, employment and fundamental healthcare. To improve the quality of life requires the joint efforts of policymakers, leisure professionals, and public and private sector program providers. Program efforts include publishing *World Leisure Journal,* world and regional congresses and training opportunities, advocacy through international declarations and position papers, and consulting services.

• *International Association for the Society and Natural Resources (IASNR).* The IASNR exists primarily to support its annual conference, International Symposium on Society and Resource Management. It is held every year, usually in North America. The symposium serves as a venue to discuss pertinent issues associated with the human dimensions of outdoor resource management and the environment. Members include academic researchers, government personnel, land managers, NGO representatives, students, and other individuals interested in human dimensions. The organization publishes a research journal called *Society and Natural Resources*.

Other professional organizations also exist, but these examples highlight some of the major groups associated with recreation services specialties.

A Code of Ethics

Another step in the process to becoming a profession is to establish a code of professional ethics. Ethics are usually part of a profession's philosophy that considers moral issues and judgments related to standards of expected behavior. For recreation professionals, a focus on ethics provides a framework for distinguishing between right and wrong conduct, and a way to rationally critique beliefs and practices that become the foundation for the profession.

The code of ethics established by a profession acts as a contract with society. This code is a pledge between a professional and the people served that duties will be performed within an acceptable moral frame. The types of ethical situations can be between individuals (e.g., guarding the welfare of the participants), the community (e.g., following the laws), or the environment where recreation occurs (e.g., promoting stewardship of the environment).

For most professionals, a code of ethics is compiled and promoted through the efforts of professional associations. For example, the American Camp Association (ACA) has a code of ethics for all members of the association as well as a statement of exemplary ethical practices for camp owners, directors, and executives (see Table 16.1). Each member must agree to abide by this code if he or she wants to maintain a professional affiliation with ACA.

A code cannot identify all practices or concepts and does not guarantee that all persons will behave in ways deemed ethical. However, a code is built on a commitment to integrity, truthfulness, and fairness to all persons. The code of ethics can also be linked to certification of the professional where a standard of behavior has been predetermined. If the recreation

Table 16.1 Code of Ethics for All Members of the American Camp Association (ACA)

1. I shall conduct myself in a manner consistent with the association's mission to serve organized camps, affiliated programs, and the public by promoting better camping for all.
2. I shall recognize my responsibility for the welfare of others in my care.
3. I shall abide by and comply with the relevant laws of the community.
4. I shall be a member in the proper ACA classification as currently defined by the ACA National Board of Directors; and I shall disclose my affiliation with ACA only in a manner specifically permitted by the association.
5. I shall speak for the association only when specifically authorized to do so and will otherwise make clear that my statements and actions are those of an individual member.
6. I shall respect the confidences of ACA members, camps, and other constituents within the camp community; however, I shall accept responsibility to pass on to the appropriate ACA official information I deem reliable that will help protect the camp community against unethical practices by any individual.

Exemplary Ethical Practices for Camp Owners, Directors, and Executives
The association recognizes the camp owner, director, and executive as the primary professional persons assuming the greatest responsibility for actual camp practices. Therefore, in addition to the Code of Ethics for all members, any member operating a camp accredited by or affiliated with the American Camp Association agrees to subscribe to the following:

7. I shall endeavor to provide an environment conducive to promoting and pro-tecting the physical and emotional well-being of the campers and staff.
8. I shall seek to instill in my staff and campers a reverence for the land and its waters and all living things and an ecological conscience which reflects the conviction of individual responsibility for the health of that environment.
9. I shall follow equal opportunity practices in employment and camper enrollment.
10. I shall endeavor to employ persons based upon factors necessary to the performance of the job and the operation of the camp.
11. I shall be truthful and fair in securing and dealing with campers, parents/guardians, and staff.
12. I shall provide a written enrollment policy for all camper/family applicants including fees, payment schedules, discounts, dates of arrival and departure, together with a clearly stated refund policy.
13. I shall provide for each staff member a written job description and employment agreement including period of employment, compensation, benefits, and exceptions.
14. I shall promptly consult with parents or guardians of any camper or minor staff member as to the advisability of removing him/her from camp should it be clear that he/she is not benefiting from the camp experience or the camper's or minor staff member's actions have created this need.
15. I shall make arrangements with the parents or guardians for the return of their camper(s) or minor-age staff member(s).
16. I shall pay the correct national and section fees as established by the ACA National Board of Directors and the ACA Section Board of Directors.
17. I, or my agent, will promptly respond to any and all complaints received by me and make a good faith effort to resolve all such complaints in accordance with generally accepted good business practices and the ACA Code of Ethics.

Adopted 2/26/95; Revised 3/2/97; 2/25/00; 2/23/02, ACA Council of Delegates. Used with permission.

professional does not meet the ethical expectations set by the credentialing organization, the practitioner may lose credential status.

A Specialized Body of Knowledge

The fourth mark of a profession is the existence of a definable body of knowledge. This knowledge is built over time as information is gathered through research and evaluation based on practice and theory. Theory provides the basic principles that serve as the foundations for conceptualizing key aspects of the field. These principles guide ongoing research as well as the development of professional leadership. The basis for this textbook, for example, is the body of knowledge about recreation services including information emanating from research and best practices related to the specialties of the profession.

Recreation professionals master a specialized body of knowledge that enables them to provide valuable services to society. Although recreation professionals should be knowledgeable about information from other disciplines such as sociology, psychology, business, medicine, and natural resources, the profession is built upon a body of research and literature applied to leisure behavior and recreation leadership, programming, and management issues. This body of knowledge serves as the basis for professional preparation programs in colleges and universities, continued research and evaluation efforts, the revision of ethical practices, and the further development of professional programs of accreditation and certification.

Common ways to remain current with this body of knowledge after going through a professional preparation program as an undergraduate or graduate student is to read the recreation research journals published by professional organizations (e.g., *Journal of Park and Recreation Administration, Therapeutic Recreation Journal*), attend professional meetings and conferences, and engage in continuing education opportunities.

Programs of Professional Education and Training

Identity and the professionalizing of recreation services has also been reflected and influenced by programs of professional preparation for recreation personnel. The need for professionally educated persons to administer and operate recreation services was recognized during the formative years of the movement at the beginning of the 20th century. As early as 1911, short courses and training manuals for instruction of playground workers were prepared.

The growth of recreation, parks, sports, and tourism parallels the acceptance of recreation services as a career field. In 1960, prior to the expansion of the outdoor recreation interest, only 62 colleges and universities offered instruction in parks and recreation, and the majority of these programs were housed in departments of Physical Education or in Forestry (Sessoms, 1993). With the growth of the recreation field, and the expanded involvement of all sectors in facilitating recreation services, the number of positions in recreation services grew more rapidly than did the supply of professionally prepared graduates.

Currently, almost 300 schools offer degrees in parks, recreation, tourism, and leisure services. These degrees range from technical Associate level degrees at community colleges to Ph.D. programs at some of the major research universities in the country. These degrees are based on the need to develop practitioners, educators, and researchers with varied breadth and depth of knowledge about all areas of recreation services.

In addition to professional education, many opportunities exist for continuing education within the profession and from other fields. Conferences offer cutting-edge sessions and specialized schools exist for training, such as NRPA's Oglebay Park schools (e.g., Directors' School, Supervisor School, Revenue School) in West Virginia. In addition, numerous webinars are now available through the recreation services organizations described earlier. Many of these professional training opportunities offer Continuing Education Units (CEUs) that are often required to maintain certifications in various areas.

Professional Standards

Professional standards of practice as another mark of a profession have resulted in the establishment of programs for accreditation (i.e., for higher education institutions as well as community agencies) and certification for recreation professionals. Agencies are accredited and individuals are certified.

Accreditation

Accreditation symbolizes a professional concern for meeting the criteria of a specified set of best practices within a recreation services organization. For example, the American Camp Association has a long-standing voluntary accreditation program for any camp that wants to go through the process. Based on the body of knowledge and current research, the ACA standards address particular areas (e.g., health and wellness, program activities, personnel, transportation, and site and facilities) deemed important for a high-quality camp experience. If a camp meets the standards as determined by a visitation team, it can advertise that they are an accredited camp.

A major effort of the National Recreation and Park Association (NRPA) was to have recreation accepted as a field through the initiation of two accreditation programs focused on universities and on public agencies. The Council on Accreditation of Parks, Recreation and Tourism (COAPRT) administers the accreditation of university programs of study related to recreation and leisure. North Carolina State University was the first institution to be accredited in 1977. Today almost 100 colleges and universities throughout the United States have accredited recreation-services curricula for undergraduates. Reaccreditation of these programs occurs every three years.

In the 1990s, an accreditation program was initiated for public park and recreation programs referred to as the Commission for Accreditation of Park and Recreation Agencies (CAPRA). The purpose of this accreditation is to assure high-quality recreation and park services and experiences for community members. Agency accreditation is available to all entities administering park and recreation systems, including municipalities, townships, counties, special districts and regional authorities, councils of government, schools, and military installations. Over 100 units in the United States have gone through the extensive self-study and visitation by peers, which comprises this accreditation. The number of agencies involved is growing rapidly. Accreditation is usually for a set period of time such as five years, and then the process is repeated to ensure continued compliance and updating.

Certification

Professional certification is similar to accreditation in that the concern is for best practice. Certification, however, focuses on the individual professional. The individual completes professional development training (i.e., academic professional preparation program or continuing education) and is expected to meet selected baseline criteria that indicate individual competence and skill. For example, NRPA offers certification of professionals through the Certified Park and Recreation Professional (CPRP) and more recently the Certified Park and Recreation Executive (CPRE) program.

Certification associated with recreation services can also occur in other ways not associated with the profession but may be necessary to assure participants that employees are qualified. Examples might include a certified lifeguard, certified canoe instructor, or a certified horse riding instructor, certified fitness trainer, or certified youth coach. Regardless of the type, certification should assure the public that paid as well as volunteer staff conducting recreation programs have adopted a specified standard of practice, and that certified individuals have made efforts to keep their skills current and at a high level.

All these areas discussed (i.e., alliance with a social concern, professional associations, code of ethics, body of knowledge, professional training, and professional standards) provide a basis for arguing that recreation and its associated specialty areas are indicative of professional status. Some people may not agree that recreation services are a profession, but these efforts over many years have shown that professional status is warranted. The next unit of this book discusses the specialties within this recreation services profession.

Reflection Questions

1. How would you describe the overall role of professional associations within recreation services?

2. Most people would argue that receiving a Bachelor's degree from a college or university is only the beginning of one's education. Explain what this statement means for a professional.

3. A few of the many professional associations are described in this chapter. In the next unit, more examples are discussed. Why are there so many associations connected to recreation services? Are all these organizations necessary?

4. What would an individual consider in deciding whether or not to apply for professional certification in an area?

5. Some people might not believe that people who work in recreation services can really be called professionals. How would you counter this perception?

6. How important is research in recreation services? What topics do you believe should be further researched?

7. Do you believe a distinct body of knowledge exists in recreation services or do professionals just borrow most of the knowledge base from other fields and professions?

Chapter 17

Opportunities
in Recreation Services

Professional careers in recreation services encompass an array of possibilities emphasizing recreation activities and leisure experiences for people of all ages and abilities. Unit Three focuses on professional career and employment opportunities available to people interested in the recreation services profession. Generally, these service sectors are categorized into public, nonprofit, and private business, but a great deal of overlap may occur among the sectors as well as across the traditional and emerging career specialties within recreation services.

Public recreation services, for example, are available to all citizens and supported mostly by public tax dollars. Typically, public services are not mandated to make a profit. A city, however, might operate a golf course at a profit so that the municipality can provide low-cost services that are not self-supporting such as after-school programs. A nonprofit agency such as the Girl Scouts relies on membership fees and donations for its operating budget. Nonprofit organizations, however, commonly partner with agencies and businesses in other sectors. Most youth-serving as well as religious organizations are nonprofit. A private business organization usually operates for a profit, but also may partner with organizations from any of the other sectors. Many tourism organizations are private businesses.

Some specialties within recreation services may be found across the sectors. For example, camps can be private, nonprofit, or public. Other specialties including therapeutic recreation, sports management, event management, and services for older adults might be facilitated by any of the sectors.

The future of recreation services will bring new and different interrelationships between and within recreation service providers. This Unit provides an overview of the career possibilities related to specialties such as parks and recreation, youth-serving organizations, outdoor recreation, tourism, sports management, events management, and many more. This chapter focuses on an overview of all sectors and specialties.

The Job Market

When people employed in recreation services tell others what they do, they sometimes get a quizzical look with a remark like "that must be fun." Many people choose a specialty in recreation services because they enjoy particular activities and want to help other people experience engagement and fun in their lives. Recreation professionals facilitate a great gift to people. Although fun is a major outcome of the efforts, the recreation profession is a serious occupation and many career opportunities exist now and will exist in the future. Further, as Unit One shows, the benefits of leisure experiences and recreation services are *endless*.

Since the 1980s, the field of recreation has grown steadily. Jobs related to recreation, leisure, sports, and tourism are expected to comprise almost half of the job opportunities in the United States by the mid-21st century (Begun, 2000). The jobs will exist in all the three sectors and professionals will have a variety of job titles and descriptions. The common element in all these jobs is the concern for facilitating leisure experiences for people, whether through providing parks, offering arts management, or promoting travel. People may experience many benefits from their involvement in recreation activities, but the core is that they enjoy their lives in ways that they could not if these opportunities did not exist. Regardless of the career area chosen, all professionals must believe that recreation services *do* add to people's well-being and to the quality of life of communities.

The public sector offers opportunities in city, county, state, and the national governments. Since the majority of public recreation spending comes from government taxes, people employed in public recreation work for the government and the citizens of the community, state, or nation. Numerous jobs exist in local parks and recreation departments, including such opportunities as recreation director, recreation supervisor, older adult programs supervisor, aquatics specialist, athletic director, outdoor educator, community center supervisor, recreation inclusion supervisor, youth outreach director, and the list goes on. In the state and federal governments, most jobs are related to natural resources and might include park ranger, park superintendent, park planner, campground manager, or naturalist/ interpreter. Besides parks, opportunities in state government also exist for therapeutic recreation specialists in state institutions and correctional facilities. Campus recreation positions exist in most public and private universities in the country. The U.S. military complex also has a huge number of civilian employees who work in recreation services around the world.

The nonprofit sector addresses specific social issues through organizations that raise money primarily through memberships or fundraising. Many nonprofit organizations do not have recreation as a mission, but most use recreation as a primary modality to reach those goals. The Boy/Girl Scouts and Y (formerly the YMCA) are common examples that fall into this sector. In the past, many of these nonprofit groups have been concerned primarily with youth issues, but the field of nonprofit management related to recreation has expanded to all age and ability groups as well as to environmental groups. The jobs in these organizations might include center director, youth leader, church ministries leader, camp director, adventure programmer, chief executive officer, program coordinator, recreation therapist, or program leader. Professionals working in this sector might be employed by organizations such as Boys and Girls Clubs, Salvation Army, Easter Seals, Sierra Club, or local charitable foundations.

The private business sector, sometimes also called the commercial sector, includes primarily for-profit organizations related to tourism, sports, and outdoor opportunities, for example. The focus of these groups is to provide recreation opportunities that generate a profit for the owners or the business operation. This sector is rapidly growing throughout the world with many possible jobs. Recreation business opportunities exist within a community such as golf course manager, bowling lanes manager, miniature golf manager, restaurant operator, corporate fitness manager, and employee recreation manager. Tourism opportunities include jobs such as a cruise line recreation director, theme park manager, fitness center director, marketing specialist for sports teams, or resort manager. Keep in mind that these job titles might also be associated with any of the other sectors as well. The difference with private businesses is that profit is the bottom line, although hopefully never at the expense of environmental degradation or social injustice.

In all these sectors, numerous part-time jobs and volunteer opportunities also exist. Many students interested in exploring careers in recreation services gain valuable experience and insight through volunteer, part-time, and seasonal jobs. Students can focus on these opportunities to move into professional positions as they gain knowledge and experience. An individual interested in a career in any area of recreation services must obtain the appropriate education and experience to be in the best position to pursue desired job opportunities.

Curricula in Professional Preparation for Recreation Services

Changes have occurred in the past century regarding the ways students have been educated for careers in recreation services. These changes reflect the ways that careers have evolved.

As noted earlier, university curricula existed separately related to parks and recreation until the mid-20th century. The focus up to that time related to recreation was mainly focused on providing activities. University curricula emerged in places like the University of Minnesota and the University of North Carolina-Chapel Hill in the 1930s that involved courses in the social sciences and physical activity, and these curricula were nested in other university departments such as physical education or sociology. Park-oriented students were prepared to be resource managers and administrators of land holdings, preserves, and municipal park systems primarily in departments of forestry. Students' preparation related to parks involved design, landscaping, architecture, horticulture, and the plant sciences. Park curricula were focused more on natural resource management than on the human dimensions of parks.

The coming together and prevalence of recreation and parks in the public sector in the 1950s and 1960s led to new programs of professional preparation in universities that were no longer connected to parent departments such as physical education or forestry. Typically these departments were more concerned about the core of management and administrative practices (whether related to social services or natural resources) than activity provision. In addition, in the 1970s, curricula became associated with leisure sciences and leisure studies as the common core of knowledge.

The growing foundation of leisure behavior was a way to connect recreation services as a profession. The *Journal of Leisure Research* was established by the National Recreation and Park Association in 1969 and *Leisure Sciences* followed 10 years later as an independent publication. Leisure studies became a way to describe all the aspects of curricula related to what activities people did in their free time. Some community programs changed their names to include *leisure services* and many university curricula added *leisure studies* into their department titles and to the names of majors. However, the term leisure was (and remains) highly misunderstood by the public in general. When the specializations began to multiply, leisure was removed from academic as well as public recreation titles beginning at the end of the 1980s. Whether leisure is the core and foundation of recreation services remains debatable and controversial today.

An interesting note regarding curricula includes the evolution of therapeutic recreation. After World War II, rehabilitation services were needed for war veterans. This concern for war veterans resulted in the recognition that many people with disabilities and illnesses were living in communities and institutions and needed recreation services. Federal grants became available to universities to educate students to apply various types of therapy including recreation therapy. Therapeutic recreation professionals associated themselves with health consciousness and the growth of allied health professions. Coursework included health sciences, assessment and evaluation methods, marketing, and leisure theory. Many educators realized that therapeutic recreation had commonalities with parks and recreation because of the focus on improving the well-being of individuals through rehabilitation as well as community inclusion. Although therapeutic recreation has many facets, it became a part of the core recreation and park curricula in many universities beginning in the 1960s.

The current and ongoing pattern in recreation curricula in higher education is the evolution of *specialties* beyond community parks and recreation. Many people believe that students need specialized education so they can get desirable jobs. This movement toward specialties began with the addition of hospitality, travel, and tourism curricula to traditional parks and recreation departments in the 1980s. Because of the projected growth of these areas along with the related area of private and commercial recreation businesses, universities turned to focus on the private for-profit sector of society. In the past 25 years, the career specialties in recreation services have exploded, as discussed in this book. All specialties have different missions, but they also share some commonalities in the professional competencies that are required.

Professional Competencies

Individuals seeking careers in recreation services, regardless of the specialty, should possess some common professional competencies. Before considering a career in this field, students should be aware of the broad skills that are required. Some of these competencies may be inherent in an individual's personality, but others are skills that can be learned, practiced, and mastered. The competencies needed can be categorized as people, conceptual, and technical skills.

Most individuals entering positions in recreation services will be working directly with *people*. Therefore, recreation professionals must have a compassion for people. They must possess communications skills including speaking, listening, writing, presenting information clearly and concisely, and working one-to-one as well as in groups. Many of these skills can be developed and learned in classes, but really liking people is an important prerequisite. Further, the more practice an individual has in working with others, the better the human skills can become.

Recreation professionals also need *conceptual* skills regarding ways to analyze how groups work and how organizations and communities function. These individuals need to be creative problem-solvers able to plan, implement, and evaluate recreation programs and processes. They also need to be people who understand how disciplines such as psychology, sociology, biology, economics, philosophy, and/or political science come together to facilitate recreation services. These individuals must to be aware of how society changes and the implications those changes have for leadership, programming, and management.

Technical skills include the ability to do such job requirements as activity analysis, planning a budget, doing a risk management plan, promoting and marketing a program, and/or maintaining recreation facilities. Many of these skills can be learned in coursework as well as through internships, on-the-job training, and continuing education opportunities.

Ideally, programs of professional preparation in recreation services at the baccalaureate level should address these competencies by: 1) providing students with a broad general education, 2) equipping them with the skills and methods of the profession and the specialty, and 3) affording them practical experiences through internships and supervised field practicums.

At the graduate level, most recreation curricula offer one or more specialties such as community recreation, human dimensions of outdoor recreation, sports management, or therapeutic recreation services. Most recreation educators agree that graduate study should be distinctly different from undergraduate study. The development of philosophical, analytical, and problem-solving skills at the graduate level characterizes that difference. Students desiring a Ph.D. and likely entering a career in higher education generally should have a broad base for teaching as well as a research specialty that enables them to contribute to the body of knowledge.

A final general note about careers in recreation services may relate to various civil service systems. In some states, civil service systems and their counterparts determine the procedures to be used in the selection and employment of personnel for recreation positions. These systems generally include specific eligibility requirements such as residence requirements, examination scores, educational and experience requirements, and other personal and skill requirements consistent with the rules of equal employment opportunity. A few personnel systems have included graduation from accredited curricula and/or certifications or registrations as an eligibility requirement for specific position titles, although this practice is not widespread.

Recreation services specialists, like other professionals, increase the quality of service because of the education received. In addition to preparation through college degrees, professionals should recognize that they will need lifelong learning. New information and best practices emerge each day. Therefore, although a solid foundation is needed and opportunities exist for certification, professionals should always be learning. Changes in society are constant. Rather than attempting to prepare students for a wide range of positions within the recreation services field, universities and colleges generally emphasize the entry-level positions at the baccalaureate level that have a specialized professional orientation.

Career opportunities within the profession of recreation and leisure continue to grow. All opportunities share a common commitment to enable people to experience leisure to enhance their well-being and contribute to a better quality of life in communities. People should have many choices in their recreational pursuits if they are to experience the value of leisure. Recreation services professionals, regardless of the specialty, strive to provide people with both quantity and quality of recreation choices.

Reflection Questions

1. What do you believe are the most important skills needed by a recreation professional? Would the skills differ based on the sector or specialty area?

2. Besides curricula, what other ways could a young person prepare him- or herself for a career in recreation services?

3. Why do you think job opportunities in recreation services will increase in the future?

4. Why would an individual with an undergraduate degree in some area of recreation services choose to get a Master's degree?

Chapter 18

Government Involvement in Recreation Services

Many career opportunities in recreation services have been and continue to be associated with the public sector and government involvement. The government's concern for citizens' health and welfare and the necessity to use natural resources carefully have become the legal basis for involvement in recreation services at all levels of government. For example, the federal government is a major supplier of outdoor recreation opportunities through the programs of the Departments of the Interior (e.g., National Park Service) and Agriculture (e.g., U.S. Forest Service). Government also has been a stimulator of culture and creative interests, an advocate of cultural heritage, and a dominant force in influencing public opinion on matters pertaining to leisure, recreation, and conservation. We can look to the Declaration of Independence for these mandates:

> We hold these truths to be self-evident, that all men [sic] are created equal, that they are endowed by their Creator with certain unalienable Rights, that among these are Life, Liberty, and the pursuit of Happiness.

Further, in the Preamble to the U.S. Constitution, the text declares that the government has a responsibility to "promote the general welfare." This general welfare generally relates to making provisions for the health, peace, morality, and safety of its citizens. These phrases related to pursuit of happiness and general welfare have been used as the rationalization for public park and recreation opportunities at all levels of government.

The major focus of this chapter and the two that follow is to examine public parks and recreation as a career field. However, this chapter sets the stage for articulating why government and people's taxes should support recreation services. The next two chapters describe the career opportunities.

Justifying Government Involvement

Many reasons justify governmental involvement in the delivery of recreation services related to the *pursuit of happiness* and *general welfare*. Most reasons support a social ethic of common responsibility for the quality of life in communities, which includes the well-being of all citizens. The following list provides some of the most commonly accepted rationales for government involvement at the local, state, level:

- Government is the agency supported by and for all people.

- Government has financial resources (i.e., through taxation) to acquire, establish, improve, and operate facilities—for every tax dollar paid to a governmental body, a small portion of it can be earmarked for recreation purposes.

- Government has the authority of *eminent domain* that allows acquisition of private lands for a greater public good, if in the best interest of the general public.

- Government provides a source of continuity and permanency.

- Legal precedent has been set over the years.

Although public recreation services are primarily funded through tax receipts, most government agencies also generate earned income. This income is a result of fees and charges to the users of the programs and/or facilities. Another source of income for public recreation is from contractual receipts such as rentals and concessions. For example, when buying a souvenir from a shop in a national park, that operator has paid a certain fee to the government for the privilege of setting up business in the park.

Government carries out societal functions in an orderly fashion. Without government, anarchy and chaos could engulf communities. The United States has chosen a representative democracy form of government to meet the needs of its people. Although the patterns of governing have varied from time to time and among government levels, ultimately government does for people collectively what they are unable to do individually. Since democratic governments are concerned with the well-being of their citizens, and since recreation experiences contribute to that well-being, recreation services are a responsibility of government.

Government is the only agency that is supported by, and can serve all segments of the population without discriminating according to characteristics such as age, gender, race and ethnicity, religion, ability, and socioeconomic condition. It is usually in the best position to develop the basic policies for effective recreation services at a minimum unit cost. The mission of government is to serve the public inclusively without excluding anyone from its programs.

Recreation Functions of Government

The government provides a myriad of functions related to public recreation services. Some of these functions vary by level of government or the particular branch of the government, as discussed in the next two chapters. Five functions, however, seem to be common to all levels:

- Management of land and natural resources

- Provision of technical assistance

- Financial assistance

- Direct service delivery

- Enactment and enforcement of regulations

The most visible and widely recognized function of public recreation has been the *management of natural resources*. For example, the creation of the National Park Service established the legitimacy of government in outdoor recreation. At the federal level, the United States has millions of acres of publicly managed lands. States also have their own network of parks and other outdoor recreation facilities and resources. Outdoor recreation may be individually pursued or may take place in an organized recreation setting.

Technical assistance is a function of federal and state recreation providers. Technical assistance refers to providing advice, consulting, and training related to a particular topic (e.g., recreation land management). With the availability of federal grants to local communities for the acquisition and development of outdoor recreation resources, many state agencies provide technical assistance and consulting capacities. The best approach to ensure interagency cooperation and a systematic development of recreation resources on all levels and among all sectors is to combine resource management and technical assistance functions. Organizations that provide technical assistance can influence the legislative process, provide government departments with needed data, and increase the public's awareness of the recreation field as a profession.

Financial assistance is provided to public recreation services from the government. These monies are available for land acquisition, facility development, restoration of historic areas, trail development, staff training programs, and program services such as artistic grants that benefit the public. This assistance often is established as a component of legislation or regulatory actions. For example, the Land and Water Conservation Fund (LWCF) was established in the 1960s as a way to preserve outdoor spaces. For many states and communities, access to additional sources of money outside of their own taxation revenues is imperative to the acquisition and development of recreation services. Other examples of financial assistance are described in the next two chapters.

The fourth major responsibility of governments in recreation services includes *direct service activities*. Some services are of a cultural and social nature while others involve physical activity and health. The major purpose of most community (i.e., towns, cities, counties) park and recreation departments is to provide direct services to the people of the community. However, some states operate state fair or exhibition facilities used year round to accommodate private and commercial businesses, including boat shows, horse shows, and music concerts. Other state services may include major sports areas, zoos, aquariums, performing arts centers, and museums. Direct recreation services at the state and federal level may also involve providing recreation at institutions such as Veterans' Hospitals, state hospitals, or prisons.

The final role of the government is to provide *regulations* and to enforce those regulations. Some of these regulations are made directly by recreation divisions in government and others come from other governmental units but apply to recreation. For example, in the first case, regulations regarding grazing on national forest lands would be regulated and enforced by managers in the U.S. Forest Service. An example from another government agency is the enforcement of the Americans with Disabilities Act (ADA), which requires that people with disabilities have access to recreation facilities and experiences without being segregated or asked to pay more for services needed to enjoy the recreation activity. The ADA was not written by recreation services agencies, but they are required to adhere to the law in the provision of services.

Recreation services, whether under governmental auspices or not, are influenced by state and local laws. For example, a recreation business such as a theme park must adhere to the health and sanitation laws of the state. The seating capacity of a theater must conform to state or local laws and ordinances concerning fire regulations and hours of operation. Further, laws establish the dates for hunting and fishing, and set limits on the number of species killed or caught. An understanding of the relationship between law and recreation and park services is essential because the legislative process affects all recreation programs at the local level.

These functions result in many career opportunities within public recreation. These possibilities are discussed further in the next two chapters.

Reflection Questions

1. Did the founders of the U.S. government assume that "pursuit of happiness" and "providing for the general welfare" included public recreation services?

2. Why did governments get involved with providing recreation services over 100 years ago? Are those reasons still valid today?

3. What is the most important function that governments provide? Could some of the government functions be better done by the nonprofit or private business sectors?

Chapter 19

Community Recreation and Parks

Community recreation and parks agencies, comprised of city and county departments as well as schools, have been important providers of recreation services for almost a century in the United States. Most of these local agencies are combined recreation and parks organizations, so this term will be used to describe this career specialty focused on community recreation. Recreation and parks services were initially an urban phenomenon. As cities grew, so did the need for recreation opportunities. Today, recreation and parks services are available to people living in rural areas and small towns as well as cities. Although local government services do not meet the recreation interests of every facet of public life, they do guarantee a basic level of support to meet people's recreation needs and interests. People have come to expect that local governments will provide parks, trails, facilities, and programs for people to meet and play.

Community recreation and parks agencies receive their authority from state-level enabling legislation. All states have these laws. Enabling legislation grants the local community the right to establish, organize, administer, and conduct recreation and parks programs. These enabling acts are permissive and not mandatory. They do not require the establishment of recreation and parks systems but allow local governments the right to expend public monies for recreation services.

For the most part, public recreation and parks departments are financed by the general fund of the community (i.e., monies which come from taxes levied on property) or from special recreation taxes. State and local laws and ordinances determine the funding sources. These monies almost always are supplemented by revenue derived from fees and charges, grants, gifts, and special assessments. In addition to these sources of support for daily operation, recreation and parks departments generally rely on bond referendums to fund their capital development projects (e.g., facility and land acquisition).

Organizational Structures

Local park and recreation agencies may have a variety of organizational structures. No single pattern for administering local public recreation services exists. The organizational structures reflect the historical origins of the recreation movement, the attitudes of the profession, and the experience and traditions of each community. Further, each local program is determined by the type and wording of the state-level enabling legislation that allowed the community to become an incorporated body that could tax and provide services.

In most cases, local recreation and parks services are provided through the offices of county or municipal government that makes these services a local government responsibility. Another local government approach is to fund recreation and parks as a special recreation and/or park district. These districts, found mainly in Illinois and Missouri, function as separate governmental units with the power to levy taxes for recreation and parks services. These districts function like municipalities except that they have the sole responsibility of providing recreation and park services.

A third approach to the provision of local recreation and parks services is the county recreation and park approach. Counties, like municipalities, draw their power from the state legislature and constitutional documents. With the growth of suburbia and urban sprawl, recreation services have become an accepted function of county government. Although similar in structure to municipal recreation services, county recreation and parks systems often have more of a parks focus than activities focus because the geographic area served is greater and the population density is usually less than in a municipality.

A fourth approach is to nurture leisure opportunities and administer local recreation services through public school systems. In rural areas, the school unit is sometimes the basic provider of recreation services. School districts generally function much like special recreation districts with the power to tax and administer services. Because the school is an essential and influential institution in every community, school officials and authorities cannot avoid dealing with recreation. They provide direct services for the millions of children and adults who spend a major portion of their lives each day within the confines of school facilities. Schools have other possibilities for addressing leisure in their structure as well as in their mission.

The role of schools, for example, involves shaping attitudes, developing leisure skills (e.g., music, physical education), and providing opportunities for practicing those skills (intramural and extramural sports, chorus, band). In addition to the educational mandate, the public school system is a significant owner of public property and facilities. Most schools have gymnasiums, arts and music facilities, playgrounds, and athletic fields. Some schools have swimming pools and stadiums. Most of these facilities can and should be made available for recreation pursuits or might be made available to the public through joint-use agreements.

Further, schools fulfill their recreation opportunities with three basic methods: community school and school-park programs, contractual agreements with counties and municipalities, and extracurricular activities. The community school component suggests that school buildings should be available to the public. The school park concept is a situation where a school is built in or immediately adjacent to a park and where the school as well as the community has access to using the park. Schools and other community groups including local recreation and parks departments sometimes enter into partnerships or contractual agreements to provide recreation opportunities for children and adults. Recess and extracurricular activities, including interscholastic sports, music, and dramatic activities, are other ways that schools link to leisure and recreation on a local level. Further, millions of families attend school-sponsored sporting events. Schools have an important role to play in leisure education and offer partnership opportunities with other recreation-service providers.

Operating Structures

Municipal and county governments, special park districts, and school districts may administer recreation services and all hire recreation professionals. Communities, however, structure their recreation and parks services in different ways, which lead to a plethora of employment opportunities. The most dominant pattern of local organization is that of the combined recreation and parks department, which has been the structure of choice for most communities since the early 1960s.

Combined recreation services are characterized by a focus on recreation and parks as an integrated function. This structure is usually the best approach to maximize the natural relationship that exists between programs, facilities, and areas. Proponents of this structure argue that when recreation and parks services are administered jointly, coordination of maintenance and program schedules is enhanced. The combination broadens the base of political support since each facet of recreation and parks has its own constituent groups (e.g., conservationists, naturalists, sports enthusiasts, social advocates).

Single-function operating structures include either a recreation activity service or a parks natural resource management mandate. The two functions operate independently of each other. When recreation services are being provided as a single function, they emphasize programs and leadership. If the park system is operated by a separate park unit, the focus is generally on land acquisition, development, and maintenance rather than on providing activities. Single function organizations are less common than combined recreation and parks organizations.

In recent years, the need for more coordination of governmental services at the local level has stimulated interest in new designs for administering recreation services. For example, various units concerned with cultural programs, social services, information, education, and related free-time activity might be brought together and will hire specialists to run these programs. Such agencies might be called departments of community services or departments of recreation and cultural services. These service agencies typically administer the libraries, the park system, the cultural arts programs, senior citizen programs, community buildings, recreation program, and sometimes even community cemeteries. The advantages of this bigger structure are largely economic and political, but such agencies are not commonly found.

One important aspect of any type of local public recreation services is the role of local boards or commissions who are policymaking and/or advisory in nature. By having citizens elected or appointed to direct the public recreation and parks services, citizen input and control is ensured. The recreation services department is directly responsible to the community. Having citizens involved in the determination of policy tends to make policy decisions more acceptable and politically appealing than when policies are formulated by a single individual (e.g., the director or city manager) or by a group (e.g., a city council) who may not have recreation and parks as the primary concern. Because recreation is often viewed as an important but not essential governmental function, advocates are needed and this advocacy is often achieved through advisory boards and committees.

Future Directions for Local Recreation Services

The relationships between public recreation services, nonprofit, and private businesses are dynamic. In some communities, these relationships are cooperative while in others they are adversarial. Some public recreation professionals believe it is their responsibility to provide a cafeteria of activities and services to the public without regard for possible competition with the programs and actions of other sectors. Other professionals say their mission is to complement those sectors. Some local government providers approach services in a supplemental way with public recreation services offered only if they do not exist elsewhere in the community.

With the growth of a business model applied to the provision of public recreation services, the relationship between the local government and other recreation services providers has become more complementary. Public agencies have developed market strategies to ensure program success. Operating stables, marinas, golf courses, and fitness centers with a middle and upper middle class appeal have enabled some public recreation agencies to recover costs, be totally self-sufficient, or make a profit. Those revenues might be applied toward other activities that are not self-sustaining, such as programs for youth from high-risk communities. Local public providers have also contracted with the other recreation entities to develop and operate services such as concessions or outdoor adventure activities. These arrangements expand the offerings of local departments without adding to the operational costs or liability of the unit.

Unfortunately, public recreation and parks have not always received adequate financial support in recent years. Most people want public recreation services. However, recreation and parks are sometimes not perceived as essential in communities when budgets are tight. New models of facilitating recreation and parks are emerging because of some of these cutbacks. For example, the outsourcing of services to private businesses is not uncommon (e.g., a business leasing a marina at a lake rather than the marina being managed by the local government). Similarly, more services may be provided by the nonprofit sector or private businesses based on contracts. For example, a local YMCA might be contracted to handle the aquatic programs at local swimming pools that were once directed internally by a recreation and parks agency. These changes are major when compared to the way agencies have traditionally operated. However, these changes allow services to continue to be offered to citizens in a community, with a different administrative structure.

Most people are influenced by recreation services at the local level. Regardless of the varied arrangements structured to provide public recreation opportunities, most cities and counties have focused on making their services available to everyone. If recreation is the right of all people, then the local government must be instrumental in ensuring that those opportunities exist. These services are also successful depending on the competencies of the professionals who work in these areas.

Prospects for
Local Recreation Services Employment

Clearly a range of recreation services has been and continues to be offered at the local government level. Services can include elaborate park systems such as those in cities like New York City or Dallas to the direct involvement of local municipalities in managing professional athletics. For example, Durham, North Carolina, owns the athletic park where professional baseball teams play. In Phoenix, Arizona, the library system is administered by the Recreation and Park Department. In other cities, community theaters are a function of local recreation agencies. The type of program and services offered to the public locally depends upon factors such as tradition, other service providers in the community, public expectations, and the philosophy and preferences of the professional recreation staff.

Professional leadership for recreation services is essential in communities regardless of the structure, functions, or activities. Most people who direct public recreation services or work full-time in these agencies have a college education. Often this education is in an area of recreation and parks, but specialists in areas such as nature centers or park planning may have education in other academic areas. Nevertheless, recreation programming and park management are at the heart in most local communities. Therefore, many opportunities exist related to park management, recreation facility management, sports programming, outdoor leadership and coordination, special events management, and arts programming, to mention only a few.

The outlook for employment in community recreation and parks programs appears stable. Huge growth occurred in the 1970s, but then leveled off in the 1980s. Most communities have public recreation and parks services, so the numbers of new programs are not growing. With the increasing growth of the U.S. population, more demands will likely be placed on local recreation and parks services. Many citizens are highly supportive of recreation and parks even though the local budgets have been cut along with other community services. Although the number of jobs may not grow, there is likely to be consistent opportunities available in general recreation programming, park management, and in specialty areas (e.g., outdoor programs, sports, festivals, arts).

Local recreation and parks services are for all citizens. Thus, many populations and activity areas are addressed. As Karen Brady describes in Table 19.1, the benefits are endless related to the numerous local participant groups served through public recreation and parks programs.

Table 19.1 "Changing Lives, Impacting Communities"

"Changing Lives, Impacting Communities"
By: Karen Brady, Business Manager, Fayetteville-Cumberland Parks & Recreation

The North Carolina Recreation and Parks Association motto, "Changing Lives, Impacting Communities," is right on target. What you do matters every day. You do change lives. You do impact your community. Don't think so? Well . . .

- Children who play sports learn sportsmanship and teamwork, discover their passion, and how to play for the love of the game. They are active, making memories of happy times spent with friends and family. They develop new skills and learn life lessons. And most importantly—they are not in front of a TV or a computer screen. YOU give them that spot on a team.
- People of all ages are outside! In parks, on playgrounds, on walking trails and greenways—outside! Walking, running, exercising, playing! Getting rid of stress, shedding extra pounds, or simply enjoying nature. Safe, peaceful places that recharge and relax lives. . . . YOU plan, design, build, and take care of these for people to enjoy.
- Seniors have places to go, people to see, and things to do! They can enjoy activities and each other through programs offered by your department. They continue to learn, socialize, laugh, and support each other as their lives change. Senior trips now include things like whitewater rafting and hiking, along with the old stand-by—the motorcoach tour! Whether passive or active, YOU allow seniors to stay in touch, stay involved, and stay connected.
- People with disabilities are doing more than ever—thanks to you! No more watching, sitting on the sidelines, left out . . . but trying, learning, pushing their limits. Wounded warriors, mentally challenged, and physically disabled individuals are now part of the action and it's changing their lives. YOU show compassion, dedication, and the ability to adapt activities for those who want to try.
- No matter age, income, or stage of life, opportunities are available at the local community recreation center through programs that teach new skills, improve fitness, or offer support. A recreation center can be a place to discover a new hobby or provide a place to volunteer. YOUR ideas bring folks in the door and YOUR hard work keeps them coming back! To a young recreation programmer who gets bogged down in details, to the parks worker who tires of mowing and marking and planting, to the supervisor who sees nothing but endless paperwork, to the administrator doing more with less—please remember that what YOU do matters. Every single day, YOU CHANGE LIVES AND IMPACT COMMUNITIES.

(Used with permission from *NCRPA Online News*, June 2012, Vol 7, no 6, page 1)

Reflection Questions

1. If no parks existed in local communities, how would the quality of life be diminished in those communities?

2. How has the current focus on "no child left behind" in schools affected the role of schools to facilitate recreation opportunities for children in the community?

3. What was the organizational structure of providing recreation services in the local community where you grew up?

4. What are some ways to engage citizens in supporting recreation and parks services in communities?

5. In what ways would you argue that recreation and parks are essential community services along with other services like police and fire protection?

Chapter 20

Recreation Services, State, and National/Federal Governments

National government involvement in recreation services began in the 19th century with the establishment of Yellowstone as the first national park. Around this same time, states were also setting aside land for parks. Policy and the relationships among federal, state, and local government roles were sometimes unclear. How much financial involvement and control the national and state governments should have with recreation compared to local involvement was debated. Some people suggested that the federal government should be setting standards and monitoring the quality of state and local services. Other individuals did not believe that state or federal government should be involved with local recreation programs at all.

These differing opinions continue to reflect the public's view of recreation services as a governmental responsibility and the growing concern for environmental and consumer protection. Over time government responsibilities for recreation services have evolved, as has been discussed earlier in this Unit. In this chapter, the ways that national and state government agencies are responsible for managing land, providing technical assistance, offering financial assistance, providing direct services, and enacting and enforcing regulations are discussed, as are potential career opportunities. Many of the roles of state and national governments relate to outdoor recreation.

The term *outdoor recreation* has been used to describe activities of a recreational nature that normally take place in natural environments and depend primarily on that environment for recreation experiences. Table 20.1 provides a picture of some of the outdoor activities that provide opportunities for participation. Distinctions in outdoor recreation activities sometimes are based on the degree to which the environment is the focus of the activity. The two common conceptualizations are *resource-oriented/ nature-based* and *activity-oriented* outdoor recreation.

Table 20.1 Participants in Outdoor Activities: 2006
[In millions (34 represents 34,000,000). Numbers rounded to the nearest million.
For persons 16 years old and over engaging in activity at least once in 2006.]

Activities	Millions
Total Sportspersons[1]	34
Total Anglers	30
Freshwater	25
Excluding Great Lakes	25
Great Lakes	1
Saltwater	8
Total hunters	13
Big game	11
Small game	5
Migratory birds	2
Other animals	1
Wildlife watchers[1]	71
Away from home[2]	23
Observe wildlife	22
Photograph wildlife	12
Feed wildlife	7
Around the home[3]	68
Observe wildlife	44
Photograph wildlife	19
Feed wildlife	56
Visit public parks	13
Maintain plantings or natural areas	15

[1] Detail does not add to total due to multiple responses and nonresponses.
[2] Persons taking a trip of at least 1 mile from home for activity.
[3] Activity within 1 mile of home.

Source: U.S. Fish and Wildlife Service, *2006 National Survey of Fishing, Hunting, and Wildlife Associated Recreation*, October 2007. See also: http://wsfrprograms.fws. gov/Subpages/NationalSurvey/nat_survey2006_final.pdf

Outdoor recreation activities that depend on the use of natural resources for the activity are usually classified as resource-oriented/nature-based recreation. In all resource-oriented outdoor activities, the environment is a critical component to the pursuit even though it may be somewhat controlled. Activity-oriented outdoor recreation emphasizes the pursuit of certain activities such as softball, golf, tennis, and other outdoor sports where the environment is of secondary concern. Many of these activities could be done indoors as well as outside. For the most part, the national and state governments have focused on resource-oriented or nature-based recreation, but not always as discussed in this chapter.

State Government Involvement in Recreation

Every state draws its power from the U.S. Constitution and may provide activities that citizens deem vital to their well-being. The Tenth Amendment to the U.S. Constitution guarantees to states that "the powers not delegated to the United States by the Constitution, nor prohibited by it to the States, are reserved to the States respectively, or to the people." Recreation is one of those areas of state power.

The categories of recreation services in states include management and protection of natural resource areas, the establishment of natural resource policy, and the distribution of information about recreation opportunities within the state boundaries. In addition, some states have established zoos, aquariums, museums (e.g., art, natural history), state fairs, symphony orchestras, and performing arts centers as part of their interpretation of their powers and responsibilities.

The role of state governments related to parks and recreation services is varied. States are a direct provider of program services when they operate fairs, state parks, and museums. State governments also directly influence behaviors through the regulatory legislation enacted and administered by state governmental units. The role of state governments is in how the state interfaces with both the federal government and local jurisdictions.

A significant development in state governments in recent years has been the expansion of public services to include a focus on tourism. The promotion of tourism has resulted from the growth of recreation as a public good and especially as a way to enhance economic development.

The recreation services provided vary from state to state but generally include the following activities:

- Acquire, develop, and manage land and water resources for conservation and outdoor recreation (e.g., manage state parks and state trails)

- Market recreation resources and attractions through state tourism bureaus and economic development commissions

- Enact permissive legislation to enable communities and districts to mobilize their resources for recreation services

- Establish state recreation commissions, boards, departments, or divisions as units to coordinate the development and management of state parks and recreation services

- Employ recreation services personnel in state agencies such as youth services, public instruction, natural resources management, state hospitals, and disability services

- Enact laws and establish policies to protect natural resources and wildlife and to regulate certain individual recreation behaviors (e.g., regulate hunting seasons or catch limits)

- Develop technical assistance programs to aid local communities in establishing, improving, and developing recreation services

- Appropriate public funds to manage state park systems and grant funds to support local recreation services systems

The management of natural resources has been influenced by political trends, intergovernmental and intragovernmental relationships, historical events, and current management concepts. No governmental agency alone can address the problems of urban planning and recreation resource management. The growing concern with the preservation of natural and cultural resources, the acceptance of recreation as a major economic and social force, and the expansion of tourism ensures further support for the appropriateness of state involvement. A challenge for the future will be for staff to provide sustainability in meeting the varied needs of diverse constituencies in the changing natural environment.

Numerous opportunities exist for employment in a variety of jobs in state government, especially related to natural resources and state parks. However, the recreation services that states provide related to therapeutic recreation in state hospitals, special events management (e.g., State Fairs, State Games), and management of state-supported programs such as zoos and symphonies offer additional job opportunities.

National/Federal Involvement in Recreation Services

Dozens of federal agencies have programs that deal with aspects of recreation services. Some are obvious, such as the National Park Service (NPS). Other agencies have other primary responsibilities in addition to recreation services, such as the Armed Forces. The role of the national government has been dynamic and ever changing. For example, in the earlier years of the park movement (circa 1916–1926), governmental units promoted environmental preservation and encouraged states to establish their own park systems. During the Depression and war years, the federal government actively developed recreation programs and services for young adults. Later, in the 1960s and 1970s, it became involved in grant activities and financial support for outdoor recreation and with programs for people with disabilities. The role and responsibility of the national government for services as it relates to spending tax money changes from time to time and is often debated. Nevertheless, the federal government makes a number of contributions to facilitating recreation services. Some of the most visible organizations are discussed briefly.

Department of Interior

The Department of Interior usually is considered the most visible federal agency concerned with recreation services primarily related to the outdoors. The Department's responsibilities include protection of natural resources, regulation of hunting and fishing activity, caring for cultural and historic sites, and management of facilities designed primarily for recreation purposes. The Department of Interior also offers technical assistance to local and state governments, conducts research investigations, and stimulates the development of recreation resources through various grant programs. The most visible recreation services role that the Department of Interior plays is the administration of the National Park Service.

National Park Service (NPS)

The NPS was established in 1916, even though several national parks had been designated prior to that time. The NPS provides a system for managing national parks and monuments, national historic areas and memorials, national seashores and lake shores, parkways, river ways, and recreation areas. The mission of NPS is "to promote and regulate the use of the . . . national parks . . . to conserve the scenery and the natural and historic objects and the wildlife therein and to provide for the enjoyment of the same in such manner and by such means as will leave them unimpaired for the enjoyment of future generations." (National Park Service Organic Act, 16 U.S.C.1). This mandate preserves and interprets national areas while making them available to the public for enjoyment. In 2011, the NPS was managing 379 units, encompassing over 84 million acres with over 280 million visitations each year.

The NPS system is organized according to several basic functions. One area is *resource management*, which includes land, water, and wildlife resources within a given administrative unit. Another area is *visitor services* including activities that ensure the comfort and protection of the visitors to the NPS units (e.g., concessions, food, lodging, safety, and traffic control). The NPS also strives to stimulate the public's interest in the historical, geological, biological, and cultural aspects of the resource through *interpretation services* such as tours, exhibits, film presentations, publications, museums, websites, and demonstrations. About half of the financial resources of the NPS are devoted to the *maintenance and development* functions. Trail systems, roads, visitor and information centers, and historic buildings must be maintained in a reasonable manner if they are to provide the visitor with a safe, positive outdoor experience. Another function is *administrative services*, which includes the management of personnel, planning, budgeting, inter-agency cooperation, public relations, and the development and dissemination of data.

The NPS is currently responsible for the administration of the **Land and Water Conservation Fund** (**LWCF**). This national program was established by Congress in 1964 to provide funds and matching grants to federal, state, and local governments for the acquisition of land and water areas for the benefit of all Americans. The primary source of income to the fund is fees paid by companies drilling offshore for oil and gas. Congress regularly diverts funds from this source to other purposes, but some funds remain available for recreation efforts and are available to local communities through a matching grant program. Over the past three decades, funding for LWCF has been consistently challenged.

The NPS is concerned with areas other than traditional national parks. Only Congress can establish a national park, whereas the President or the Interior Secretary may designate national recreation areas. Because of the power and the actions of recent presidential administrations, a new controversy has arisen. In response to the demands for recreation areas, various Presidents and/or Interior Secretaries have increased the number of areas within the NPS system. Unfortunately, appropriations for the NPS have not kept pace with expansion and demand. Consequently, some of the resources that might have been used for maintenance and development of national parks have been expended for the development and operations of national recreation areas. Despite the general feeling that the services provided by the NPS are important, not enough money has been allocated to the continued maintenance and operation of park areas. The role of the national parks will continue to be debated in the coming decades as conservationists, concessionaires, and citizens advocate their positions.

Regardless, the NPS is gearing up for its 100th anniversary in 2016. In preparation for that benchmark, a plan entitled *A Call to Action: Preparing for a Second Century of Stewardship and Engagement* has identified specific actions. The actions address how to better connect people to parks, advance educational opportunities, preserve America's special places, and enhance organizational excellence. Among the report recommendations are developing a comprehensive National Park System plan, analyzing the total economic value of all NPS programs, engaging youth and education partners, addressing the impacts of climate change, launching a national parks endowment, and enhancing cultural diversity throughout the park system and among visitors.

Other Department of Interior Roles

The **Bureau of Indian Affairs** (BIA) was established at the turn into the 20th century primarily to oversee Indian reservations and maintain a positive relationship between American Indians and non-Indians. The BIA has developed and operated various recreation facilities such as campgrounds, ski resorts, casinos, museums, restaurants, and hunting and fishing areas on Indian reservations. These services are primarily for tourists who happen to be visiting Indian lands. The BIA also oversees more typical community recreation programs for American Indians on reservations, including community centers, playground facilities, and programs for special populations.

In 1946, the **Bureau of Land Management** (BLM) was established to oversee all federally managed public lands not under the jurisdiction of other agencies such as the NPS, the U.S. Forest Service, or the Army Corps of Engineers. The BLM was empowered to sell unreserved non-mineral lands to other political subdivisions for recreation and park purposes. It also leases or sells small tracts of land to individuals for camps, cabins, and other recreational uses. Like the U.S. Forest Service, the BLM has a multiple-use philosophy that underscores the simultaneous development and use of areas for recreation, mining, and resource exploration.

The **Bureau of Reclamation** was established primarily to oversee the development of water resources in the western United States. Active participation in outdoor recreation activities is encouraged for water sports such as boating, fishing, and swimming. It also works jointly with the NPS and states in planning, developing, and promoting outdoor recreation facilities. State or local government organizations may administer or develop recreation resources on Bureau of Reclamation lands.

The **Fish and Wildlife Service** (FWS) is both a regulatory and a resource management agency. It has two major responsibilities: (a) the protection and development of fish and wildlife resources including the enforcement of federal game laws, and (b) the management of recreation areas associated with national wildlife refuges and national fish hatcheries. These refuges and fisheries are open to visitors primarily for photography, picnicking, and sightseeing. The FWS also gives financial assistance to state fish and game departments for projects to restore, conserve, and manage fish and wildlife resources.

Department of Agriculture

The U.S. Department of Agriculture (USDA) is one of the federal government's providers of recreation services primarily through the U.S. Forest Service, Federal Extension Service, and Soil Conservation Service. This Department has provided technical and educational assistance, outdoor recreation resources, and has encouraged and enacted regulatory policies to protect the quality of the environment and the recreation experience. Although established to serve rural America, the USDA also has urban program areas.

The **U.S. Forest Service** manages 155 national forests and 20 national grasslands that encompass 193 million acres in the United States. The philosophy of the Forest Service has been one of multiple uses with compatible activities occurring simultaneously at the same resource. These national forest lands are open for recreation, grazing, hunting, and mining. Recreation is an important use and the Forest Service has developed areas for picnicking, camping, hiking, and boating. Millions of persons visit the national forests each year to engage in their favorite outdoor recreation activities. Private investors also are able to develop resorts on public lands. Many of the well-known winter ski and sports resorts are located in national forests. Hunting and fishing in national forests, except in a few areas, are controlled by state laws.

The **Federal Extension Service** (FES) provides a range of technical and educational assistance programs including information on the design and development of recreation areas, youth and family programs, and on the operation of tourist attractions. These functions are implemented through 4-H clubs, the work of county agents, and the activity of the extension programs housed in land-grant colleges and universities. The extension service in most states includes the employment of full-time youth, recreation, and tourism specialists.

The major purpose of the **Soil Conservation Service** (SCS) is conserving land, but this national organization also encourages camping, picnicking, hunting, fishing, and other forms of outdoor recreation. Under the provisions of the Watershed Protection and Flood Prevention Act, the SCS has entered into cost-sharing arrangements with local organizations for the development of lands for public recreation and for fish and wildlife conservation.

In addition to those services mentioned above, the USDA has conducted research activities directly related to outdoor recreation behavior and natural resource management through its agricultural experiment station network. The Forest Service specifically operates multifaceted recreation research programs. The research findings have influenced the design, maintenance, and construction of recreation sites and have offered models for recreation resource management.

Department of Defense

The Department of Defense provides recreation opportunities for armed service members through **Morale, Welfare, and Recreation Services** (MWR). The recreation programs operated by the military branches are similar to those typically found in local recreation departments or in employee recreation services. MWR professionals employed by the Department of Defense have many of the same job descriptions as local recreation professionals such as assessing needs, facilitating recreation programs, and evaluating their services.

The previous Unit in this book notes that since World War I, the military has been concerned with morale, welfare, and recreation programs needed to promote the physical, social, and mental well-being of military personnel and their families. Each branch of the service (e.g., Army, Navy, Air Force, Marines, and Coast Guard) has its own pattern of recreation services administration. All branches attempt to serve the military personnel (i.e., active, Reserve, and Guard), their families, civilian employees, and military retirees. Activities offered include sports, library services, arts and crafts centers, musical and theatrical programs, and youth and family services. All rely heavily on tax money appropriated by Congress as well as self-generated revenue resulting from the operation of post exchanges and on-base clubs.

Recreation programs exist in the military to induce enlistment, promote increased levels of productivity, encourage sustained morale, and allay the possible loneliness associated with military service. The military branches often employ civilian personnel as recreation specialists to conduct recreation programs on military bases and to work cooperatively with adjacent communities. Recreation programs exist on almost all military bases in the United States and around the world. More about careers in military recreation is discussed later in this unit.

The **Corps of Engineers**, a branch of the Army, has functions similar to the U.S. Forest Service and National Park Service. The Corps is a provider of outdoor recreation opportunities through the development and maintenance of recreation areas. Although the primary responsibility of the Corps of Engineers is to develop and maintain rivers and waterways in the interest of flood control, the Corps has built picnic areas, hiking trails, public boat launching and docking facilities, campgrounds, and other recreation facilities for public use. Federal legislation in the 1940s and 1960s authorized the Army Chief of Engineers to construct and maintain public park and recreation facilities at Corps water resource and development projects. The laws also provided that the Corps financially assist local groups and governments in the development, operation, and maintenance of project land and water areas for recreation as well as fish and wildlife enhancement.

Department of Education

The Department of Education promotes the cause of education throughout the nation by collecting and disseminating information, awarding grants, and providing consulting services. Recreation and play are recognized as a part of education, and the involvement of public school systems in the provision of quality recreation opportunities is encouraged.

The Department of Education has had a special influence on recreation services for people with disabilities. The **Office of Special Education and Rehabilitation Services** (OSERS) *has as its mission to "provide leadership to achieve full integration and participation in society of people with disabilities by ensuring equal opportunity and access to, and excellence in, education, employment, and community living."* OSERS supports personnel training, program development, and efficacy research.

The **Rehabilitation Services Administration** (RSA) is associated directly with OSERS and oversees grant programs that help individuals with physical or mental disabilities to obtain employment and live more independently through supports such as counseling, medical and psychological services, job training, and other individualized services such as recreation. RSA maintains close liaison with federal counterpart agencies such as the Social Security Administration, the Department of Labor, National Institute of Mental Health, the President's Committee on the Employment of Persons with Disabilities, the Office of Special Education

Programs, the Office of Adult and Vocational Education, and the National Institute on Disability and Rehabilitation Research.

Department of Health and Human Services

Several bureaus and programs within the Department of Health and Human Services (HSS) influence the recreation and leisure services system. The most prominent are the Administration on Aging, the Children's Bureau, and the U.S. Public Health Service Commissioned Corps.

The **Administration on Aging** was established in 1965 as part of the Older Americans Act. The purpose was to encourage and financially assist with establishing comprehensive program services, including recreation, for older persons. Under the Older Americans Act, funds have been expended for recreation related purposes such as the renovation and repair of facilities, payment of salaries, and the operation of continuing education, recreation, and outreach programs.

The **Children's Bureau** was established in 1912 and is one of the oldest federal agencies involved in recreation. The Bureau has largely concentrated efforts in the development of literature pertaining to the play environments of children and has worked cooperatively with state, national, and non-governmental organizations to promote services for youth.

The **U.S. Public Health Service Commissioned Corps** is a team of public health professionals dedicated to delivering the country's public health promotion and disease prevention programs and to advancing public health research. The historical contribution to recreation is in the areas of safety and environmental protection. However, with the current concerns about obesity and physical inactivity, the Corps is an ally to recreation services focused on promoting physical activity.

Department of Housing and Urban Development

The Department of Housing and Urban Development (HUD) is primarily concerned with the comprehensive planning and development of American cities. Recreation concerns are part of the planning process. HUD has encouraged the development and use of planning standards for recreation and parks and the necessity for effective evaluation of recreation delivery systems. HUD has made efforts to include space for recreation in public housing areas but has not assumed responsibility for administering recreation programs within these areas. Activity programming has generally been facilitated by local public and nonprofit recreation agencies.

Department of Veteran Affairs

The Department of Veteran Affairs (VA) was established as a cabinet position in 1989. It administers hundreds of VA medical facilities, clinics, and benefits offices and is responsible for administering programs of veterans' benefits for veterans, their families, and survivors. A major connection to recreation services is evidenced through therapeutic recreation programs at each VA facility. Programs include activities and services directed by therapeutic recreation specialists. The objectives for these therapeutic recreation programs are to aid veterans in adjusting to hospitalization and treatment, to contribute to morale during hospitalization, to facilitate recovery and rehabilitation, and to aid in the veteran's return to life in the community.

Other Federal Programs

In addition to the described federal departments that have programs related directly and indirectly to recreation services, several other agencies and activities are important to note.

The **National Endowment for the Arts** assists individuals and nonprofit tax-exempt organizations in the development and promotion of arts, dance, literature, music, and theater. This program was created in 1965 to aid local communities in the creation and support of performing and visual arts. Although funding has been reduced over the years, the program has been sustained through private philanthropic support.

The **President's Council on Fitness, Sports and Nutrition** was established in 1956 because of concern for the lack of fitness of American youth. Since then, the Council has aggressively promoted the cause of fitness and sports in the United States. It disseminates information on the importance of fitness to general well-being, sponsors national forums, and encourages the development of fitness, sport, and nutrition programs through school systems as well as other public and nonprofit organizations. The Council works primarily through existing agencies rather than by providing direct services.

The **Tennessee Valley Authority** (TVA) was established during the Depression to oversee the development of hydroelectric power in the Tennessee Valley and to monitor the flood control and navigation aspects of the Tennessee River. Even though recreation was not a major concern initially, the TVA has been a force in the development of recreation resources and activities in that region. It develops recreation facilities such as boat docks, fishing camps, resort sites, and lots for vacation cottages.

The Future and Employment Outlooks

Despite the numerous programs and services that exist, no single national agency is solely concerned with recreation services. Some people feel that a federal agency primarily concerned with leisure opportunities and recreation services should be established to coordinate the efforts of the federal government. Furthermore, these individuals argue that this new agency should have cabinet rank. They would argue that since a Department of Labor exists, a Department of Recreation would be warranted. Others argue that the present system of many federal agencies involved in parks and recreation services is ideal because of the variety of options and support.

Although governmental funding is a continual concern, many of the established groups that provide recreation services are likely to continue. Getting enough funding to meet the goals of the programs will be a challenge.

As this chapter shows, many recreation services are supported through the federal government. Many opportunities exist for employment in national agencies that support parks and recreation. All the websites of these organizations offer information about job opportunities and how to apply for federal service jobs. As can be seen from these descriptions, the opportunities are broad. Similar to all recreation services organizations, federal employers are always eager to hire enthusiastic, educated, and committed professionals.

Reflection Questions

1. A Department of Labor is part of the federal government. What would be the advantages and disadvantages in having a national Department of Recreation?

2. Are there too many or too few agencies in the federal government involved with recreation? What do you think is unnecessary? Are there additional services that the national government should be providing related to recreation?

3. Each state is free to design its own systems for recreation services. Do you believe there should be more consistency from state to state?

4. Do most people know the difference in jurisdictional responsibilities when they are in a local, state, or national park? In other words, do they know the differences among the three types of park systems? Does it matter whether they do or not?

Chapter 21

Nonprofit Recreation Services

Alexis de Tocqueville (1945) argued in his classic work, *Democracy in America*, that voluntary associations were the backbone of American society and that the future of the country would depend on these associations. Today, such associations continue to be an integral part of American society. They have played an important role in the recreation movement in the United States. Virtually every industrial country has nonprofit groups that fill a gap in services not provided by the public or private sectors.

The sector termed 'nonprofit' in this book includes voluntary associations, public charities, private foundations, third sector agencies, non-governmental organizations (NGO), not-for-profit, or independent associations or agencies. 'Nonprofit' is the generic term that describes all these types of groups. In 2009, there were more than 1.5 million registered nonprofit organizations in the United States, with 56,000 listed as social or recreational clubs (http://nccsdataweb.urban.org/PubApps/profile1.php). This chapter will focus on the nonprofit sector related to organizations that address recreation services as part of their mission.

Justifications for Nonprofit Organizations

Salamon (1999) identified several reasons why nonprofit organizations were established in the United States. He noted that groups formed to meet the needs of their communities long before governments became involved. For example, playgrounds, volunteer fire departments, schools, and adoption agencies were informal nonprofit associations before they became functions of the government.

Another reason for nonprofits to form was what might be called a market failure. The private business sector of the economy is good at providing individual consumable goods and products, but less effective at providing collective goods and services such as clean air or safe neighborhoods. Nonprofit agencies provide a context in which groups of individuals pool resources to produce collective services and programs they desire but cannot convince government or private businesses to support.

Further, the government has limitations in funding and cannot provide directly for all the needs of individuals. By granting nonprofit status to agencies and organizations through the Internal Revenue Service, the government assists non-governmental organizations in addressing the public good and meeting important community needs. Nonprofits encourage individual initiative for the public good just as corporations encourage individual action for the private good. Most major social reforms including recreation, civil rights, environmental, child welfare, and women's rights movements in American society began by using nonprofit associations.

The strength of nonprofit organizations is joint collective action. Nonprofit organizations emerge as a result of people's willingness to volunteer to work together to meet a need. As discussed in Unit Two, the roots of the contemporary recreation movement in America grew from the work of social reformers who developed responses to the collective needs of children and immigrants for structured recreation opportunities. Nonprofit organizations historically played a pivotal role in the development of needed services that eventually led to public recreation services. They continue to enhance leisure experiences and facilitate leisure experiences for targeted groups in communities.

Nonprofit organizations generally fall into two major categories called *member-serving organizations* and *public-serving organizations* (Salamon, 1999). Member-serving organizations have some public benefit, but their primary purpose is to directly benefit the members of the organization rather than to the public at large (e.g., soccer clubs). Public-serving organizations exist primarily to serve the public-at-large rather than just members. They may provide health and education services, recreation services, sponsor cultural or religious activities, advocate for social or environmental causes, or aid disenfranchised citizens.

Among the many community organizations and groups comprising nonprofit organizations are youth-serving voluntary agencies, employee recreation groups, special interest groups (e.g., Sierra Club, Audubon Society), religious organizations (e.g., churches and synagogues), and specialized recreation associations (e.g., neighborhood clubs, soccer clubs, running clubs, hobby clubs). Most nonprofit groups focus on participants who are members and volunteers.

Myths about Nonprofit Organizations

Three common myths about nonprofit organizations sometimes influence the way people think about this sector. These myths are important to address in considering possible employment in recreation services in nonprofit organizations.

First, many people mistakenly assume that nonprofit means that an organization cannot make an actual profit. Nonprofit organizations may make profits. What distinguishes this type of agency from a private business or commercial for-profit venture, however, is that these agencies may not distribute profits to individual stockholders. Nonprofit agencies must put any profits gained at the end of the fiscal year back into the organization.

Second, some people believe that employees working for a nonprofit organization do not make any money. Some people believe that it is almost impossible to survive on nonprofit salaries. Although working in the private sector may result in higher salaries, individuals who work in nonprofit agencies can and do make a living wage. Some of what characterizes a salary in this sector, as in all sectors, is job location. People who live in urban areas will likely earn what others in comparable positions make based on the cost of living for a particular region of the country.

Third, some people believe that one of the advantages of association with a nonprofit organization is that these organizations do not pay taxes and that all donations are tax-deductible contributions to their organization. This statement is partially true. The Internal Revenue Service has developed more than two dozen different tax codes for nonprofit agencies and organizations. Many agencies are exempt from paying taxes. However, unless a nonprofit formally applies to receive tax-exempt status, the agency will not automatically receive this designation. The majority of nonprofit organizations apply for a tax exemption, but some do not. However, only one tax code, 501(c) (3), allows an agency to not pay taxes and to receive tax-deductible contributions from individuals and corporations.

Commonalities among Nonprofit Organizations

The contributions of nonprofit organizations in communities are varied and extensive relative to recreation services. In some communities, nonprofit recreation providers supplement and complement public recreation offerings. In other areas, nonprofit agencies may be the basic provider of the community's organized recreation opportunities. Nonprofit organizations can be seen as competitors with public agencies and private businesses in some communities, but the growing need to form partnerships is mitigating some of that competition.

Nonprofit organizations are different than public agencies or private businesses in several ways (Salamon, 1999). These organizations are separate from government but can receive government support, and many do. They are self-governing and not controlled by outside entities. In addition, nonprofit organizations often rely on volunteers to supplement the work of paid staff in conducting the agency's activities or in managing its programs and policies. Most nonprofits have a voluntary board of directors.

Any group interested in joining together to address a community problem or meet a community need can form a nonprofit organization and apply to receive tax-exempt status. A typical structure would include a Board of Directors, Executive Director or Chief Executive Officer, paid staff, and volunteers. Nonprofit organizations range from having no or only part-time staff (e.g., a neighborhood association) to organizations that have thousands of paid employees (e.g., The Y). The size of the organization and the purpose will depend on the scope of the organization's mission. A neighborhood association with 100 residences would obviously be different than the Sierra Club with its hundreds of thousands of members.

Most nonprofit organizations receive community support in several ways (e.g., United Way, community foundation grants, individual donations, funds solicited through special events, membership fees). Individuals are the largest source of funding for most nonprofit organizations. According to *Giving USA*, total charitable giving in the United States reached more than $303 billion in 2009. Of that amount, 75% came from individuals (http://nonprofit.about.com/od/fundraising/a/fundraising101.htm).

The United Way of America is another source of income for some established agencies. The United Way, referred to as the Community Chest, United Fund, Federated Funds, or Combined Campaign in some communities, provides a way for people to make contributions through their employer to affiliated agencies. Donors can earmark particular organizations, or local boards of the United Way can determine how the donated money will be distributed in communities.

Nonprofit agencies may supplement donations by charging fees for membership and/or services. These fees are typically moderate and financial assistance is often available for persons unable to afford the fees. Other funds may be obtained through structured fund-raising efforts such as direct mail, phone, and face-to-face solicitations; fund-raising events such as golf tournaments or live auctions; or grants from corporations, foundations, and the government.

Volunteers in Nonprofit Organizations

Nonprofit organizations often rely heavily on volunteers for the operation of their programs. The spirit of volunteerism is a hallmark of America's national identity. Recent estimates indicate that 26% of Americans of all ages (i.e., over 60 million citizens) volunteered an average of 34 hours per year to various charitable and other organizations from 2008–2010. (http://www.volunteeringinamerica.gov/index.cfm).

Two major types of volunteerism can be found in nonprofit as well as some public recreation programs: structured and unstructured. These types might also be classified as *regular* versus *lend-a-hand* volunteers, or long-term versus short-term (i.e., single event) volunteers (Tedrick & Henderson, 1989). These descriptions refer to the amount of training that might be required and how many hours a volunteer commitment might entail. People are generally looking for volunteer positions that meet their personal needs as well as contribute to an organization or a cause that interests them. They may be seeking to change the system or maintain it, to work for their special interests or for others, to give monetary gifts or help solicit from others, or to feel good about making contributions to society.

Paid professional staff members who work in nonprofit organizations will often devote a great deal of time to working with volunteers—training, supervising, evaluating, and recognizing their efforts. Learning to manage volunteers is an essential skill for a recreation professional interested in working in the nonprofit sector.

Examples of Nonprofit Recreation Providers

In addition to youth-serving agencies that are discussed in the next chapter, three examples of nonprofit groups that offer opportunities for recreation are faith-based groups and organized religions, employee recreation services, and advocacy organizations.

Faith-Based Groups and Organized Religion

The statistics differ somewhat, but it appears that over 335,000 religious congregations exist in the United States. Between 20% and 40% of the U.S. population participate in organized religious activities (e.g., church, synagogue attendance) each weekend (http://hirr.hartsem.edu/research/fastfacts/fast_facts.html). Organized religion in the United States is a powerful social institution. Religion shapes people's values and attitudes and is a critical force in the lives of millions of Americans. Religious organizations also provide a variety of recreation and social experiences for many of their members. Major coordinating organizations of religious bodies in the United States, including the National Council of Churches, the National Catholic Welfare Council, and the Jewish Welfare Board, have proclaimed recreation to be an important part of church life as a means for bringing congregations together.

Churches have assumed three basic responsibilities in relationship to recreation services. First, they have aided and shaped the development of community recreation programs through the positions they have taken on recreation issues and their attitude toward specific leisure experiences. The *blue laws* that limited what activities can be done on Sundays are one example of how churches historically influenced recreation in some communities.

Second, they are a provider of direct recreation services for their members with their recreation centers, recreation activities, and recreation programs. Church officials often combine recreation with education and worship programs. Further, the religious environment lends itself to the promotion of certain types of recreation pursuits. Many local churches have constructed gymnasiums as part of the church facility and have operated sports leagues and teen clubs. In 1994, the Association of Church Sports and Recreation Ministers (CSRM) was formed with a vision to equip local churches to change lives through sports and recreation. This group focuses on mobilizing local church staff and volunteers to build bridges in their communities using sport, recreation, and leisure activities to lead people

into a personal relationship with Christ (http://www.csrm.org/purpose.
html). In addition, probably no group in the community is more involved
in music and drama than church groups. Religious holiday celebrations
also are commonly shared in many communities (e.g., Christmas parades,
Easter egg hunts).

Finally, organized religious organizations often provide recreation
opportunities for the public at large, especially by making their facilities
available for youth and civic group meetings and through the public availability of many of their programs (e.g., Bible School and day camps). Many
churches operate conference centers, camps, and other outdoor recreation
facilities. As a part of recreation services in communities, organized religious groups can add to the quality of life in the community and ensure the
relationships among spirituality, play, leisure, and recreation. More about
faith-based recreation careers is discussed later in this book.

Employee Recreation Services

Numerous U.S. industries and businesses provide recreation and fitness
services for their employees. These services have gone by different names
but generally have employee health and morale as their goals. Employee
morale managers, as they are currently called, generally work in human resource departments in organizations or businesses. They are responsible for
managing employee services that include recreation programs, community
services, event planning, childcare/eldercare services, and travel opportunities. The Employee Morale and Recreation Association (EMRA) was
founded recently as an association to enhance employee services (http://
www.esmassn.org).

Employee recreation is the broad application of recreation services to
a particular clientele (e.g., employees of a particular business/organization
and their families) sponsored by a corporation or agency. Employee recreation may be provided by the employer and/or by the workers themselves.
Although private companies and corporations generally conduct these
services, many of these employee services run like nonprofit entities. For
many employees and their families, employee programs offer leisure and
fitness opportunities such as sponsored athletic teams, camping and resort
facilities, dramatic and musical productions, pre-retirement and leisure
counseling, and tours or special travel arrangements for their employees.

In recent years, the trend has been toward the development of fitness
and wellness services in businesses and corporations. Organizational wellness programs can usually be categorized into two types: fitness only and
comprehensive. Fitness-only types might include offering a fitness center
on-site or providing membership discounts to off-site community fitness

and health clubs. Comprehensive programs include the fitness component as well as educational programs such as seminars about various aspects of wellness and healthy living. These comprehensive programs may also include special events and opportunities such as *take the stairs day*, walking programs, and family fun days.

Corporation executives, labor unions, and industrial sociologists generally agree that recreation activities can contribute to worker productivity and well-being. If employee recreation and fitness programs reduce absenteeism, worker turnover, and workplace accidents, then they are a good business investment. If these services add to the well-being of workers and their families, enhance the quality of the work environment, and provide opportunity for personal fulfillment, then employee services can be profitable to individuals, businesses, and communities.

Advocacy Organizations

Many nonprofit organizations and agencies exist to provide direct services for their membership. Some organizations also impact recreation services and leisure opportunities through their advocacy missions.

Examples include environmental organizations such as *Nature Conservancy*, which purchases ecologically significant lands and holds them in escrow until those lands can be acquired by governmental organizations as parks and preserves. *The National Trust for Historic Preservation* operates museums and advocates the acquisition and preservation of historical areas. The *National Audubon Society* also offers educational programs, lecture series, and support for wildlife sanctuaries. The Joseph P. Kennedy, Jr. Foundation is known for its work with people with mental retardation through *Special Olympics. AARP*, formerly called the American Association of Retired Persons, advocates for the needs and interests of the aging population including addressing recreation services. The list of nonprofit advocacy organizations is huge and many of these organizations have employment opportunities for individuals interested in facilitating recreation services for people with a diversity of backgrounds.

In addition to these organizations, countless nonprofit organizations support specific recreation interests as is shown in Table 21.1. Some of these use professional staff to manage the organizations and others are staffed primarily by volunteers. These examples provide a flavor of the ubiquity of nonprofit recreation activity organizations.

Table 21.1 Recreation Interest Groups

Academy of Model Aeronautics www.modelaircraft.org	American Federation of Arts www.afaweb.org	International Mountain Bicycling Association www.imba.com
Access Fund www.accessfund.org	American Hiking Society www.americanhiking.org	International Quidditch Association www.internationalquid-ditch.org
Amateur Athletic Union www.aauathletics.org	American Iris Society www.irises.org	
Amateur Softball Associa-tion of America www.softball.org	American Library Association www.ala.org	Izaak Walton League of America www.iwla.org
American Amateur Baseball Congress www.aabc.us	American Model Yachting Association www.theamya.org American Power Boat	The Knitting Guild Association www.tkga.com Little League Baseball, Inc.
American Association of Community Theatre www.aact.org	Association www.apba.org American Rose Society	www.littleleague.org Musical Dog Sport
American Barefoot Water Ski Club www.barefoot.org	www.ars.org American Theater Wing	Association www.musicaldogsport.org National Collegiate Table
American Birding Association www.aba.org	americantheatrewing.org The Antique Outboard Motor Club, Inc.	Tennis Association www.nctta.org National Field Archery
American Canoe Association www.americancanoe.org	www.aomci.org Casual Gaming Association	Association www.nfaa-archery.org
American Casting Association www.americancastingas-soc.org	casualgamesassociation.org Comic Book Collecting Association	National Audubon Society www.audubon.org National Federation of
American Contract Bridge League www.acbl.org	www.comiccollecting.org The Contemporary A Cappella Society	Music Clubs www.nfmc-music.org
American Crossword Association www.crossword.org	www.casa.org Hip Hop Association www.hiphopassociation.org	National Field Archery Association www.nfaa-archery.org

Table 21.1 Recreation Interest Groups (cont'd)

National Garden Clubs, Inc. www.gardenclub.org	National Speleological Society www.caves.org	United States Handball Association www.ushandball.org
National Horseshoe Pitchers Association of America www.horseshoepitching.com	National Wildlife Federation www.nwf.org	United States Kenpo Karate Federation www.uskka.com
National Model Railroad Association www.nmra.org	The Nature Conservancy www.nature.org	United States Lawn Bowls Association www.uslba.org
The National Quilting Association www.nqaquilts.org	Puppeteers of America www.puppeteers.org	United States Lawn Tennis Association www.usta.com
National Rifle Association www.nra.org	USA National Shuffleboard Association www.national-shuffle- board-association.us	United States Parachute Association www.uspa.org
National Scrabble Association www.scrabble-assoc.com	Sierra Club www.sierraclub.org	United States Sudoku Association, Inc. www.unitedstatessudoku. com
National Skeet Shooting Association and National Sporting Clay Association www.nssa-nsca.org	Unicycling Society of America www.uniusa.org	
National Ski Association nationalskiassociation.org	United States Bowling Congress www.bowl.com	World Folk Music Association www.wfma.net

Careers in
Nonprofit Recreation Services

The nonprofit sector, which focuses on services for members as well as special interests, is a critical element in the recreation services system. The role of this sector regarding recreation has varied depending on public attitudes, fads, leisure interests, and patterns of governmental involvement. However, this sector has not always been considered an integral part of the recreation profession, even though methods for addressing social issues often involve recreation programming and policy. Nevertheless, the beneficiaries of nonprofit services often receive recreation opportunities that lead to their well-being and a better quality of life in communities. Recreation services are only one aspect of many nonprofit organizations and professional employees may have backgrounds from the social or behavioral sciences as well as from among recreation majors.

People interested in careers in nonprofit organizations need organizational management, fund-raising, and public relations skills. These organizations also seek professionals and volunteers with leadership and programming skills. Regardless of whether these nonprofit organizations associate directly with recreation services, they clearly enhance leisure opportunities in communities. In the coming years, these organizations will continue to be major employers of recreation graduates as well as individuals interested in other areas of human services and natural resources. Recreation services in the United States would be quite different if this myriad of nonprofit organizations did not advocate for people's well-being and the quality of life in communities.

Reflection Questions

1. The United States has thousands of nonprofit organizations. Why have so many organizations existed for so long in the United States? Why have they been called the backbone of American society?

2. Many nonprofit organizations use recreation as a means to accomplish other goals in their organization. Why is recreation such a successful means for addressing other goals?

3. What are the advantages to a business in offering opportunities for employee recreation?

Chapter 22

Youth Recreation Services

Youth recreation services cut across all sectors. The most familiar youth organizations like the Girl Scouts or the Campfire Boys and Girls are nonprofit organizations. However, many communities offer government-sponsored youth programs through parks and recreation services. Issues concerning youth have been central in the recreation movement throughout its history. As discussed in Unit Two, recreation services in communities were initiated over a century ago largely because of a concern for children and youth.

The social welfare movement of the late 19th and early 20th centuries served as an impetus for recreation development in both the public and nonprofit sectors. Philanthropists responded to the needs of youth in urban areas by creating agencies and services for children and youth. Although recreation was not the central reason for the development of many of these organizations, it was central to the success of the programs. For youth, recreation is often the means to reach other desirable ends related to youth development. Recreation activities remain a major focus for hundreds of national as well as local youth-oriented organizations in the United States. This chapter describes some of the meanings of recreation for youth, how organizations have addressed the needs and interests of youth, and potential career opportunities in this field.

The Nature of Youth Services

Children and youth are a primary target for recreation programming in U.S. society, regardless of the sector. However, youth services are most often associated with the nonprofit sector. Educational groups, family life agencies, fraternal and patriotic orders, and religious bodies have youth programs. Probably the best known and well-established are the Y (formerly called the YMCA), YWCA, Boy Scouts of America, Girl Scouts of the USA, Camp Fire USA, and 4-H. Dozens of organizations exist for youth sponsored by national nonprofit organizations (e.g., American Red Cross, Boys and Girls State, Young Men's and Young Women's Hebrew Associations, Habitat for Humanity, Junior Achievement), and thousands exist at the local levels (Youth Councils, Student Councils, Teen Centers).

Often this youth movement is directed by youths themselves with organizational support from public schools and public recreation agencies. Many of the youth opportunities appeal to older adolescents, but the programs of the more established national organizations have children as their focus.

Some organizations stress services to youth of color, the urban poor, and/or youth from high-risk communities. Nonprofit organizations such as the Police Athletic League and the Children's Aid Society are found primarily in metropolitan areas working almost exclusively with these groups of children. Recreation activities are generally used as a means for preventing delinquency and enriching the lives of young people. Recreation opportunities are important to all age groups, but youth generally have an abundance of time and energy available to pursue recreation interests. Recreation has also been viewed as developmentally important as young people find their identities and move into adulthood.

Regardless of the population or the types of recreation activities, the contemporary focus on youth generally relates to positive youth development. This youth development encompasses processes that prepare young people to meet the challenges of adolescence and adulthood by providing supports and activities that contribute to their growth. Positive youth development is based on theories of human development and links these theories to environments that promote youth development (Eccles & Gootman, 2002; Lerner, Lerner, Almerigi, & Theokas, 2005). Recreation services are one of those environments.

Positive Youth Development

Positive youth development is a relatively new idea. Although in the 18th century Rousseau was one of the first thinkers and writers to influence how societies began to think about and view adolescents, his view was tempered by the reality that children and youth of all ages were needed to carry out the work required for living in agrarian cultures. With the emergence of social and school reforms in the late 19th century, the lives of children and youth in America were dramatically changed.

Social reformers, including many of the early proponents of the recreation movement, were concerned about child labor. These progressive reformers realized that children and youth had nowhere to play and, often, nothing to do. They also believed in the value of structured recreation opportunities. The ideas of the social reformers coincided with the efforts of educators interested in legal reform that required children to attend school and limited their participation in the workforce. The convergence of issues led to how Americans constructed adolescence in the 20th century, including a movement to provide children and youth with opportunities for free play and structured recreation, and the institutionalization of education for all children. These issues led to interest in youth development and occurred concurrently with the creation of the contemporary recreation movement in the United States.

Many people believe that young people should be taught to follow the rules and do what is expected of them. A phrase, "youth-at-risk," was constructed to categorize problem youth and/or youth who were considered to be delinquent in some way. Youth-at-risk permeated the national consciousness in the latter part of the 20th century, with efforts directed to responding to this segment. Curricula, videos, workbooks, and handbooks were developed on how to deal with young people identified as being at-risk for drug abuse, teen pregnancy, violence, and generally not likely to make a successful transition from childhood to adulthood.

This focus made youth a problem while often ignoring other issues that might contribute to the negative situations that young people faced, such as poverty, inadequate educational opportunities, institutionalized racism and sexism, physical and sexual abuse, and a culture that devalues children and youth. Today youth leaders recognize that all young people may be at-risk and the focus should not be on the problems but on how youth can develop positively. Unfortunately, education, after-school programs, and other governmental programs that can help young people develop positively have often been under-funded.

Emerging Youth Services

The original goal of many youth programs was to be diversionary and give young people something positive and structured to do to get them off the streets. Over the years, however, these programs have changed in their focus toward developmental outcomes such as physical, cognitive, and emotional growth. Structured recreation programs were important, as were youth-related health promotions such as teen pregnancy prevention and drug/alcohol prevention.

In the mid-1980s, after-school programs for elementary school children and some middle school-age children began to emerge throughout the United States. Typical after-school programs offered components such as homework assistance, tutoring, free play, and structured recreation opportunities. Today, many agencies market their youth programs to attract a wider audience by promoting overall health and well-being for young people as well as personal empowerment.

One new curriculum in the 1990s centered on the idea of developmental assets. According to the Search Institute in Minnesota (Leffert et al., 2006), about 40 developmental assets such as honesty, good communication skills, and ethical decision-making can help young people make successful transitions from childhood to adulthood. The idea with this approach—present also in others—is that if recreation professionals know what structured activities might be most developmentally beneficial, they can plan and implement programs and/or develop mentoring programs that will assist young people in reaching adulthood successfully.

Further, recreation professionals working with young people have emphasized including youth in the planning process and have actively sought their feedback through focus groups and their participation on advisory or teen boards that oversee their own programs. In addition, people have identified that recreation activities, along with school, family, work and religious affiliation, are an important context for identity development and formation. The more committed and engaged a young person becomes through participation in recreation opportunities, the more likely that young person will internalize the social identity associated with that activity (e.g., an athlete, actor). When program planners understand how to structure recreation programs so that young people will internalize developmental aspects, then these extracurricular and free-time activities can have greater influence on the positive development of young people.

Youth services are an important component of recreation services, and vice versa. However, several issues regarding young people should be noted. For example, some parents, educators, and youth workers are concerned about *overscheduling* young people. Further, with the proliferation of video games, computers, and other digital gadgets, youth may be beginning to lose their ability to be spontaneous and creative. They also may be spending more time indoors, which has created what Louv (2005) called, *nature-deficit disorder.* Finding balance between structured programs and opportunities for young people to learn how to play on their own without relying on technology remains a challenge.

Youth Services Organizations

Numerous ways can be used to analyze and describe youth recreation services. Youth-serving groups can be viewed regarding their service focus (e.g., outdoors-oriented, social service-oriented, church-oriented, educational-oriented), their appeal to one sex or the other or to both, their organizational structure (e.g., national affiliation, local autonomy), their management approach (e.g., group work-oriented, facility-based), or their leadership structure (e.g., adult-directed with professionals, adult volunteers, youth-directed). The leadership factor provides the basis for grouping organizations that provide recreation services into adult-directed and youth-directed.

Adult-Directed Organizations

Youth-serving agencies often have policies and structures established by adults with paid professional staff to administer the program services. Most of these groups are well-known by the public and generally have a long history. Most have a positive youth development focus and often operate their own facilities. Many have large memberships and visibility in the United States. Further, professional employment opportunities in youth services are available in these organizations:

Boys & Girls Clubs of America

The Boys Clubs of America and the Girls Clubs of America merged in 1990 to become the Boys & Girls Clubs of America (BGCA). After over a century of services, the BGCA now has 4,000 clubs and over 4 million participants across the United States. The mission of the organization is to enable youth to reach their full potential as productive, caring, and responsible citizens. The organization guides urban boys and girls in their physical, intellectual, emotional, and social development by offering education and career, health and lifestyle, arts, and sports, fitness, and recreation programs. The national organization furnishes services to the largely urban-oriented clubs on matters pertaining to the organization, administration, and operation of the club facilities. Local clubs offer professional employment opportunities in youth development, management, and executive leadership.

Camp Fire USA

Camp Fire was established in 1910 and is one of the oldest organized youth programs for girls. The original mission was to promote the spiritual ideals of the home and stimulate the development of good health and character for girls. In 1975, membership was opened to boys and now about 46%

of the members are males. Today's mission is to build caring, confident youth and future leaders. This mission is accomplished through programs offered in local communities during out-of-school time hours. Camp Fire contributes to the community by engaging youth in a small group atmosphere with trained volunteer adults who use educational, enrichment, and service-learning programs to address social issues and build life skills. Further, Camp Fire also provides day and overnight camps, trip and travel programs, and adventure challenge and environmental education sessions. Over 85 Councils across the United States employ professional staff to supervise their programs.

4-H

The four H's stand for Head, Heart, Hands, and Health. This youth organization was founded at the turn of the 20th century primarily for rural youth. Then and today, 4-H leadership is primarily from Cooperative Extension Service staff employed in virtually every county in the United States through agreements with the U.S. Department of Agriculture, state land grant universities, and county governments. 4-H is one of the largest youth development organizations in the United States, with over 6 million young people residing in urban neighborhoods, suburban communities, and rural areas. 4-H focuses on *learning by doing* through wide-ranging projects related to science, citizenship, and healthy living. Over a half million volunteers and 3,500 professional staff are involved with 4-H, and the organization boasts of over 60 million alumni.

Girl Scouts of the USA

Similar to the other youth organizations described above, Girl Scouts (GSUSA) was founded in the early 20th century (i.e., 1912). The mission is to build girls of courage, confidence, and character who make the world a better place. Today, the over 3 million Girl Scouts includes 2.3 million girl members and almost 900,000 adult members working primarily as volunteer leaders. In the United States, over 100 Councils exist with professional leaders who support the volunteers in the area. GSUSA is primarily a group-oriented program. Many people are familiar with Girl Scout Cookies. The $760 million Girl Scout Cookie Program is the largest girl-led business in the country and generates income to support troops' chosen activities for the year, fund community service and leadership projects, attend summer camp, travel to destinations in the United States and around the world, and provide events for girls in their communities. Although adult professionals and volunteers provide leadership, the girls themselves (in what is called "girl planning") undertake much of the programming and planning, especially within the older troops.

Boy Scouts of America

The Boy Scouts of America (BSA) is one of the largest and most prominent values-based youth development organizations in the United States. BSA provides a program for young people that builds character, focuses on active citizenship, and develops personal fitness. It was established in 1910. The original intent was to promote character building and citizenship training for young males through group-oriented outdoor recreation activities under professional and volunteer leadership. Today, BSA has broadened its base and provides urban-oriented programs and service activities. Some troops for older youth accept female members. Around 115,000 civic, faith-based, and educational units operate Boy Scout units to deliver programs to their youth members as well as the community at large. These units provide meeting spaces and volunteer leadership. Basic leadership is coordinated through the efforts of professional scout executives. About 2.7 million young people are involved in scouting with 1.1 million volunteer leaders. Almost half of those youth attend a camp or high adventure outdoor program each year.

The Y(MCA)

The Young Men's Christian Association (YMCA) is one of the oldest youth-serving organizations; the first U.S. operation was established in Boston in 1851. In 2010, the Y revitalized its brand to extend its reach, and began officially referring to itself by its most familiar name—the Y. The Y estimates that it engages 9 million youth and 12 million adults in 10,000 communities across the United States. The Y considers itself a cause-driven organization aimed at youth development, healthy living, and social responsibility. It is primarily a facility-based operation. Although early Ys were established as Christian groups with a restricted membership based upon one's sex and age, they no longer function in that capacity. The Y is for everyone—youth and adults, males and females, and any religious affiliation. The programs and services enable young people to realize their potential, prepare teens for college, offer ways for families to have fun together, and empower people to be healthier in spirit, mind, and body. Each Y functions autonomously but with a strong relationship with the national organization. About 2,600 Y programs employ 20,000 full-time staff and manage 500,000 volunteers across the country. Many professional career opportunities exist in Ys.

The Young Women's Christian Association

The Young Women's Christian Association (YWCA) emerged in the United States shortly after the YMCA. It was originally designed to meet the needs of young women working in urban environments. The YWCA serves over 2 million women, girls, and families in the United States today. It is a multiracial women's movement with major goals of empowering women, eliminating racism, and promoting peace, justice, freedom, and dignity for all. The focus is broader than just youth as the YWCA promotes the good health, education, and social awareness of women and their families. YWCA facilities vary greatly from community to community but may include housing opportunities, multipurpose recreation centers, camps, and social activity areas. Professional leadership is essential for the YWCA's success.

Jewish Community Centers

Jewish Community Centers (JCC) are recreational, social, and fraternal organizations serving the Jewish community in cities. JCCs promote Jewish culture and heritage through holiday celebrations and Jewish education. However, JCCs are open to everyone and many of the facilities have extensive recreation and fitness programs. The JCC movement includes more than 350 JCCs, Young Men and Young Women Hebrew Associations (YM-YWHA), and camp sites in the United States. A typical JCC operates social, cultural, and athletic programs for all age groups. Culture and performing arts activities are also stressed, as are child-care programs and programs for special populations and teens designed to strengthen religious and cultural heritage.

Other Groups

Several other youth services sponsored by adult organizations merit mentioning. These auxiliary groups often are directed by volunteers who are members of the parent organization. Typical among them are fraternal and patriotic societies and national civic organizations such as Junior Order of Elk, the Order of DeMolay of the Masons, branch organizations of labor unions, the Junior American Red Cross, the Junior Legion of the American Legion, and the Key Club of the Kiwanis International. These types of programs range from sponsoring a youth recognition day to actively supporting a comprehensive youth service organization within a community. Although recreation is not the basis of these programs, it is a key element. The parent organizations have found their youth programs to be a way to promote citizenship and introduce youth to the values and benefits of the parent organization. Since volunteers generally drive these groups, few professional opportunities seem to exist.

Youth-Directed Groups

Some youth programs and organizations are planned and directed by youth. These groups might be a program of the public parks and recreation department, a program established by the mayor or county commission, a private community-based nonprofit organization, or may be autonomous. All these programs emphasize the self-directed aspects of the program, with youth providing their own leadership with a minimum of adult advice and supervision. They are known by a variety of names but most frequently as Teen Centers and Youth Councils.

These youth councils may be organized in a plethora of ways. In the United States, youth councils have been formed by nonprofit organizations and at all levels of government. Forms of youth councils may include *youth advisory* councils that provide input and feedback regarding adult-driven decision-making, *youth research* councils that are responsible for assessment and evaluation of youth and community programs, and *youth action* councils designed to either be youth/adult partnerships or youth-led activities.

Although a national youth council organization does not appear to exist, various states have taken steps to assist with the organization of youth councils. For example, in 1992 Utah State University formed the Association of Youth Councils (AYC) to provide youth with opportunities to develop citizenship, leadership, a personal sense of achievement, and an understanding of the government.

Organized Camps

One important area of youth services for almost 150 years is organized camps for children and youth, which can include residential (i.e., sleep-over) and day camps. Many young people are involved in camp opportunities, and positive youth development is central to the operation of these camps. The American Camp Association (ACA), the professional association for people involved with organized camping, defines camping as a community of people living together as an organized group, usually in the outdoors, under the direction of designated leaders. The focus is on each camper's mental, physical, social, and spiritual growth.

'Camp' is sometimes a term used broadly. The above definition of organized camping generally requires an interaction with the natural environment. Activity camps that stress the pursuit of a specific activity such as basketball, music, dance, or cheerleading generally do not meet the traditional definition associated with traditional camp programs, even though the living arrangements and designated leadership may be similar. Nevertheless, they are called camps and address the goals of camp experiences. The focus on youth development through a camp-like experience can be highly beneficial regardless of the setting.

Like other recreation services, the organized camping movement gained momentum in the late 1800s. Organized camps have had several emphases ranging from an earlier concern for physical fitness and activity to a more recent concern for outcomes-based quality programs (Meier & Henderson, 2012). Today, camps take many forms and offer a range of experiences and benefits.

Organized camps encompass an array of organizational structures and programs. Sponsors can include governmental organizations, voluntary agencies, civic and fraternal organizations, churches and synagogues, corporations and labor unions, and private business enterprises. Some camps operate for profit and others do not. Some organized camps are only for boys and men, while others are only for girls and women or operate a coed system or have a family orientation. Some camps offer day camping where the camper leaves the site to return home each evening while other operations offer resident or travel camps. Camps can offer sessions that last a few days or up to eight-weeks. Some camps offer trip programs or extended outdoor experiences. Special camps have been designated specifically for people with disabilities. With the implementation of the Americans with Disabilities Act, all camps are encouraged to respond to the needs of people with disabilities and focus on inclusive camping.

Camps, as all forms of recreation services, depend on leadership, facilities, programs, and finances. The success of the camp program depends on the quality of its leadership. Leaders range in experience and backgrounds from high school students who may serve as junior counselors to experienced professional camp administrators. Effective programming involves the careful planning, execution, and evaluation of activities and experiences.

The exact number of camps is unknown, but it appears that at least 12,000 camps are operated in the United States and some of these camps and conference centers operate year round. Job opportunities exist in year-round camp administration as well as in seasonal summer employment.

Youth Services Issues

The aim of recreation services focused on youth, regardless of the organizational structure, is positive development. To reach this goal, however, requires being aware of several issues. For example, structural issues such as funding and duplication of services influence youth services. Funding for services comes from different sources that vary among groups. Further, funding often dictates the programs offered, especially when staff depend on community or grant funding. Providing high-quality services with adequate funding, particularly those services that are adult led, will continue to be a challenge in the future. Although some concern has been expressed about duplication of services for youth in communities, it is unlikely that too many youth services will ever exist. In addition, many opportunities now exist for partnerships so that several agencies in different sectors might come together to address the needs and interests of youth.

Program viability is also a persistent issue for youth services especially in traditional adult-led structures. The needs of families and youth are constant, but the means to address those needs and interests change. Attention to changes is evident in the way that the organizations described in this chapter have evolved to stay current with missions that address today's world. Although youth organizations may perpetuate basic core values, the means for organizing programs must be continually evaluated. Providing programs that meet the interests of young people is always a challenge.

All trends suggest that youth-service organizations are seeking a broader base of support. In addition to working with youth from high-risk communities, more attention focuses on co-recreational activities, family activities, nonathletic activities, and short-term projects and activities rather than only long-term club membership. Youth are becoming more involved in planning and conducting those programs and services designed for them.

Youth services offer education and recreation opportunities for young people. Youth organizations were one of the first ways that recreation was provided to young people over a hundred years ago. The goals of those original programs are similar today with youth programs aimed at helping young people develop life skills, providing outlets for energy, and giving a supportive environment for growing up. Recreation professionals seeking careers in youth services should be aware of the numerous employment opportunities in youth-serving organizations, public recreation programs, and organized camps.

Reflection Questions

1. How would you define positive youth development? What would be the outcomes of such development?

2. Were you a member of one or more youth organizations when you were a child? What were your positive experiences with these organizations? What could these organizations do to have improved their services?

3. What are the advantages of adult-directed youth organizations? What are the advantages of youth-directed organizations?

4. Do you believe that all youth are "at-risk"? Explain your reasoning.

5. Some people have suggested that working with youth results in a high burn-out rate. Why might this be the case? How could burn-out from employment in youth services be avoided?

6. What challenges exist in trying to meet the needs of youth in communities?

Chapter 23

Private Business
and Commercial Recreation

Recreation services are an important part of the private sector of the economy, with new markets, services, and products appearing constantly. The terminology used for these types of for-profit businesses has traditionally been called commercial recreation within recreation circles. In this chapter, both terms are used to illustrate the focus on businesses run for profit by individuals or corporations. Private recreation services should not be confused with personal leisure, although they might be related. Private refers to the independent organizations associated with recreation. Business refers to the traditional profit focus in U.S. society.

Recreation is big business in terms of its ubiquity and expenditures. As shown in Table 23.1, in 2009 almost a trillion dollars was spent on recreation. These expenditures represented about 9% of what is available for the average consumer to spend. The biggest expenditures were for video and audio equipment, followed by sports-related consumption. Much of this consumption is a result of the offerings of private recreation businesses, although the public and nonprofit sectors also sell some of these services and products.

Unlike the public and nonprofit sectors, however, the mission of a private recreation business is explicitly to generate a desired rate of return on the investment, which is commonly called profit. These recreation services are market-driven. Providers may also have a split personality. Owners of and investors in recreation businesses do not always identify themselves with the recreation profession. Instead, they see themselves as business people who provide goods and services to customers at prices determined by market factors. Owners and investors often have business backgrounds, attend their own specialized trade meetings, read specialized trade publications, and evaluate the performance of their enterprises using criteria like rate of return on investments, market growth potential, and profit margins.

Table 23.1 Personal Consumption Expenditures for Recreation in 2009
(in Billions of Dollars)

Total recreation expenditures	897 .1
Percent of total personal consumption (9%)	
Video and audio equipment, computers, and related services	265.2
Video and audio equipment	107.1
Information-processing equipment	64.7
Services related to video and audio goods and computers	93.4
Sports and recreational goods and related services	196.9
Sports and recreational vehicles	41.7
Other sporting and recreational goods	150.0
Maintenance and repair of recreational vehicles and sports equipment	5.2
Membership clubs, sports centers, parks, theaters, and museums	126.5
Membership clubs and participant sports centers	32.7
Amusements parks, campgrounds, and related recreational services	41.8
Admissions to specified spectator amusements	45.6
Motion picture theaters	10.4
Live entertainment, excluding sports	14.5
Spectator sports	20.7
Museums and libraries	6.4
Magazines, newspapers, books, and stationery	105.1
Gambling	109.3
Pets, pet products, and related services	67.1
Photographic goods and services	17.7
Package tours	9.2

(Taken from http://www.census.gov/compendia/statab/2012/tables/12s1233.pdf)

Many recreation business employees, however, do see themselves as part of the recreation movement in providing goods and services that people want during their free or leisure time. The goal of recreation business people is to gain happy satisfied customers who will come back again and tell friends about their good experiences. This might be the goal of professionals in public and nonprofit services as well, but the need to make financial gains is the bottom line of private businesses.

Recreation business owners and employees have a variety of backgrounds in academic areas such as recreation, economics, business, or hotel and hospitality management. Many successful business people have also learned through on-the-job experience. Some have college degrees and some do not. Many part-time jobs also exist in recreation businesses in communities.

The Structure of Recreation Businesses

Private and commercial recreation businesses are a collection of industries that provides a range of recreation, entertainment, and/or amusement services. These enterprises may vary in size from local *mom- and-pop* businesses (e.g., a town's bowling operator) to huge multinational corporations (e.g., Nike). Examples range from amusement and theme parks to professional sports, show business (e.g., movies, TV, and the legitimate theater), tourist attractions, manufacturers of recreation apparel and equipment, health spas and sports clubs, and elements of the transportation and food industry.

One term often associated with businesses is entrepreneurism. Entrepreneurism is not only the prerogative of business people and is a term that can be applied widely to mean anyone who is innovative and willing to take a risk. The common definition associates entrepreneurism with a new venture, service, or product aimed at making a financial gain. However, entrepreneurs also can be individuals who want to launch something new and are willing to take responsibility for the outcome. An entrepreneur is willing to take a moderate risk, which is often but not always financial. An entrepreneur may challenge the status quo by doing or starting something new or different that does not currently exist. Therefore, professionals in any area of recreation services might be entrepreneurial. However, entrepreneurs are most often associated with private businesses and commercial recreation.

To describe and classify the components of commercial recreation, Bullaro and Edginton (1986) developed a traditional scheme with five overlapping service domains: entertainment services, nature-based services, retail outlets, hospitality and food services, and travel and tourism services. Examples of businesses in each of these domains are shown in Table 23.2. These service domains also reflect the areas where full-time (and part-time) employment exists.

Although this classification scheme is helpful in illustrating the scope of private recreation, these five service domains are not mutually exclusive. Overlap exists. When people go to see a movie, for example, they may also have dinner at a restaurant. Tourists patronize local businesses and not just travel and tourism businesses. Tourism provides a good example of the overlap not just of the five service domains in the private sector but also the overlap of recreation with other sectors of services. For example, many components of tourist services (e.g., parks, campgrounds, historical sites, and cultural facilities) are provided by the public and nonprofit sectors.

Table 23.2
Private (Commercial) Recreation Classification Model (Illustrative List)
[Adapted from Bullaro and Edginton (1986)]

Travel and Tourism Services	Retail Outlets
Airlines	
Tour promoters/operators	***Products:***
Tour boats (cruises)	Product showrooms
Tour buses	Discount stores
Travel agencies	Home shopping network
	Specialty (recreational vehicles,
Entertainment Services	athletic equipment, specialized
Amusement/Theme parks	boutiques, video rentals) shops
Bowling lanes	Shopping malls
Carnivals	Variety/department stores
Circuses	
Entertainment bureaus	***Services:***
Movie theaters	Aquatic centers
Nightclubs	Dance studios
Billiard rooms	Equestrian centers
Professional athletics	Fitness clubs
Racetracks (horse, dog, NASCAR)	Golf clubs
Rodeos	Ice rinks
Special events and festivals	Racquet clubs
Waterparks	Roller rinks
Gambling casinos	
Symphony performances	**Hospitality and Food Services**
Broadway and regional plays	Catering services
	Convention centers
Nature-Based Services	Guest houses/Inns
Beach/Waterfront	Hotels
Campgrounds	Motels
Hunting preserves	Resorts
Liveries	Restaurants
Marinas	
Resident camps	
Ski resorts	
Zoo/Aquarium/Wildlife parks	

Similarly, sports tournaments that attract out-of-town visitors might be sponsored by public or nonprofit recreation organizations. The following sections discuss four of the five service domains. Travel and tourism services are discussed in the next chapter.

Entertainment Services

Entertainment services intend to provide recreation that offers diversion and escape from people's daily lives. These services may include amusement and theme parks, special events, spectator sports, and cultural opportunities. Examples of organizations serving professionals in this service domain are the International Association of Amusement Parks and Attractions, the International Association of Fairs and Expositions, and the Association of Events Management Education.

Amusement parks began in England in the late 1800s and appeared in the United States shortly thereafter (Wilson & Wilson, 1994). Coney Island was among the earliest amusement parks. To stimulate both sensory and psychological pleasures, they featured lights, moving objects, rides, and games of competition. By 1950, however, most amusement parks were in disrepair and faced financial difficulties and a poor public image.

The amusement park industry was revitalized in 1956 when the theme park Disneyland opened in Anaheim, CA. Theme parks are what their names imply. Careful planning of the physical and interior layout of the park and its component parts create a specific atmosphere. Even the dress and attitude of employees reflect the park theme. Theme parks have been successful because they offer more than amusement. They invite guests of all ages to escape by immersing themselves in the fantasy. Attendance at amusement and theme parks has increased in recent years as new attractions are continually added. For example, Universal's *The Wizarding World of Harry Potter* debut at the Islands of Adventure theme park at Universal Orlando resort in 2010 was highly popular.

Theme and amusement park developers apply the concept of clustering to increase the attractiveness of their facilities. Developers encourage rather than discourage adjacent recreation developments. With a choice of opportunities available to them, visitors are more likely to prolong their stays in an area or to return for repeat visits. In those cases, they spend more money. When opportunities are multidimensional and supported by attractive food service and accommodations, return visits are more likely. Clustering requires planning and cooperation between the public and private business sectors. For example, Orlando, FL, Branson, MO, and Myrtle Beach, SC, have been successful with such an approach. The clustering technique also has been applied in the development of recreation, entertainment, and shopping zones in cities such as Harbor Place in Baltimore, MD, and the Riverwalk in San Antonio, TX.

Special events are a second major category in the entertainment services domain. Special events have become such a huge part of communities that a professional field of event management has grown as part of recreation services. These opportunities as they exist in the public, nonprofit, and private sectors are discussed in more detail later in this text.

Spectator sports and cultural opportunities make up two other categories in the entertainment services domain. Spectator sports, in particular, have enjoyed an extended period of growth. Spectator and the cultural categories might also include circuses, traveling shows, and various theatrical or musical productions. Many people attend cultural events such as jazz concerts, classical music and opera performances, musicals, plays, and ballet performances. Recreation professionals are more often prepared to program for participation rather than spectating, but spectator event businesses employ sport and arts managers to assist with marketing, scheduling, and event management.

Nature-Based Recreation Services

Although many people associate outdoor recreation with the public sector, nature-based recreation services are a major component of the private recreation business sector. Private campground owners and operators provide over half of all campsites in North America. For example, Kampgrounds of America (KOA) began business in 1964 and operates hundreds of franchises across the United States. Further, about 7% of the U.S. population downhill skied and 6% snowboarded in 2010. All these people were involved in nature-based recreation and spent money in some way, whether on entry fees, equipment and supplies, equipment maintenance, guides, or lessons. Activities such as rock climbing, hang gliding, zip lines, parasailing, and wind surfing include needs for specialized equipment, knowledge, skills, and instruction.

An emerging area related to nature-based recreation businesses is extreme sports, which are often called action sports or adventure sports. These activities are perceived as having a high level of danger because of the speed, height, level of physical exertion, and highly specialized gear needed. Most of these activities often occur in natural areas. These sports gained in popularity in the 1990s when they were highlighted by marketing companies to promote the X Games. Athletes in these activities compete not only against other athletes, but also against environmental obstacles and challenges. These environmental variables are frequently weather- and terrain-related. Because of the nontraditional nature of these sports and the implications for liability, they tend to be offered by private businesses rather than the public or nonprofit sectors.

Retail Outlets

Retail outlets sell products and services directly to customers. The volume of sales related to leisure and recreation is astounding, as is noted in Table 23.1, with $107 billion spent on audio and video equipment and $50 billion on sporting goods, for example. For many people, retail shopping in and of itself is a recreation activity.

Products

One important tie between retail sales and recreation is the proliferation of shopping strips and malls. Malls are designed to make visiting less like a shopping trip and more like a leisure experience. People go to these places in their free time to buy or window shop, to people watch, meet friends, and absorb the atmosphere. Larger malls sometimes hire special event planners or coordinators to plan opportunities to entice people to come to malls and to stay and shop. Malls often provide performance space and facilities for concerts, art exhibits, craft shows, and fashion shows. Children's entertainment (e.g., free rides, game arcades) may be available to encourage parents to bring their children and shop. Some malls offer free rides for smaller children and amusement arcades with video games to attract older youth. Coffee shops and specialty food vendors attempt to re-create a sidewalk café environment within malls where shoppers can relax. Open-air markets, farmers' markets, and even flea markets use some of the same techniques to attract customers.

Another tie with sales is the link retailers provide in connecting merchandise and recreation activities. Salespeople have always advised customers on appropriate equipment and its proper uses. Some specialized retail outlets (e.g., outdoor equipment retailers) employ skilled recreation participants to sell merchandise, since the availability of expert advice is an incentive to buy from such retailers (e.g., outdoor stores, bicycle shops). Retailers often also provide services in addition to their products and may sponsor workshops and demonstrations to educate existing and potential customers about specific recreation activities and equipment. Some retailers, particularly larger ones, now provide recreation trips as well as merchandise. Companies such as Recreation Equipment, Inc. (REI), for example, offer everything from weekend excursions to major expeditions.

Recreation sales volume has consistently grown over the years. Caution is necessary, however, when interpreting these figures. For example, not everyone who buys jogging shoes intends to use them for jogging. On the other hand, people who buy bicycles or weightlifting equipment probably intend to ride or lift, but researchers found that only about half (52% of bicycles and 49% of weight equipment) were in use a year later (Brooks, 1988). Organizations as the National Sporting Goods Association and the American Recreation Equipment Association provide useful information and support to recreation product retailers.

Services

Service providers generally focus on a specific activity. Examples of recreation services offered are aquatic centers, fishing ponds, fitness centers, bowling lanes, martial arts studios, aerobic dance studios, video arcades, and billiard rooms. These recreation businesses increase their market shares by using a variety of marketing strategies, although they may be vulnerable to changing market conditions. Long-term viability depends on distinguishing fads from long-lasting trends, and responding accordingly.

Recreation businesses need good marketing data. The key is to understand the motives that determine individual recreation behaviors and the forces that modify them. A range of information sources are available to help, including government agencies, universities, general trade and business groups, and industry-specific trade organizations such as the International Health, Racquet, and Sportsclub Association and the National Golf Foundation.

Hospitality and Food Services

Private recreation businesses provide lodging, food, and other services to local community residents as well as travelers. Resort communities, for example, have become a major component of the private recreation domain. Resorts are frequently planned around activity clusters (e.g., performing arts, gambling, the visual arts, skiing, golf, tennis), but aim to provide a total recreation experience. Resort communities have a dual nature, including home for permanent residents and travel destinations for temporary residents and tourists. Two types of recreation professionals may be found in resort communities: professionals who provide services for the permanent residents of the community, and professionals who work with temporary residents and tourists. Ideally, all recreation professionals work together to plan and use a community's resources effectively.

Another hospitality/resort business that has enjoyed success is the cruise ship industry. Its popularity can be traced to factors including nostalgia, strong marketing, and favorable sociodemographic trends (e.g., more single professionals, more double-income married couples, and a rising number of healthy and affluent older adults). Cruise ships provide millions of passengers with experiences as varied as traveling the Mississippi on paddle wheelers, island hopping in Hawaii or the Caribbean on luxury liners, and scenic and educational tours along the coasts of British Columbia and Alaska. One trade group serving this industry is the Cruise Line International Association.

Issues Surrounding
Private Recreation Businesses

Private businesses differ from the public sector with respect to organizational motives, job characteristics, and work motivators. Studies reveal many participants perceive differences both between the type of services and facilities offered by public and private sector organizations and between the people employed in the two sectors (Bogle, Havitz & Dimanche, 1992).

Customers may also be different. The private recreation business sector is, for example, perceived as more responsive to changing market conditions than is the public sector. They must be responsive if they are to remain in business and attract customers, and thus make a profit. Recreation businesspeople can make large capital investments that can be lucrative, but they also can expose owners and investors to financial risks.

Safety and legal issues can be another significant difference between private and other sectors providing recreation services. Recreation business operators generally push risk boundaries more than their public and nonprofit sector counterparts. They treat recreation as an end rather than as a means toward desirable outcomes, although these purposes are not necessarily mutually exclusive. Recreation businesspeople may regard some activities like drinking or gambling as acceptable that would be regarded as unsuitable for public-sector agencies. The ability to capitalize on market opportunities characterizes the history of the private sector.

The three sectors of recreation services usually have different missions as described early in this book. Public and nonprofit recreation agencies emerged to meet specific social needs. Most public and nonprofit recreation professionals continue to believe that even if market-based approaches to the delivery of recreation services must be implemented, their services must nonetheless be sustainable and socially and environmentally beneficial. Public recreation professionals are accountable to elected officials and ultimately to the citizenry. Public professionals also operate under the scrutiny of the media, appear at public hearings, respond to citizen advisory boards, and comply with requirements for open meetings.

The private recreation sector, on the other hand, generally faces none of this external oversight. These business professionals and employees receive less pressure to consider the social and environmental consequences of their programs, goods, and services. Some private recreation operators consider themselves less obligated to educate and inform customers than to "give them exactly what they want." Retailers of jet skis, snow machines, and all-terrain vehicles, for example, quite likely have different views on the value of those products than public employees charged with preserving both natural resources and the civil peace. Because a product *can* be sold or used does not mean it *should* be. Many private recreation business owners and operators, however, do have high ethical standards regarding the products and services they provide. Being employed in private recreation business does not mean that social and environmental sustainability are not important, and many professionals recognize this concern.

Unlike the public and nonprofit sectors, private recreation providers may have less responsibility to serve underrepresented or disadvantaged members of the community. Private recreation providers target individuals who are participating in particular activities who are willing and able to pay for products and services. As emphasized, the inevitable bottom line is that private recreation enterprises generally must be concerned with profit margins.

Many entrepreneurial and employment opportunities exist in the private recreation sector. This area continues to grow. Knowledgeable and socially responsible professionals are needed for these businesses. The mission of most private recreation providers is market driven and may be different than the mission of the public or nonprofit sectors, which focus more on social services. All sectors, however, have a role to play in providing a variety of recreation opportunities for people in communities. Their relationships must be complementary, not competitive.

Reflection Questions

1. Think about the past week. What businesses have you associated with that might be considered private or commercial recreation providers?

2. Have you known any people who might be called entrepreneurs? What characterized them?

3. What products or services might private recreation businesses be better able to provide than public or nonprofit organizations? Conversely, what services might be better provided by the public and/or nonprofit sectors?

4. Compared to other recreation services sectors, what advantages might be associated with owning one's own recreation business?

5. Sustainability related to social, economic, and environmental aspects is the focus of this book. If the economic outcomes are a primary goal of private businesses, how would social and environmental issues support this economic focus?

Chapter 24

Sustainable Tourism

As an area of study within recreation services, tourism is a relative newcomer. Prior to 1980, a chapter in an introductory book on recreation services that dealt specifically with tourism and travel was not likely to be found. Today tourism is recognized as a vital element related to people's leisure experiences, and is a popular specialty within recreation services.

As noted in the previous chapter, tourism is often associated with private recreation businesses. However, similar to other career opportunities in recreation services, tourism can be connected to the public and nonprofit sectors. This chapter focuses on what tourism is and how it can be sustained. Sustainability is concerned with long-term maintenance with an emphasis on social, economic, and environmental dimensions. The thesis of this book is that sustainability should apply to all aspects of recreation services, but it may be especially important for tourism because of the frequent reliance on the natural and built environments.

Descriptions of Tourism

The field of tourism is difficult to define with its many facets. Several university departments across the United States have a title like the *Department of Recreation, Parks, and Tourism Management*. Some educators, however, argue that tourism should be an area of study in business schools because it is a collection of profit-focused industries. Others see tourism as part of the hospitality field. Others view tourism as a commodity or profession in its own right. The way that tourism professional preparation should be structured is debatable but there is no doubt that tourism is a major industry tied to leisure behaviors and interests. For the discussion in this book, the strong tie to recreation services is assumed.

Travel for trade and religious purposes dates back to ancient times. Tourism as a form of behavior is a more contemporary purpose. Tourism has become a major economic force and is possible for millions of people due to both technological advances and affluence. Tourist behavior ranges from trips to the beach to sunbathe and shop to trips to Antarctica to study its fragile ecosystem. It can involve traveling to an outdoor destination to ski, swim, or hike, but it can also mean taking city trips to Las Vegas to gamble, to New York City to attend a Broadway play, or to London to shop at Harrods. Traveling for pleasure, or tourism, has become popular enough in the past 100 years that it now warrants a system to manage and accommodate it.

Tourism is an outgrowth of people's desire to see other cultures, visit other environments, and have new and different experiences away from their everyday routines. **Tourism activities** with the greatest level of interest among U.S. adults in 2009 were in order of importance:

- visiting friends and relatives
- sightseeing
- going to beaches/waterfronts
- visiting zoos/aquariums/science museums
- going to natural areas such as a state or national park
- going on a cruise
- recreating in theme parks
- visiting a city
- visiting a mountain area (http://www.ustravel.org/news/press-kit/travel-facts-and-statistics)

Given the complexity of tourism, most professionals tend to define it by its characteristics or elements rather than by a single description. The elements most frequently mentioned are: distance traveled, motives of travel, and the time required for the visit.

The first characteristic of tourism generally involves a distance traveled. The United Nations (U.N.) definition of tourism requires one to cross an international border, while the U.S. Census Bureau defines a trip as traveling one hundred miles away from home. Both definitions are problematic. For example, skiers traveling from Denver to many of the Colorado ski resorts would go less than a hundred miles, but their behavior and impact on the local economy would be similar to those skiers coming from points several hundred miles away. On the other hand, it is highly unlikely that the residents of Juarez, Mexico, feel as if they are tourists when they cross the border each morning to work in El Paso, Texas.

The second characteristic is the reason for the trip. The U.S. Travel Data Center includes in its definition all motives for travel except those related to commuting to and from work, school-related travel, or travel involved in operating a vehicle such as a plane, train, or truck as part of employment. All the motives cited for other forms of recreation may hold true with tourism—a desire to relax, learn, and to have new adventures. Tourism also is perceived to have high status. Given the opportunity to travel, many people enjoy it. When they are unable to travel for tourism purposes, typical reasons include the costs involved, lack of free time, health limitations, fear and safety factors, or family situations.

The final consideration in tourism is the length of time away from home. Most definitions of tourism include a time frame such as the U.N.'s definition that requires a stay of at least 24 hours. Such a restriction, however, would eliminate many day trips in excess of a hundred miles for recreational purposes. In these day trips, the traveler exhibits the characteristics of a tourist. Consequently, most people who study travel and tourism are less concerned about the duration of the trip than the motives and distance traveled.

Given these parameters, a tourist would be defined as an individual who travels to a destination for recreation purposes. This definition allows a business traveler to become a tourist when a portion of the travel is recreational rather than work required. All tourists are travelers but not all travelers are tourists.

Forms of Tourism

Tourism can occur in numerous forms. *Mass tourism* has appealed to the majority of recreational travelers in the past. Mass tourism is convenient. Tourists generally are not required to adapt to the culture of the host when they see attractions or explore an area during mass tourism. Further, this travel may be with a tour group or individually planned. It may be organized or spontaneous and is system-dependent, relying heavily on promotion materials, tour guides, transportation systems, and hotel and motel chains.

Ecotourism, nature tourism, appropriate tourism, ethical tourism, and responsible tourism are some of the tourism descriptors emerging in recent years. These descriptors have overlapping and imprecise meanings, but all might be grouped under *alternative tourism* with the focus on sustainability. Alternative tourism is much different than mass tourism and is most often associated with ecotourism. The appeal of ecotourism is the opportunity to see and possibly become connected to threatened and endangered cultures, lands, and animals. Properly practiced, ecotourism is multifaceted with its low-impact, small-scale structure that educates the traveler. Ecotourism can also provide funds for conservation, help empower local communities, and foster respect for different cultures and human rights.

Niche tourism is a popular new form of tourism. A niche is a specialized interest that is shared by a small but interested group of people. Many forms of niche tourism can exist such as: culinary tourism, wine tourism, heritage tourism, LGBTQ tourism, medical tourism, religious tourism, slum tourism, nautical tourism, space tourism, war tourism, dark tourism, and weather tourism. Each niche has a particular area of emphasis. For example, dark tourism involves visits to "dark" sites such as battlegrounds, scenes of horrific crimes or acts (e.g., concentration camps, mass murder scenes). Motivations for dark tourism might relate to mourning, remembrance, education, macabre curiosity, or even entertainment.

Agriculture tourism, sometimes called agritourism, sustainable agriculture, or agritainment, is a form of niche tourism that has rapidly grown in recent years. It involves any agriculturally-related activity that brings people to a ranch or a farm. It may mean staying on a farm or ranch overnight, or coming to participate in activities or events related to hay rides, feeding barnyard animals, pick-your-own fruits and vegetables, fishing, horseback riding, pumpkin patches, corn mazes, or buying directly from farmers.

Another emerging area relates to *volunteer tourism*. This type of tourism is also called volunteer travel, volunteer vacations, or voluntourism. The essence is to travel and volunteer for a charitable cause. These vacations can vary greatly from low-skill improvements to natural areas (e.g., maintenance of trails) to high-skill medical aid (e.g., volunteering in a clinic in a rural area). Some types of travel might also engage people with scientific research. Regardless of the volunteer opportunity, participants want to do good while also experiencing new cultures and challenges. Participants usually pay for the opportunities to engage in these types of projects.

Sports tourism is another big interest that some people have. Sports tourism might include travel to participate (e.g., to play in a tournament, run a marathon, or some other active involvement), to spectate (e.g., football bowl games, Olympics, Commonwealth Games, Asian Games, FIFA World Cup), or to go to sport museums or iconic places associated with sports (e.g., Sports Hall of Fame or a former site of Olympic Games such as a stadium or a bobsled run). For large participant or spectator events, travel companies often gain tickets or entry allocation and then sell them in packages that include flights, hotels, and excursions.

The Tourism Industry

Other than the recreation activities, tourism is also dependent on infrastructure, accommodations, and services. People need transportation to get to tourist destinations and require accommodations and dining opportunities once they arrive. Although many people travel for business, many hotels would not exist without tourists and mass tourism. Table 24.1 shows the billions of dollars spent on various aspects of the tourism industry within the United States.

Table 24.1 Real Tourism Output in the United States: 2009
[In billions of dollars (574 represents 574,000,000,000)].
Numbers rounded to the nearest billion.

Commodity	Direct Output (Current Dollars)
Total	**699**
Traveler accommodations	131
Food services and drinking places	112
Domestic passenger air transportation services	67
International passenger air transportation services	45
Passenger rail transportation services	2
Passenger water transportation services	11
Interurban bus transportation	2
Interurban charter bus transportation	1
Urban transit systems and other transportation services	4
Taxi service	5
Scenic and sightseeing transportation services	3
Automotive rental	31
Other vehicle rental	1
Automotive repair services	15
Parking lots and garages	2
Highway tolls	1
Travel arrangement and reservation services	35
Motion pictures and performing arts	12
Spectator sports	7
Participant sports	10
Gambling	41
All other recreation and entertainment	17
Gasoline	51
Nondurable PCE[1] commodities other than gasoline	96

[1] Personal consumption expenditures.

Source: U.S. Bureau of Economic Analysis, "Industry Economic Accounts, U.S. Travel and Tourism Satellite Accounts for 2005–2009," http://www.bea.gov/industry/

In addition to the basic elements of the travel industry (i.e., hotels, transportation), tourism requires the additional component of attractions. Activities, sites, and relationships bring tourists to a given destination for recreation purposes. The activities might include shopping, sightseeing, dining, active participation (e.g., skiing, horseback riding, attending the opera), spectating, or structured tours. The success of tourism largely depends on the successful interaction of travelers, hosts, private businesses, and governmental policy.

People who reside permanently in tourist destinations are called *hosts*. Depending on the importance of the tourist industry to them, hosts often have a love/hate relationship with tourism. Sometimes host community residents are not universally happy to see their area become a travel destination. They understand the positive economic impact tourism brings to their communities, but they also know that with the travelers come longer lines at local restaurants, crowded highways, potentially increased criminal activity, and inflated prices on local goods and services. They understand the symbiotic relationship that exists between travelers and the host environment with its services and attractions. The degree that local citizens are involved in tourism planning and development may directly relate to the attitude the hosts have toward its visitors and the visitors' view of the community's hospitality.

From a marketing standpoint, local *private businesses* usually differentiate the host from the tourist. By knowing the tourists' origins and behaviors (e.g., their cultural traditions, interests, income, and motives), local merchants can prepare for them. These businesspeople also know if these products and services will be needed or wanted by local residents and can make adjustments accordingly. In addition, these business people may provide various incentives (e.g., reduced rates) to attract guests.

Local governmental officials also are interested in tourism. Tourists have an influence on government services such as police and fire protection, public transportation, health and sanitation, water treatment, and local parks and public areas. Officials in local governments must consider the impact of tourist activities before embarking on a course of action to attract visitors. For example, the building of a sewage treatment plant with a capacity many times greater than that required by the local residents may be necessary to meet the demands of its seasonal visitors.

The social, economic, and environmental impact of tourism is significant. Government and businesses must work closely to assure controlled tourism development and to minimize host and visitor conflicts as well as environmental degradation. Infrastructure must be considered. Highways, nearby airports, and parking lots, for example, are all needed for tourism to be successful. A tourist destination must be able to accommodate visitors with adequate water and sewage systems, police, fire, and medical services. In addition, people need to eat. Many people enjoy new cuisines when travelling but others prefer food that gives them a sense of security and familiarity (e.g., McDonald's, KFC).

Social Issues and Tourism

Like all industries undergoing growth and change, tourism has social challenges. The federal government addresses both regulation and promotion concerning tourism. Regulations to protect the safety of tourists, whether in the United States or traveling abroad, are important. How much tourism promotion is done to attract people to an area is also important. Some politicians believe that tourism promotion should be left to the private sector and should not involve the government. Others believe the government should be concerned because of the economic impact that tourism has on local communities and states.

Another problem confronting tourism, which is also an asset, is its variety. The tourism industry comprises many subsystems. At the local level, each state has its own set of laws governing operations, health, and safety. Coordination among levels of government, among private businesses, and between businesses and governments is critical to the operation and growth of the tourism industry. This coordination does not always exist as well as it could.

The effect that tourism has on social systems and culture is a third issue that has become more prominent with discussions about sustainable tourism. Many people view tourism as a savior for economically depressed areas, especially if the region has a strong natural resource base as one of its attractions. However, potential negative costs must be considered as well as economic gains. Pollution, infrastructure costs, and seasonal unemployment issues can occur. An underdeveloped infrastructure or poor labor market can negatively affect a destination in much the same way that under-capitalization may negatively affect a start-up industry.

Before a community embarks on the path of becoming a tourist destination it should carefully weigh the gains and losses. Cases exist where tourism has transformed or destroyed local social traditions and crafts. Rather than reflecting the values and interests of the community, local traditions can come to reflect the market. In some cases trinkets have replaced native crafts, or the demand for inexpensive souvenirs has caused a decline in craft quality. The designs of many Amish quilts, for example, may no longer have meaning to the Amish if they become the designs most popular with the tourists. Dance rituals of American Indians once performed for their own sake are now sometimes done at specific times for monetary reasons just to please crowds.

Freedom of movement is taken for granted in the United States. This freedom, however, is not universal. Even the U.S. government restricts the travel of citizens to certain countries during periods of unrest or political disagreements. Cuba, for example, in the 1950s was a major tourist destination for thousands of Americans but was placed off limits to travelers once the U.S. government broke off diplomatic relations. In 2011, some of the restrictions on travel to Cuba were eased. Nevertheless, international tourism requires agreements covering who can enter a country, air and ground transportation, what products can be taken across borders, and what tariffs must be paid.

Economic Impacts

From a global perspective, the tourist industry is worth trillions of dollars. Tourism in the United States is valued at more than $700 billion and ranks among the top five private employers in the country. It employs more than 10 million American workers. Spending by travelers is responsible for more than $113 billion in tax revenues alone that are used to support a number of projects in communities (http://www.poweroftravel.org). In addition, Americans spent $110 billion in travel to countries outside the United States in 2010 (http://data.worldbank.org/industries).

At the local level, the economic impact of tourism can be significant. For example, the Charlotte, North Carolina, Chamber of Commerce estimated that the National Basketball Association's all-star game in a recent year had a $15 million impact on the Charlotte region and that the sales tax generated from visitors to the Coca-Cola 600 stock car race was equal to having 22 new property owners paying property tax.

From an incidental economic perspective, consider the laundry operator who has a contract with a local convention hotel, the food wholesaler who provides hamburgers or salad materials to a theme park, or the furniture company that provides beds, carpets, and television sets for a regional motel chain. Probably none of these workers (i.e., the food producer, the furniture maker, the local laundry worker) would consider himself or herself being employed in the tourist industry. Yet their jobs economically relate directly to tourism.

Environmental Issues and Tourism

A great concern expressed by many individuals interested in sustainability is the impact of tourism on the natural environment. Tourism depends almost wholly on the environment. If the environment degrades, many forms of tourism may diminish. Sustainable tourism development can be the impetus for structural change within society by moving away from a strictly economic focus toward not compromising the future socially or environmentally (Fennell, 1999).

Sustainable tourism relates to not consuming natural resources at a higher rate than they can be replaced, maintaining biological diversity, recognizing and valuing the aesthetic appeal of an area, following ethical principles that respect local cultures, and involving and consulting local people (Williams, 1998). Mass tourism is typically not sustainable in many of these ways. The principles of ecosystem management and human ecology must be considered for tourism to remain sustainable (Fennell, 1999).

Ecotourism was described earlier in this chapter. The premises of ecotourism are built solely on sustainability. Further, people who earn their living from ecotourism are more likely to defend natural resources against destructive activities. Many of the most remote corners of the earth are now accessible by modern transportation. Using ecotourism to create awareness that these areas exist might help protect them. The assumption is that ecotourists will fight to keep wild places wild because they have seen these areas and have been touched by their beauty and the life forms that exist there.

Tourism professionals must consider how to adopt a greener agenda. A green agenda is appropriate for all recreation services, but since tourism is so dependent on natural as well as built environments, green agendas are necessary for the future. Fennell (1999) suggested that perhaps the most important aspect facing tourism planners and managers is *not* to insert small numbers of environmentally aware people into pristine environments, but to improve the sustainability of ethical and responsible mass tourism. One role may be to demonstrate the ability of the tourism industry to become more ecologically accountable.

Further, tourism is often influenced by climate and weather. For example, hurricanes on the seacoast can cause billions of dollars of damage and negatively affect tourist destinations. Sometimes even the possibility of natural disasters such as hurricanes keeps people from visiting a potential destination. Tourists have the choice to go or not to go to a locale, but the destination itself cannot move due to weather or natural disasters. These environmental issues cannot be controlled but they should be considered relative to tourist behaviors.

New forms of tourism will bring new challenges and more demanding standards for sustainable tourism development. The industry and professionals facilitating tourism must appreciate and manage change to address the ethics of sustainability.

Tourism and Employment in the Future

Tourism will likely remain strong in the United States as well as throughout the world. Globalization brings the world ever closer and the media continues to generate interest in opportunities for adventure near and far. The service economy continues to grow. Further, social changes may influence the types of tourism activities available. For example, with the aging population in the United States, package tours (i.e., having the travel agent attend to all the travel details so all the tourist has to do is participate) may become more important. Turning the details over to someone else may be why the cruise ship industry has been so successful. Tour planning is likely to be a fruitful area of employment for interested individuals in the future.

Big corporations like hotel chains and Walt Disney World are involved in tourism, but the majority of the tourist operations in the United States are operations employing 25 or fewer persons. The small operators serve as the backbone of the industry. Within tourism, countless opportunities exist for professionals who want to try their entrepreneurial skills by providing travelers with information, offering services to destination, and programming and managing for tourists at their destinations.

Tourism affects everyone. Although not all recreation professionals are involved directly with tourism activities, most will be tourists from time to time. Like some other recreation businesses, tourism can be criticized for contributing to pollution, immorality, urban blight, and related social problems. On the other hand, it also has the potential for bringing to the public creative stimulating experiences and aesthetic surroundings. Tourism has the potential to foster cultural understanding and possibly, world peace.

Sustainable tourism can be maximized when all sectors of society work cooperatively to provide quality leisure experiences and recreation services. Every time a community develops an attraction for visitors, additional recreation opportunities are made available for citizens. When a community develops public recreation areas or encourages private entrepreneurs to operate attractions, the area may become attractive as a tourist destination. The systems are interactive and interdependent. The future of tourism will lie in how it can be sustained in a way that results in economic development but also maintains human and environmental integrity. Well-educated and creative professionals will be needed in this area of recreation services.

Reflection Questions

1. When were you most recently a tourist? Where did you go? What did you do? Why did you make this choice?

2. If you had the choice of any type of tourism experience, would you be more interested in a mass tourism opportunity or an alternative form of tourism? What appeals to you about that choice?

3. Why is it important to be able to define the characteristics of a tourist?

4. What are the advantages and disadvantages of tourism to a local community?

5. Should state and local governments be involved in marketing tourism or is this the job of the individual tourism businesses? What advantages might exist in each case?

6. What are some ways that a greener agenda might be applied to tourism?

Chapter 25

Therapeutic Recreation Services

Leaders in the recreation movement held from its beginnings over 100 years ago that recreation opportunities should exist for all people. The values of play and leisure experiences are well-documented. Unfortunately, not all citizens have had equal opportunities to participate in recreation services. Conditions such as limited economic resources, racial and ethnic prejudices, transportation difficulties, age and gender discrimination, and disability can create inequity, resulting in groups becoming marginalized and lacking access to the benefits of recreation services.

All professionals in recreation services have an ethical responsibility to increase recreation opportunities for persons with marginalized status. However, therapeutic recreation professionals have been on the forefront of advocating that people with disabilities as well as other marginalized individuals have access to leisure opportunities whether in communities, the outdoors, or through sport and tourism activities.

The purpose of this chapter is to discuss how therapeutic recreation specialists can facilitate leisure experiences for people with disabilities. Career opportunities in therapeutic recreation exist in clinical settings as well as in communities. Therapeutic recreation specialists work with clients of all ages, from children all the way to older adults. They work in public parks and recreation programs, nonprofit disability-focused groups, and in public and private hospitals. They work with people having a range of physical and mental disabilities. Further, these specialists use all forms of recreation activities (e.g., sports, arts, outdoors) in their work. A group that has received particular attention in recent years is the veterans with disabilities returning from the Afghanistan and Iraq wars.

People with Disabilities and Inclusion

People with disabilities make up approximately 17% of the U.S. population. With the growing older adult population, this percentage may increase in the future. Disability is defined as the inability to perform one or more major life activities of self-care, range of motion, manipulation, communication, learning, working, cognitive processing, or maintaining relationships. A disability may be physical, cognitive, mental, sensory, emotional, developmental, or some combination of these areas. Most people will experience some type of disability in their life, even if it is only temporary (e.g., a broken arm). Regardless of whether a disability is short-term or permanent, it may interfere with the ability to experience leisure and participate in recreation services to the fullest extent possible.

The treatment of people with disabilities has changed over the years. At one time, people with some disabilities (e.g., people with developmental disabilities, people who were blind) were placed in institutions where they had little contact with the outside world. This approach ended with a new philosophy that people should have services available to them in the community. Regarding recreation, many public recreation departments focused on people with disabilities through "special recreation." This term is no longer used since the new philosophy and mandate of the Americans with Disabilities Act (ADA) focuses on the inclusion of people with disabilities in all recreation services.

The ADA specifies that no one shall be denied opportunities, segregated, or otherwise discriminated against based on their disabilities. Along with housing, employment, and transportation, the law specifically identifies recreation (i.e., public, nonprofit, and private business) as areas to address. Public services, such as parks and recreation programs and public accommodations (e.g., restaurants, hotels, movie theaters, museums, zoos), must ensure that people with disabilities are not unnecessarily separated, omitted, or discriminated against. As a result, activities that previously separated people with disabilities from those without disabilities have had to be reevaluated to ensure equity (i.e., fairness) and to establish that people are not segregated or discriminated against based on disability.

The ADA requires that agencies evaluate their facilities and services before renovating and plan proactively about architectural changes and modifications to include people with disabilities. Human-made and natural barriers can pose restrictions. Ramps, doors large enough to accommodate wheelchairs, curb cuts, and well-defined walking areas improve access. These improvements benefit all participants (e.g., parents with strollers, older adults) but especially enhance opportunities for people with disabilities.

Rather than offering special programs as the only option for people with disabilities, the trend is to provide supports within all recreation programs to increase inclusive opportunities. For most individuals, providing recreation-program accessibility through the elimination of the economic, physical, and social barriers reduces the need for special programs.

Inclusion, however, is more than placing people with disabilities in a group of people without disabilities. Inclusion involves social interaction as well as physical integration. Providing support includes expressing an acceptance of a person and their abilities and enhancing participation at the individual's desired level of independence. Although making a recreation environment physically accessible is important, if participants do not feel welcome in the setting, inclusion cannot occur.

Not only should the public sector respond to increased recreation services for people with disabilities, but private businesses and nonprofit organizations have ethical responsibilities to consider how inclusion can be facilitated. For example, some travel resource guides explain accommodations and access for people with disabilities seeking air travel, cruises, and admittance to theme parks. Museums and theaters have headphones and tapes that describe the objects of art in a gallery or the movements of dancers on the stage for those with visual impairments. Ski resorts now rent pull sleds, outriggers, and monoskis (i.e., ski equipment that does not require the use of legs) for skiers with orthopedic impairments such as amputations and paralysis. Wheelchair designers have streamlined and adapted chairs to facilitate wheelchair activities such as tennis, basketball, and marathon racing. A bowling ball ramp can help anyone, from small children to those with temporary back problems, to participate in bowling. The investment often is small for businesses but a big benefit to the users.

Although inclusion is important, in some cases specialized services are necessary and desired. The continuum of recreation services for people with disabilities cannot be easily dichotomized into specialized or inclusive programs. People may be anywhere along the continuum. People with disabilities should be able to choose differing degrees of inclusive participation. Thinking about how support can be provided, and not necessarily how to provide specific activities, is key to understanding the difference between specialized and inclusive recreation. Choice is the core of both approaches. For many of the specialized services, Certified Therapeutic Recreation Specialists are needed.

Goals of
Therapeutic Recreation

All recreation activities can be therapeutic. In thinking about the benefits obtained from recreation services, all recreation professionals contribute to therapeutic gains. However, a specialty area in recreation services focused specifically on people with disabilities and their rehabilitation and enhanced quality of life is called therapeutic recreation.

Therapeutic recreation, which is also called recreation therapy or recreational therapy, is a process where activities and experiences are chosen and implemented with specific purposeful goals for individuals with disabilities. Therapeutic recreation may occur in public agencies in communities, nonprofit agencies and hospitals, and in private businesses and clinical settings.

Therapeutic recreation services involve the use of recreation activities, education, and personal support to enhance the lives of people. Services may support the improvement or maintenance of functional daily living skills, social skill development, and/or health and wellness. Professionals involved in offering recreation therapy attempt to modify or reinforce behaviors through recreation and play experiences.

The goals addressed in therapeutic recreation are as varied as the participants or clients involved. Goals generally relate to enhancing functioning in life or leisure skills, increasing personal choice, gaining control over one's own life and community membership, and the maintenance or improvement of optimal health and quality of life. The prevention of illness and the promotion of healthy behaviors are also important goals of therapeutic recreation. These goals usually address the four domains of function: cognitive, social, emotional, and physical. The goals of recreation therapy also depend on the philosophy and function of the agency offering the recreation services, and the importance of these goals to individual needs and desires. The recreation therapist must assume a variety of roles to reach therapeutic goals.

Recreation therapists are also educators. Within the framework of therapeutic recreation services, leisure education includes helping individuals increase their leisure and recreation awareness, identifying attitudes and values, developing decision-making and problem-solving skills, and becoming knowledgeable of the recreation resources in communities.

Therapeutic recreation has evolved relative to some goals during its history. Therapeutic recreation started as mainly a diversion for children in pediatric units of hospitals in the 1920s. In the late 1940s providers of therapeutic-recreation-type services united through organizations such as the American Recreation Society and the National Association of Recreation Therapists to advance the field, especially after men returned from WWII with disabilities.

Today, the American Therapeutic Recreation Association (ATRA) is the primary professional organization supporting recreation therapists. To become a Certified Therapeutic Recreation Specialist (CTRS), a professional must successfully complete certain educational requirements, including a supervised internship under a certified recreation therapist and pass the therapeutic recreation certification examination. This certification is monitored through the National Council on Therapeutic Recreation Certification (NCTRC). Similar to other certifications, professional continuing education is necessary to retain the CTRS status.

The Scope of Therapeutic Recreation

A CTRS wears many hats depending on the needs of the individuals with disabilities and the mission of the employing agency. The CTRS educates individuals about leisure options, personal interests, barriers, needs, resources, and/or acquisition of functional skills. The CTRS may also facilitate recreation experiences conducive to the individual making choices, applying knowledge, or practicing newly acquired recreation as well as decision-making skills.

Several assumptions exist about therapeutic recreation. First, individuals needing therapeutic recreation services generally have some barrier (e.g., physical, mental, emotional, or social) to life fulfillment. Second, the individual population addressed through therapeutic recreation is not homogeneous. A variety of impairments, levels of functioning, and needs for intervention exist. Although most therapeutic recreation specialists work with people with disabilities, services might also be appropriate for people confronting lifespan transitions such as divorce, retirement, or as a preventive intervention for persons who are workaholics.

Just as individuals vary, so do settings where therapeutic recreation occurs. Changes in healthcare—such as reduced length of stay in hospitals and emphasis on services in the community—are resulting in more jobs for therapeutic recreation specialists outside traditional hospital settings. Therapeutic recreation occurring outside hospital settings is not a new concept. A recreation therapist in a community center providing a program for cancer survivors aiding them with their recovery to health is just as much therapeutic recreation as is the recreation therapist leading an anger management group in a psychiatric hospital. The majority of CTRSs work in institutional and hospital-type settings.

Inpatient facilities in hospitals, rehabilitation centers, healthcare centers, and correctional institutions exist because community services do not exist. In these facilities and settings, the CTRS works as a member of a team that will include doctors, nurses, physical therapists, occupational therapists, social workers, and nutritionists. Together these professionals provide a range of both group and individual interventions that address the functioning of individuals.

One of the fastest growing areas of employment for therapeutic recreation specialists, however, is with older adults in long-term care and skilled nursing facilities. Job growth in that area is projected because of the aging population in the United States. Regardless, only 5% of the population of this country resides in an institution at any given time. Thus, many persons are receiving therapeutic recreation services in agencies based in the community. These agencies include local mental health centers, outpatient clinics, public recreation departments, schools, and through home-based care providers.

Some public recreation departments and nonprofit organizations employ CTRSs to work not only toward inclusion but with specialized groups. These programs often have a training or skill-acquisition focus to help participants gain abilities to pursue inclusive recreation. These programs may also use trained volunteers to assist with the programs. Programs might include wheelchair tennis clinics or ballet for people with developmental disabilities. Social clubs or Friday night dances may be popular recreation programs often marketed to persons with particular disabilities. Examples of nonprofit organizations that offer specialized recreation programs include Special Olympics, Wheelchair & Ambulatory Sports USA, and the National Sports Center for the Disabled.

Special Olympics (SO) is an international program of year-round sports training and athletic competition for children and adults with mental retardation. SO began in 1968, and today athletes from all 50 states and over 150 countries compete with other athletes of similar ability. The intent of SO is for athletes to have an avenue to test their skills, be motivated to continue to grow and develop, and share friendships and experiences.

Wheelchair and Ambulatory Sports, USA (WASUSA) began in 1956 to provide competitive opportunities for wheelchair users, including many WWII veterans. Today, WASUSA provides athletic experiences for athletes with disabilities paralleling those of the able-bodied, from novice through elite levels. Formerly only for wheelchair athletes, the organization now includes people with blindness, cerebral palsy, and amputees. The organization is a member organization of the United States Olympic Committee and elite athletes can qualify for the Paralympic Games.

The **National Sports Center for the Disabled** (NSCD) began in 1970 with ski lessons for children who had amputations. Today it provides therapeutic sports and recreation programs for thousands of people of any age or mental/physical ability. NSCD serves people each year at ski slopes, mountain trails, and playing fields to experience the adventure of outdoor recreation and sports.

CTRSs and other recreation professionals as well as volunteers working with people with disabilities in communities clearly provide important recreation services. However, progress has been slow regarding inclusion with barriers such as money, transportation, awareness of need, and inadequately trained staff (Devine & Kotowski, 1999). The ADA has affected recreation services for people with disabilities, although much of that act has yet to be fully implemented in communities.

Therapeutic Recreation Opportunities

Therapeutic recreation is a process of working with individuals with a variety of disabilities to determine strategies for accomplishing goals to enhance their well-being. Professionals working in the field of therapeutic recreation appreciate the potential that every individual has. These professionals also believe that medicine is not only about treating illness but preventing health problems in the future.

Although therapeutic recreation is a relatively small field, opportunities for employment are broad. Many types of disabilities exist that need professionals with professional education and a commitment to serve. As noted earlier, the number of older adults who require institutional care will grow in the future. In addition, the awareness of the medical problems, both physical and mental, of returning veterans is resulting in new therapeutic services. Therapeutic recreation may not be as visible as physical or occupational therapy, but it offers benefits that cannot be found in other therapies.

All recreation activities can have benefits. Therapeutic recreation, however, is the use of the inherent and structured benefits of a recreation activity to address functional deficits. Both community and facility-based clinical recreation opportunities are necessary to provide a full range of options for people with varied physical, social, mental, and cognitive disadvantages.

Reflection Questions

1. Do you believe all recreation is therapeutic? Support your opinion.

2. What is the difference between specialized and inclusive recreation services for people with disabilities?

3. The Americans with Disabilities Act was passed over 20 years ago. Why do you suppose it has taken so long for the act to be effective?

4. Professionals working with people with disabilities have the option to become Certified Therapeutic Recreation Specialists. Getting the certification means an individual must meet basic requirements, take an exam, and pay a fee. What would be the advantages to obtaining this certification?

5. Will the day come when there is no longer a need for specialized services? When might specialized services be more desirable than inclusive opportunities?

6. How do the goals of therapeutic recreation differ from the goals of other specialties?

Chapter 26

Sport and Golf Management

Sports are huge in the United States and around the world. They are everywhere—in schools, on the playground, on television, and in sports stadiums. The sports industry is complex and encompasses a range of participants from young children to professional athletes. Sports can occur in informal ways (e.g., backyard baseball) and as major events (e.g., NCAA basketball tournaments, Olympics). Social, political, and economic forces shape sports from the local to the international level. Further, golf is a specific sport activity that has received academic standing because of the efforts of the Professional Golf Association.

Sport management, as well as golf management, grew as important fields of study in the latter half of the 21st century. Once associated primarily with physical education, sport management now has its own curriculum and growing body of knowledge. Sport management is not always associated with recreation services curricula, since it may have its academic home in sports sciences or business management. However, sport as well as golf management offer many recreation benefits for both spectators and participants. The focus of this chapter is in providing an overview of sports and specifically sport management as a component of recreation services. Golf management is also discussed as a career specialty.

Sports Background

Sports include a range of activities that involve rules, physical exertion, and/or coordination and competition between individuals or teams. Sports generally require demonstrating physical prowess, and the rules of a sport determine the outcome of the activity (i.e., winning or losing). However, sports are sometimes used to describe any type of competition regardless of physical prerequisites (e.g., NASCAR). Sports can have elements not related to physical ability, but these examples are less common than the assumption of some type of physical exertion (i.e., either watching athletes or active participation).

The difference between *sport* and *sports* is somewhat unclear, as they are used interchangeably. 'Sports' most often refer to particular activities, while 'sport' connotes the all-encompassing concept. Sport also can refer to organized entertainment (i.e., spectator) opportunities. Although the duality of physical participation and entertainment is a false dichotomy, they offer two ends of a spectrum related to thinking about sports and sport management. Regardless, both have implications for leisure behavior whether as a spectator or active participant.

Sports and competitive games in some form have existed throughout history. The early Olympic Games in Greece, for example, were undertaken centuries ago with an emphasis on individual performance. Almost all team sports that are played today, however, can be traced to England (Masteralexis, Barr & Hums, 2011). During the 18th and 19th centuries, nobility in the British Empire had a sporting culture that spread throughout the U.S. colonies. Even sports that did not originate in England, like basketball and golf, initially employed English sport organization and management styles largely in the form of Sports Clubs.

In the United States, the traditional English system did not work as well, since the aristocracy was not as invested in the financial support of sports. In addition, the Industrial Revolution in the United States resulted in leisure becoming a part of the lives of the masses. People from all walks of life became interested in sports. Sports as we know them in the United States today were well on their way to being established over a century ago. Every popular sport today has a rich history regarding its evolution. However, the involvement of women as well as people of color in sport has a much shorter history related to the most popular sports. People of color as well as women have been involved in sport in the past (e.g., the Negro Baseball League, the sports leagues for women sponsored by factories and mills), but these opportunities did not receive widespread promotion or publicity. Needless to say, today sports are a marker of American culture from the perspective of enthusiastic participants as well as loyal spectators.

Sports participation is available for people of all ages. Most people, however, participate most in sports when they are children. Fewer adults are involved in sports participation, but the amount of involvement varies by sport. In addition, the popularity of sports tends to wax and wane. Table 26.1 shows the percentage of the U.S. population that participated in sports in 2010. It also indicates the relative change in the activity from the

Table 26.1 2010 Sports Participation Rates
(Participation means doing the activity at least once for anyone over 7 years old.)

Activity	Percent of Participants	Percent of Change*
Exercise Walking	95.8	2.6
Backpack/Wilderness Camp	11.1	-9.3
Exercising with Equipment	55.3	-3.4
Softball	10.8	-8.4
Swimming	51.9	3.4
Volleyball	10.6	-1.0
Camping (vacation/overnight)	44.7	-12.0
Dart Throwing	10.5	-14.1
Bicycle Riding	39.8	4.3
Football (tackle)	9.3	4.8
Bowling	39.0	-13.3
Skateboarding	7.7	-8.5
Aerobic Exercising	38.5	16.3
In-Line Roller Skating	7.5	-5.4
Hiking	37.7	10.9
Scooter Riding	7.4	-9.4
Workout at Club	36.3	-5.3
Skiing (alpine)	7.4	5.6
Running/Jogging	35.5	10.3
Mountain Biking (off road)	7.2	-13.5
Fishing	33.8	2.8
Archery (target)	6.5	-8.3
Weightlifting	31.5	-8.8
Paintball Games	6.1	-2.7
Basketball	26.9	10.1
Snowboarding	6.1	-1.2
Billiards/Pool	24.0	14.8
Kayaking	5.6	14.8
Golf	21.9	-2.0
Target Shooting (airgun)	5.3	2.4
Yoga	20.2	28.1
Hunting (bow & arrow)	5.2	-16.7
Boating, Motor/Power	20.0	-16.2
Water Skiing	5.2	0.6
Target Shooting (net)	19.8	0.3
Gymnastics	4.8	23.5
Hunting with Firearms	16.3	-13.5
Hockey (ice)	3.3	7.9
Soccer	13.5	-0.3
Muzzleloading	3.1	-19.6
Table Tennis	12.8	-3.7
Wrestling	2.9	-0.9
Baseball	12.5	8.9
Skiing (cross country)	2.0	19.5
Tennis	12.3	13.2

* Percent Change is from 2009
Source: http://www.nsga.org/files/public/2010Participation_Ranked_by_-
TotalParticipation_4Web.pdf

previous year. Walking is the number one activity, which could be argued regarding whether or not it meets the definition of a sport. Nevertheless, it is an important activity that can be done by most people and may be a way to become fit enough to participate in many of the other activities that are listed.

Sports spectating is also a huge recreation activity as well as a major economic impact on communities. Table 26.2 shows the changes in number of participants in selected sports comparing 1990, 2000, and 2009. The numbers of people attending continue to increase each decade with most of these spectator sports.

A Model of Sport Development

As has been emphasized so far in this chapter, sports provide a plethora of opportunities. Green (2005) provided a pyramid model of sports development that may show how sports can link recreation with big business. Figure 26.1 (see p. 258) shows an adaptation of the model. The pyramid does not suggest that elite sports is the epitome of involvement (i.e., at the top of the pyramid), but relates more to the relative numbers of people who might be involved at the various levels of sports. Although elite sport may have fewer athletes, the number of people who are spectators is huge, as noted above. However, on the bottom foundation of the pyramid, the ubiquity of sports is evident in how many people participate in recreational sports in schools and communities across the country.

Green (2005) contends that this pyramid is essential for providing a means to facilitate sports that can lead to elite opportunities. These levels allow for people (i.e., athletes) to begin, to continue, and to excel in sports. Providing these opportunities for involvement requires planning and evaluation on all levels by professionals with expertise in sport management. On the other hand, however, elite participation is of little interest to most people. Most people enjoy sports and the competition but are never going to be elite athletes.

Perspectives on Sport Management and Professional Education

Sport management as a career field can also be linked to the pyramid example of sport development. Career opportunities are available in recreational sports (e.g., through youth sports or community recreation programs),

Table 26.2 Selected Spectator Sports 1990, 2000, and 2010
[55,512 represents millions or 55,512,000 participants]

Sport	1990	2000	2009
Baseball, major leagues[1]			
Attendance	55,512	74,339	74,499
Regular season	54,824	72,748	73,054
National League	24,492	39,851	40,890
American League	30,332	32,898	32,164
Playoffs[2]	479	1,314	1,210
World Series	209	277	244
Basketball [3,4]			
NCAA-Men's college	28,741	29,025	32,821
NCAA-Women's college[5]	2,777	8,698	11,135
National hockey league[6]			
Regular season attendance	12,580	18,800	20,996
Playoffs attendance	1,356	1,525	1,702
Professional Rodeos[7]	754	688	570

[1] Source: Major League Baseball (previously, the National League of Professional Baseball Clubs), New York, NY, National League Green Book, and The American League of Professional Baseball Clubs, New York, NY, American League Red Book. [2] Beginning 1995, two rounds of playoffs were played. Priori years had one round. [3] Season ending in year shown. [4] Source: National Collegiate Athletic Association, Indianapolis, IN (copyright). [5] For women's attendance total, excludes double-headers with men's teams. [6] Source: National Hockey League, Montreal, Quebec. [7] Source: Professional Rodeo Cowboys Association, Colorado Springs, CO, Official Professional Rodeo Media Guide, annual (copyright).

competitive sports, and in elite performance sports. Individuals interested in recreation services would mostly align with recreational sports. However, individuals interested in facilitating spectator opportunities could work at competitive or elite levels as sports managers.

Sport management majors in colleges and universities did not begin until the 1960s, but by the mid-1990s these majors had become common in higher education. Prior to that time, community sports programming and management including youth sports were career options within a general recreation degree. New majors in sport management were prompted by the need for educated managers but also they were a way for traditional curricula in universities to attract students (Masteralexis et al., 2011). Whether there are enough professional jobs available for the number of sport management graduates is an issue that remains debatable.

As a professional field of study in the past several decades, however, sport management has tended to the business or management side of sports

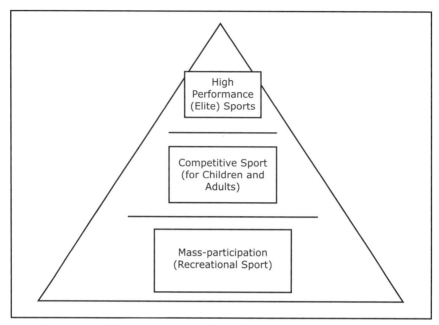

Figure 26.1 Adapted Pyramid Model of Sport Development (Green, 2005)

with the emphasis on sport as entertainment that needs to be managed. Most of these sport management programs are not necessarily associated with recreation services. According to the North American Society of Sport Management, sport management focuses on business applications to sports that may include sport marketing, employment perspectives, management competencies, event management, leadership, sport and the law, personnel management, facility management, organizational structures, fund-raising, and conflict resolution. Most of these applications by this definition relate *indirectly* to helping the public be more physically active and to promote physical health. Compelling reasons exist in today's society, however, to consider more directly the relationships among physical activity, sports, and health promotion whenever possible.

The philosophy of the university curriculum in which the sport management degree or emphasis exists may determine whether the focus is more on recreational sports participation or sport business management. Because of the attractiveness of sport management, some traditional recreation services faculty have been concerned about this field competing for recreation students. Dustin and Schwab (2008) likened this situation to a metaphor about a bird stealing the nest of another bird and taking over. Concerns have been expressed that sport management will subsume recreation management. Other researchers, however, (e.g., Gibson, 2008,

Edwards & Peachy, 2010) see the sport management curricula as highly compatible with recreation services.

A recent study by Schwab, Timmerman, Wells, and Dustin (in review) examined sports management programs housed within recreation, parks, and tourism academic departments and found that students had several perceptions regarding their sport management major:

- 89% of the students said they loved sports and wanted to work in the industry

- 69% said they enjoyed watching sports

- 67% said they enjoyed playing sports

- 48% said they were interested in the issues revolving around sport

- 39% said they thought there were many job opportunities in sport management

- 16% said they were interested in community-based sport programming

Although the reasons involved for pursuing sport management have a broad range, the skills necessary to be a successful sport management professional relate to behavioral as well as business skills. Masteralexis et al. (2011) identified some of those areas as human behavior, organizational skills, ethics, marketing, communication, finance, economic, and legal and governance aspects. A Master's degree in this area requires similar background skills along with research and evaluation competencies.

As in other areas of recreation, this knowledge base can be learned in a classroom. However, sport internships are a means to ensure that students have an opportunity to apply skills in actual situations under the advisement and guidance of practicing professionals. The more experience individuals can gain in terms of volunteer as well as part-time/seasonal work, the better prepared they will be for the professional world.

Career Opportunities

The sport industry has grown dramatically and is likely to continue to expand. Jobs in marketing and promotions, sports information, academic student services, and development within intercollegiate sports are available. Many communities offer youth sport programs through local park and recreation programs, schools, nonprofit youth organizations, and private club organizations (e.g., swim clubs, soccer clubs).

Universities offer sports opportunities through intramural sports as well as athletics administration. Other employment opportunities exist in professional sports with event management, facility management (e.g., arenas, stadiums, convention centers) and community relations. Further, employment options could include sporting goods manufacturing, sports agents, arena management, and sports tourism. Although not always considered part of sport management, the health and fitness industry is closely tied to sports. More about careers in this area are discussed in chapter 29 of this book.

The 2011 study by Schwab et al., uncovered that 70% of the students majoring in sport management were interested in athletic administration, 62% in personnel management, 57% in marketing, 47% in public relations, 42% in coaching, 32% in recreational sport programming, and 18% in retail. Further, when asked about their career goals after completing their sport management studies, interests included 26% professional sports, 15% pursuing an MBA or graduate school, 10% law school, 8% coaching, 8% collegiate sport, 6% athletic administration, 4% community recreation, and 12% did not know.

Consistent with the goals of sport management majors, Schwab et al. (under review) also found among sport management graduates that less than 20% currently worked in traditional park and recreation settings, 57% of sport management graduates worked in specific sport management settings, and about one third went into other related areas, but not sports. The coursework in curricula related to all the areas of recreation services resulted in competencies that could be applied to human services of many types.

Continuing Education Opportunities

Just as in other recreation services careers, many opportunities exist for continuing education. Several professional organizations and numerous interest groups provide support for individuals working in sport management. As mentioned earlier, the North American Society for Sport Management (NASSM) is directly related to the sports industry. Similar to other professional organizations, the purpose of this group is to promote, stimulate, and encourage study, research, scholarly writing, and professional development of sport management in both theoretical and applied areas.

Sports organizations have been formed across the globe; New Zealand and Australia have national organizations, and others exist in Europe, Asia, and Latin America.

Many magazines and journals are available that provide information about promising practices in management as well as research. The leading research journals are the *Journal of Sport Management* and the *Sport Management Review*, although there are many specific journals related to such aspects as sports business, sports marketing, sports behavior, and sports medicine. Many of these journals are relatively new because the field of study is still in early stages.

Certification is available in a variety of specific areas within sport management. Examples of certifications that can be obtained include sports coaching, sports fitness, personal training, sports strength and conditioning, and bodybuilding, to mention only a few.

University programs in sports management can also be accredited. The Commission on Sport Management Accreditation (COSMA) is a specialized accrediting body that promotes and recognizes excellence in sport management education in colleges and universities at the baccalaureate and graduate levels. The purpose of this accreditation is the same as has been discussed for other recreation services such as public parks and recreation. Accreditation assures the public of the quality of the education and provides a way to continually improve quality. COSMA was jointly established by the National Association for Sport and Physical Education (NASPE) and the North American Society for Sport Management (NASSM) in July 2008.

Golf Management

Golf management is a specific focus within recreation services. This major and the opportunities associated with the academic preparation have emerged in the past 20 years. This degree is highly specialized in universities and is sponsored and partially funded through the Professional Golf Association (PGA). The major exists in only 20 universities in the United States. However, just because an individual does not have a degree in golf management does not mean that opportunities are not available in this field. Nevertheless, the PGA sponsored curricula have been quite successful and have led to improving the quality of golf programs throughout the United States.

Sports historians usually trace golf's origins to a type of land hockey played in the middle ages. Three Scotsmen witnessed the game and took it home to Scotland where it took root. Traditionally golf has been played by wealthy individuals who could afford both the expensive materials and access to the desirable places to play. To some extent golf retains this upper-class image although now inexpensive or rental equipment is available as are publicly accessible golf courses, which along with the visibility of people of color and women in the sport have popularized the game (http://www.historyofsports.net/history_of_golf.html).

The PGA golf management program aims to create leaders in the golf industry. Professionalism and business concepts are applied directly to the golf industry. The PGA golf management university program is a 4.5- to 5-year college curriculum for aspiring golf professionals. The curriculum usually includes both general education and core golf requirements including such areas as turf grass management, food and beverage management, and golf course architecture.

The major often appeals to individuals who are interested in business management as well as sales and marketing and who want to make a positive impact on others through sport, recreation, and golf. The program provides students the opportunity to acquire the knowledge and skills necessary for success in the golf industry through classroom studies and internship experiences.

Examples of the types of employment that can be found in golf management include head golf professional, director of golf, teaching professional, ownership and executive management, golf clinician, college golf coach, golf retail, golf course planning and development, golf course maintenance, broadcasting and journalism, golf manufacturing manager, sales representative, tournament director, consultant, rules official, and golf equipment specialist.

The field of sport management is quite broad, as this brief introduction shows. Individuals interested in a specific area of sport management will find many opportunities to gain experience and academic coursework that can lead to a successful career in this area of recreation services.

Reflection Questions

1. What kinds of sports do you participate in? Did you begin this participation when you were a child? How has your sport participation changed over time?

2. Sport management majors can be found in different departments in universities. What advantages exist depending upon

whether sport management is a part of recreation services, sport sciences, or business management?

3. Golf management is a new area of study within recreation services. Why has this area developed as a specialized sport focus? Why do universities not have majors such as football management or tennis management?

4. Sport as entertainment or sport as participation can have similar leisure outcomes, but can also be quite different. What are the similarities and differences regarding the benefits an individual might receive from these two encounters with sports?

Chapter 27

Events Management

Thousands of special events occur annually in many places. For example, even though the United States has become urbanized and suburbanized, people still enjoy activities like agricultural fairs, rodeos, and folk festivals. Many small towns across the country have 4th of July celebrations, street fairs, and arts and crafts festivals.

Special events include popular well-known events (e.g., New Year's Eve in Times Square, Mardi Gras in New Orleans, Kentucky Derby in Louisville, Boston Marathon, Indianapolis 500) as well as sporting events and tournaments (e.g., NCAA Basketball Tournaments). Events can also be on a smaller scale such as corporate picnics and weddings. Regardless of the size, events create a sense of excitement and opportunity among visitors (i.e., guests) and local residents.

Special events are not new—think of the huge events occurring in stadiums in ancient Rome. Further, managing special events is not a new activity related to recreation services. However, it emerged as an important industry in the 1970s. In recent years it has become a rapidly growing area of emphasis within recreation services. Although these events may occur in all sectors of society, many special events rely on partnerships that are nurtured and developed. Basic skills of event management, regardless of the size, sector, or number of partners, include programming, leadership, and administration, as is common for most areas of recreation services. In this chapter, approaches to events planning and management are explored.

Defining Special Events

'Special events,' 'event planning,' and 'event management' are terms used interchangeably. Events by definition usually refer to a significant or important occurrence of some type. It also implies an activity that is exciting and perhaps unusual. Jackson (1997) defined special events as "extraordinary, non-spontaneous, planned occurrences designed to entertain, inform, or provide enjoyment and/or inspiration to audiences and/or spectators" (p. xii). He also suggested that advocacy of a product, service, message, or group can be a characteristic of these events. Volunteers are usually enlisted for these events and many events rely on financial sponsors. Event planning is described as the process of managing a project such as a meeting, convention, tradeshow, ceremony, or party.

The event manager, therefore, is the person who plans and executes the event. The Institute of Event Management described event management as comparable to directing a live stage performance. Event managers and their teams are often behind the scenes, running the event and coordinating every detail. They may also be involved in brand building, marketing, and implementing communication strategies. The event manager is an expert in the promotional and operational elements that enable an event to be successful. The ultimate purpose of any event is to create positive, lasting memories among the participants.

Special events can be classified or categorized in several ways. As noted above, however, these are always events that occur out of the ordinary. For example, a weekly bowling league would not be considered a special event. However, if a bowling tournament is hosted over a weekend once every year, the tournament might be considered a special event. Events can be grouped into several categories that describe the scope of activities (Jackson, 1997).

One category of events might be called neighborhood events. These are events put on by a group such as a homeowners association, a school, or a church. These events are usually quite limited in their scope and may be designed only for the audience involved with that group. For example, every 4th of July in my small neighborhood of 150 houses, a parade is organized. Children and adults simply show up with their parade equipment (i.e., bicycle, scooter, pet in a costume) and they promenade on the two main streets in the neighborhood.

A second category relates to personal or private events. For example, wedding planners are available to individuals who wish to have this type of event assistance. Planners can also be contracted to host large parties for children as well as adults, universities' social events, and family reunions. Private event planners customize the events to the needs of the client and provide a range of services. These events generally do not involve sponsorships but may include working with a number of informal volunteers to carry out the activities.

Corporate events may be considered a category of events, but can vary greatly from organizing a large national trade show to coordinating a local company picnic to recognize employee achievements. Corporate events are sometimes used to launch a new product or to retain loyal customers or loyal employees. A ground-breaking ceremony or a dedication ceremony for a new building might be examples of corporate-type events.

Another category is community or metropolitan events. These events are larger than neighborhood events and may encompass several neighborhoods or a whole city or county, or even several cities within an area. Examples might be community food festivals (e.g., Greek Festival, Hog Days), races (e.g., Race for the Cure), commemorations such as a Memorial Day service, amateur athletic events, music festivals, or job fairs.

Some events are statewide in nature. For example, many states have Senior Games that feature a statewide competition for older adults. Political parties typically have statewide conventions. Many other professional organizations also have state organizations that meet regularly at an annual conference. Tournaments for high school athletes usually have statewide involvement.

Regional and national events are also common. A regional event includes a number of states but may not include the entire country. National events are generally large events that draw many participants. Convention bureaus in cities across the country vie for national conferences and meetings. All types of religious, political, artistic, medical, and civic groups, to mention only a few, have national gatherings that draw crowds and that may have budgets in the millions of dollars.

International events are yet another area. The Olympic Games or the World Cup are well-known examples. However, many groups hold international competitions and gatherings related to a variety of global issues and special interests.

Skills in Managing Special Events

Basic core skills in recreation services management will be a necessary starting point when considering a career in event management. However, several competencies will be particularly important for event managers.

One important area relates to event marketing. Since special events do not occur on a weekly or monthly basis, participants have to find out about the special opportunity. The 4 P's of marketing commonly discussed apply to the skills needed: identifying the product, appropriate pricing, accessing the right place, and promoting the event. Each of these key ingredients is necessary to make an event work. Promotion is particularly important related to getting free publicity from the news media, advertising (i.e., the purchasing of time or space in media), and considering other forms of creative promotion that might excite people about participating.

An important attribute of successful event management is the ability to manage people including full-time, part-time, and volunteer staff. Although part-time and seasonal staff as well as volunteers are commonly found in recreation services, many events require volunteer personnel to make the event successful. Managing individuals to get the most from them and to help them feel like they are an important part of an enterprise is crucial. Another aspect related to participation relates to how to oversee large numbers of participants and audiences, which may include security and crowd control.

Many events rely on financial sponsorships. Therefore, an events management professional must be able to market events not only to potential participants but also to sponsors. Many businesses are willing to support special events, but most do not just walk in the door and offer to give the event a donation. Sponsors need to be approached, asked, and sold on the benefits of their sponsorship. Sponsorships by companies and corporations have been growing steadily for special events, but planners must know how to appeal to potential sponsors by offering them benefits such as positive publicity, heightened visibility, enhanced image, improved customer relationships, opportunities to sell their products directly, increased employee morale, and strategies to address targeted audiences.

Managing special events also requires an entrepreneurial spirit. Some event managers may work for other groups that contract services. Some event planners will work within organizations to sponsor such events (e.g., many public parks and recreation departments offer annual community festivals). Some individuals will establish their own special-events consulting businesses with the intent as an entrepreneur to sell services for a profit. All approaches require creativity and a drive to start and maintain something that will be exciting to participants.

These events also require the ability to oversee operations necessary for the event. This skill requires being able to see what is needed, secure the appropriate equipment, arrange transportation and parking, secure the physical site, arrange for decorations and food, coordinate communication, and consider the safety of all people associated with the event, to mention only a few of the tasks. A planner must be able to anticipate all the needed logistics for a successful event.

Finally, an events planner must be able to evaluate realistically and be ready to make changes and improvements in the future. Many tools exist for evaluation but the bottom line is that evaluation must take place. The operations must be evaluated as must the impact of sponsorships. If specific objectives for an event have been set, and they should be, then the objectives can be evaluated and benchmarked. Other aspects to consider evaluating are the attendance, demographics of participants, media coverage, and cash intake. Ways to evaluate might include attendance counts, surveys or polls, media impressions, and product sales (Schmader & Jackson, 1997).

All these characteristics of event managers are important. On the downside, however, individuals interested in careers in event planning and management must recognize how demanding the work can be (i.e., the hours can be long and irregular). Event managers must be good at multi-tasking, setting and meeting deadlines, and working with diverse groups of people.

Professional Opportunities

Special events management as an emphasis area related to recreation services is growing rapidly. Although the United States is slightly behind in curriculum development, other countries such as Australia have the majority of their students in recreation services curricula focused on events management. In addition to academic courses, associations and societies provide courses on the various aspects of event management such as catering, logistics, decor, study of law and licenses, risk management, and budgeting. Certifications can be acquired such as Certified Trade Show Marketer (CTSM), Certified Manager of Exhibits (CME), Global Certification in Meeting Management (CMM), Certified Meeting Professional (CMP), Certified Special Event Professional (CSEP), and Certified Wedding Planner.

Individuals who want to learn more about event management have several additional sources of information. One organization that exists is AEME, the Association for Events Management Education, which was established in 2004 with the mission to advance the education of the public in the subject of events and events management. The aim of the organization is to support and raise the profile of the events profession through the sharing of education and best practices.

The International Special Events Society (ISES) fosters management performance through education while emphasizing ethical conduct. It is comprised of 4,000 professionals in over 35 countries representing special event producers ranging from festivals to trade shows. The International Festivals and Events Association (IFEA) is a voluntary association of events, event producers, event suppliers, and related professionals and organizations whose common purpose is the production and presentation of festivals, events, and civic and private celebrations. IFEA officially represents members in 38 countries on 5 continents. In addition, the International Institute of Event Management offers educational opportunities, job listings, and certification opportunities in event management and wedding planning.

A journal called the *International Journal of Event Management Research* is available. It is a peer-reviewed e-journal that has as its purpose to enhance, disseminate, and promote research findings and good practice in all aspects of event management. Similar to other professional journals, the editorial staff encourages scholarly debate with a focus on understanding facets of event management.

The Future of Event Management

The area of event planning and management and all its associated possibilities is without a doubt one of the fastest growing emphasis areas within recreation services. Event management has become a big business around the world. One aspect that is gaining favor relates to sustainable event management (also known as event greening). This process can be applied to produce an event with particular concern for social, economic, and environmental issues. Social and environmental sustainability are consciously incorporated into decision making about the planning and implementation of events. Event greening must start when an event is first conceived and should involve all stakeholders in the event.

Job opportunities in event management exist in all sectors and the possibilities continue to expand. Most event management focuses on concerts, parades, parties, conventions, and special events and a professional can work for corporations, governments, nonprofit organizations, or in his or her own private business. Opportunities exist in public park and recreation programs as more communities use festivals and sports tournaments as part of their programs. Many nonprofit organizations use event managers to assist with fund-raising events. The tourism and hospitality industry recognizes the role that events can play in drawing people to particular locations and venues. Many corporations as well as universities also employ full-time event managers.

Reflection Questions

1. Think back to the past year. What special events have you attended? Were they large or small? Who was responsible for conducting the events?

2. What makes special events different from the daily recreation activities that you might do?

3. How do the skills required to be an events manager differ from skills required for other recreation services specialties?

4. How can events of all sizes be "greened"?

Chapter 28

Gerontology and Older Adults

Regardless of where you work or play, you will probably interact with older adults. The aging of America's population will both challenge and invigorate recreation services in the future. Most of today's older Americans will enjoy longer lives and better health than did previous generations.

Gerontology is the discipline associated with aging and older adults. Gerontology refers to the social, psychological, and biological aspects of aging. Because of the aging process, people modify their behaviors as they get older due to these changing aspects. Individuals interested in working with aging populations in recreation services focus on the implications that social, psychological, and biological changes have on leisure behavior. The efforts are quite interdisciplinary.

The terms used to describe older people vary, and they include 'older adults,' 'senior citizens,' 'seniors,' 'older Americans,' and 'the aged.' For this book, the term 'older adult' is used. Typically this older adult or senior citizen status begins at 65 years. This age distinction, however, also varies, as it might be defined at 50 years (e.g., AARP), 55 (e.g., Senior Games), 60 (e.g., for some senior citizen discounts), 62 (e.g., when people can get a Senior Pass to all U.S. public lands such as National Parks), 65 (e.g., the current age to receive Social Security, although it will change shortly), or 66 (e.g., the age for Social Security and Medicare for most Baby Boomers).

Age, however, is not the sole determinate of what might be considered *old*. Many people are old when they reach 60, whereas others are young at 80 years. A common saying these days is "60 is the new 40." Physical characteristics like gray hair and wrinkles may indicate the physical aging process, but the mind and spirit may suggest something different. Therefore, defining older adults and their recreation interests and needs will be highly variable in the future.

In this chapter, the status of older adults is discussed along with the continuum of recreation services for older adults that will be needed in the future. Services will range from therapeutic recreation for older people with illnesses and disabilities to community recreation programming so that older adults can find enjoyment in casual recreation opportunities just like younger populations.

The Aging Population

Historically, the U.S. population has been triangular, with the greatest number of persons being young and the fewest number being very old. This pyramid will dissipate into a rectangular graphic of age cohorts groups as childbirth continues to decline and more people move into older-age categories. Never before has any society faced a situation where the oldest age groups equal the numbers of persons in the youngest age groups.

The Baby Boomers are turning 65 and people are living longer than in the past. Figure 28.1 shows the increase in the older population both related to individuals over 65 and those over 85 and their projections into the future. The AARP (formerly called the American Association of Retired Persons) states that people over the age of 65 years are the fastest growing segment of the U.S. population, and persons over the age of 85 years represent the greatest growth of all groups.

People who are currently 65 years old can expect to live another 17–20 years, and will be joined by the surge of Baby Boomers entering older adulthood each day. According to the Administration on Aging, by 2030 almost 22% of the U.S. population will be over 65 years. Further, the percentages of persons over 65 who are minorities are growing at a rate faster than whites.

Older adults make up a heterogeneous collection of individuals with differing interests, values, experiences, health, income, and education. Many myths exist about older adults in society. Many of these myths are not true because of the great diversity among older adults. For example, not all older adults are feeble and live in nursing homes. In reality, approximately 95% of older adults live in the community and the majority own their own home. Most of the 5% who live in nursing facilities are over the age of 80 years. However, minority older adults are less likely to live in a nursing home since many of these older adults live with family members.

Additionally, not all older adults are poor, lonely, or have debilitating impairments. Although about half of persons over age 65 years have some type of chronic impairment such as arthritis, hypertension, or hearing loss, the majority function independently in activities of daily living such as self-care, mobility, and leisure. Many older adults living in the community

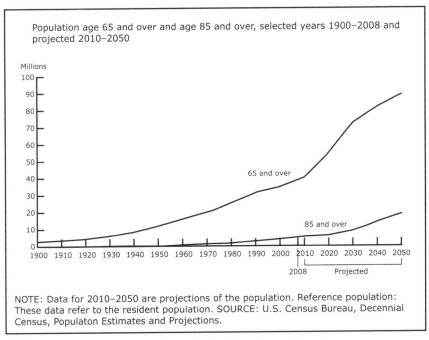

Population age 65 and over and age 85 and over, selected years 1900–2008 and projected 2010–2050

NOTE: Data for 2010–2050 are projections of the population. Reference population: These data refer to the resident population. SOURCE: U.S. Census Bureau, Decennial Census, Populaton Estimates and Projections.

Figure 28.1 Indicator 1 - Number of Older Americans

describe their health as good to excellent, although that perception and reality does change as people grow older.

As a greater percentage of the population reaches old age, issues of family caregiving also will increase. Men are more likely than older women to be married or living with a family member. Thus, adult women are increasingly faced with the role of caregiver for a spouse or a parent. As society ages, the probability of an older person being the caregiver for another older person also increases greatly. Caregivers will have recreation needs to help reduce their stress about the responsibility for continual care for others. They must not be forgotten in thinking about recreation services for older adults. Caregivers perceive that they lack time or they feel guilty so recreation opportunities are often difficult to negotiate. This issue is not the concern of only individuals working directly with older adults but also for other types of recreation services providers in the community. Partnerships will be necessary to bridge the gaps, work with faith-based organizations, develop resource guides, and market opportunities for caregivers.

Many older adults are economically independent. Programs such as Social Security have enabled older adults to live above poverty lines. However, a greater percentage of older adults of color live in poverty than do whites. Social security is the major source of income for some older adults. Although some of the monies in the Social Security fund were deposited during the working life of today's older adults, the viability of this program is influenced by the current working population. The Social Security dependency ratio is the proportion of working adults (aged 18–64 years) compared to the number of persons over the age of 65. In 1910, the ratio was approximately ten working people for every older adult. Today that ratio has decreased to five working adults for every older adult, and it is expected to continue to decline well into the 21st century as birth rates remain low and numbers of older adults increase (Hooyman & Kiyak, 1999). The age when people can begin to receive Social Security has risen and other changes are also likely to occur. The role of Social Security in the future is highly speculative because of the differing political views surrounding it. Nevertheless, many older adults have sufficient resources aside from Social Security to be able to spend part of their income on recreation services.

Implications for Recreation Services

The changing numbers of older people, their health, their interests, and government programs including Social Security's future will affect the opportunities for leisure and the provision of recreation services in the coming years. These demographics raise issues of what successful aging means and how recreation and active engagement are a part of aging.

Figure 28.2 shows the ways that older adults use their time. They are involved in a variety of daily activities including leisure activities. Figure 28.3 shows the range of leisure activities. When thinking about the interests of older adults, stereotyping must be reserved. Older adults enjoy activities similar to younger people, but the way that they engage in these activities may change as they get older and experience additional health issues.

Work and leisure issues often are magnified in retirement. With people living longer and having adequate retirement resources, some older adults will experience more years of retirement from work than in the past. Many people dream of retiring and living what they define as the good life. Because of economic conditions, however, some people may choose to work longer than they would like. In addition, some people now consider working part-time rather than taking full retirement because of economic constraints or because they are looking for meaningful activities, which work can provide.

Noted earlier was the idea that disability increases with age. In addition, people with lifelong disabilities are now living to old age. This trend

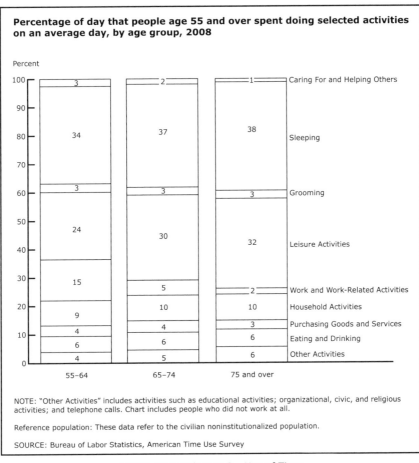

Percentage of day that people age 55 and over spent doing selected activities on an average day, by age group, 2008

Figure 28.2 Indicator 2 - Use of Time

means that service systems for older adults as well as services for persons with disabilities will need to work together. Until recently, few persons with a developmental disability were expected to live to old age. Further, many had never worked so retirement had no meaning. Systems are now needed to support the retirement options of persons with disabilities including access to community senior programs (Mahon, Mactavish, Mahon, & Searle, 1995).

As the number of older adults continues to grow, recreation professionals will be faced with changing policies and programs to meet these needs. The demographics of the older adult population will become more diverse, as will examples of how people age successfully. For example, older adults do not suddenly begin to participate in recreation activities focused on exclusively seniors just because they turn 62, or 65, or even 70 years

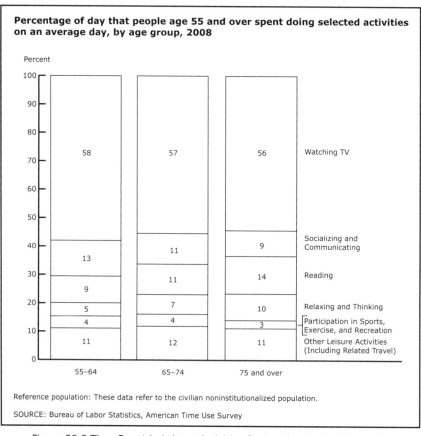

Figure 28.3 Time Spent in Leisure Activities for People Over 55 Years Old

old. Rather, people tend to continue activities developed during earlier adulthood although they may become more selective in their activities over the years. Programs just for older adults may be desired, but older adults will continue to participate in the same activities as they have in the past and will desire to participate in inclusive activities with middle-aged and younger people.

Interesting changes are occurring in senior centers that have traditionally been part of parks and recreation as well as nonprofit programming (Beard, 2012). The centers are more than a place to serve meals or offer Bingo. Café-type settings have great appeal to older adults in communities. These settings are designed for social interaction and are flexible enough to provide a variety of indoor activities for active engagement. Some centers also rely heavily on outdoor areas for activities such as pickle ball courts and lawns for bocce as well as places for older adults to sit and socialize. Because older adults vary so much in their needs, senior centers are moving toward offering a continuum of services such as front desk concierge-type assistance, group tours, walking clubs, billiards rooms, libraries, kitchens, and fitness areas to mention only a few. Many of these centers are trying to market to the young older adults who do not yet see themselves as aged in any way. People who are actively engaged in life and leisure are likely to remain healthy longer than those who are not engaged. The opportunities for creative programming for older adults are highly diverse.

Career Opportunities in Recreation Services for Older Adults

Opportunities for working with older adults abound in all sectors of recreation services going into the 21st century. A key factor in the expected job growth in the field of aging, besides the obvious demographic bulge, is the shift away from viewing aging solely from the illness and disease model toward focusing on ways that successful aging can occur. Recreation and active engagement are important components of successful aging.

Many older people continue to reside in the community as they age. For individuals who are mobile and in fairly good health, many public recreation departments employ older adult specialists to coordinate programming with older adults. Some of these program opportunities have been facility-oriented senior centers and are an extension of the traditional community recreation center concept. Professionals in these settings offer activities but many times the participants themselves are highly involved in the planning. Further, opportunities exist for part-time employment related to instruction in areas such as dance and fitness. Intergenerational programs and opportunities for older adults to volunteer in community events also can be facilitated through public recreation programs.

In addition, retirement villages and independent living opportunities for older adults abound. These living situations enable older adults to maintain a high level of independence, but provide programmed activities (e.g., clubs, special events, local and beyond trips and tours) that older adults can enjoy with other older adults.

At some point, however, the health and abilities of older people often deteriorate. Some of these older people with health problems live with family members who provide assistance with daily living tasks such as dressing, eating, and money management. For those unable to stay in their homes unattended during the day, adult day care or senior day care facilities provide an option for family caregivers. Older adults can attend these facilities during the day when no one is home to assist them. The adult day care facilities combine recreation with daily living assistance. In addition, these adult day care programs give caregivers a respite from the demands of their roles.

Nonprofit associations and senior clubs for older adults also continue to grow. For example, the AARP provides various travel and recreation opportunities. Road Scholars, formerly called Elderhostel, has been a nonprofit leader in educational travel since 1975, with educational tours offered in all 50 states and 150 countries. Road Scholars experience in-depth learning opportunities ranging from cultural tours and study cruises to walking and biking opportunities. Senior Games is an Olympic-like nonprofit program for persons over the age of 55 years. In addition to athletics events, Senior Games activities may include contests in art, dance, and music in competitions held locally, regionally, and nationally. Other local Senior Games programs have included spelling bees, dance contests, and holiday celebrations. All of these organizations have opportunities for professional employment to facilitate the experiences of older adults.

Other jobs working with older adults occur in long-term care facilities, nursing homes, and rehabilitation programs. Many of these services may be closely associated with functions that might be performed by therapeutic recreation specialists. Most care facilities and nursing homes provide activities for residents that not only provide some rehabilitation but offer opportunities for social interaction and entertainment. Recreation opportunities may be offered in cooperation with other service providers in centers that address a full spectrum of needs. Combined services might include counseling, healthcare screening, and legal aid.

Individuals may choose careers in working with older adults for many reasons. Many professionals find older adults interesting and inspiring as positive role models. Other professionals choose this area because of the numerous growth opportunities in the future. Regardless, working with older adults by facilitating recreation services requires a desire to work with people and apply skills in leadership, programming, and administration.

Reflection Questions

1. Think about an older adult that you know (e.g., a grandparent). What does that individual enjoy doing for recreation? Do you think his/her recreation has changed over time?

2. Do you believe that most people dream of retiring throughout their working lives? How important is retirement to middle-aged people?

3. If you are a young person reading this book, how can you prepare for retirement even though that option may be decades away?

Chapter 29

Other Recreation Specialties

The chapters in this Unit have focused on some of the traditional and/or popular specialties associated with recreation services. In addition to the primary employment areas related to the government (i.e., local, state, and federal), nonprofit and youth organizations, sports, tourism, events, therapeutic recreation, and older adults, several other career specialties in recreation services were mentioned in previous chapters but not discussed in detail relative to career possibilities.

Five areas will be highlighted briefly in this chapter: health and fitness, military recreation, arts management, faith-based recreation, and outdoor adventure leadership. Each of these areas represents an opportunity to combine the basics of recreation services with other disciplines such as health, arts, theology, and the environment.

Health, Fitness, and Aquatics

As noted in the chapter on sports and golf management, the areas of health and fitness are a growing area that is associated with sports but goes beyond sports to include other ways that people are physically active. Some people thought the fitness boom of several years ago was a passing fad. However, the value of health clubs, fitness opportunities, and aquatic facilities continues to be highly desired and needed in communities. The obesity epidemic among children and adults necessitates a vigilant concern for how recreation services can contribute to health and fitness.

People's choices to engage in physical activity and fitness opportunities are complex. The Nike slogan of "just do it" is not as simple as it suggests. People need to be intrinsically motivated, but that motivation often depends on other factors. Health professionals have used a model in recent years referred to as the social ecological model, which was introduced in Unit One.

The social ecological model suggests that in addition to individual or intrapersonal motivations and interests, behaviors such as being physically active also depend on social, community, organizational, and policy dimensions. For example, having an activity partner and/or supportive others may be necessary for some people to be active. In addition, having places to be active in the community (e.g., parks, trails, gyms, swimming pools) is important. Organizations can provide a basis for participation such as the programs available through community or fitness centers. Recreation services organizations in all sectors have a role to play facilitating health by considering the elements of the social ecological model.

Communities contribute to this model through programs that may be available across all sectors. Some fitness opportunities are facility based and provide spaces and equipment for people to use. Some of these facilities may have trainers available who can assist with developing individualized programs. In addition, offering classes for group fitness is commonly done.

Health and fitness clubs as well as many recreation centers may offer physical activities such as yoga, Pilates, zumba, salsa dancing, kick-boxing, Tai chi, cycling (aka spinning), step aerobics, muscle conditioning, cardio sculpt, Nia, power yoga, martial arts, stretch and tone, iron ballet, belly dancing, HIT High Intensity Training, interval training, and stretching. These opportunities change as the interests and needs of participants change. A recreation professional working in the area of health and fitness must be aware of the changing interests.

Health and fitness centers may also offer training programs (e.g., run your first marathon) as well as classroom sessions related to wellness, nutrition, and weight control. Many centers also have swimming pools, whirlpools and Jacuzzis available. Some offer therapy sessions for various types of rehabilitation while others include spas that may provide health treatments and massage. Health and fitness centers also may be associated directly with healthcare through partnerships with medical centers and hospitals.

An important area related to health and fitness is aquatic activities. Many communities have swimming pools that require management, maintenance, and supervision. Other aquatic activities may be available at outdoor venues such as for boating or paddle boarding. Individuals are hired as professionals to supervise aquatics in organizations in all sectors. Common job responsibilities might be: directing activities related to lifeguarding staff and aquatic operations; coordinating aquatic programs such as swim lessons, swim teams, and aquatic special events; developing aquatics policies, procedures, rules and regulations and ensuring their enforcement; monitoring technical aspects of swimming pool operations and maintenance; interviewing, selecting, and training employees; and monitoring records of revenue and expenditures.

Health, fitness, and aquatics facilities and programs may be found in business establishments, public parks and recreation agencies, nonprofit organizations (e.g., the Y), hospitals, and at schools and universities. They may have different target audiences such as families, children, older adults, or women-only. Some also offer child care services for parents who want to exercise.

Careers in the health and fitness field, similar to other areas, often begin with part-time or summer work experience. Opportunities for full-time work generally do not become available without higher education and some work experience. Obtaining a job in this area generally requires a combination of health and fitness skills as well as management background. Working in these areas is comparable in commitment and salary to any type of service industry that focuses on meeting the health needs and interests of individuals.

Military Recreation

The philosophy of military recreation is that military personnel should have the same quality of life as anyone else in society. The military must be ready to defend the country, which requires hard work and training. However, service members need a balance of work and play. Military recreation goes by many names across the Services: Army Morale, Welfare, and Recreation (MWR), Marine Corps Community Services (MCCS), Navy MWR, U.S. Air Force Services, and Coast Guard MWR. Regardless of the name, all branches provide service members and their families with recreational programs on and off the military base.

The military has offered some form of morale, welfare, and recreation programs since it began. Services for military families, however, are relatively new, having been created within the past 50 years. Army Community Services was not created until 1965. In 1968 a Youth Activities Program was established and, in 1971, an Outdoor Recreation Program was begun (http://www.armymwr.com/commander/aboutfmwrc.aspx).

The MWR Program within the U.S. military is a worldwide system of services and activities provided by civilians that supports soldiers and their families. Many of the activities found in a local parks and recreation center would be the same as those offered to service members on military bases.

In addition to outdoor activities (e.g., climbing, aquatic sports), sports and intramurals are available along with arts and crafts programs and numerous activities for youth. Assistance with travel plans and vacations can be provided. Various entertainment opportunities such as concerts and theatre often are made available to service members and their families. Many bases have fitness centers that provide exercise and weight rooms, saunas, and sports fields and courts. Some posts have community pools as well as parks and playgrounds. In addition to outdoor programs, some bases rent gear such as bicycles, picnic and camping gear, trailers, fishing equipment, and canoes and kayaks. Most bases also have craft shops that offer photography, pottery, and woodworking, which are available for the whole family.

Internships in military recreation are also widely available both in the United States and globally. Young recreation professionals are often interested in internships as well as military positions because they give them a chance to gain valuable experience while also visiting countries around the world. Each branch of the military (i.e., Air Force, Navy, Marines, Coast Guard, and Army) provides recreation services. Listings of full-time career civilian positions can be found on the web pages of each branch.

Arts Management

Although maybe not as well-known as sports, the arts are important in U.S. communities. If arts are defined broadly, virtually everyone is involved with the arts on a somewhat regular basis if they go to movies, read books, listen to CDs, go to museums, or go to live theater or concert performances. Arts audiences as well as arts organizations spend billions of dollars related to arts each year (Carpenter & Blandy, 2008). In addition, many people travel as tourists to visit cultural events. Table 29.1 shows a breakdown of the attendance rates of Americans in various types of arts during 2008.

Sometimes arts have been overlooked as an aspect of recreation services because sports are so closely associated with recreation. However, arts and cultural programs are a part of all great communities. Successful arts organizations are able to plan and implement cultural arts experiences for all citizens (i.e., children up to older adults).

Cultural arts are most commonly associated with music, literature, and drama. However, the plethora of arts can be categorized in several ways: visual arts (e.g., jewelry making, tattooing), literary arts, media arts (e.g., music videos, creating computer art), musical arts, dance and other movement arts (e.g., choreography, gymnastics, skating), performances and exhibitions (e.g., music, dancing, acting, laser shows, street performances,

Table 29.1 Attendance/Participation Rates for Various Arts Activities: 2008

(224.8 represents 224,800,000)								
Adult Popu-lation (million)	Jazz Concert	Classical Music Concert	Musicals	Non-Musical Plays	Art Museums/ Galleries	Craft/ Visual Art Festivals	Parks/ Historic Buildings[1]	Read Liter-ature[2]
224.8	7.8	9.3	16.7	9.4	22.7	24.5	24.9	50.2

[1] Visiting historic parks or monuments or touring buildings or neighborhoods for the historic or design value.

[2] Literature is defined as poetry, novels, short stories, or plays.

Source: U.S. National Endowment for the Arts, "2008 Survey of Public Participation in the Arts" (http://www.nea.gov.pub/)

circuses), media, selling art objects, collecting and preserving, teaching about arts and culture, and administrative works (Carpenter & Blandy, 2008). The variety of arts programming is huge and offers an important leisure experience for children and adults.

People are considered cultured if they have knowledge about the arts. Arts, however, are for everyone, and not just the elite. Children learn about art in schools but adults continue their education about art through community venues. Facilitating appreciation of the arts is often how recreation services connect with the arts.

Involvement in the cultural arts has numerous benefits for adults and children. These benefits can occur through participation in projects and performances or by being a supporter (i.e., patron) of the arts. Although crafts may not have the same sophistication as arts, they also provide many benefits. One benefit of both arts and crafts is the opportunity to foster creativity. This career skill is important regardless of whether it is applied to arts or other elements of life (e.g., creative problem-solving). Taking a raw material or an idea and making something of it provides great pleasure to people. Arts also are a way to express thoughts and emotions. Creating something can provide a sense of achievement and satisfaction. A related benefit is the dexterity and physical coordination that can be developed through the use of tools (e.g., scissors, brushes, clay, paints, colored markers, beads, or knives) necessary for some art projects. In addition, producing art requires concentration and perseverance, which can be skills that will be used in many domains of life. Further, involvement in the arts often includes the development of planning and practice skills.

Being a patron or supporter of the arts usually means going to concerts, theater performances, or art museums. These leisure experiences offer benefits related to relaxation and reflection. They can provide joy and entertainment. Many people view arts involvement as a way to reduce stress in their lives. When people are immersed in their own creativity or the creativity of others, they can forget life's problems, even if only briefly. From a community perspective, arts also can stimulate local economies and improve the quality of civic life. People often travel to communities to attend concerts and theater productions. While there, they may need lodging and will likely dine in the area. They may also come to a community to attend an arts event but also combine it with visiting other attractions in a community.

Arts management is an area considered part of recreation services. Although arts management degrees often are offered through business or art schools, individuals with backgrounds in recreation services may also be interested in cultural arts employment opportunities. Appreciating arts is important and management skills are necessary for arts organizations to operate effectively and efficiently.

Some parks and recreation programs have individuals that manage community art centers or coordinate cultural arts within a community. Public recreation organizations also have made spaces for arts in parks such as band shells and outdoor performance areas. When thinking about all the elements that might be included as art or cultural arts, many opportunities exist for professional, part-time, and volunteer work.

Similar to other recreation services, the general duties of an arts administrator can include staff management, marketing, managing budgets, public relations, fundraising, program development and evaluation, and board and volunteer relations. The arts manager is focused on the business and administrative side of the arts and usually is associated with the daily operations of programs, organizations, or facilities. Opportunities in arts management can be found in public recreation agencies, theaters, galleries, museums, arts festivals, arts centers, arts councils, dance companies, community arts organizations, and disability arts organizations.

Faith-Based Recreation Ministries

Although the primary purpose of faith-based organizations is not to provide recreation, many churches and synagogues use recreation as a key element in creating religious communities. These services may be called youth ministries or outdoor ministries, or they may just be part of the life of the faith organization.

Several foundations underlie recreation and religion. One's faith is serious, but playfulness can yield important spiritual benefits and enable individuals to witness for their faith. Many of the traits fostered in healthy play such as honesty and fairness are basic to religious teachings. Games and recreation opportunities can bring people together and provide emotional and spiritual uplift.

Specific religious groups and denominations may view the ministry related to recreation in different ways. In some Protestant churches, but not all, a recreation ministry is carried out by an ordained minister or pastor. However, in other cases especially related to youth, the recreation opportunities may be carried out by someone skilled in youth or outdoor ministries or even by a layperson or by a volunteer. Titles might be youth minister, youth pastor, or youth worker. In Catholic churches, youth work is usually carried out by someone who is not a member of the clergy. Youth ministry is now an area of study in some Christian universities and colleges. Individuals interested specifically in recreation and sharing their faith may find this area of recreation services appealing. Although youth is often the focus, recreation in faith-based organizations is also facilitated for adults.

Many outdoor programs such as camps, retreat centers, and outdoor conference centers are supported by faith-based organizations and provide full-time as well as seasonal employment. Outdoor ministries generally encourage spiritual growth for the whole person by providing encounters with scripture, recreation experiences, and care for the environment through involvement in worship, recreation, and relationship development. Further, outdoor ministries offer a wide array of programs that provide growth experiences for people of all ages.

Some large churches and synagogues operate recreation programs similar to what a local community might provide. It is not unusual to see opportunities in sports (e.g., softball) offered as co-ed activities or for men (or women) only. Dance lessons for couples as well as seasonal dances might be offered as a church activity. Day camps might be available for youth in such areas as soccer, basketball, cheerleading, and glee. Some churches have cycling clubs or running/walking clubs. Many churches sponsor Cub Scout and Boy Scout troops. Further, many of these recreation programs are open to all community members and not just church members. Recreation is often seen as a way to attract young and old people to a faith-based community.

Individual denominations as well as local churches and synagogues offer opportunities for recreation ministries in a variety of ways. As is true in other organizations, having part-time, seasonal, or volunteer work experience may provide a foundation for gaining full-time careers in faith-based recreation ministries.

Outdoor Education and Adventure Leadership

An area that has grown in the past 50 years relates to outdoor leadership. This area is called by names such as adventure education, outdoor adventure, outdoor learning, experiential education, adventure therapy, outdoor leadership, outdoor education, or camp administration/management. Each of these areas has nuanced differences but they all relate to providing challenging educational experiences in the outdoors that contribute to human growth and development. The context is the outdoors and the focus is on programs and leadership, and not necessarily resource management, as is the focus of most state and federal programs. These outdoor programs also may involve residential or journey-based experiences in which students (i.e., both children and adults) participate in outdoor activities such as hiking, climbing, canoeing, ropes courses, and group games.

Individuals working in outdoor leadership usually have expertise in program administration, leadership and group dynamics, problem solving, and environmental ethics. These individuals generally love being in the outdoors and want to instill this interest, appreciation, and commitment to environmental stewardship in others.

The field of organized camping is discussed in the chapter on youth development. For decades children and adults have gone to camp to experience group living in the outdoors. Thousands of young adults are employed in camp leadership each summer. Hundreds of professionals work full-time in this area.

In addition to camp directors, career titles associated with outdoor leadership might include outdoor program coordinator (in universities as well as some schools, public agencies, and nonprofit groups), outdoor/environmental educator, wilderness instructor, outdoor adventure guide, outing club supervisor, ropes/challenge course facilitator, and outdoor education instructor. Regardless of the organization or the philosophy, all these programs focus on the influence of natural environments on human beings, the experiential role of challenge, and educational learning. Many individuals start as instructors, counselors, or guides in outdoor organizations and then may move into administrative positions.

These five specialties are offered to further emphasize the breadth of recreation services as well as the interdisciplinary links that recreation has to many other areas such as education, psychology, theology, or environmental studies. As has been emphasized throughout this unit, many common competencies and abilities are needed for any specialty in recreation services but each job opportunity also requires specialized skills.

Reflection Questions

1. Colleges and universities are involved with health, fitness, and aquatic opportunities for students and faculty. What opportunities do you have on your campus?

2. Colleges and universities are also involved in providing arts opportunities. What cultural arts events are occurring on your campus this semester?

3. Why are arts often associated with the elite? How can that perception be changed?

4. Do the benefits found in faith-based recreation program participation differ from the benefits found in any other type of recreation activity? Is recreation more of a means than an end related to faith-based recreation opportunities?

5. Colleges and universities are sometimes involved in providing outdoor programs. What is available on your campus related to the outdoors? Why are outdoor activities seen as important for college students?

Chapter 30

Recreation Services
and Higher Education

If you are reading this book, most likely you are associated directly with higher education. Some of us who are faculty in recreation programs in higher education obviously enjoy this environment. Personally, I believe there is nothing more exciting than the "life of the mind." Those of us who get to spend our lives in the atmosphere of intellectual challenges are highly privileged. Not all recreation services in higher education involve teaching and research, but all offer opportunities to work with bright young adults. In this chapter, specialties related to student services and campus recreation are discussed. The advantages of graduate education and the opportunities for careers in college/university teaching and research also are introduced.

College/University
Student Services

Although the purpose of colleges and universities is to provide education, providing recreation and entertainment for students as well as for the community where the university is located is an aspect of a college or university's mission. For example, many campuses make their facilities for concerts or other cultural events open not only to students but also the entire community. Musical events, theater, botanical gardens, art museums, planetariums, and sports events are only a few examples of the ways that colleges and universities might provide recreation opportunities for students, their families, and local citizens.

Colleges usually focus their efforts directly with students through the student services offered, which consist of activities and programs that support the academic and personal success of students in colleges and universities. Common areas within student services are enrollment services, student health, counseling and psychological services, and student life.

The area most closely related to recreation services is a component of what many universities call student life. This area can also be quite broad, but some of the common activities related to recreation services are special event ceremonies (e.g., convocation, graduation), fraternity and sorority life, athletics, health and wellness, student unions, and intramurals and recreational sports. People from a range of disciplines are employed in these areas but recreation services related to event management, arts management, and sports can tie into these services.

University administrators as well as other university employees who support these recreation services must be able to articulate why these student amenities are needed. Both public and private colleges and universities are scrutinized with concerns about higher education costs and how students use their time while in college. Therefore, the rationale for the resources put into student life must be justified. Administrators in higher education must have responses to criticisms about the perceived country-club nature of some universities that have built large recreation facilities. Universities and colleges have invested in resources as a response to student demands as well as a recognition that leisure opportunities on campus (i.e., rather than just the party and bar scene) can increase the likelihood of students' successful completion of college (Astin, 1993). Growth and development of the students as persons is an important part of the college experience. In addition, the emotional health of students must be considered.

Career opportunities related to recreation services exist in some areas of student life. For example, event planners may be involved with special campus activities related to students and faculty. Student unions operate by managing spaces for students to congregate and meet. They also serve as a hospitality and hotel opportunity on some campuses. Professional personnel are needed who can work with student groups like sororities and fraternities. Opportunities exist on campuses to be involved in arts management through music, theater, and art productions. Health and wellness may refer to counseling and support services but are also a part of the campus recreation program. Athletics are central on many campuses not only for the opportunities that students have to participate and receive scholarships, but also as a means of connecting alumni and the community back to the campus through sports competitions that encourage spectators (i.e., tourists). Coaches and athletic administrators provide opportunities for students and visitors to experience university life. Some of these activities also serve to attract and recruit students to campus. The most common aspect of student life related to recreation, however, is campus recreation.

Campus Recreation

Many campuses in the United States have made provisions for student involvement through recreation, outdoor recreation, fitness, and intramural opportunities. These programs usually are administered through student life or student affairs on each campus. The aim in most campus recreation programs is to promote the pursuit of healthy lifestyles by providing facilities and programs to encourage social interaction and physical activity.

The traditional focus of campus recreation has been intramural sports. Intramurals are usually defined as sports activities that are designed for a particular targeted group, such as students who attend a specific university or college. Extramural sports would refer to intercollegiate sports where competition occurs with others outside the university. Intramurals are organized between individuals or teams who are somewhat equivalent in terms of age and athletic ability. These sports provide students who cannot compete on varsity teams a chance to promote their physical activity and find enjoyable competition.

Intramurals are typically organized with league play as well as tournaments. Students are paid on a part-time basis typically to run the events and serve as officials. Full-time professionals direct or manage these programs. The National Intramural Recreational Sports Association (NIRSA) is the professional organization that provides a network of more than 4,000 professionals, students, and associate members in the recreational sports field throughout the United States, Canada, and other countries.

Many campuses offer fitness centers, aquatic centers, sports fields, running tracks, climbing walls, and gyms that students use for structured intramurals programs, but that also offer them opportunities during their own free time. Fitness centers generally provide equipment to use and often offer group exercise classes as well as personal trainers. Campus recreation programs frequently offer places to check-out or rent sports equipment.

Another option within campus recreation is sports clubs. These clubs give students an opportunity to interact with others of similar interests. The clubs are student run, but a professional may oversee the groups to ensure that they are following university policies. These sports clubs include typical team and individual sports (e.g., basketball, wrestling, softball) but on many campuses the offerings can be whatever students find of mutual interest, such as aikido, cricket, ultimate Frisbee, ballroom dancing, or cycling.

Some campuses have a vibrant outdoor recreation program affiliated with campus recreation. Outdoor opportunities might include challenge courses, Frisbee golf courses, running and biking trails, and/or organized outdoor trips and expeditions. Outdoor equipment (e.g., tents, stoves) can often be rented through these outdoor programs. These programs are usually student-led but outdoor leadership professionals may provide the administration of these programs.

Campus recreation is a diverse area within the broad division of student life in colleges and universities. Career opportunities exist in all the sport formats described above. Similar to other areas, a student desiring a career in campus recreation should get as much part-time experience as possible through working in university recreation programs. In addition, most job descriptions call for a Master's degree, especially for professionals in higher education who direct or administer the campus recreation programs.

Graduate Degrees in Recreation

The Bachelor of Arts (B.A.) or Bachelor of Sciences (B.S.) is usually considered the entry-level degree for professional employment in most recreation services. Entry-level positions may not always require a degree in recreation services, but depending on the particular job within an organization, a college degree in some area usually is necessary. Depending on the position, previous experience in part-time, seasonal, or internship positions is highly desired for any position in the field. Fortunately, all accredited recreation curricula require experiential learning through classes, practicums, and internships.

Having a Master's of Arts (M.A.), Master's of Science (M.S.), Master's of Education (M.Ed.), or some other professional Master's degree may or may not be helpful in gaining the first job, depending on the area of recreation services. Educators vary on the advice that they give to young people regarding going directly from a Bachelor's degree to a Master's degree without a break between degrees. My personal observation has been that students coming back to get a Master's degree, after a break in their education and with some full-time work experience, find the Master's degree more beneficial. They can often better direct themselves to get the most out of the additional time spent in college. Other students, however, perform well going from a Bachelor's program directly to a Master's program as long as they realize that a Master's degree is more than a fifth year of undergraduate education. Some with a Master's degree, however, without previous experience (e.g., part-time or volunteer) may not be more likely to get an entry-level job than an individual with a Bachelor's degree who has previous experience. = more likely to get a job

The purpose of a Master's degree is to become a "master" or a specialist in an area of study. A Master's degree in the field of recreation services may focus on applied research and/or professional practice. Degrees that are often not thesis-based are referred to as professional Master's or terminal degrees, which can be likened to getting an MBA (Master's in Business Administration). These professional Master's degrees in recreation services might be a degree such as Master of Parks, Recreation, and Tourism Management (MPRTM), which we offer at North Carolina State University. Although basic research methods and evaluation skills are an important part of a professional degree, the focus is on becoming a reflective practitioner.

Some individuals seeking a Master's degree may choose to get a research-based degree, which means that a thesis is required for graduation. Some of these individuals may also intend to go into recreation services in a variety of organizations, but others may intend someday to do research and/or get a Ph.D. A thesis is often required before an individual can be admitted to a Ph.D. program.

People also have different opinions about whether a Master's degree in recreation is needed if an individual already has an undergraduate degree in recreation. As noted, getting a Master's means that you have gained a breadth and depth of expertise. Others might argue that expanding one's horizons such as getting a degree in Business or some other applied area would be useful if one already has finished a degree in recreation. If a student does not have an undergraduate degree in recreation but has experience in recreation services, he/she should be well-positioned for obtaining a Master's degree in recreation. This decision may depend on an individual's personal situation as well as on professional interests and experience.

Getting a Master's degree may be necessary to be considered for promotion in some recreation services organizations or for availing oneself of opportunities to move into administrative positions. Therefore, obtaining a Master's degree can be useful for the future.

Admission into graduate school usually requires having had a successful undergraduate experience with a GPA of around 3.0 (based on a 4.0 scale). However, the GPA cut-off differs across universities. Some Master's programs may require the Graduate Record Exam (GRE) or another somewhat equivalent exam, such as Millers Analogy Test (MAT). The GRE measures verbal, quantitative, and writing skills. The MAT measures problem-solving skills using analogies. Scores can generally be improved on these tests by going through tutorials and being familiar with the kinds of questions asked.

Choosing whether and when to pursue a graduate degree is a personal choice. Factors that go into the decision relate to career goals, family considerations, and economics. A growing number of universities are offering distance education degrees for individuals interested in an advanced degree. Although these degrees require a huge commitment of time (i.e., we estimate that for every 3 credit course, a student will need to devote 8–10 hours a week toward study and preparation) and money, an individual can remain "at home" and many students continue with full-time jobs while involved in their Master's education.

Other individuals may choose to go to graduate school full-time. At many universities, graduate assistantships are available for resident students. Although these assistantships may not cover all costs, they frequently cover tuition and most living expenses. Most of these degrees can be completed in two years. A student may want to weigh whether getting a Master's degree is worth the time, money, and effort. For the most part, the degree is likely to open doors that may not be available without an advanced degree.

Academic Careers in Teaching and Research

Some individuals may want to go beyond the Master's degree to get a Doctorate (i.e., Doctor of Philosophy, a Ph.D.). In some areas of recreation services, such as in the federal land management agencies, a Ph.D. will enable an individual to be involved in higher levels of management and research in federal and state governments. For most students interested in recreation services, however, a Ph.D. is sought to gain the knowledge needed to remain in higher education as a teacher and scholar.

The types of positions in higher education will vary greatly depending on the university. Most universities that offer Ph.D. programs are research intensive. In other words, if you are a faculty member at one of those universities, you are expected to make a major time commitment to research and obtaining research grant funding. This expectation does not mean that an individual does not teach, but faculty in research-intensive universities may teach less than in a university that offers only Master's or Bachelor's degrees and does not have research as a central mission. Some colleges and universities may not require a Ph.D. for teaching if the individual is hired as an instructor or lecturer, but the majority require this degree.

Faculty in the United States and Canada are employed at various ranks. These ranks may differ slightly but usually are described as adjunct instructors, instructors/lecturers, assistant professors, associate professors, and (full) professors. Adjunct faculty members are part-time and usually teach only one course a semester. Instructors and lecturers are generally not considered tenure track, but the other three ranks are tenure track. Tenure means that the individual meets certain expectations that guarantee a permanent job in a college or university. Extenuating circumstances can terminate an individual from tenure but usually faculty members have this protection when they receive tenure. Although many debates exist about whether or not tenure is a good thing, it was originally instituted to ensure that faculty members were not fired from universities because their philosophical perspectives were not the same as their supervisors' perspectives.

Faculty members typically spend 5–6 years as an assistant professor before they go forward for tenure and promotion. Requirements differ among universities, but generally an assistant professor must demonstrate scholarly competence and teaching proficiency. Service as it relates to the university, profession, and community is part of the requirement but is generally not nearly as important as research and teaching, depending on the mission of the university. Although good teaching is important, successful research and publishing is required in major universities. Promotion includes going to the status of Associate Professor. Failure to gain tenure means that an individual must leave the particular university and go to a different university. Individuals may be appointed to Professor after another period of several years in which the Associate Professor demonstrates that he or she can continue to do excellent research and teaching and develops a national and international reputation for the research, teaching, and service undertaken.

Obtaining a Ph.D. is a huge undertaking. The culminating experience of the Ph.D. is a dissertation, which is a major project that demonstrates a student's ability to do independent research. In universities, students have numerous opportunities to explore topics in-depth and develop research skills that can be applied to the dissertation. Ph.D. students have advisors and committee members to assist, but they also must demonstrate their ability to conceptualize and write independently. Not everyone is suited to obtain a Ph.D. but someone who is intelligent, diligent, disciplined, academically curious, and creative can be successful.

The rewards of higher education are many. Shaping the next generation of professionals is exciting. Undertaking research projects to add to the body of knowledge as well as to improve the quality of life of individuals is challenging and gratifying. Being in constant contact with students and colleagues creates opportunities for continual learning. Higher education is not for everyone, but many people (hopefully your instructors) find each day highly interesting as well as challenging.

Reflection Questions

1. What types of experiences have you had with student life at your university?

2. How would you justify to someone outside the university that many benefits can occur as a result of participation in campus recreation?

3. What are the advantages and disadvantages to going directly from a Bachelor's degree to a Master's degree?

4. If an individual wants to work in some specialty in recreation services in the community, how will doing a thesis be useful?

5. What are the characteristics of faculty members who are successful as teachers in higher education?

Chapter 31

The Mission of Recreation Services

Most people do not possess crystal balls, so they cannot be absolutely sure of the future. However, professionals can be knowledgeable about what may lie ahead in the future if they are reflective practitioners and if they believe that the obligation of a professional is to be a continual learner. People gain insight into the future by considering what issues are on the horizon and thinking about how those challenges can be confronted to shape the desired goals for the future.

To be productive, you must decide your goal and preferable future. If you want to work professionally and full-time in some area of recreation services, you know that you need to go to college, choose a major, and graduate with a degree. You know this path will be challenging and you do not know if everything is going to work out for you, but you do know that you will need to study hard, get volunteer and part-time work experience, and complete your degree. The issue is your future and desire to have a meaningful career, the challenge is to get an education, and the action required is to shape your college experience so that you can reach your goal. You create your future each day by the actions you take.

This same approach applies to thinking about professional issues and challenges related to sustainable recreation services for the future. In this Unit, several specific issues are identified. The challenges are described, and then some possible directions for action for recreation services professionals are offered to meet those challenges. Sixteen areas that may be professional challenges are discussed briefly in this Unit. Many more exist, and others will pop up in the coming years. For now, however, these issues are offered for your consideration. The future of recreation services will depend on the actions that professionals take now and for the future.

In a static society with no change, the future is like the present. In a dynamic society, the future is being created each day and requires individuals and professionals to modify their behaviors accordingly. In the 21st century, recreation services are a part of a big world that must be made sustainable. Further, if recreation professionals believe that leisure is the right of all people, then strategies must be developed to ensure that recreation services are inclusive. Envisioning the desired future and not just leaving it to chance is important.

Recreation services have been described broadly in this text, but most professionals interested in this area identify most closely with a specialty. Although specialty identity is important, I believe that professionals should also have a broad perspective about the recreation services profession and the commonalities that exist among the specialties. Strength exists in unity. The purpose of this first chapter is to reiterate a common mission related to leisure behavior and reinforce core values that cut across all sectors and specialties in recreation services.

Issues

Some professionals believe that the future of sustainable recreation services may hinge on determining what the commonalities or common mission is across specialties (Henderson, 2010; Stebbins, 2011). Professionals in some of the specialties may argue that their area has little to do with other specialties or with a broader mission. For example, what does operating a bowling alley have in common with recreation therapy? One could argue very little, but others might say that both are aiming to contribute to the leisure well-being of individuals.

If professionals in specialty areas of recreation services do not believe they have anything in common with other areas, then the field will likely splinter, as some people believe has already happened. That fragmentation may not be bad and may be the outgrowth of a growing field. On the other hand, many of the specialties within recreation services are small in terms of the numbers of employees (e.g., military recreation) and being affiliated with a larger mission may add strength and additional credibility.

Further, being able to speak with confidence about the purpose of recreation services and how a specialty contributes to social good is part of what constitutes a human services profession. Therefore, a preferable goal is that professionals will speak in a unified voice about the benefits of leisure to individual well-being and the contributions to the quality of life in a diversity of communities.

In a society dominated by the work ethic, leisure experiences and recreation services have often appeared to be secondary in importance and sometimes even considered frivolous. Leisure researchers have had to struggle to establish the legitimacy of their field of study despite the rigorous approaches used. Further, much of the leisure research as well as practices in recreation services are borrowed from other disciplines (e.g., psychology, business). The questions that can be asked: "What is distinct, or special, about the outcomes of recreation services?" "Why are the specialty areas not subsumed in other disciplines or fields such as sport management in business schools, tourism in economic development departments, outdoor resource management as a part of forestry, public parks and recreation aligned with public administration, or therapeutic recreation as a unit within allied health?

The relationships among these specialty areas of recreation services can be better understood by articulating a philosophy and encouraging professionals to examine core beliefs about the role of leisure in people's lives. Exploring the unity and coherence may be important regardless of the recreation specialty.

Challenges

The main challenge in examining the unity of the recreation services specialties is to determine a collective identity and apply it. I suggest that no other professional area that currently exists focuses specifically on the human behavior of *leisure*. I would argue that leisure behavior is what makes recreation services specialties different from other fields and professions such as business management, public health, or social work. The philosophy is what is distinct since many of the ways recreation practice and leisure research are undertaken use the same approaches and theories as these fields.

In the United States, a targeted focus on the institution of public parks and/or recreation defined the field initially (Sessoms & Henderson, 2009). The mission of parks and recreation as a social service in communities changed when the market potential related to fields such as sports, tourism, event management, and private business was recognized. Dustin and Goodale (1999) have lamented that the profession has lost its mission and become a highly segmented and disjointed collection of curricula driven by the political economy (i.e., what majors will attract the most students and which specialties will contribute the most to the economic development of a state). Rose and Dustin (2009) also identified the "sell out" of leisure researchers and universities to neo-liberal issues related to this political economy.

In 1985, an argument was put forward by Burdge that leisure studies should be separated from parks and recreation in higher education. He suggested that different preparation is needed for undergraduates (i.e., a focus on training) than graduate students (i.e., focus on theory), that faculty in the two areas (i.e., leisure studies verses recreation services) had different orientations, and that no linkage existed between leisure research and the needs of recreation professionals working in the various sectors. The respondents to Burdge were unanimous in disagreement and leisure studies and recreation services have remained loosely tied together for the past 30 years.

The question of the relationship of leisure studies and recreation services is currently being raised again across the world (Henderson, 2010; 2011). I contended that figuring out what "holds us together" is the challenge. Focusing on enhancing the leisure lives of individuals can be done regardless of whether focused on sports, arts, special events, or the outdoors.

However, I also think a challenge that exists may not be thinking of recreation services as reliant on leisure studies, but examining how leisure behavior and professional specialties (i.e., parks and recreation, event planning, sports, therapeutic recreation, and tourism) are at two ends of a continuum. Putting these perspectives on a continuum enables discussions about where intersections and interdependencies *may* exist. (See Figure 31.1).

This continuum allows for *both/and* thinking as contrasted to *either/or* thinking. A continuum allows for discussion along many points and allows for varying perspectives. Thus, the challenge is to understand leisure in society and to see how professional specialties promote the positive benefits of leisure. If the areas of specialty described in this book do not find common ground, then this broad field of recreation services will become fragmented and applications to leisure likely will fade away. On the other

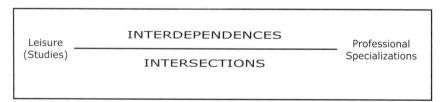

Figure 31.1 A Continuum of Leisure and Professional Specializations
(adapted from Henderson, 2011)

hand, maybe common ground was an artifact of the 20th century and now needs to change.

Strategies for Action

Four approaches might be considered in pondering the value of unity within recreation services (Henderson, 2010):

- Embrace change
- Articulate an identity among specialties
- Celebrate the contributions of leisure
- Identify collaborators

Change is inevitable but not uncontrollable. Professionals can recognize that all knowledge is relative to changing social, cultural, and historical contexts. Rowe (2002) contended that, "The future of leisure studies is bound up in changes that far exceed the powers of its practitioners to control. What they can do is to recognize these circumstances and seek to mold them, contextually, to their advantage" (p. 10). The mindset is to anticipate change before it becomes a crisis. In addition, change is the *new normal* for society as well as recreation services.

Because change is inevitable, recreation services professionals can consider the evolving identity and goals. Without a collective identity, fragmentation is inevitable. Leisure is about enhancing the lives of people through enjoyable activity. This value can make leisure behavior common to all recreation services specialties.

By recognizing change and articulating an identity, the contributions the specialties can make to society, universities, knowledge systems, and students will be obvious. Opportunities within recreation services should contribute to what makes life meaningful and professionals should be able to describe those benefits and contributions confidently.

Finally, the future of sustainable recreation services will depend on collaboration and establishing partnerships—across the specialties as well as with other professions. Recreation services do not exist in isolation and will not survive without identifying integral connections with others. Partnerships are discussed later in this Unit, as they are paramount to the future and will provide a way to promote the value of recreation services regardless of the specialty.

Reflection Questions

1. Do you believe that leisure behavior unites all the specialties? Justify your answer.

2. What are the specialty areas in your academic department? Are there other departments on your campus that are supporting recreation services with the professional preparation that students are receiving (e.g., is sport management housed elsewhere)? What are the advantages and disadvantages of the way academic recreation services are organized on your campus?

3. Change is a fact of life, whether related to a field like recreation services or in an individual's own life. What are the best ways to cope with change?

4. What is your preferred future regarding your particular recreation services specialty?

Chapter 32

Time for Recreation

Time is equal for all people. No one gets more than 24 hours in a day and 168 hours in a week. Time is also the scarcest and most valuable of any of the resources people have. A sense of control over time and having sufficient time contribute to people's satisfaction with life (Campbell, Converse, & Rodgers, 1976). Most people want enough time at their disposal and want to be able to choose how to use it. To understand leisure behavior and why people make choices about recreation services requires a further discussion about time.

Issues

With the emergence of the Industrial Revolution in the 18th and 19th centuries, workers, employers, politicians, social reformers, and economists struggled with how long people should reasonably be expected to work. Resolving this question proved to be difficult because it involved conflicting economic, moral, political, religious, and social interests.

By 1900, when the U.S. workweek was approximately 60 hours (Hunnicutt, 1985), work hours reduction was a central issue for the U.S. labor movement and for many social reform organizations. The length of the workweek was reduced to 42.7 hours by 1948 and to 42.5 hours in 1975 (Owen, 1976). Today in the United States, the average worker spends 36–42 hours each week in paid work.

What would the preferable future resemble related to time? No one says that people should not work for pay. However, economists in England recently recommended that moving to a 21-hour standard workweek could address problems with unemployment, high carbon emissions, low sense of well-being, entrenched inequalities, overworking, family care, and the general lack of free time (http://tedxghent.blogspot.com/2012/06/

anna-coote-on-21-work-week.html). More people working, albeit working on a three-day-a-week schedule, would be a huge change but also might address some of these social issues. The likelihood of reducing work hours dramatically is unlikely in the United States. However, enabling people to find meaningful experiences in their nonwork hours is part of the role of professionals in recreation services.

Not all time, however, can be dichotomized as either work or leisure, as discussed earlier in this book. The U.S. Bureau of Labor Statistics (http://www.bls.gov/news.release/atus.nr0.htm) presented several interesting findings about how people spent their time during 2011:

- For the first time ever in 2011, data were collected about eldercare. About 16% of the adult population was involved in unpaid eldercare.

- On average, 21% of employed persons did some or all of their work at home, with men and women almost equal in the amount.

- On an average day, 48% of women and 19% of men spent some time each day doing household activities (e.g., housework, cooking, lawn care, household management).

- At least 95% of adults said they did some sort of leisure activity (e.g., watching TV, socializing, exercising) every day. Of those that engaged in leisure, men (5.8 hours) spent more time than did women (5.2 hours). Watching TV accounted for *half* of this leisure time. Socializing or visiting with friends or attending social events was the next most common activity.

- Men were more likely than women to participate in sports, exercise, or active recreation—1.9 hours for men compared with 1.3 hours for women a week.

- Individuals aged 15–19 read an average of 7 minutes a day and spent 1.2 hours playing games or using a computer for leisure.

- Adults living in households with children under the age of 6 spent about 2 hours a day doing primary childcare (i.e., direct contact with the child such as physical care like bathing or feeding a child). Women spent four times more time doing this caregiving than men who lived with young children.

These selected statistics provide a snapshot of the time use of adults and children. Just how much people work for pay, do unpaid home-related activities, and how much leisure they have comparatively has been widely debated. For example, although many more professional women are now in the workforce, the amount of unpaid household and childcare work that remains expected of them has only diminished slightly. Hoschild and Machung (1990) referred to this phenomenon as the *double shift* for women. Schor (1990) argued that people perceived that work hours and time pressures were increasing substantially in American society. Although some researchers agree that work hours have increased, no consensus exists on the size of the increase or how the additional work hours are distributed. Perhaps the perception of time pressures is more salient for people than the actual amount of time they have in work or leisure.

Challenges

The work ethic remains high in the United States. Therefore, to suggest that work is not important is both economically and socially problematic. Obviously, people need to have some means for making a livelihood. People need to make money to survive. The question that needs to be considered is, however, how much money is enough? People need an adequate standard of living and discretionary income to use for their recreation. However, some people may take a second, usually part-time, job because they do not always know what to do with their time and working is a socially sanctioned activity. Nevertheless, when people are asked whether they would rather have more time or more money, many choose more time although great variability usually exists in that response. Unfortunately, many low-wage earners must take a second job to make a subsistence living for their families. A full-time job paying only minimum wage will not support a family.

Another challenge to time for recreation is that people with higher levels of education on average work longer hours than people with less education. These people also make higher wages but not due necessarily to working longer hours. Some people have argued that while technology has enabled people to work more efficiently, technology also suggests that people can do more. In addition, the ways that people are now connected to work 24/7 through technology also may mean that no professional employee is ever completely unobligated from their work, which contributes to people believing they are working longer.

Workers in the United States also are bound to policies that exist about time away from work. Paid vacation days are a benefit that organizations voluntarily provide to employees and is generally accrued based on years of service in the organization and the level of the position. Unlike many other countries, especially in Europe, no Federal laws in the United

States require an employer to offer paid vacation days as a benefit. Earlier in this book the differences in vacation among countries was contrasted. The number of vacation days is also controversial in terms of how it could slow down an economy. Nevertheless, getting Federal regulation of uniform vacation days could be a way to encourage more time for leisure for everyone.

Therefore, at the beginning of the 21st century and despite all the progress made with technology, people do not perceive that they have more time for recreation than in the past. Work hours do not follow a uniform pattern in society and have not continued to decrease as many people anticipated. Regardless of economic boom or recession, work hours tend to increase among the well-educated while at the same time secure employment remains elusive for many workers. As people work longer hours, whether they earn more money or not, they surrender more of their scarcest resource, time. Most people want more time for leisure and want choices in recreation services where they can use that time for leisure.

Strategies for Action

Recreation services cannot provide more time for people. However, the services can be of high quality so that people feel they have made good choices in using that time. How an individual chooses to use his or her time is a personal choice, although usually highly influenced by family and friends. Recreation services in all the sectors offer choices that people can choose or not. Several strategies aimed at individuals as well as professionals may be worth considering.

The reason people almost always give when asked why they do not participate more in leisure is that they "don't have time." Individuals cannot create more time but they can prioritize what time is available. They need to know their options so they can decide how to use their time. The role of recreation services organizations is to create opportunities and ensure that people are aware of what is available. Although part of what is wonderful about leisure is that it can be spontaneous like play, the reality is that many people have long "to do" lists. If a recreation activity is really important, it needs to be prioritized and put on the list.

Often, if people decide they will exercise or take a walk when their work is done, they will not have any time left over. An analogy relates to saving money. People who are able to save money each month take out the amount (e.g., $100) at the beginning of the month and don't just hope

save $ analogy

they have $100 left over at the end of the month. The money is seldom there. The same is true with time for leisure. Determine what it is that gives enjoyment and then set aside time for it. Write it on your calendar. In addition, schedule weekends for special activities and plan for annual vacations. If an individual does not plan for recreation activities, they may not happen. Or when time becomes available it will be spent doing something like watching TV since it requires little effort. TV watching is usually not a very meaningful recreation activity.

Related to priorities is setting boundaries. That means paying attention to physical and emotional limits and knowing when to slow down when feeling overly stressed or overwhelmed. This advice is certainly easier to give than to take, but it can allow more time to do the things a person really wants to do. Some people may also want to think that their work must be perfect. Sometimes deciding that a task undertaken is good enough is more important than making it perfect.

Finally, individuals need to think about leisure as a right that everyone has. As noted in earlier chapters, leisure is not without responsibility to yourself and others, but having time to recreate is essential. Sometimes people need to give up potential feelings of guilt for doing something that they really enjoyed. Everyone deserves to have enjoyment in their lives.

From a social policy perspective, an initiative that has begun to help people is called *Take Back Your Time*. Its purpose is to challenge the epidemic of overwork, overscheduling, and time famine that now threatens people's health, families and relationships, communities, and the environment (http://timeday.org). This group has put together what they have called a "time to care" public policy agenda that focuses on perceptions of lack of time, also called time poverty.

- Guaranteeing paid leave for all parents for the birth or adoption of a child. Today, only 40% of Americans are able to take advantage of the 12 weeks of unpaid leave provided by the Family and Medical Leave Act of 1993

- Guaranteeing at least one week of paid sick leave for all workers

- Guaranteeing at least three weeks of paid annual vacation leave for all workers (the European Union requires that workers receive at least 20 days of paid leave per year (http://www.time.com/time/world/article/0,8599,2109263,00.html#ixzz24es7HIZU).

- Placing a limit on the amount of compulsory overtime work that an employer can impose

- Making election day a holiday with the understanding that people need time for civic participation

- Making it easier for people to choose part-time work by prorating benefits (e.g., vacation time, health benefits)

These proposals aimed at changes in time spent in the workplace will influence recreation services. Having more time is the responsibility of individuals as well as society. Valuing time for leisure and having meaningful opportunities for recreation can enhance people's well-being and the quality of life in communities in the future.

Reflection Questions

1. Do you feel you have enough time to undertake all the tasks you need to do as well as want to do each day? Explain. How could you be more efficient in the use of your time?

2. Given a choice and you had adequate amounts of money, would you rather have more time or more money?

3. One of the problems with a work/leisure dichotomy is acknowledging that work is more than just paid work. Many tasks of daily living fall in neither the category of work nor leisure all the time. How do you classify tasks in your life such as eating, preparing meals, shopping, doing laundry, sleeping, taking a shower? How might they be more like work? How might they be more like leisure?

4. What issues would U.S. society have to address if a 21-hour work week was mandated (assuming the wages earned were above a subsistence level)?

Chapter 33

Changing Demographics

Social changes are constant in society, and many of those changes are connected to changing demographics. Some examples of how changing populations influence recreation services have been highlighted in this book (e.g., older adults, youth culture). In the past 50 years, the size, age, and diversity of the population of the United States have changed dramatically (Sheffield, 2012) and will likely continue to change. A brief focus on selected populations may be useful, since the growth and change will require investments in recreation to meet the needs, interests, and preferences of new audiences. The population is growing in the United States, and the nature of that population is changing regarding disability, racial and ethnic diversity, age, gender, socioeconomic status, sexual identity, and religious affiliation. These demographic changes raise opportunities to focus on social sustainability and balancing personal autonomy with social good.

With a larger population base comes the need to provide more recreation services. Similarly, greater participation requires continuing innovation and evaluation for program improvement. Alternative funding may be necessary in all sectors to ensure balanced opportunities. As the world changes, recreation services professionals will need to consider the implications for these changes. The goal will be to meet the multitude of needs and interests of individuals in society in ways that are meaningful, inclusive, and sustainable. Committing to leisure as a right of all individuals can influence the future of recreation services.

Issues and Challenges

Several demographic groups will be discussed briefly to illustrate some of the changes and the implications for recreation services. People with disabilities are discussed elsewhere in this book.

Age Groups

As noted in the chapter about older adults, Baby Boomers are beginning to retire. Also noted was the great diversity that exists among Baby Boomers. Yet, as a cohort going from youth to old age, they continue to influence society. Further, they are likely to live longer than any previous U.S. generation, so they will be involved in recreation services in all sectors for many years to come. People living longer and healthier will likely change patterns of participation as recreation activities become lifelong pursuits. Recreation professionals will need to consider safety and access as they program for these individuals. Further, the Baby Boomers have grown up expecting more opportunities for themselves, and they will continue to have those expectations from recreation services into the future.

In addition to the Baby Boomers, three other generational cohorts will seek recreation services. A generation cohort is a group that shares birth years, age, location, and significant life events at critical developmental stages. Variations in the group can be the result of whether people were born at the beginning or the tail end of the birth years. The Silent Generation, also called the Traditionalists, includes the oldest individuals in communities. They were born prior to the end of World War II and represent what might be called the *old old* in society. Generation X (i.e., 1965–1981) and Generation Y or the Millennials (i.e., 1982–2002), compose the other two main groups.

All four generations differ based on their attitudes, behaviors, expectations, habits, and motivational buttons. For example, the Millennials have also been referred to as Generation We, Global Generation, the Net Generation, and the Echo Boomers, which all describe some of their characteristics. These individuals have also called themselves Non-Nuclear Family generation, the Nothing-Is-Sacred Generation, the Wannabees, the Feel-Good Generation, Cyberkids, the Do-or-Die Generation, and the Searching-for-an-Identity Generation http://rtc.umn.edu/docs/2_18_Gen_diff_workplace.pdf).

Much has been written about these generations and their characteristics, which has implications for recreation services in the future. Generation Xers, for example, appear to aspire more than the Boomers or Traditionalists to achieve a balance between work and leisure. They also tend to be more independent and self-reliant (e.g., they were the latchkey children). They are strongly loyal to their family and friends. They may care more about what they are doing than how much time something takes.

The Millennials, on the other hand, have been greatly shaped by hovering parents, computers, and huge technological advances. They are highly comfortable with technology, but also value teamwork and diversity. Like

Generation X, they desire a more balanced life, but at the same time are multitaskers. Being aware of some of the age markers of people in communities can give some sense of what they may want regarding their recreation services as well as how they wish to be communicated with and organized.

Socioeconomic Status

Although many people in the United States are economically well off, many are not. Income inequality is an issue due to lack of training, lack of education, or inability to adapt to the changing job market. Many lower-income people are clustered together in communities whether in urban areas or rural enclaves. Bifurcation (i.e., the *haves* and the *have nots*) also occurs regarding access to recreation services. People who are economically disadvantaged continue to be marginal participants in the *good life* enjoyed by many Americans. Their traditional organized recreation opportunities often have been affected by their lack of resources.

Like other populations, great diversity exists among people with limited economic means. Some are alone while others are in family units. Some have physical, social, and/or mental disabilities and could benefit from ongoing assistance, while others find themselves only in short-term crisis situations. Some people are homeless, while others live in subsistent housing. In the United States today, unfortunately, people with lower economic means continue to be over-represented by racial minorities, and many of the individuals in poverty are women and children. The gap has become wider rather than narrower due to the economy's downturn. Recreation services professionals should keep these disparities in mind when pressure is placed to make people "pay to play."

Women

Women have made great gains in their status in the past 50 years. However, issues remain to be addressed related to equity in time to be used in leisure, as illustrated early in this unit. Many of the inequities pertain to the historical treatment of women. For example, prior to the 1960s, jobs were advertised as for males or for females and it was not until 1963 that laws prohibiting unequal pay were passed. Although women had opportunities to go to college for decades, it was not until the 1960s that women had their choice of attendance at co-educational institutions. The laws have changed and the attitudes toward women and their capabilities have improved, but the reality for many women is that they remain disadvantaged in ways that include their work and recreation.

Women's pay, for example, has not changed radically. In 1963 women earned 59% of the wages earned by men. In 2008 they earned 77% of men's wages. This represents an improvement of about half a penny per dollar earned every year. At this rate, it will be another 50 years before women earn the same percentage as men. The good news is that conditions are changing since women under the age of 25 now make 93% of what men make. But why don't they make 100%? Clearly issues persist. Although income does not completely define one's leisure, it does have an effect on the options available, especially for recreation services. The more resources that women have, the more likely they will be able to participate in recreation opportunities.

Ethnic and Racial Groups

The "color" and ethnic cultures of U.S. society are changing. The United States has always been diverse since it is a nation of immigrants. Today African Americans, who are mostly descendants of slaves, constitute the largest racial minority in the United States. However, Latinos constitute the largest ethnic group. (Note: race relates to physical characteristics of individuals and ethnicity concerns the culture and language of a group.) About two-thirds of Latinos are of Mexican descent. The Latino population is rapidly growing due to immigration and the tendency for Latino families to be large (http://www.usa.org/demographics). With current trends, whites of non-Hispanic origin will be a minority group in the United States by 2050.

The changes in the ethnic and racial composition of the United States will obviously have implications for the recreation services. Family and individual recreation patterns and preferences are shaped by cultural influences. Based on cultural background, people have different desires. For example, picnic areas in many city parks have been designed with a table here and a table there, assuming that a traditional nuclear family will be using the site (i.e., two parents, two children). Many Latinos, however, consider the family to be extended to aunts and uncles and all generations. Therefore, when a Latino group visits a park, often they want several tables grouped together where the entire family can eat and relax. Changes are occurring in some of these park designs, but this example illustrates how recreation services will be challenged to change as the racial and ethnic composition of U.S. society continues to evolve.

Sexual Identity

Same-sex attractions and behaviors are not new in U.S. society or in any part of the world. However, in the past half-century, lesbian, gay, bisexual, transgendered, and queer (LGBTQ) individuals have become more visible. Sexual identity is the term used here to refer to how people think about themselves related to their sexual and romantic attractions. In the past, terms like sexual preference (i.e., choosing to be with the same sex) and sexual orientation (i.e., fantasies and longings for the same sex) have been used. Sexual identity seems to be a useful term in the 21st century because it allows an individual to define him- or herself.

Regardless, the visibility of LGBTQ identity is part of the U.S. culture. The "Don't Ask, Don't Tell" policy in the military has been ended recently, and a growing number of states allow same-sex marriage or domestic partnerships. Although some people see sexual identity as a moral issue, many people are now acknowledging the human rights that LGBTQ individuals deserve.

The exact number of individuals in the United States who are LGBTQ is difficult to know. Different studies have shown the percentage is between 4.5% and 10%. However, how people define their identity varies and people experiment and change over time. Nevertheless, LGBTQ individuals represent about 1 of every 10 Americans. Many of these individuals reside in cities across the United States that are perceived as "gay-friendly." However, LGBTQ people live everywhere.

Many LGBTQ people do not necessarily want different recreation opportunities than anyone else in society. However, LGBTQ is a culture and opportunities to share that culture through Gay Pride festivals, gay sports leagues, gay bars, gay businesses, gay churches, gay travel agencies, and gay arts groups are not uncommon in most cities in the United States. Catering to LGBTQ interests is a growing business and certainly these people want recreation opportunities for the same reasons as others. The growing number of gay families also cannot be discounted nor, unfortunately, the possibilities of the bullying of gay young people in communities. Recreation professionals in all sectors should be aware of the recreation interests and needs that LGBTQ individuals have in communities.

Religious Affiliations

Religion is an element of culture that is also highly visible in the United States. Discussions about the influence of religion on work and leisure, spirituality as a benefit of recreation experiences, faith-based organizations, and careers in recreation ministries are discussed in this book. However, a bit more can be said about the importance of religion in the United States and connections to ways of thinking about recreation services. Although people in the United States have been primarily influenced by the Judeo-Christian tradition, the history and philosophies of Eastern religions, as well as other Western religions, are useful to examine as a basis for understanding more about leisure experiences and recreation services.

Religious doctrines, practices, and philosophies have played a role in determining cultural attitudes and behaviors towards the natural world and toward leisure. No one religion is better than another, but each teaches its followers how to best live in the world. For example, each religion has rituals (e.g., prayers, Sabbath, pilgrimages) that people value in their daily lives and in times of anxiety. Most religions have history and traditions that serve as templates for action. Collectively, religion helps understand the nature of reality and gives people a basis for how they should live their lives.

Religious beliefs both enhance and constrain recreation involvement. For example, the Western religions of Judaism, Christianity, and Islam all espouse action and a belief in the importance of performing good works. Judaism and Christianity both maintain that caring for one's body, as God's creation, and maintaining good health are aspects of religious practice.

Eastern religions (e.g., Hinduism, Confucianism, Taoism, and Buddhism) share the commonality of an Asian heritage. Hindus, for example, believe that all forms of life are to be respected and protected, and this idea relates to the dignity of individuals and to the earth in all activities including recreation and leisure. Confucians believe that the universe is constantly changing, unfolding, and filling with vital force or power called *chi*. Leisure is important as it contributes to chi and to social harmony. Leisure and play have significance as they help people relate better to one another. Taoists believe the environment determines the condition for one's own actualization or enlightenment. Taoists also value simplicity and spontaneity, which are embodied in anything undertaken, including leisure.

An interpretation of any religion and the meanings it portrays for leisure is much more complex than it may appear on the surface. Knowing something about what people from different religions believe about living, however, may help in thinking about what recreation services might offer, whether within a faith-based organization or in the broader community.

Strategies for Action

Although recreation services are not the panacea for social ills, recreation and leisure have been used throughout history to maintain social order. Empowering all people regardless of their demographic characteristics through recreation aids in the development of individuals and can give a sense of community.

Recreation services can be designed by considering the behaviors and constraints of potential participants. If people are economically disadvantaged, or older adults cannot come to the recreation site, then recreation professionals could consider how transportation might be provided. If the users do not speak English, staff interaction and instructional materials should be in their native language. By having some swimming periods available to all free of charge, while also having at the same location some swimming sessions for which there is an admission fee, recreation departments can accommodate both those who want a degree of exclusiveness and those who cannot afford such an economic luxury. A trend in the past has been to automatically reduce fees for older adults or people with disabilities. Just because an individual has a disability or is older, however, does not mean that he or she lacks economic resources.

Program accessibility is a concern that involves both access and omission. Cultural competence is an area that recreation services professionals should address. Most professionals do not wish to offend or exclude anyone, but their actions might be unintentionally or unconsciously insensitive. Sensitivity is necessary regardless of the group and regardless of the specialty within recreation services.

Culturally competent and sensitive leadership is the key to successful recreation programming for all people. Able-bodied college graduates with middle-class value orientations often staff recreation services, and human nature suggests that professionals are inclined to understand the value of recreation services for people like themselves. Consequently, potential participants who want activities similar to their own cultural interests and traditions may not be interested in traditional program offerings.

Part of the education of future recreation professionals (both in the curricula of undergraduate programs and in postgraduate courses) must include the development of cultural competence applied to all groups that may be marginalized in society. The first step is to learn about community groups and cultures. Secondly, recreation professionals can facilitate equitable opportunities in recreation for all individuals when a philosophy of choice exists. Successful recreation services require professionals who are sensitive to people's interests as well as barriers that prohibit them from participation. Cooperative strategies to work with different groups and to involve these groups in planning will be necessary to facilitate meaningful leisure experiences.

Reflection Questions

1. How does a future or current professional learn more about diverse groups of people and develop cultural competence?

2. What are the greatest challenges to recreation professionals in trying to meet the interests and needs of different groups in society? What can be done to address those challenges?

3. Not only will the population of the United States change in its composition, but more people overall will desire recreation services in the United States. How can the field meet the challenge of this greater demand?

Chapter 34

Social Inclusion

At the end of the 20th century, many people were optimistic about the future. They had hopes for a better society where tensions and divisiveness around characteristics such as race, gender, (dis)ability, age, income, sexual identity, and religion would be in the past. However, segregation and prejudices have not gone away. For example, many communities remain segregated by race as well as class. Although discrimination is illegal, people tend to not mix readily with others who are not like them. A challenge to recreation professionals in the future and an important aspect of social sustainability is to address social inclusion. This inclusion includes the groups described in the previous chapter as well as other marginalized groups.

This chapter examines the idea of social inclusion and how recreation services might be made more inclusive. 'Inclusion' is a term often associated in the United States with people with disabilities. The term has been useful for this population, but it also has broader significance for thinking about the right that all people have to recreation services.

Issues

Two terms that have been used for over two decades in other parts of the world are 'social inclusion' and 'social exclusion.' Exclusion identifies how all people regardless of markers such as ability and economic level might be segregated in their communities. Social inclusion offers a broad base for understanding the value of recreation services for all groups. Socially-inclusive recreation means that individuals, regardless of their position in society, have opportunities to find meanings and connections through socially responsible and sustainable recreation opportunities.

Inclusion assumes a concept of social justice. The notion of inclusion has been linked to *just recreation*, referring to the idea that leisure and recreation should contribute to social and environmental justice (Henderson, 1997), as discussed earlier in this book. To do harm to any group through unethical leisure behavior or inequitable recreation services diminishes everyone. When discussing social inclusion, the concepts of equality and equity are important to understand. The metaphor of restrooms serves to illustrate these concepts, as Molotch (1988) explained:

> In many public buildings, the amount of floor area dedicated for the men's room and the women's room is the same. The prevailing public bathroom doctrine in the United States is one of segregation among the genders, but with equality the guiding ideology. . . . Such an arrangement follows the dictum that equality can be achieved only by policies that are "gender-blind" (or "color-blind" or "ethnic-blind") in the allocation of a public resource. . . . Women and men have the same proportion of a building to use as restrooms.
>
> The trouble with this sort of equality is that, being blind, it fails to recognize differences between men as a group and women as a group . . . (such differences include hygiene needs, different physiological functions, and the use of toilets versus urinals). . . . By creating men's and women's rooms of the same size, society guarantees that individual women will be worse off than individual men. By distributing a resource equally, an unequal result is structurally guaranteed (pp. 128–129).

Molotch goes on to describe the specific situation of intermission time at a theater where long lines for women and no lines for men are not unusual. The *liberal* policy or solution is to make women's rooms larger than men's. An alternative solution (one he calls *conservative*) would be for women to be more like men and to change the way they use restrooms, rather than for society to change the structuring of restroom space. In other words, a conservative approach would say there is no need to overturn the principle of equality of square footage among the genders. Instead, women need to use their allotted square footage more efficiently. This conservative argument, however, discounts the role that some men have had related to the problem. What if the issue is not that some women primp in the rest room, but that men expect them to be beautiful? Another possible solution, which might be called a *radical* approach, would allow women to decide for themselves what they will need for restroom space and how they will use it.

Molotch (1988) concluded that determining equality and equity is not a matter of arithmetic division, but social justice. Equality is a matter of fact (i.e., women have as many restrooms as men, or women have the same sports programs as men) and is basically objective. Equity is a matter of ethical judgment (i.e., women need more restrooms than men because of the way they use restrooms, or women need more sports skills development opportunities than men because many women did not have the same learning opportunities when younger) and takes subjective assessments into account. Therefore, equity is equated with fairness. The equal treatment of groups may create inequity issues for others. The story provides a foundation for examining the goals of social inclusion in all sectors of recreation services.

Challenges

Inclusion cannot occur without acknowledging the power of privilege and the diversity among people. For example, differences between men and women are one aspect as are differences among women, and among men. Recreation professionals in the future will need to focus on gender, race, class, and ability inclusivity rather than neutrality. Arguing that no differences exist draws attention away from actual differences in power and resources among groups (Rhode, 1990). Affirming the similarity between women and men, black and white, gay and straight, able-bodied and disabled, or other heterogeneous groups may inadvertently universalize or validate norms of the dominant social groups. These assumed norms often have not addressed diverse interests, experiences, and perspectives for groups participating in recreation activities.

The goals of social inclusion are reflected in a philosophy of recreation services that allows individuals (e.g., low income, people with disabilities, or females) to go from roles to rights, from best interests to choice, from paternalism to self-determination, and from invisibility to visibility (Rioux, 1993). As Molotch noted, fairness rather than sameness is required to achieve social inclusion. Recreation services should be intentional acts deliberately designed to bring about the development of the best qualities in individuals. If inclusion is to occur in recreation and leisure experiences, then it must be a goal and not just assumed to happen. As noted earlier, leisure and recreation are not inherently good. They must be intentionally framed for inclusion if the opportunities are to be just.

Strategies for Action

Recreation professionals in all sectors can challenge themselves to teach and provide recreation opportunities for community groups that will enable those groups to become empowered, not only in their leisure, but also in other areas of their lives. Inclusive recreation services means that all participants will be encouraged to participate and to undertake enjoyable activities because they possess the confidence and skill levels necessary to be successful. This philosophy has been commonly discussed for people with disabilities largely because of the American Disability Act, but has implications for all nontraditional and marginalized groups.

No magic formulas exist to help recreation professionals facilitate social inclusion, but some approaches are better than others. Traditionally, the recreation field has followed the liberal philosophy of treating people equally. This approach, however, is almost always defined according to the dominant culture's terms, with minority groups striving to get more of what the dominant group has always had. The approach offered in the name of equality has been effective in offering more opportunities for particular groups and for calling attention to the inequalities that have existed. However, professionals cannot assume that all activities are important to all individuals just because they are important to some. Activity does not have to be the same for all, but everyone should have a choice.

Another approach to programming for inclusion is based on an equitable education model (Bailey, 1993). Achieving equity means equally recognizing and rewarding the achievements of all individuals. For example, "a wider range of choices will be genuinely available to girls only when an equally wide and nontraditional range of choices is available to boys as well" (Bailey, 1993, p. 322). This model also seeks to counter stereotypes and behaviors that diminish the value of recreation. Frequently when a person from a marginalized group does not perform in some way, attributions are made to that person's group affiliation. For example, if a woman cannot shoot a bow and arrow well, the assumption is that females can't shoot well. If a man cannot shoot a bow and arrow well, he's just not a good shot. Recreation professionals will be challenged with addressing stereotypes they hold, which are also held by others in society.

Although any individual involved in leisure experiences can examine the implications of his or her behavior for social and environment justice, recreation professionals who facilitate these experiences have, in my opinion, a mandate to reflect on how recreation services contribute to or are detrimental to the social good. This notion of the social good relates to assuring the social, economic, and environmental sustainability of recreation services. Several suggestions may give some guidance.

First, professionals ought to examine the philosophy and mission of their organizations. This examination may relate to considering what recreation means as well as who the beneficiaries of the services are. Are programs conducted and opportunities offered that are available to all and that do not stereotype people? Do the leisure opportunities create the least possible environmental impact? Can the services be sustainable over a period of time?

Second, an awareness of leisure's significance and the possibilities for recreation services must lead to some type of action. After examining recreation services critically, then action should occur to right any possible wrongs. The challenge lies in finding ways to try new approaches, take risks, and engage in activities that go beyond stereotypical or socially proscribed boundaries (Kivel & Kivel, 2000).

Third, professionals need to be able to see the "big picture." All recreation services organizations are influenced by the larger society. Part of sustaining recreation services to promote inclusion and justice relates to realizing the connection to larger social issues (e.g., poverty, technology, changing demographics).

Society has many challenges to address about inclusive leisure. Addressing exclusion problems is difficult, especially when groups such as the Boy Scouts can legally deny gay leaders a place in their organization. Hate crimes and sexual assault can make people fearful. Therefore, some groups of people would rather participate in activities with like groups because it is easier, more comfortable, and safer. Recreation professionals, however, must be aware of these larger social issues and attempt to make sure that leisure services do not contribute further to the social problems that exist.

Recreation and leisure can make a difference in the quality of life in communities in ways that can bring people together, rather than isolate and separate. Making recreation programs inclusive depends on consistent and concerted efforts. When all individuals in our society confront comparable life, leisure, and employment choices, no need will exist for discussions about inclusion and justice—inclusion and justice will be automatic. If recreation and leisure are to contribute to a more sustainable world and a higher quality of life, all recreation professionals must be concerned about inclusion.

Reflection Questions

1. Give some additional examples of how equality and equity may produce different outcomes, such as what was described in the restroom example.

2. How is social exclusion of benefit to some people? How can this benefit be mitigated?

3. When an equal treatment model is applied, who decides what 'equal' means?

Chapter 35

Education and Advocacy

Recreation professionals believe in the value and benefits of leisure experiences and recreation services. They also should believe in the right of all people to freely choose and participate in recreation opportunities. The opportunities are embodied in recreation services but often people can benefit from education that will enable them to make informed choices. Helping others who are not professionally employed in recreation services to see the educational benefits of leisure is necessary in enlisting advocates for the recreation services field.

Although recreation is sometimes thought of as only fun and games (and there is no denying that it should be enjoyable), it is also an avenue for personal development. A major outcome that recreation may offer is opportunities for education and learning for life. In a similar vein, the greatest impact of education may be when it is designed to be more like recreation. John Dewey (1939) stated, "Perhaps the most deep-seated antithesis which has shown itself in education history is that between education in preparation for useful labor and education for a life of leisure." In many ways, education and recreation in their finest forms are one and the same (Henderson, 1981). Education for leisure should include not only instruction about leisure awareness, attitudes, and knowledge, but also a focus on personal and social values and how values influence leisure choices and decision-making skills. To advocate means to support these goals.

Issues and Challenges

A leisure age, which has obviously not come to fruition, was forecast almost 60 years ago. Concerns were raised in the 1960s about whether people could handle leisure for the good of themselves and their communities. Leisure was envisioned as a commodity with access for everyone, but was also viewed as problematic. Free time could make for personal well-being, but a concern existed that those opportunities would not happen without adequate structured services in schools and communities. The leisure age did not come to pass, but many professionals believe today that an awareness and appreciation of leisure can be developed in numerous ways through educational approaches as well as recreation services.

Leisure education as a means for improving people's lives has existed since the 1970s. World Leisure (2005) has defined leisure education as primarily a subject in schools:

> The main aim of leisure education in educational frame-works is to help the individual, the family, the community, and the society to achieve a suitable quality of life and good health by using leisure time intelligently, by developing and cultivating physical, emotional, spiritual, mental, and social aspects, each individually or combined, as they relate to the aims of education in the country and its cultural heritage.

On the other hand, the former American Association for Leisure and Recreation (2003; now called the American Association of Physical Activity and Recreation) differentiated leisure education as potentially the subject of leisure (e.g., education about and for leisure) from leisure as the context of education (e.g., education through, during, and as leisure). The latter approach relates to informal and non-formal settings within recreation services where education through, during, and as leisure occurs, whether consciously addressed or not.

Leisure education as a subject has not been mainstreamed into schools despite the efforts of some individuals. It has been used formally in thera-peutic recreation settings and offered in some programs for people with disabilities. Further, the recommendation to some of the problems people have in being unable to find meaningful leisure is sometimes to suggest that leisure education is needed, which is often nonspecific. Interestingly, leisure education has not been an explicit goal related to recreation services, even though it is often implicit in the outcomes that individuals receive through recreation services.

Leisure and recreation attitudes, abilities, aspirations, and skills are learned experiences (Godbey, 1989), and thus, recreation services can be a context for education about leisure. Some forms of recreation involve physical or mental skills while others do not. People generally prefer doing recreation activities in which they feel competent. Thus, learning specific skills cannot be disassociated from appreciation and enjoyment in experiences. People with higher levels of education often have more leisure aspirations because the process of education itself exposes them to new activities and socializes them into these activities. Therefore, the availability and meanings of leisure experiences vary greatly often because of the relationship between leisure and education.

An emerging aspect of education relates to learning from technology. This area is sometimes called edutainment (i.e., educational entertainment or entertainment education). It is designed to educate as well as amuse. One well-known example is *Sesame Street*. Edutainment seeks to change behaviors by making learning fun. Leisure also may occur in edutainment in the form of educational computer games, educational toys, and infotainment.

By participating in recreation services, people learn about opportunities, other people, and themselves. Thus, recreation is a context for learning about leisure. Schools have supported leisure and life choices in major ways. For example, appreciation of leisure is often the outcome of learning through music, arts, reading, physical activity, and extracurricular activities. Education for leisure, however, is more than teaching specific activity skills or providing facilities for extracurricular activities. Education implies developing attitudes about life that free individuals to discover who they are and what is meaningful to them. Leisure education also suggests developing the attitudes and skills necessary for future explorations and involvement in new recreation pursuits.

Strategies for Action

Most people can define leisure in a taken-for-granted manner but have not thought about the value of leisure and recreation services in their lives. The notion of leisure rarely elicits deep reflection or contemplation for average people, although many people say they do not have enough time for what they consider to be leisure. Without an understanding of the value and role of leisure in life, people may have trouble making it a priority or identifying leisure resources. Increasing people's understanding of leisure in their lives and improving their attitudes toward it can be a foundation for taking control of recreation choices, reducing stress, and enjoying life more fully.

What to do with unstructured free time can be uncomfortable if choices are not available to people. Sometimes turning on the TV or the computer and being entertained is easiest. Having choices among recreation activities, or being free to participate sounds like a simple concept. Individuals, however, must be aware of the multitude of recreation opportunities available, as well as the benefits of those choices. All recreation professionals have a role to play in helping people appreciate and enjoy recreation activities.

Advocating for leisure and for recreation services is certainly the role of professionals in the field, but it is also important to get others (e.g., citizens, clients, customers, business people, educators, policymakers, elected officials) to be advocates if recreation services are to be sustained. Advocacy is always political because it is about expressing beliefs about something that is valued as good. Advocacy is a means to move a cause forward. Lobby groups, for example, are a form of advocacy where a direct approach is made to legislators on an issue that plays a significant role in community life. The Internet has become a tool of advocacy for people who support particular causes. Advocacy also can include activities that a person or group undertakes including media campaigns, public speaking, and research and evaluation.

Recreation professionals are advocates when they emphasize the benefits of leisure experiences and recreation services. They are advocates when they recognize the educational value of recreation. To encourage advocacy from others, good information is needed (e.g., education about leisure) so that its benefits can be understood and people can see how their own personal leisure contributes to their well-being and how recreation services are necessary for the quality of life in communities.

Reflection Questions

1. What characteristics do recreation and education share?

2. What is the difference between leisure as an educational subject and leisure as a context for education? Is one more important than the other?

3. How are education and advocacy connected?

4. In what ways can you be an advocate for recreation as leisure, or for any other benefit that might exist as a result of recreation services?

Chapter 36

Technology and Leisure

A recent story about technology unfolded like this:

> It was just a bowl of soup, but it meant so much more to Brandon Cook. He called Amherst Street Panera Bread looking for a bowl of comfort for his dying grandmother. She wanted some Panera clam chowder in a bread bowl. He called on Monday and found that the soup was only served on Fridays. He asked to speak to a manager who took his call. After hearing the story, she got the soup for Brandon's grandmother and gave it to him free of charge, and she included a box of cookies.
>
> Brandon posted the story to his Facebook page because he was so grateful to the manager. His mother saw the post and was so grateful to Brandon and to Panera that she reposted Brandon's Facebook comment to the Panera Bread Facebook page. The post went viral with over 500,000 likes and more than 10,000 comments in the first week alone.
>
> Because of Facebook, Brandon Cook's gratitude for the chowder was magnified many times over. The manager says that the real hero is Brandon because he asked and cared. Brandon said that if his grandmother had not been so sick, he would have shown her all about Facebook and how many "friends" she had, and how many prayers were being said for her. (http://nashua.patch.com/articles/a-bowl-of-soup-and-a-simple-gesture-of-kindness)

Technology is ubiquitous. It has huge influence on people's free time and work. This technology can offer amazing advantages, as shown in the story above, but it also can have drawbacks. The future will necessitate finding ways to use technology for enhancing leisure and recreation services, without making it the complete focus of free time.

Free time is frequently necessary for recreation to occur. Unobligated time, however, becomes difficult to address as American life speeds up in response to a greater focus on productivity, communication, and technology. Technology was supposed to make life easier for workers, but rather it has created the expectations that a professional should be able to do more. In addition, many people are connected to their technology (i.e., smartphones, tablets, laptops) almost 24/7. This constant availability of technology has also resulted in doing more than one thing at a time or multitasking, which Godbey (1997) called time deepening.

No question exists that technology greatly impacts the way people live, work, and play in the 21st century, as noted in the story above. Technology influences recreation in terms of the individual's leisure pursuits and the recreation professional's viewpoint. Advances in technology have given people new ways to communicate, innovative places to play, better equipment to facilitate their adventures, and new activities to pursue. Some of the advances have helped recreation professionals streamline or remove tedious work tasks like league scheduling, improve communication efforts with participants, and manage services more efficiently and effectively. Many of these positive advances, however, have come with often overlooked costs. The purpose of this chapter is to explore some of the benefits and challenges of technology as it relates to leisure experiences and recreation services.

Issues

The influence of rapidly evolving technological changes will continue to have dramatic effects on people's lives. For example, the separation between where people work and where they live will likely be blurred in the future. Technology has allowed many professionals to do more of their work from their homes rather than travel to an office. The rise in technology has contributed to making recreation and leisure opportunities commodities. The mass consumption of movies, e-books, DVDs, MP3 music, and computer and video games consumes the time of many individuals.

The influence of technology has greatly influenced communication. Although people continue to socialize in person, texting someone or checking out their status on social media sites has made the amount and nature of communication different than in the past. Ironically, the consumption of technology that was once billed as bringing people closer together can have opposite effects. A Twitter message with 140 characters is efficient, but it may not be sufficient in some cases. Short and to-the-point statements may allow for more communication, but the quality of the communication must be considered. Technology can also make people impatient with each another. Since we know we can get in touch with one another at a moment's notice, we expect others to respond immediately, and we often expect that the world around us including cars, traffic, and lines in stores will also speed up to keep pace with everything else that moves so quickly.

Every person is influenced by technology. Many households in the United States have televisions with cable or satellite dishes (i.e., often one in every room of varying sizes with TiVo or DVRs), high-speed Internet service, digital telephones, and a DVD or Blu-ray player. These households also may have a confusing number of remote controls. People buy recreational vehicles like personal watercraft, motor homes, and the latest bicycles, tennis rackets, and inline skates to enhance their recreation opportunities. People make vacation reservations, access maps, and find yellow page information over the Internet. More people are doing activities like backpacking, climbing, and paddling because technology has improved the equipment needed to make the activities more comfortable and safer, which attracts a wider range of individuals. The next time you put on your high-tech clothing (e.g., Gore-Tex, a Coolmax shirt, Fleece, or Tencel) remember how much even the clothes people wear is influenced by technology that was developed to enhance the recreation experience.

Many examples exist of technological advances that help people to access information and pursue new recreation interests. The Internet has become the biggest information center in society. Within seconds, people can access information about new hobbies, places to do these activities, and connections (i.e., meet ups) with other people interested in the same activities. People can access websites to buy the needed equipment or supplies, make reservations, acquire permits, or just chat with other interested people. Advances in fiber optics, laser technology, and other forms of transmission continue to make this access faster, easier, and cheaper.

Technology has also led to new recreational activities and significant changes in some traditional forms of recreation. For example, dozens of new leisure pursuits are directly related to the prevalence of computers such as virtual reality gaming centers, online auctions, and just surfing the Net. Improved recreational equipment is available for playgrounds and play surfaces. Some old recreational activities have been technologically enhanced by the development of new materials such as titanium for softball bats, bicycles, and backpack equipment. Technology is used to make equipment stronger and lighter, clothing warmer or cooler, and activities more exciting and innovative. Athletes commonly use heart monitors to aid in their training. Sonar is used to locate fish and target equipment is produced for activities like paintball. Rock climbing can be done indoors on artificial walls. These activities would have been unimaginable a few years ago. By the time you read this book written in 2013, you will probably be aware of more technological innovations that influence people's leisure experiences.

The technology has also allowed new opportunities for all people, including people with disabilities. For example, some people with physical disabilities can ski, run, climb, garden, paint, and lead an active life because of technological advances that facilitate their movement, their senses, and their personal interactions. Since many service members in the Iranian and Afghanistan wars incurred physical injuries that have been life-changing, new prostheses that allow walking and running as well as other devices have been made available to these veterans as well as others. People with communication impairments have computers that can speak for them.

Technology influences the way people travel and visit other people and places. People around the world want to experience different cultures, visit historic areas, and see the natural beauty of the world. For example, people are now able to visit the penguin colonies of Antarctica, trek in the remote areas of Nepal, and float the Amazon River to see some of the remaining rain forests. Tourism has emerged as one of the leading economies in many countries because of the ease of travel due to technology that has made travel faster and more comfortable. Who knows what may lie ahead for tourism when the possibilities of space travel are further explored?

Challenges

Technology has left its mark on recreation activities, but not everyone views all the advances positively. For example, although some people value forms of recreation such as jet skis and hang gliders, other people view them as negative due to their environmental impact. This equipment appears incompatible to some people's leisure ideals because of the noise, pollution, resource depletion, and habitat destruction they can cause. Some people even believe some types of technology should be banned from the general public.

Technological developments are often touted as labor-saving devices that free people from the drudgeries of manual work. Technology, however, has often taken away many physical demands of life and offered passive opportunities instead. For example, many experts are increasingly alarmed at the lack of physical activity of Americans and often link this passivity to television viewing and computer-based entertainment. In 2012, adults spent an average of four hours a day watching television and children spent over three hours each day watching television, which does not count other types of screen time. (http://www.csun.edu/science/health/docs/tv&health.html).

Although TV watching has declined slightly, the use of computers for entertainment has grown steadily. Rather than use free time to pursue active leisure pursuits, more people and especially children spend many passive hours in screen time. The positive aspects of television and computers have been highlighted, but the negative impacts on physical activity cannot be denied. Physical and mental health concerns as a result of less physical recreation are a direct challenge brought about by responses to the easy access to computer technology.

Violence also arises from increased technology related to leisure and recreation. Historically, violence has been evident in leisure for centuries (e.g., the gladiators of the Roman Empire). Concern exists that some recreational activities promote violence, and technology exacerbates this violence. For example, violence has been associated with sports like football and soccer, and with the advent of televised games, millions of people view these events. In addition, the number of murders seen on TV by the time an average child finishes elementary school is 8,000, and this jumps to 20,000 by the time a child reaches the age of 18 years (http://www.csun.edu/science/health/docs/tv&health.html).

Parents also worry that violent computer games with realistic blood and gore send a message of permissible violence, especially when reinforced by similar images on television and lyrics in popular songs. Pornography accessed through the Internet is just one more way that some people suggest violence against women is perpetuated. Blaming violent behavior on technology alone is simplistic, but these behaviors raise the ethical issue of whether a person should be free to access and pursue violence through technologically enhanced leisure experiences.

Increased consumerism also has a direct tie to technology. As more activities and equipment are developed, many people feel they need the latest, biggest, or fastest version available. Further, every day new advances come on the market and possessing them can suggest expertise, wealth, and status. The message is that even if you are not good at an activity, you can at least look the part. The slogan that appeared on a t-shirt several years ago, "He who dies with the most toys, wins" has become a metaphor for the consumerist culture. All of this equipment and gadgets deplete the available environmental resources. If the entire world had access to the same lifestyles as most Americans, our planet would be unable to sustain life.

The issue of social isolation during free time can be linked to technological advances, as can the ways that technology links people in very different ways. As noted earlier, telecommunication advances have allowed people to live in electronic cottages. People can email, fax, text, talk on cell phones, send photos instantly, and search the world's databases from almost anywhere, including their homes. Some people who work outside the home return at night and do not leave until the next day. People can buy groceries and shop online with the products delivered directly to one's door. With technological advances, many people can choose to have minimal contact with other people. With reasons that vary from weak interpersonal skills to being too tired from work demands, people have become more isolated socially even though more technically linked interpersonally. Social isolation can be seen as a matter of individual choice especially related to leisure, but this isolation can result in a decrease in civic participation with negative influences on people who lack social support groups and companions. On the other hand, media such as Facebook can connect people in ways not thought possible before.

Strategies for Action

Technology clearly impacts individuals, but it also has implications for recreation services among all the sectors and specialties. Technological changes have occurred in the management of recreation services. For example, almost all recreation organizations have websites developed for information and marketing. Online registration is expected by most people. Documents can be scanned and emailed to people instantaneously, even if the individual is thousands of miles away. Professionals with smartphones can be in contact with anyone in the world 24 hours a day. GPS (geographical positioning system) units are common in the field, with the professionals taking advantage of the extensive mapping systems available to help them to understand their communities and resources. Professionals can conduct training or take continuing education courses online or through interactive webinars.

Ever-changing recreation activities have placed new demands on many agencies for programs and facilities. For example, participants want state-of-the-art fitness centers with spinning bikes, saunas, and weight-training machines. Participants also want trained personnel to operate and to teach them how to use this equipment. Professionals respond to consumer expectations for such amenities by updating websites daily, providing downloadable maps of local parks, and getting immediate web results posted after tournaments or other events.

For many people, including recreation professionals, the challenge for the future will be how to balance the demands and expectations that arise from technological advances without losing the personal touch that has been the foundation of people's lives and the recreation profession. Further, recreation professionals must not focus only on the quantity of opportunities but also the quality. Recreation professionals will need to be continually aware of how people are informed about options through the communication and educational tools they use. Further, they will be challenged in some cases to get people to leave their homes and virtual communities and to find opportunities to recreate in communities.

Reflection Questions

1. Have you ever tried to go for a day without using your smart-phone, tablet, or computer? What would your world be like without these technological devices? If you could only have one device, what would you choose and why?

2. Has technology raised the expectation that people can do more and that they should be able to multitask easily?

3. What are the advantages that this technology provides for people? What are the potential disadvantages?

4. How will technology continue to influence leisure behavior in the future?

5. Does social media have advantages over interacting with people face to face? Disadvantages?

Chapter 37

Humans and Nature

The significance of outdoor activities and people's desire to be connected to nature has been important to people for generations. This desire, for example, was the impetus for the parks movement in the United States. In addition, many people enjoy backyards and gardens where they can connect to nature. Sport Utility Vehicles (SUVs) are popular and have been marketed to appeal to people's sense of adventure and the *potential* to go into the rugged environments while riding in luxury. As discussed in the previous chapter, clothes originally designed for outdoor experiences are now found on racks in most stores and are worn on city streets.

Although outdoor recreation is popular, some concerns exist that people, and especially children, are less connected to nature than in the past. Further, the impact of humans on the environment and the implication for sustainable recreation are also of concern. This chapter raises some issues about how humans connect to nature and the following chapter will explore the environmental implications.

Issues

Outdoor areas have typically been seen as places for people to visit and play where they can become challenged physically, engaged socially, and renewed spiritually. Natural environments ranging from wilderness areas to people's backyards provide a foundation for a variety of leisure opportunities. The preservation and conservation of outdoor spaces and natural areas for the public is central to the government's involvement in recreation services. Outdoor areas have been managed and protected as spaces available for everyone's use. At the same time, these resources are finite, and preserving them so others can enjoy in the future is important.

Physical, mental, and spiritual benefits have been associated with the outdoors. Most people feel relaxed and happy when they are in the outdoors, weather permitting. Further, Vitamin D exposure from the sun is known to help prevent a host of diseases as well as treat and prevent depression. Free play in the outdoors encourages children to be creative and to appreciate nature. In addition, the more exposure to nature that people have regarding its beauty and benefits, the more likely they are to want to ensure that nature-based recreation activities are available for future generations.

Several concerns have been raised about humans and nature. One includes the perceived decline in the use of the outdoors, especially related to visitation to national lands. Another concern is that young people are experiencing *nature-deficit disorder* (Louv, 2005) and are not connected to the outdoors in the ways they once were. A third issue relates to safety.

Visitation

Getting exact figures about the number of visitors to parks is not easy. Visits are measured as visitations and not number of visitors. For example, an individual might go to a city park to walk his or her dog almost every day, while another individual might only visit that park once a year for a family picnic. The number of visitations is important but so is the number of people coming to an outdoor area. Nevertheless, statistics about visitation are important to consider. Although the percentage of change of visitors seems to fluctuate yearly and differs among particular parks, the overall trend in national parks has been a slight decline since 1999.

Several reasons might be noted for these declines in national park visitation. Some relate to the economy. Gas prices have continued to rise and with the recession beginning in 2008, people have less discretionary income. Interestingly, however, with the decline in visits to national parks in the past several years, state parks have seen an increase suggesting that maybe people are just not traveling as far as they once did. Most of the iconic national parks are in the western part of the United States and not near large population centers. Therefore, a decline might be expected given the economy and cost of travel.

People who manage parks have also been concerned about the lack of diversity often seen in parks. With the growing numbers of people of color in the United States, a proportionate number would be expected to visit parks. However, many of the faces in parks, especially in national and to some extent state parks, are white. The use of parks in cities based on race and ethnicity has not been a major concern. Discussion continues about why some racial groups such as African Americans are not visible in national and state parks. Many people of color have not had the same traditions in outdoor activities as have middle-class white people. With the predictions discussed earlier of white non-Hispanic citizens becoming the minority in the United States in the coming decades, the support and advocacy from all racial and ethnic groups are needed.

Children and Nature

Recreation professionals are also concerned that if children from all racial and ethnic groups do not have exposure to the outdoors, they will likely not support outdoor policies in the future. In addition, if children are disconnected from nature, they will miss important contributions to their well-being.

Louv (2005) coined the term *nature deficit disorder*, not as a clinical diagnosis, but as a way to highlight the changing relationship between children and nature. Louv noted that in one century, citizens in the United States have gone through the stages of direct connection to nature, romantic attachment to nature, and now detachment from nature due partially to the influence of technology on people's lives. Louv stated, "That which cannot be Googled does not count" (p. 61).

Louv (2005) also noted that the amount of screen time that children now spend using electronics compared to in the past has greatly changed their relationship with the outdoors. Young people do not know how a world ever existed without computers and instant communication. Urbanization has also influenced how children experience direct contact with nature. Parental fears in urban as well as rural areas result in not allowing their children to go outdoors unless supervised. Children's lives are structured differently than back in the times when children were told to "just go play outside." Therefore, if children are to be connected to nature, it is through family influences or structured recreation activities such as at day or resident camps. Unfortunately if adults care less about going outdoors, they are not likely to take their children for these experiences. Recreation services that address outdoor opportunities may become more important than ever before, and they have always been quite important.

Safety

Perceptions about safety related to outdoor use cannot be discounted. Crime has increased in society and outdoor spaces are not exempt from this trend. Women as well as children may be perceived as at more risk for personal physical violence in outdoor pursuits. Perceptions of unsafe areas, regardless of whether a real danger exists, influence what people do. Some of the problems of fear and violence are larger social issues that have no easy solution. However, outdoor spaces (e.g., parks, trails) are safer when they are filled with people who are enjoying recreation.

In addition, if people can be convinced that they have some owner-ship of outdoor areas and facilities, empowered citizen groups can organize themselves to address problems of vandalism or crime in parks. Safety issues and issues of fear, unless addressed directly by recreation professionals, may be one of the major constraints to people's outdoor involvement in the future.

Challenges

The future of outdoor spaces as well as environmental sustainability will depend on the successful advocacy efforts of citizens. People will defend a cause if they feel directly connected to it. They will also advocate if they experience the benefits of being in the outdoors—benefits such as op-portunities for physical activity, stress reduction, and spiritual reflection. Although these benefits might be found in other activities, the outdoors can become special compared to activities undertaken indoors. If children develop an appreciation and respect for nature as they grow, they are more likely to advocate for wild and outdoor spaces when they become adults. Further, with the changing racial and ethnic demographics of the United States, all citizens will be called upon to support the funding for public lands. People who do not appreciate the outdoors and wilderness areas are less likely to support preservation and conservation policies.

Strategies for Action

Fortunately, recreation services offer many ways to be connected with the outdoors. All sectors can have a role in educating people about the outdoors and its values. Connection to the outdoors can occur through structured recreation programs as well as providing spaces where adults and children can experience nature and develop a sense of appreciation for all that nature has to offer. Some specialties within recreation services specifically use the outdoors as a context for their programs, but most all specialties use the outdoors in one form or another. The goal of enjoying the outdoors while reducing the environmental impact is essential to consider.

Nature is everywhere. Encouraging opportunities for connections between human and nature is a task for many groups in addition to rec-reation services organizations. Helping individuals develop a land ethic (i.e., treating outdoor resources with respect and stewardship), gaining knowledge about how ecosystems work together including the negative as well as positive impact that people have, learning to feel comfortable in the outdoors, and seeing outdoor opportunities as lifelong pursuits cannot be done by any one organization.

Schools were a focal point for much of the early education in the outdoors, but today many other educational opportunities exist. Schools, unfortunately, have a minor role to play. The most widely recognized programs for outdoor leadership, particularly in wilderness areas, are Outward Bound and the National Outdoor Leadership School (NOLS). Outward Bound is an adventure-based program that provides challenging opportunities in wilderness settings that foster self-discovery and leadership training for people of all ages. NOLS offers courses that develop fundamental knowledge, skills, and experiences necessary for minimum-impact use and enjoyment of wilderness environments by emphasizing safety, judgment, leadership, teamwork, outdoor skills, and environmental studies.

Liability issues will need to be considered in thinking about outdoor experiences offered through recreation services in the future. No one is immune from lawsuits. Safety in the outdoors is a paramount concern. Some outdoor experiences that offer great benefits are also associated with risk including adventure activities and extreme sports such as rock climbing, hang gliding, and whitewater paddling. The challenge for now and the future is how to offer these activities in a way that allows excitement but minimizes the risk to the recreation service organization or the environment.

Providing support and opportunities to connect people to nature is important for numerous reasons. As discussed in the next chapter, however, facilitating enjoyment as well as personal and social benefits must be coupled with environmental sustainability.

Reflection Questions

1. What evidence might suggest to you that people are less connected to nature today than they have been in the past?

2. Why is getting more people to visit public lands (e.g., national parks, state parks, county parks) important?

3. Some people suggest that the perceptions people have about safety are often not consistent with the reality. How do people develop their perceptions about how safe an area might be?

4. Should public schools be promoting outdoor education more than they currently do?

Chapter 38

Environmental Impacts

The dynamics between the natural environment and humans have been an ongoing source of concern for decades. Aldo Leopold (1949) summarized the situation over 60 years ago in the classic book, *A Sand County Almanac*: "We abuse the land because we regard it as a commodity belonging to us. When we see land as a community to which we belong, we may begin to use it with love and respect" (pp. xviii–xix).

Therefore, addressing environmental impacts and sustainability means planning and facilitating recreation services on a daily basis, with full consideration regarding how environmental factors affect long-term goals. This chapter extends the previous chapter to explore sustainability as it relates to selected environmental impacts.

Issues

Two broad views about the environment have been associated with American culture. These views reflect the heritage and spiritual connection of people who cared about the environment. Native American and Transcendentalists celebrated the environment in ways that sought harmony with all life and natural elements. Western traditions promoted a belief in the superiority of humans to all other life and a belief that the universe exists to serve human needs (Driver, Dustin, Baltic, Elsner, & Peterson, 1996).

The Native American philosophy links the spiritual experience directly to the environment. Most indigenous Native Americans view themselves not as the masters, but as a part of a balanced universe. In this belief system, they often perceived an imbalance caused by humans, so they developed ceremonies that would retain and reestablish the harmony with nature. These rituals and ceremonies maintained a belief in the unseen powers and the unity with fundamental life forces inherent in all things (Ibrahim & Cordes, 1993).

The Western view often portrayed nature as dangerous or something to be used and dominated. Other life forms were important only in terms of their usefulness to humanity, especially when development and profit motives were foremost. Spirituality became tied to beliefs that civilization, not nature, conveyed the sacred lifestyle. Nature as a spiritual connection became further removed from daily existence as this Western view dominated.

These views provided juxtaposition for the way that the environment is perceived today. The topic of environmental impacts is far-ranging. The major issues identified for this brief discussion, however, are use versus preservation of outdoor areas, climate change, and the greening of recreation services.

Challenges between Use and Preservation

Considerable interest has developed during the past 25 years in protecting the outdoors and the environment from pollution, unneeded industrial development, rampant residential urban sprawl, and wanton destruction of natural resources. This protection and conservation movement has taken different forms. Special interest groups such as the Sierra Club, Defenders of Wildlife, the Audubon Society, and the Wilderness Society have mounted large public information efforts. Preservation of natural environments includes maintenance of long-term ecological processes and management to protect the resource from human influence (Hendee, Stankey, & Lucas, 1990). Conservation is usually associated with renewable natural resources and using resources in the most beneficial manner over time while avoiding waste. Conservation involves a cycle of intelligent use and timely replenishment of resources as they become damaged or partially depleted. In general, conservation has been the focus of recreation services, since use can be encouraged in environmentally conscious ways. The preservation as well as conservation of resources in the future will be challenged by the conflicting demands between people and the environment.

People who use the outdoors to pursue recreation interests exert stress on these outdoor areas. Just by going into the outdoors, some environmental impact occurs. People have been accused of "loving the wilderness to death." Simultaneously, the environment receives extreme pressures from industries, developers, and citizens who demand the amenities provided by the exploitation of natural resources. This clashing of perceptions about the environment results in heated debates about how best to manage environmental resources for both preservation and conservation.

Accessibility, availability, and the use of the natural resources in contrast to the preservation of these areas are controversial. The amount of use an area can withstand before severe or irreparable damage is done (i.e., carrying capacity), whether an area is left entirely in its natural state or developed for recreational (e.g., camping, fishing) or business enterprises (e.g., timber harvest, mining, oil exploration), and visitor management must be considered. Carrying capacity implies that a resource has a natural level of productivity that must be controlled for the resource to be sustained. Recreational carrying capacity refers to the relationship between the recreational experience sought and the recreation resource. In other words, identifying the maximum number of people and type of use an area can sustain without negatively impacting the environment or the visitor's experience is important.

Visitor management also has been a concern of recreation land managers. As noted in the earlier chapter, not having enough visitors to public lands may be a concern. However, the negative impact of large numbers of people to an outdoor environment can result in pollution from vehicles, garbage and sewage concerns, crime and vandalism, deterioration of facilities and areas, and increased presence of emergency medical care and rescue. Park managers confront increasingly complex management decisions at a time when fiscal and human resources are often lacking.

The multiple uses of land for recreation and other activities is also an issue. One recent concern is fracking on public lands. Fracking is the process of drilling for natural gas by injecting millions of gallons of water and chemicals underground and then fracturing rock layers to release natural gas that can be gathered. Natural gas may be an important energy source, but its long-term implications for the environment and for the use of land is highly controversial. The co-existence of fracking and quality recreation experiences requires serious attention in the future.

Challenges Regarding Climate Change

Climate change is a long-term issue that will affect everyone. Sometimes referred to as global warming, climate change is a more accurate term. Global warming includes the recent and ongoing rise in average temperatures caused by increasing amounts of greenhouse gases. It can translate into climate change, which is defined as any significant changes lasting over several decades related to temperature, precipitation, wind patterns, or other effects (http://www.epa.gov/climatechange/basics).

Many places have seen changes in rainfall, which has resulted in more floods, droughts, intense rain, and/or more frequent and severe heat waves. Oceans are warming and becoming more acidic, ice caps are melting, and sea levels are rising. As these changes become more pronounced in the future, recreation opportunities will be affected.

Extreme weather events have particularly influenced the provision of recreation services. For example, extreme heat over a prolonged time does curtail outdoor activity. This extreme heat also stresses plants and trees and may be associated with drought conditions. Dry conditions can also result in increased insect manifestations that can also kill trees. Trees dying in parks can affect maintenance budgets, cause ecological disruption, and may create fears for public safety. Dead trees also seem to contribute to wildfires in all types of landscapes. Tree die-offs also result in closures of campgrounds, trails, and picnic areas in public parks. On another extreme, heavy rains can cause flooding and permanently change landscapes in urban and rural areas.

Changes in temperature can also affect activities traditionally done during particular seasons. Impacts from climate change will vary among recreation activities such as skiing, camping, boating, fishing and hunting, outdoor sports such as golf, and wildlife viewing (Morris & Wall, 2009). For example, ski seasons may be shorter due to warmer conditions. Longer and warmer summers likely will increase the demand for outdoor recreation including hiking, fishing, hunting, camping, and beach visits. Rising sea levels could reduce the size of beachfront recreation areas and national seashores. High temperatures may make programs in the outdoors far less appealing. Further, more rain instead of snow in the winter could mean an earlier spring runoff into streams and reservoirs, which could mean less fresh water flowing in the summer months when sport fishing and boating are most popular. Lower water levels in other places could mean fewer duck populations for hunting.

Research studies are being undertaken to explore the implications of climate change and how it might be mitigated. However, the conditions currently caused should be understood by recreation professionals as they manage programs, facilities, and outdoor areas into the future.

Challenges Regarding Green Recreation

Sustainability as it relates to the *green* environment is being addressed in recreation services in all sectors and in specialties including parks and recreation, sports, and tourism. The green aspect refers to supporting environmentally friendly products and services as opposed to those that pollute or harm the environment. This movement is not new, but the idea of green has received greater emphasis in recent years. The green movement is an extension of the environmental movement that began over half a century ago. *the green movement*

Several examples exist of what can be done to address the challenges of facilitating green recreation. Recycling should always be an option at recreation centers as well as in parks. Many communities hold regular environmental clean-up events that are sponsored by public and nonprofit organizations. The emphasis on eco-friendly products (e.g., green cleaning products) that do less harm to the environment than others is worth considering. In addition, energy-efficient lighting might be considered along with green buildings. New constructions and major renovations of facilities can be designed to receive LEED (Leadership in Energy and Environmental Design) certification. LEED buildings are accessed related to aspects such as sustainable sites, water and energy efficiency, materials and resources used, innovative design, and indoor environmental quality. More ideas that work are being discussed every day.

A different example of green recreation is the emerging opportunities to promote gardening. Not everyone has a backyard where they can associate with the natural world. Public as well as nonprofit groups are promoting community gardens. These gardens are usually on public lands and are planted and grown by a collection of people. These gardens can provide fresh produce for healthy eating as well as opportunities for physical activity, neighborhood improvement, a sense of community, a connection to the earth, and a means for communities to become greener. Many of these gardens grow vegetables but gardening also might relate to preserving a natural area with flowers or in beautifying street corners. The environment is much more than a large open space. The more green undertakings that occur in communities, the more the natural environments will be valued. *community gardens*

Strategies for Action

The future offers opportunities and challenges regarding the environment and those involved with recreation services. Environmental concerns, however, also must be considered within the broad spectrum of sustainability that includes social and economic aspects. Although some management and environmental practices can save money, money is often needed to implement the changes.

The foundation for addressing environmental sustainability in the future will start with strategic plans that make environmental management central to everyday operations. This approach is a form of prevention in that in addition to addressing the environmental consequences, steps are taken to avoid these consequences in the future. For example, ecotourism is discussed in this text as an emerging form of tourism that revolves around the meanings and importance of the environment to visitors as well as to the community hosts. Ecotourism is one way to mitigate the problems associated with some forms of mass tourism.

The National Park Service (NPS) recognizes that applying principles of sustainability can lower long-term maintenance and operating costs as well as improve the quality of life for citizens. The NPS is also striving to be a model for sustainability. Recommendations have been adopted concerning policies, partnerships, and the education of the workforce to make sustainability integral to park operations. NPS is making the education of the public about the benefits and values of sustainable recreation a high priority. In addition, the NPS is committed to monitoring its own ecological footprint to ensure that the organization is not contributing further to environmental issues. Some parks have already implemented best practices concerning environmental sustainability, but a systematic approach is necessary.

Sports organizations have also begun to focus on green environments and sustainability. Many examples exist but one is between the Honda Center and the Anaheim Ducks in southern California. In a recent 18-month period, the Honda Center recycled more than 28 tons of cardboard, glass, aluminum, plastic, and paper. The center uses compostable cups, popcorn, and trash bags, as well as recyclable beverage and food carry trays. The restaurant in the Honda Center uses locally grown produce and meat and seafood from sustainable sources. Additionally, the Ducks donate all unused food to a local food bank (http://greensportsalliance.org).

Environmental sustainability as it is connected to social and economic sustainability offers challenges that will not be easily addressed. As already noted, no environmental impact can be addressed by any one organization.

All sectors and all recreation specialties must be involved in planning for environmental preservation and conservation. Nevertheless, professional leadership is important in setting an example and showing commitment to the environment.

Reflection Questions

1. A number of college campuses have become committed to being a "green" campus. What efforts are occurring on your campus?

2. What is the difference between conservation and preservation, and how might policies based on these differences influence the outdoor recreation opportunities that are available to people?

3. What can be done to mitigate the environmental impact that participants in outdoor recreation might have?

4. What can individuals do to mitigate the effects of climate change? What can recreation services professionals do to mitigate the effects of climate change?

WHO

Chapter 39

Health and Wellness

Health and wellness have always been the goals of recreation services either directly or indirectly. Health is defined as more than the absence of illness or disease. The definition most often used for health comes from the World Health Organization (WHO), who describe health as a state of physical, mental, and social well-being. Well-being obviously refers to good health but also includes being happy and prosperous, as discussed earlier in this book. Wellness intentionally focuses on optimal mental, bodily, and spiritual health.

Positive leisure lifestyles can result in improved physical and mental health. These lifestyles can result in increased life expectancy in addition to well-being. Payne (2002) advocated that recreation agencies should be considered part of the healthcare system. Recreation services that emphasize health promotion and physical, mental, and spiritual outcomes can contribute to the prevention of illnesses and disease. Healthcare tends to focus on interventions to "cure" health issues, whereas recreation services, as part of the healthcare system, focus on preventing illness and injury. Therefore, this chapter examines the relationships that exist between leisure experiences, recreation services, and health and wellness and why people are more concerned about health than ever before.

Issues

The patterns of health and illness in the United States have changed. Historically, people died of infectious diseases such as smallpox, diphtheria, and yellow fever. Today, people are living longer and affected more by chronic degenerative illnesses such as heart disease and cancer (Whitman, Merluzzi, & White, 1999). These diseases are directly connected to the lifestyle problems of overweight/obesity and physical inactivity. Being

why overweight happens

overweight or obese is a result of energy imbalance when more calories are consumed than are expended. The contribution that recreation services can make to healthcare and prevention of illness and disease is to enable people to find ways to be physically active. Other lifestyle activities affect people's health such as tobacco use, drug and alcohol abuse, and sexual behavior. However, physical activity is part of many recreation activities and can have major influences on health.

Numerous studies have demonstrated that physical activity decreases health risks for cardiovascular disease including high blood pressure, obesity, and high cholesterol. Physical activity also contributes to increased energy, body strength, and self-esteem as well as decreases tension and symptoms of depression. Most people know the benefits of physical activity, but getting them to find ways to be active is the challenge.

Broadly speaking, physical activity is the movement of the body caused by skeletal muscle contractions. More specifically, physical activity includes movement that results in health benefits. Physical fitness and exercise are also associated with physical activity. Physical fitness is the capacity of the body affected by physical activity. Exercise usually refers to activity done specifically to attain fitness. These differences are important, since physical activity is aimed at physical as well as mental outcomes. For example, stress is also linked to physiological and mental health and has become a prevalent problem today. Stress reduces productivity, causes accidents, and results in fatigue, headaches, and anxiety (Golen & Hanlon, 1995).

how intensity can be measured

Getting optimal health benefits from physical activity depends on the activity undertaken, the duration, frequency, and intensity. Some recreation activities provide more intensity. This intensity can be measured in metabolic equivalent of a task (i.e., MET). Playing golf at a driving range results in less than 3 METs. Race walking consumes 6 or more METs. How long someone participates (e.g., 10 minutes versus 30 minutes) affects health, as does the frequency of the activity (e.g., once a week compared to every day). Although most professionals in recreation services do not get involved with the physiology of physical activity, having a basic understanding can be important relative to impacts on the body as well as on the brain.

adults get 150m vigorous or moderate activity each week

The Centers for Disease Control and Prevention recommend that adults get 150 minutes of vigorous (i.e., activity that results in sweating and greatly elevated heart rate, such as running or swimming) or moderate (i.e., activity that results in breaking a sweat and elevating heart rate, such as walking or gardening) physical activity each week, along with strength training and flexibility exercises. Children and youth are recommended to get at least 60 minutes of vigorous or moderate activity each day. People need to have some motivation to be active, but more importantly, they need

youth need @ least 60min /day

recreation spaces and places where they can move. Further, most people will stick to doing physical activity if they enjoy it. Recreation services professionals should be helping people find *enjoyment* in movement.

Health and wellness also address people's social connections. Social belonging is an important part of being healthy that is not discussed as much as physical and mental health. People do not seem to be joining civic groups, churches, or other organizations as frequently as in previous years. Despite, the influence of social media, people seem to be less connected to their communities in today's society. This lack of social connection can be a problem, since social belonging directly relates to overall well-being. For example, older adults with strong social ties live longer than people without social connections, regardless of other risk factors. Recreation providers can offer opportunities for social interaction in many of the activities facilitated, which can contribute greatly to well-being.

In addition, recreation activities frequently enable individuals to get together to have a good time. Laughter activates muscles and increases heart rate and oxygen exchange similar to the desirable effects achieved through exercise. Laughing heartily releases endorphins that elevate people's moods. Further, a good strong laugh reduces muscle tension and thus, stress. Laughing can be a mini-workout for the internal organs. Further, laughing is inherently associated with play. Cousins (1979) contended that adults forget how to laugh and play, and this lack of spontaneous enjoyment is related to physiological and psychological ills. Clearly health and wellness are outcomes of many types of leisure experiences.

Strategies for Action

Individuals who care about health and wellness have advocated for a shift from the medical model that focuses on treating diseases (e.g., usually with drugs) to a focus on prevention and opportunities for wellness leading to an enhanced state of well-being. Prevention is cheaper than treatment or cures, but that thinking has not necessarily been reflected in the current health system in the United States. Shifting from treating disease to health maintenance clearly positions recreation services as part of the healthcare system. Recreation professionals can then collaborate with other organizations in communities that also have health promotion as their mission. If the new paradigm of healthcare is holistic, preventive, and focused on healthy lifestyles, then recreation services can have beneficial impacts on the whole of people's health including physical fitness, social connections, and stress relief.

Improving the wellness of citizens will increasingly become the responsibility of multiple service providers. Partnerships with health organizations will be an important effort for the future. The social ecological approaches discussed earlier in this book relate to how individuals, social groups, organizations, communities, and policymakers all have roles in health promotion.

Brown, Heath, and Levin Martin (2006) edited a guide for promoting physical activity in communities. They identified how behaviors could be changed in three ways: informational approaches, social and behavioral approaches, and environmental and policy approaches, consistent with the social ecological model. They offered suggestions such as community-wide campaigns (e.g., a "walk to work" day). Social approaches could include an organization or business putting together a noon walking group or planning family events that focus on being active together. Policy approaches might relate to a school and community group or nonprofit organization putting together a joint-use agreement so that gyms in schools, for example, could be used by the public over the weekend. The approaches are almost endless if addressing physical and mental health is the goal of recreation services organizations.

Other organizations such as the American Council on Exercise (ACE) have also examined how people can be more physically active in the future. ACE emphasized the need for groups within communities to work together. They also discussed access for all community members, which may mean thinking about fitness and exercise in broader ways such as by encouraging dancing and group activities. Low-income communities are particularly at risk of having greater health disparities and of being *park poor*. ACE sees emerging opportunities in the workplace to reward employees who strive to be healthy. Many of the needed changes require funding, which may come from nonprofit charitable foundations in the future.

As described throughout this book, choice is central to leisure enjoyment. As recreation professionals approach ways to handle future needs related to health and wellness, they must focus on giving people information and choices. Some people can get exercise by walking, gardening, or dancing more easily and enjoyably than by going to a fitness center. However, people of all ages should be able to choose. This freedom to choose should provide a powerful avenue for people with differing interests and abilities to find a route toward improving their overall life and preventing future health problems.

Reflection Questions

1. Do you meet the daily requirements for physical activity? What do you do? Where do you participate? Who do you participate with?

2. Being a student can be a stressful situation, especially at certain times of the semester. What do you do to manage your stress in a healthy way?

3. The saying sometimes goes that "laughter is the best medicine." How have you experienced the benefits of laughter in your life? When was the last time you had a really good laugh?

4. How would you describe what a positive leisure lifestyle would look like?

5. What organizations can you name in your community or on your campus that focus on promoting health and wellness? What do these organizations do? Are they effective?

Chapter 40

Globalization

Leisure is a global issue. Any discussion of leisure around the world must start with a willingness to step outside of one's own cultural viewpoint. Many people reading this book grew up in the United States where the political focus has been on individuals and their rights. The definitions used to describe leisure as a state of mind point to the individual nature of leisure experiences. Further, as noted earlier, the work ethic that has been so prominent in the United States also influences people's view of leisure experiences and recreation services. The foundation of this book is to examine leisure experiences and recreation services from a U.S. perspective. However, with the globalization occurring, ideas about leisure are important to understand from different viewpoints.

The focus of this chapter is on globalization and its relationship to leisure and recreation services in countries outside North America. Knowing about other cultures often helps us understand our own culture better.

Issues

'Leisure' and 'recreation' are terms used around the world with a variety of meanings. More collectivist societies as well as those societies not driven as centrally by industrialization models may view leisure as less individualistic. The emphasis of leisure in developing countries is often not on the individual, but rather on the family or community—a cultural perspective. Leisure from a collectivist viewpoint is less about the rights of the individual to pursue self-benefiting experiences but more about the shared benefits occurring within a larger social structure (e.g., extended family, neighbors, community).

The words used to describe leisure and recreation also vary in other countries and cultures. The word 'leisure' may not be a familiar concept in some countries other than as a synonym for free time. North American views have tended to define leisure in more psychological ways related to state of mind and personal experiences. In some Latin American countries, no equivalent for the term 'leisure' can be found. The closest word is similar to the American words 'free time' or 'play.' The word 'recreation' is not used as commonly in many parts of the world that do not have English as the primary language.

Further, although the idea of parks is gaining importance around the world, parks and recreation have not been linked in the same way, especially in non-English speaking countries. In the United States, the term 'park' is used to include any size of park, yet some countries views parks as associated with only large tracts of land. Much as was true in the United States prior to the 1960s, in some countries parks and recreation are completely separated from one another.

In addition, recreation professionals in the United States usually make a major distinction between sport and leisure as well as tourism and leisure. In other countries such as the United Kingdom, Turkey, and many Asian countries, leisure is synonymous with sport and/or tourism. However, with the globalization occurring around the world, the understandings of these words are becoming more universal.

'Globalization' is a term that has emerged in common discussions over the past 20 years, but it is an idea that has slowly been taking form for many years. Globalization describes how the world has "shrunk" due to advanced technology and its influence on communication, travel, and economies. In one word, globalization now describes the *connectedness* that exists across the globe. The distribution of information, people, goods, and services has helped to define globalization. Globalization also refers to the international relations and social relations that are influenced by ideologies and popular culture. What happens around the world influences everyone, whether related to civil unrest, human rights, environmental disasters, or new pop music groups. No country is an island. Leisure has been influenced by globalization because of how quickly ideas and trends can sweep across the globe. The Internet and satellite television have given ready access to information about events of all kinds nearly everywhere in the world.

Many people have debated the pros and cons of globalization. It has served to break down barriers to travel and created the need to establish political relationships among countries (http://globalizationprosandcons. com). Globalization has given people a chance to trust and understand others when they are able to share directly in their worlds, whether related to celebrations such as the Olympics or in disasters such as tsunamis. Concerns that were once only the problem of one nation can now be felt by all.

Globalization has numerous implications for economies. Many national economies have been influenced by globalization, in that the recession that occurred in the United States in 2008 impacted the entire world. Similarly, the potential bankruptcy of a country in Europe has direct implications for the stock market in the United States. Markets of all kinds are now shared throughout the world. Further, the production capabilities of companies and their ability to go anywhere in the world allows them to customize their efforts. On the downside, however, corporations using cheaper labor in other countries have been criticized for their outsourcing jobs away from the United States. In some ways less labor is needed because of what technology can do. Also, a concern has been raised that a brain drain may occur in the United States if skilled people can be recruited to work all over the world, regardless of where they live.

The primary emphasis of globalization has been on the economic implications, but as was discussed, globalization also has social implications. The loss of national identity due to globalization is a concern of some people. Others, however, see the idea of world citizens as a potential way to encourage world peace. Further, globalization has resulted in the possibilities of both information as well as epidemics spreading quickly across the Earth.

Challenges

Many Western cultures have significant technological development, stable economies, and a history of world leadership. Countries such as the United States, Canada, Australia, and the United Kingdom as well as countries in Western Europe tend to value leisure for its enhancement of the well-being of individuals and quality of life in communities as well as the contributions to development and economies. These Western countries share to some degree a similar cultural heritage strongly influenced by Christianity, a work ethic that is related to leisure, and an emphasis on national pride due to excellence in sports and cultural arts.

Media have influenced Western societies greatly. Because of globalization, the media are also influencing many other cultures around the world. Media shape the messages about leisure by the programs aired on TV, opportunities available through the Internet, types of music created, books produced, and through cultural and performing arts. On the other hand, leisure also informs the media. The demands by the public for certain media opportunities for their leisure have fueled the desire for satellite TV with hundreds of channels that guarantee something for everyone and that can be broadcast around the world.

Western societies have typically had a consumerist approach to leisure, and that notion is growing throughout the world. In this sense, recreation opportunities are viewed as a commodity to be bought and sold. This leisure market sector has generated millions and billions of dollars for national economies through private business recreation opportunities that include entertainment, sporting equipment, spectator events (e.g., concerts, sport events, theater), travel, and tourism.

Across the world, symbols of leisure such as possessions and travel opportunities represent high status. People everywhere have access to media that show the standard of living as typically held by people in Western countries, and most people aspire to those lifestyles. Although leisure was once thought to be something primarily for the rich and wealthy, opportunities for leisure experiences and recreation services seem to be desired by many people regardless of their economic status or geographical location. A life of leisure is becoming a global dream, assuming that subsistence levels are met.

Interestingly, however, people in many developed countries feel they have more work and stress with less time and less emphasis being placed on relaxing, fitness, social responsibility, stewardship of the natural environment, and commitment to community. Having leisure and recreation opportunities represents a high quality of life to most of the world, but some Americans do not feel that this quality of life has made them any happier. Regardless, the significance of leisure as a goal for life has been exported around the globe to developing countries.

Some countries in the world are termed developing because the full productivity of their resource potential has not been realized. The concept of development implies a general level of technology, economic sophistication, and standard of living (Russell, 1996). Some of these developing countries face overwhelming issues related to poverty, education, health, and environmental degradation that result in a low standard of living and depreciated quality of life in communities. In many cases, globalization has placed pressure on traditional social structures by replacing long-standing cultural values with lifestyle standards that emulate the values of Western societies.

Although changing somewhat due to globalization, many developing countries do not have the variety of recreation services systems as in North America. Nongovernmental organizations, similar to nonprofit groups, may be more responsible for recreation in some places than are governments. Some countries have cultural or political beliefs that do not support leisure and recreation for everyone. Some countries simply do not have the economic resources to support recreation activities such as arts, sports, children's play spaces, programs for older persons, and parks. When basic subsistence is a problem or when a country is at war, these resources usually do not exist.

A prevailing attitude has been that excess and resource depletion is not a problem in Western countries. This attitude is highly problematic. If all individuals in the world had the same lifestyle as many Americans, the environment could not sustain itself. Some people estimate that it would take five Earths to sustain the standard of living at the U.S. level, if everyone across the globe had the same opportunities. Obviously, five Earths are not available, regardless of what space travel may tell us about other planets. Therefore, the implications of globalization on the environment are a serious concern that must be addressed.

Strategies for Action

Leisure within some developing countries can be viewed as a liberating perspective, but only if the realities of poverty and poor health can be addressed. Traditionally leisure has been an integral component of rural village life. The celebration of rituals and traditions through stories, dance, music, art, and games is often the cornerstone for the life of these communities. In other ways, many cultures are intimately tied to the environment where landscapes and places are sacred and cared for as an honored responsibility. The appreciation of the environment reflects a connection to nature.

On the other hand, recreation can become an exploitive tool for increasing economic gains without the concern for social and environmental sustainability. This problem occurs when recreation becomes the product being sold rather than a way of life that does not require the consumption of resources.

Although exploiting leisure and recreation as commodities may immediately alleviate some of the harshness of people's economic lives, the long-term consequences may not be fully appreciated or understood. As discussed in the previous Unit, tourism can bring economic gain to countries, but the cost of that recreation opportunity to entertain wealthy tourists may result in the loss of cultural traditions, new materialism desires, and irreparable environmental stress and degradation on fragile ecosystems. The desire of some developing countries to be like Western countries can promote social change on one hand, but can also alter the cultures and leisure of a country in negative ways.

The right to leisure is a global human rights issue. One organization that has addressed leisure across the world is the World Leisure Organization (WLO). It is a worldwide nongovernmental professional organization dedicated to discovering and fostering those conditions that best permit leisure to serve as a force for human growth, development, and well-being (http://www.worldleisure.org). WLO partners directly with the United Nations and other national associations to address global issues.

Through the efforts of WLO in cooperation with the United Nations, a Charter for Leisure was drafted and first approved in 1970 and updated over the years (see Table 40.1). This proclamation reinforces the importance and value of recreation and leisure in the lives of the world's citizens. It presents a global perspective about leisure, although is based primarily

Table 40.1 Charter for Leisure [approved by the World Leisure and Recreation Association Board of Directors, July 2000 (http://www.worldleisure.org)]

Introduction

Consistent with the Universal Declaration of Human Rights (Article 27), all cultures and societies recognize to some extent the right to rest and leisure. Here, because personal freedom and choice are central elements of leisure, individuals can freely choose their activities and experiences, many of them leading to substantial benefits for person and community.

Articles

1. All people have a basic human right to leisure activities that are in harmony with the norms and social values of their compatriots. All governments are obliged to recognize and protect this right of its citizens.
2. Provisions for leisure for the quality of life are as important as those for health and education. Governments must provide their citizens a variety of accessible leisure and recreational opportunities of the highest quality.
3. The individual is his/her best leisure and recreational resource. Thus, governments should ensure the means for acquiring those skills and understandings necessary to optimize leisure experiences.
4. Individuals can use leisure opportunities for self-fulfillment, developing personal relationships, improving social integration, developing communities and cultural identity as well as promoting international understanding and cooperation and enhancing quality of life.
5. Governments must ensure the future availability of fulfilling leisure experiences by maintaining the quality of their country's physical, social and cultural environment.
6. Governments should ensure the training of professionals to help individuals acquire personal skills, discover and develop their talents, and to broaden their range of recreational opportunities.
7. Citizens must have access to all forms of leisure information about the nature of leisure and its opportunities, using it to enhance their knowledge and inform decisions on local and national policy.
8. Educational institutions must make every effort to teach the nature and importance of leisure and how to integrate this knowledge into personal lifestyle.

on Western ideals. Nevertheless, the statement addresses a belief that the individual has the right to experience freely chosen activities that lead to self-fulfillment, improved quality of life, and the attainment of community values.

The meanings and importance of leisure and recreation services around the world varies. With globalization, the divides between countries are diminishing in some ways, but in other ways globalization has exacerbated the differences between the "leisure rich" and "leisure poor" countries.

As noted throughout this book, leisure experiences are a part of every society on Earth, with rich histories that go back thousands of years for some of the earliest cultures. However, leisure can be a double-edged sword that benefits some while exploiting others. Recreation services can have a major economic influence whether provided by governments, nonprofits, or private businesses. Regardless, sustainability based on economic, environmental, and social aspects must be central in all countries if leisure and recreation are to continue to offer their full potential for individual well-being and the quality of life of communities and countries.

Reflection Questions

1. Have you traveled outside the United States? What did you learn about other cultures? What did you learn about what leisure meant to people in other countries?

2. Is the ideal of leisure as espoused in the United States applicable in developing countries? How might it be useful? How might this ideal be detrimental?

3. Globalization is not going to go away. How can people interested in leisure and recreation use the idea to facilitate the quality of life around the world?

4. How is leisure a symbol of status both in the United States and in other countries?

5. Is the *Charter for Leisure* a realistic document to serve as a guide for both the so-called developed and developing countries?

Chapter 41

Partnerships

The phrases "two heads are better than one" and "the more the merrier" can be applied to partnerships in recreation services. All recreation-service sectors are relying extensively on partnerships among agencies, sometimes within a sector (e.g., a local parks and recreation department works with state government to develop a bicycle path) or across sectors (e.g., a pizza company provides refreshments at the end of a race run by a nonprofit organization).

The future of recreation services will depend on working collaboratively in partnerships. This chapter provides a brief background about partnership issues, their challenges, and ways to strengthen partnerships within and across recreation sectors.

Issues

Partnerships of all types will be paramount in the 21st century. Dollars for public services have been more difficult to acquire, while at the same time citizen demand for recreation services has increased. Most nonprofit organizations are increasingly relying on partnerships to reach their mission. Private businesses recognize the value of partnerships and sponsorships to enhance their visibility and potential sales. By their nature, partnerships generally involve people. A by-product of these partnerships is also a better-informed public with more people potentially working together to show support for recreation services.

The challenge of any partnership, whether it is in recreation services or in a marriage, is to ensure that each partner benefits from the relationship. Partnerships are designed to accomplish goals in effective and efficient ways. Each partner must understand the obligations and responsibilities that are necessary for the partnership to work. Some partnerships work better than others because the benefits and the costs are clearly identified in the beginning. Partners can then work diligently to make sure that the outcomes promised and the responsibilities delineated are consistent over time.

Partnerships may occur within sectors or across sectors, with two partners or numerous partners. Some partnerships include primary partners and numerous other contributors or sponsors. Just look at a t-shirt given at a road race to see examples of partnerships in action. Each event or program is likely to offer many potential avenues for involvement, but successful professionals will determine what partners are needed and how they can best work together.

Partnerships should be cost-effective. Professionals in recreation services must determine how and where to invest funds for personnel and space to provide the broadest and most inclusive services possible. In addition, without cooperation and partnerships, competition and duplication of services (and thus a waste of time and money) could occur. Communities that have adequate and effective partnerships are likely to be places where recreation services employees coordinate, communicate, and work together.

Partnerships also can add energy and enthusiasm to recreation services, programs, events, or facilities. Partnerships offer an opportunity to provide creative ways to address recreation needs and interests. They also provide a way for professionals, business leaders, and citizens to learn from one another. In essence, partnerships can allow people and organizations to contribute their strengths to a situation. Depending on the type of partnerships, other outcomes can occur, such as greater profits or sales, tax deductions, improved quality of services, and the development of a sense of ownership among the partners.

Outcomes

Challenges

Clearly define roles of partners to avoid challenges

No disadvantage is insurmountable, but the potential disadvantages of partnerships should be assessed. One of the biggest disadvantages occurs if the roles of the partners are not clearly defined. Some partnerships may be defined as one partner such as the public parks and recreation department being responsible for the actual programming of an event with another partner providing, for example, money. If one of the partners does not understand their role, problems can exist. Policy (including financial aspects) and program control must be clearly identified for each partner.

Undertaking a partnership takes time and energy to determine how a partnership will work. Questions to consider are who will be served by the partnership and how will quality standards be met. Participating in a

Q's to ask

partnership can be likened to a committed marriage or domestic relationship. People start out getting to know each other by dating before they jump into engagement and eventually marriage. Partnerships do not happen overnight, just as relationships usually do not happen overnight. Partners need to get to know as much as possible about potential partners before making a commitment. Since partnerships take time and effort to form, having a divorce after only a few weeks of being together is a waste of effort and can lead to much unhappiness.

A problem that can undermine partnerships is the perceived and actual competition that can occur in a community between potential partners. For example, if a community recreation program and a YMCA exist in a community, they may be perceived in some cases as competitors for the same participants. To some extent, these agencies may have some similar target audiences, but their missions vary and should not preclude examining how they might work together to provide better opportunities for all citizens. The success of both organizations may depend on recognition of the interdependence between sectors so the highest quality of recreation services can be facilitated.

Any partnership might result in the need to negotiate differences among the partners related to policies, scheduling, financial constraints, legal restriction on public use of private facilities (and vice versa), mutual protection of spheres of influence, available information, and the determination of specialized nature of particular groups. None of these problems are intractable but recreation professionals must take these into account when embarking on opportunities to work together.

Strategies for Action

Partnerships can develop in several ways. They usually take on forms to meet different community needs. These forms range from the need to attract or invite investment capital in a community to gaining efficiency through coordination. The joint ventures also can range from shared responsibility on the part of partners to minimal involvement by one or more of the partners. Here are some examples to consider:

- One common way to set up a partnership is for the public agency to provide facilities and a nonprofit or private business to offer services. An example would be a local business contracting refreshment services at a public athletic field, or a canoe club providing instruction at a lake in a local park. Another example is a community organization such as a Lions Club that *adopts* a park or a greenway and is responsible for litter pickup.

- Partnerships also occur in the form of lease agreements. These agreements have specific legal functions. An example is the case of a marina that might be leased for operation on a public lake owned by a state.

- Coordinating councils within communities are another example of partnerships. A coordinating council frequently consists of individuals from organizations representing different sectors. An example that occurs in several places around the United States is a community coordinating council that looks at the needs of a particular group, such as people with disabilities or youth services.

- The use of sponsorships is a common example of partnerships. Sponsorships at different levels provide the chance for several commercial businesses or other groups to work together. An example might be a road race coordinated by a specific group but offering numerous opportunities for others to be involved either with monetary contributions or volunteer services.

- Partnerships might also exist with people offering technical assistance to one another. If an organization such as an agency that serves youth has particular expertise in youth programming, they might assist another organization to set up a program or address issues that need assistance.

- Funds can be raised for special events through partnerships, including a direct solicitation for money as well as the use of in-kind donations or material goods that can be given away (e.g., free refreshments) or door prizes.

A number of other examples exist, such as loaned executive programs, loaned equipment, volunteer labor, shared facilities, joint purchases, joint public relations or advertising, and endorsements. The opportunities and options are virtually limitless given the many providers of recreation services and the needs that exist in communities.

No major formula exists for developing partnerships, but in today's society one sector alone cannot meet the recreation interests and needs of all citizens, particularly when the goal is sustainable recreation. Initial partnerships can result in opening the door for other endeavors in the future. Partnerships often have financial advantages, but they also provide a way to enhance services and develop a broader base of support for recreation opportunities so that leisure experiences become more available to all.

Reflection Questions

1. Why have partnerships become so important in the past few years?

2. What are the advantages of promoting partnerships?

3. Campus organizations often form partnerships to accomplish particular goals. What partnerships have you been involved with through your campus participation? How effective were these partnerships?

4. Communication between and among partners is a key factor in the success of the partnerships. In recreation partnerships as well as your personal relationships, what can be done to assure that communication works?

Chapter 42

Volunteers

Volunteers are the backbone of many recreation services. In the future they are likely to become more important than ever before. Even private recreation businesses work with volunteers from time to time. Understanding a bit about the issues of volunteerism may be useful for two reasons. First, volunteering, even though it is often called volunteer work, is a recreation activity and a form of leisure. People choose to participate freely and most people find volunteering to be highly enjoyable.

Second, because volunteering can be a form of leisure, examining the issues, challenges, and opportunities associated with volunteering within recreation services serves two purposes. Managing volunteers well not only contributes to the efforts of an organization but also provides a meaningful leisure activity for many individuals. The purpose of this chapter is to briefly investigate some of the dimensions of volunteering as a leisure experience within recreation services organizations.

Issues

A volunteer is someone who altruistically participates in promoting something he or she believes is good or that will improve community life. A volunteer may give time and/or money with no expectation of monetary reward, but hoping to feel good about their efforts and perhaps to gain new skills or learning.

Volunteerism was discussed briefly in the chapter about the nonprofit sector. Some nonprofit organizations are referred to as voluntary action organizations. However, many public recreation and parks programs also rely on volunteers to assist with instruction, supervision, serving on Advisory Boards, doing environmental clean-up projects, and participating in Friends groups that raise money for projects. Private businesses may pay many of their staff, but they often work with volunteers through their involvement and partnerships with other organizations (e.g., a race management company might provide the structure and timing for a road race, but volunteers may be used to assist with course monitoring, water stops, and finish-line duties).

Volunteering may be considered a leisure experience because it is not coerced but freely chosen. It generally occurs during an individual's free time and results in intrinsic feelings of value and self-worth. However, while volunteers are anticipating a positive experience, there may be drawbacks if the organization soliciting volunteers does not train and manage them appropriately. Volunteers do not just show up at the doorstep, already knowing how to contribute. Recreation professionals working with volunteers must spend considerable time in ensuring that volunteers know what they can help do.

Statistics vary, but it is estimated that between 20–30% of the U.S. population volunteer one or more times a year within some type of formal structure. The value of these services is huge when one considers what the costs would be if these individuals had to be paid. The interest in volunteering seems to be rising, because many professionals realize that the current recession requires more efforts on the part of citizens. On the other hand, people are very busy, which can curtail their volunteering.

Further, the characteristics of volunteers are highly variable, since they range from youth volunteers to retired persons. Some volunteers participate regularly, while others lend a hand when needed. This variety means that no one recipe can be given for how volunteers can be engaged with an organization. Volunteers can provide services in many ways including teaching activities and skill classes, serving on policy or advisory boards or commissions, advocating through education, fund-raising for certain causes, adopting a park, assisting in the carrying out of office routines such as distribution of pamphlets and other informational materials, serving as sponsors or advisors of recreation clubs, or providing transportation for people in special recreation services to and from recreation centers.

Challenges

Since volunteering is a leisure experience and recreation activity, and since many recreation organizations rely on volunteers, the effective management of individuals and groups that volunteer is essential. People need to know what opportunities exist and how they can take advantage of ways to make contributions to the causes that they value.

People have different reasons for volunteering. They also have different expectations. The challenge to recreation professionals is to be able to match volunteers with opportunities that they will find rewarding. Regardless of the opportunities, people want easy access to tasks for which they have the skills and abilities. Most volunteers are looking for opportunities to learn and add to their skills. Although not everyone is interested, friendship and social interaction is desired by many volunteers. Maybe more than anything, volunteers want to be appreciated and thanked for their help. A thank-you does not need to be elaborate but can just involve the recreation professional taking a minute to verbally say thank you or send a note. Volunteers want to know that someone thinks they made a difference. Recreation professionals must not forget that volunteers want enjoyable experiences—they want to have fun, which further shows the link between recreation and volunteering.

An issue that has arisen recently is the challenge regarding what to call volunteers. Some organizations have backed away from the term "volunteer" because it traditionally connotes long-term volunteering or the image of a candy-striper in a hospital. Many opportunities exist today that are short-term. Some organizations give volunteers titles associated with internships, service learning, pro bono involvement, donated services, civic engagement, board members, unpaid staff, active citizens, citizen service, activists, or community participants. The name given to volunteers may appear trivial, but some professionals are examining new ways to recruit help that does not connote traditional volunteering.

Several other trends have been identified regarding volunteering in all types of organizations, including recreation services. Some people have less interest in traditional service groups unless these groups offer shorter-term commitments. People want to know what to anticipate and how much or how little they are expected to volunteer. Many people are interested in only occasional volunteering when needed (e.g., helping with an arts and crafts fair for several hours on a Saturday once a year). 'Micro-volunteering' is a term that was coined to explain people volunteering for short periods of time without an ongoing commitment. Regardless, volunteers do not want to waste their time, so they need projects that they see as important but that also fit into their busy schedules.

Different people have special skills to contribute. Some volunteers are interested in virtual volunteering, where they might be able to contribute without leaving their house. In other cases, volunteers want to volunteer with a group of people they know (e.g., a church youth group helping with a stream clean-up). Retirees are a potential group of people that are often looking for meaningful experiences. On the other hand, students in primary or secondary schools as well as college students may be searching for volunteer opportunities as a way to develop employment skills or to be involved in service learning.

Donors are also important volunteers in recreation services organizations even though they do not necessarily give of their time directly. A donor is interested in a cause. He or she could be someone who leaves a large sum of money to a recreation organization in a will, or a donor might be someone who gives $10 online. A donor might give a laptop to an organization or offer to give furniture. Donations might come from sponsors who partner with an organization to fund, or assist with funding a program or event. Some donors and funders may be reluctant to support long-term projects but would be interested in short-term projects where the differences they make can be readily observable. Donors are no different than other volunteers in that they want to feel that they make a difference and that their efforts are appreciated. They want to be recognized in informal as well as formal ways.

Strategies for Action

A typical volunteer no longer exists. People are looking for opportunities to volunteer in family or friend groups, through online services, at all hours of the day or night, and with flexible time commitment opportunities (http://nonprofit.about.com/od/volunteers/a/Does-Your-Nonprofit-Appeal-To-The-New-Volunteers.htm).

Based on what volunteers want, recreation professionals also might be involved in helping people get civically engaged by offering them opportunities to define and solve problems that they see in their communities. Members of groups such as faith-based organizations, schools, businesses, and governmental agencies may be interested in working within their organization as volunteers (e.g., a private business might designate a project such as Habitat for Humanity or river clean-up as something that employees can do together).

Volunteer management needs to be a commitment if volunteers are to be used effectively in recreation services organization. Volunteers need guidance, and using volunteers means that an organization is committed to determining how to best guide and train volunteers for mutual benefit. Tailoring opportunities to fit people's lifestyles and changing expectations will be necessary. Although some volunteers are motivated by external rewards (e.g., their names on a plaque or a volunteer recognition luncheon), many just want to be thanked.

A huge diversity of potential volunteers exists that will be needed in the future if recreation services organizations are to get the help they need. Volunteers will not supplant staff but they certainly can augment the efforts of an organization. Further, although many volunteers want short-term projects, they also do not want to lose contact with an organization. Thus, volunteer management will require record keeping and developing a pool of potential helpers.

Volunteering is a two-way street. Volunteers must feel they gain something from their experiences. At the same time, organizations must feel that volunteers help them provide recreation services in better ways. Civic engagement, donations, and volunteer experiences will remain essential for recreation services into the future. They will also remain important leisure experiences for individuals.

Reflection Questions

1. Where have you volunteered in the past? What was the experience like for you? What did you gain? How could the organization have done a better job in working with its volunteers?

2. Do people view volunteering as a recreation activity? Does it matter whether they do or not?

3. How much difference does a name make? Would you rather be called a *volunteer* or an *active citizen*?

4. People are asked to give monetary donations constantly. How do you decide whether you will donate and how much you will donate?

5. What do you think are the best ways to recruit volunteers for particular events related to recreation services?

Chapter 43

Repositioning Recreation Services

The benefits of leisure experiences and recreation services have been emphasized throughout this book. Nevertheless, although recreation services can make many contributions to individual well-being and community life, some people regard anything related to leisure, recreation, or play as frivolous. Recreation services are sometimes viewed as nonessential services, particularly in the public sector where tax dollars are limited and other community services are viewed as more essential.

The purpose of this chapter is to address how recreation services, primarily in the public sector but also to some extent in the nonprofit sector, can be positioned or repositioned to be seen as essential in communities. Repositioning can contribute to the sustainability of recreation services. The basis for this chapter comes from the lifelong work of John Crompton, who expounds this theme in greater depth in his 2007 book, *Community Benefits and Repositioning.*

Issues

The traditional role of public park and recreation agencies has been to provide facilities and/or programs for people in communities. Since the 1970s, many public agencies have been scrutinized regarding what share of the public dollars should be allocated to them. This questioning has sometimes related to what has been described as the taxpayers' revolt. To try to show the value of recreation services when this scrutiny came, many organizations thought the solution to gaining credibility would be to more vigorously market and promote the programs (Crompton, 2007).

This marketing was based largely on a user-benefits-based approach. The marketing was about encouraging people to participate in and/or buy opportunities and services. Professionals tried to move away from the idea of activity-based management toward benefits-based management. This approach meant that professionals, mostly in the public sector but also to some extent in some nonprofit organizations, operated with several beliefs:

- Benefits meet human needs and not just recreation interests
- Benefits must be identified so that services can be designed to meet them
- Needs can be met by partnering with other organizations
- Services must be structured to address desired benefits (Crompton, 2007)

This benefits approach was useful. Identifying benefits, as discussed in Unit One of this book, is important. If a recreation professional, regardless of the sector or specialty, cannot identify the benefits of participation or involvement, then he or she will not be effective in promoting these activities. The benefits approach that is focused on outcomes for individuals provides a sound basis, but according to Crompton (2007) it is not enough. High user satisfaction is a necessary condition but may not be sufficient to sustain recreation services.

An additional way to talk about benefits is in the context of community benefits related to the three aspects of sustainability: social stability, economic prosperity, and environmental preservation. These are areas that may resonate best with decision-makers and taxpayers. As the thesis of this book emphasizes, recreation services will not be sustainable into the future unless these three aspects are repositioned as central to recreation services.

Crompton (2007) believes that recreation services should be repositioned so they are viewed as distinctive and valued in the minds of the general public and elected officials. The current position held about recreation services is that they are relatively discretionary and nonessential. The goal is to sustain recreation services so they are perceived as central to addressing social, economic, and environmental issues within a community.

Repositioning often involves helping people recognize that entrenched perceptions held that recreation is only "fun and games" need to be reconsidered. I have long argued that what really makes recreation services distinct is that we address enjoyment and fun. These outcomes define recreation and no other profession gives people the "permission to play" that recreation services do. However, positioning or repositioning means that recreation is both fun for individuals *and* meets important community needs.

Challenges

As with any new way of thinking, time is needed to implement changes. This time is needed both in helping professionals think about their field differently as well as helping citizens/participants and decision-makers see the broad scope of recreation services. Related to the time it takes, repositioning also may be met with resistance by professionals who have not thought about program structure and marketing related to the potential benefits.

The lack of adequate funding of public parks and recreation is likely to be a reality into the future. Money is tight for people and no one wants to pay higher fees or taxes. Further, people view public services such as police protection, maintained roads, and firefighting as absolutely essential. Public park and recreation services may be seen as in competition with those essential services. Therefore, positioning recreation services so people believe they are necessary will be an ongoing challenge. However, thinking about the values of recreation and finding ways to articulate them from both individual and community perspectives will be necessary to change attitudes in communities.

Strategies for Action

At least four approaches can be used for repositioning (Crompton, 2007). Real positioning means developing new services or restructuring services to explicitly address community benefits. Associative repositioning means partnering with other organizations to strengthen one's position (e.g., working with the public health department to sponsor programs aimed at wellness). Psychological repositioning means working with people in communities to change their perceptions of recreation services. Research can often be useful in this regard. Finally, competitive repositioning means showing how some recreation services can be done as well in the public sector as in other sectors.

An example from an organization that is using repositioning successfully may be useful. Lee's Summit is a community located in Missouri. Under the direction of Administrator Tom Lovell, the community has specifically focused on how the recreation services benefit the community. The motto of the department is "every age, every season," which speaks to the commitment to inclusion and opportunities. Specifically, Lee's Summit has described their park and recreation services by using the following statements:

- An average house that sells for $150K would sell for $30K more if located near a safe, well-maintained park.

- The cost to incarcerate a juvenile offender for one year is $71K. With that money, Lee's Summit Parks and Recreation could employ 5 part-time staff to work at a community center, provide 100 youth passes to Summit Waves, and offer 100 fitness memberships annually. Prevention or intervention?

- Fitness programs such as those offered in Legacy Park Community Center may be reducing healthcare costs by as much as 55%.

- Legacy Park Community Center represents a $10M capital investment in leisure services, generates $1.6M annually in revenues covering all operating expenses, employs 8 full-time and 50 part-time staff, and serves over 320K people per year

- 30% of military recruits can't pass the basic physical requirements for service. Fitness is a national security issue.

Many people are highly supportive of recreation and parks in communities. This support is evident in the high percentage of propositions and bond issues that have been passed authorizing capital expenditures for recreation services (Crompton, 2007). Many of these same people recognize the importance of having strong public, nonprofit, and private business recreation options in communities. However, these services cannot be taken for granted. Regardless of which sector or which specialty within the field, being able to describe the benefits of recreation services for individuals as well as the economic and environmental impact on communities is necessary if recreation services are to be sustainable into the future.

Reflection Questions

1. Repositioning can apply to academic programs in colleges and universities as well as in communities. What might you say are the benefits of having a professional preparation program in recreation services at your university?

2. How do recreation services meet human needs in addition to satisfying recreation interests?

3. Of the examples given in Lee's Summit, which of those reasons appears to be most important from your point of view?

Chapter 44

Management of Recreation Services

Recreation services are dynamic. What people want regarding enjoyable leisure experiences is directly related to their personal interests and their community environment (e.g., family, culture, opportunities, policies). When recreation services professionals focus on sustainability, many possibilities exist for facilitating meaningful opportunities within communities. If the field of recreation services is to maintain its viability, professionals must consider the emerging issues and develop management strategies to facilitate social, economic, and environmental sustainability.

In a static society with no change, the future is like the present. In a dynamic profession, the future is created each day and requires people to modify their behaviors accordingly. In the 21st century, recreation services are a part of a much bigger world. Significant influences such as demographics, technology, and partnerships have been highlighted in this introductory book. This chapter will highlight some recreation services management issues, including general management and challenges to economics and funding, personnel management, and research and evaluation. If you major in recreation at your university, you will examine all these areas in greater detail in later professional coursework.

Issues in General Management

Management refers to getting people together to accomplish desired goals by using the resources (e.g., human, financial, technological) that are available effectively and efficiently. Although entry-level positions in recreation services are not necessarily titled management, the job descriptions of many recreation services professionals, regardless of the specialty, involve activities such as planning, organizing, staffing, and monitoring efforts within an organization. Although one's title might be therapist, recreation leader, coach, or park ranger, aspects of general management will be fundamental.

All organizations have to be managed for success. All organizations must consider the financial bottom line, but professionals must also consider what difference they make in people's lives. Thus, being effective in making a difference but also being efficient with good fiscal and personnel management is necessary. Stubbs (1998) suggested several strategies that link organizational practices with effective management:

- Planning based on a clear mission

- Agenda focusing on priorities

- Recruitment of employees and volunteers that seek quality leadership

- Fiscal management and fund-raising organized for intended purposes

- Accountability in reaching the goals that fulfill the mission

- Responsiveness in reflecting participants' (e.g., customers, clients, citizens, visitors) expectations

Strategic planning is a necessary component for successful management. Although strategic management is not new, the process within recreation organizations in all sectors should be considered. Strategic planning includes the strategies outlined above related to setting goals, determining the best ways to achieve those goals, and laying down specific steps to reach the goals. The goals should emerge from the mission statement of the recreation services organization. Planning requires determining what personnel, funding, and functions need to be undertaken. This final aspect of strategic management requires laying down specific steps for how to reach the goals based on the priorities of the organization. Although this planning provides guidance, strategic plans should also be flexible. A plan provides a roadmap, but you never know when it might be necessary to take a detour. Effective strategic management should enable your organization to respond to new challenges and make adjustments. (http://www.allbusiness.com/management/2975129-1.html#ixzz25yPJxAGi)

People use strategic planning in their lives, but may not always realize it. For example, if a student had the goal of getting away and having a good time on spring break, he or she would consider what funds were needed, where to go, and who to go with. Then, planning would include talking to friends who might want to go, determining a destination, and then securing funds and determining the logistics of travel and lodging. If at the last minute, a friend who was going to provide the car gets sick, then a new plan would need to be developed.

Challenges Regarding Financial Resources

Regardless of the plan, economics influence how goals are reached. The economy is always an issue of concern for participants and professionals alike. Recreation services professionals in all sectors recognize the need to strengthen and broaden the base of financial support. These efforts likely will occur through the exploration of new funding sources identified through strategic planning.

Depending on the mission of the recreation service, getting more funding has to be compatible with the organizational goals. For example, public recreation services cannot rely solely on taxes for operating budgets. On the other hand, increasing fees and charges should not make programs and facilities inaccessible to people who have typically been underserved and marginalized. In addition, donors no longer reward only good intentions but want to see results. These results often rest on sound evaluations of programs to document accountability. Creative financing is a task that is essential for management regardless of the sector.

The focus of this book is not on management and finance, but recreation professionals should be aware that many options for financial support can be considered. Among the techniques mentioned in this textbook that may be used to expand recreation budgets and services are grants, trusts, endowments, bequests, gift catalogs (i.e., itemized lists of the needs of an organization with solicitation for those items), Friends of the Parks or "adopt-a-park" programs, co-sponsorships and corporate assistance, and volunteer services. Privatization (i.e., the assignment or contracting of certain functions to private business organizations) may be another alternative way to expand services, especially within public recreation services.

Political attitudes affect financing recreation services, particularly in the public sector. If citizens view recreation and parks as a necessity, they tend to support bond issues and the expenditure of tax dollars for recreation operations. They want their recreation and parks professionals to work for the betterment of the community. Therefore, recreation professionals must be politically smart, fiscally accountable, and must foster a strong loyalty from their grassroots participants if recreation is to be sustainable and on the forefront as an essential component to enhance the quality of life in communities.

Challenges in Personnel Management

In addition to financing, recreation services are highly dependent on personnel. Over 75% of most recreation organizations' budgets are used for full-time and part-time employees. Many professionals in recreation services are responsible for managing people—full-time employees, part-time and seasonal staff, and volunteers. The workforce is changing and will continue to change, especially as the bulge of Baby Boomers retires.

The diversity of the workforce reflects the changing environment. For example, many of the new employees entering the workforce are women and minorities. Newer workers will emerge from the Millennial generation. Recreation professionals who will be most successful in the future must be able to thrive within a diversified work team. In addition, they must be managed by administrators sensitive to perspectives that may vary by gender, race, ethnicity, sexual identity, disability, religion, and age (Barner, 1996).

As Baby Boomers in the workforce age and move into retirement, the new leaders and managers may represent different views of work as well as leisure. Much has been written about the work force comparing Baby Boomers (i.e., born 1946–1964), Generation X (i.e., 1965–1981), and Generation Y or the Millennials (i.e., 1982–2002). The generations were described briefly earlier in this book and people working in any organization must realize that communicating across the generations is essential.

Students reading this book are likely Millennials. Several suggestions can be offered for all members of generations to consider in working together. For example, focusing on the similarities as well as the differences among the generations is important. Change does occur, even if it feels that sometimes things move slowly or sometimes too fast. Understanding the past is often helpful in planning for the future. Asking questions rather than just making statements is a way to understand how things can be done differently. Further, all employees are admonished to avoid stereotyping of people just because of their age or because cultural or historical references may not be understood (http://www.techrepublic.com/blog/10things/10-ways-to-minimize-generational-differences-in-the-workplace/2140).

Another issue that can cut across all generations related to personnel is the part-time, seasonal, or contract employees that may work in recreation services organizations. Traditionally many recreation programs have relied on seasonal or part-time people hired in the summer, for example, to be lifeguards and camp counselors. Today, part-time employees are commonly used year-round in all the sectors. These part-time employees may be young people, but many older adults are now seeking work experiences on a part-time basis. Successful professionals will need to remain open and flexible in working with all colleagues whether they are full-time, part-time, or volunteers. Volunteers are important contributors to recreation services, as discussed earlier in this book.

Evaluation and Research

The practices of management, leveraging financial resources, and supervising employees will be enhanced through evaluation efforts and recognizing the importance of learning about best practices through research. The effective management of recreation services is more than learning from experiences. It includes the continual reforming of practices to provide the best possible services. Programs need outcome-based processes that are monitored and evaluated.

The success of recreation programs measured in the past by numbers of participants and their satisfaction is not enough in the 21st century. Recreation professionals must be able to identify the outcomes of recreation services and not just the numbers of participants who happened to enjoy a program. The focus on outcomes, monitoring, and evaluation are essential for the continued sustainability of recreation services in all sectors.

Evaluation includes the systematic collection and analysis of data based on a specified purpose or set of criteria to make judgments about the value or worth so improvements can be made (Henderson & Bialeschki, 2010). Effective evaluation means making decisions (i.e., conclusions and recommendations) based on identified questions and supporting information. Everyone is continually making evaluative judgments about the world around them (e.g., the weather or someone's hairstyle), but successful evaluation requires a systematic approach with specific purposes and outcomes. Evaluation in recreation services can occur regarding programs, personnel, policies, facilities, and participant outcomes. Further, various levels of program evaluation exist, including:

- inputs (e.g., resources and personnel allocated)

- the activities (i.e., number and type)

- people involvement (i.e., number and characteristics)

- reactions (i.e., satisfaction with facilities, leadership)

- changes in knowledge, attitudes, skills, or aspirations

- behavior change (e.g., becoming more active, developing a hobby)

- long-term impacts (e.g., life-changing influences from participation)

A reflective recreation professional recognizes the importance of evaluation plans and using data to make improvements in the services provided.

A new planning and evaluation tool now available to professionals in parks and recreation is PRORAGIS (Parks and Recreation Operating Ratios and Geographic Information System), which is an online database and GIS-mapping system (http://www.nrpa.org). It combines data from park and recreation departments including finances, resources, staffing, and programs and allows for online mapping of parks, trails, and facilities. The value is that a city or county recreation and parks unit can use the data as a benchmark for planning within their organization. These data can also be used in ways such as budget justifications, master planning, market research, revenue enhancement, and events promotion. This database allows agencies to evaluate how their facilities, spaces, administration, and programs compare to others of similar size.

For recreation services to address the needs of people in the future requires an appreciation of research. The importance of a body of knowledge in defining a profession was noted earlier in this book. The success and progress of recreation services will depend on the quantity and quality of research undertaken and how it is applied. This applied research system must involve and use resources of the academic community, private research firms, and research units of federal and state agencies. Research is essential to the development of sound public policies and effective administrative practices. Understanding leisure behavior, as well as best practices in management, will be necessary for the sustainability of recreation services into the future.

Reflection Questions

1. When thinking about the future of recreation services organizations, how important is understanding the past?

2. What will be the greatest issues facing recreation services regarding the economy and financial resources in the future?

3. What will be the greatest issues facing recreation services regarding personnel management in the future?

4. Why is evaluation important in recreation services? What aspects of recreation services will be most important to measure in the future?

5. What topics of research will be most beneficial to recreation services professionals in the future?

Chapter 45

Service Living

Service living includes lifelong action that contributes to the health and well-being of all living things (Wellman, Dustin, Henderson, & Moore, 2008). This idea is related to but not at all the same as service learning, which is a concept embraced in schools to combine classroom learning with undertaking projects in communities. Service living is about recognizing that everything that one does is connected to a larger community. The purpose of this short chapter is to summarize the idea of service living as presented by Wellman et al. in their 2008 book, and to demonstrate how this idea relates to recreation services and the lives of professionals.

Issues

The population of the United States in 2012 was 314 million people. With this many people, individuals sometimes feel insignificant and do not think that one person can make a difference. Many people prefer to retreat to the privacy of their homes and only do what is necessary to live a comfortable life. The public good is thought to be the responsibility of others such as politicians.

Hearing or reading the headline news can be disheartening when thinking about all the injustices in the world and the growing concerns about environmental sustainability. Further, with all the emphasis on consumerism, some people believe the marketplace has taken over their lives. The world appears to revolve around money. Money is important, no doubt. Other values such as friends, family, and community, however, are also important. People need to realize that they can make a difference individually and collectively in addressing problems that are omnipresent.

Service living recognizes that democracy depends on ordinary citizens making extraordinary contributions. Service living within the context of recreation services means going above and beyond job duties to focus on a bigger picture that addresses sustainability.

The goals of service living are to challenge what it means to be a responsible citizen in a participatory democracy. Service living means recognizing the responsibilities that individuals have for being part of a larger community. People have both the opportunity and the obligation to become engaged in the life of the greater community through their professional as well as their personal efforts. This idea pertains to what individuals do more than what recreation services organizations do. However, recreation professionals can view their work as service living when addressing the pressing issues of social inclusion and sustainability that go far beyond most job descriptions.

The compelling aspect about service living as it pertains to recreation services is that professionals must be committed to taking the long view of the future. Getting caught up in day-to-day hassles without keeping the goals of improving the well-being of people, promoting the quality of life in communities, and making the world a better place can result in burnout and disillusionment at work. Although most of us likely will not make contributions that will make us famous, many of us can make contributions to communities that will have long-term influences, if we keep the potential of leisure experiences and recreation services in mind.

Challenges

The book *Service Living* tells the stories of four individuals who made remarkable contributions to the country through their recreation-related work. The individuals were Frederick Law Olmstead, Jane Addams, Benton MacKaye, and Marjory Stoneman Douglas. Some of these people embodied service living partially through their employment (i.e., Olmstead, Addams) but others were primarily community volunteers (i.e., MacKaye, Douglas) who wanted to make a difference. In both cases, these individuals went much further than what might have been expected of them.

Each of these people was an ordinary citizen who suffered ups and downs and had their own insecurities, doubts, and anxiety. But, they transcended this individualism to promote the public good and leave lasting legacies.

Olmstead was a landscape architect best known for designing Central Park in New York City. He also designed hundreds of green spaces throughout the United States and is known as the father of landscape architecture in America. The principles of his ideas and designs have influenced park planning for over a century. Not only was Olmstead a great architect, but he was also a humble teacher. He shared his ideas widely and was not afraid to take risks and take action on his big ideas.

Addams was called by many people at the time of her death the "greatest woman in the world." She had also been called several years prior to that the most dangerous woman in America because of her radical ideas. Her involvement with a settlement house in Chicago called Hull House, along with her writing and speaking that addressed social work, juvenile justice, education, and recreation, defined her life. She epitomized lifelong learning and social action. She believed that to be educated meant that one must live a life of service to others.

MacKaye's life spanned the most pivotal events in American conservation history, and he was instrumental in setting aside huge tracts of public land, developing federal land management agencies, and promoting the rise of environmental organizations to protect the outdoors. He had a vision of how the American landscape should be protected. MacKaye was most visible in establishing the Appalachian Trail and inspiring the thousands of volunteers who worked to build, maintain, and manage the hundreds of miles of trails. He co-founded the Wilderness Society and promoted environmental justice long before the term was used.

Douglas was an environmentalist who will be remembered in association with the Florida Everglades. Similar to Addams and despite the constraints often placed upon women in the 20th century, Douglas stuck to her convictions and persevered to reach her goals of preserving the Everglades as a biologically diverse place that could be enjoyed by future generations. In addition, she was known as a writer with a huge sensitivity to social causes, although she did not consider herself an environmentalist for much of her life. She was 70 years old before she took up the cause of saving the Everglades. She lived a simple life with little concern for materialism. Books were her passion and though she led a solitary life, she had numerous supporters and friends.

Strategies for Action

Each of these individuals had different experiences in their lives. Each, however, believed in something much bigger than themselves. They demonstrated that democracy is a verb and not a noun. Democracy is civic-mindedness in action. The U.S. government was founded on the premise of "of the people, by the people, and for the people," and service living embodies this ideal of democracy.

The four historic figures described above lived the ideal of democracy. They did not rely on experts or politicians to tell them what to do. They saw what needed to be done and joined with others to address what they considered to be the social good. An important point is that although they are credited for making great contributions to American life, they did not undertake their projects alone. None of them could have done anything significant by themselves. They needed others and they knew how to mobilize others to share their dreams.

These individuals took time to learn as much as they could about the issues that were important to them. They were well read. They listened to the expertise and opinions of others and reflected on that information. Service living means seeing both the opportunity and the obligation to educate ourselves and others, *and* to take action. It also means being a reflective professional that knows how to evaluate and learn from all situations. Professionals as well as concerned citizens who take action for the public good are open to criticism, but they must persevere in their ethical beliefs and the necessity of being of service to others.

Stories about people such as Olmstead, Addams, MacKaye, and Douglas are inspiring to read. Their work provides models for how recreation services professionals might extend their impact. The challenge is to find ways to embody service living in our personal and professional lives. Everyone has self-doubts, insecurities, and anxieties about work, and sometimes about leisure. However, meeting those concerns straightforwardly is needed. The benefits of a life of action, engagement, and service living make for a personal and professional life worth living.

Reflection Questions

1. Do you know other people who might reflect this ideal of service living? What are they doing? How have they been successful?

2. What can you do in your personal life that will embody service living? What can you do to evidence service living in your future career in recreation services?

3. What can you do to prepare yourself for a life of service living?

Chapter 46

Becoming a
Recreation Services Professional

Recreation services are a profession. This statement has been emphasized throughout this book. People reading this book are likely students who may be interested in a career in recreation services. This chapter addresses some of the issues and challenges associated with becoming a professional.

Every person should be in a mindset of "becoming." I have sometimes thought that maybe people should not call themselves human beings, but human becomings. Regardless, becoming a professional may be hastened by considering the value of professional education, acknowledging one's professional identity, distinguishing the qualifications needed for becoming a professional leader, and emphasizing ways to be a continual learner to ensure that professionals are always on the cutting edge of the field. All professionals should be in a constant state of becoming.

Issues in
Professional Education

Professional education provides individuals with the skills and opportunities to facilitate leisure, recreation, tourism, sport, and play experiences in a structured and organized fashion called recreation services. The purpose of this professional education continues to be to prepare individuals to manage areas, facilities, and programs that will facilitate recreation opportunities for people in all types of communities. The breadth of these possibilities and the professionalization of the field have grown steadily throughout the world in the past 50 years. As noted earlier, the specialty areas have also expanded, particularly in the past 25 years. The field continues to grow and change, which is good. Any profession that stays in status quo is not likely to be sustainable.

If a student chooses a major with the hopes of a career in a specialty within recreation services, coursework will include core areas such as leadership and supervision, program planning, administration, financing, diversity and inclusion, facility management, and risk management, as well as specific courses related to the specialty (e.g., outdoor leadership, outdoor management, communication in sport, golf club management, event management, tourism). Curricula in each university will vary depending on the mission of the unit and the resources that are available. Students also have the opportunity to take general education courses that support their degree as well as elective courses across the university that may strengthen the specialty expertise (e.g., business management courses, public administration). The design of curricula supports the belief that recreation services are a professional career. Many of these core courses, however, provide foundational skills that can be applied in a range of human services.

The degree of professionalism (i.e., according to the criteria discussed in Unit Two including an alliance with a social concern; professional societies and associations; a code of ethics; a specialized body of knowledge; professional education and training; and professional standards of accreditation, certification, and licensing) varies throughout the world. Dustin and Goodale (1999) noted that more students are professionally educated in parks, recreation, and leisure studies in the United States than in all the other countries in the world combined. Professional standards such as accreditation (e.g., university curricula as well as agency practices) and certification (e.g., Certified Park and Recreation Professional) are primarily U.S. based. Efforts in developing professional education programs, however, are gaining impetus throughout the world. In addition, a growing trend is to offer professional education through online Master's programs, which can be accessed from literally all over the world.

Although certification and licensing recreation services professionals, and accreditation of academic programs as well as of public agencies are most common in the United States, not every recreation services professional in the United States takes advantage of these opportunities. Certification and licensing are acts of public protection. When certification is required, the public is assured that employees have achieved a certain level of education, training, and/or experience. Certification says nothing, however, about the quality of the individual's experience or ability to perform. Naysayers about certification argue that it is an act of exclusion because the field of recreation services may be closing out some individuals who could make a significant contribution to the profession without having a professional degree in recreation services. This issue is hotly debated. As you become a professional, you will need to decide the value of certification for your particular specialty interests.

Accreditation and certification are interwoven processes. For certification to exist, recognition of education is necessary. This recognition is best achieved when applicants can demonstrate that they are graduates of accredited programs. When accreditation exists, graduates from these programs are automatically assumed to have obtained the basic preparation for the profession, and therefore, are qualified to practice. In both instances, the public is protected because minimum levels of quality are ensured through experience and training.

Professional Identity

A preferable future and an essential aspect to sustain recreation services mandates that recreation services are valued by society based on the services and facilities offered and the individual and community benefits that are outcomes of the services. Just as personal identities are shaped by environment and experiences, the same type of forces will be encountered regarding professional identity. Some of those forces will lead to positive change, but some may not.

Professional identity within the services field will result from clearly defined roles that are different from the roles assumed by other groups, professionals, and organizations. The emerging body of knowledge obtained through research can help in establishing the recreation services profession's uniqueness. The activities of professional associations can aid that endeavor, but the burden of professionalism lies with individuals who identify themselves as professionals and act accordingly.

The field of recreation services has a long and rich history that supports interests in the preservation and use of the environment as well as concerns for social welfare programs, marginalized groups, and opportunities for individual and community development. The future professional identity will be influenced by the past and will evolve with changing economic and political climates. How recreation services will fare as a profession depends on the leadership that comes from professionals themselves.

Challenges in Professional Leadership

The question of leadership is paramount in any profession. The problem involves two kinds of leadership: 1) professional leadership that gives direction to techniques and program strategies; and 2) citizen involvement that gives the program validity and political credibility. As discussed in detail in Unit Three, recreation services as a profession offers employment opportunities for individuals with a variety of backgrounds, skills, and professional orientations. Sociologists, economists, landscape architects, gardeners, maintenance workers, computer specialists, dance specialists, and technicians are all a part of the recreation services system. The recreation professional that is prepared to give leadership to a recreation, park, sport, or tourism organization or business will be needed as the guiding force that integrates all employees into a cohesive group who can provide quality services.

The role of the recreation professional leader is distinct from the technician or activity leader. Being a professional requires broad understandings of interpersonal relationships and dynamics, interagency relationships and partnerships, the need for long-range as well as short-term planning, and the significance of leisure behavior in contemporary life. The technician or activity leader is more concerned with the implementation of day-to-day activities and making decisions based on local planning and evaluation. In the future, recreation services in all the sectors will likely increase their use of part-time workers and volunteers who will need supervision and leadership from professionals who also see the big picture.

The foundation for being a successful professional leader can be viewed in different ways, but in general several principles can apply:

- Keep things in perspective, and use laughter each day

- Put customers, members, citizens, or participants first

- Have high values and principles

- Be humble and generous (i.e., no individual can do it all alone)

- Know the business of recreation through professional preparation education as well as continuing education

- Be trustworthy (i.e., it takes years to develop trust and only a few seconds to destroy it)

- Share your knowledge willingly

- Exceed the expectations of your job

- Communicate effectively (in oral and written forms)

- Say thank you (as often as you can)

From Jan Gaden (personal communication, August 25, 2012)

If a professional keeps these admonitions in mind, he or she will maintain that professionalism as well as facilitate services that will meet the interests and needs of participants.

Another perspective for successful leadership in recreation services is to recognize the value of partnerships as well as other forms of collaborations. Partnerships were discussed in some detail earlier. In addition, recreation professionals may provide leadership by defining themselves as facilitators and educators regarding leisure. People, especially in local communities, need to feel empowered to meet their needs while the professional facilitates opportunities for personal and community growth through recreation. Recreation programs can evolve from expressed grassroots needs in addition to top-down leadership. Facilitative styles of programming and leadership will be necessary for professional leaders in the future.

The role of women, people of color, and other marginalized people is an issue that will likely influence the leadership of recreation services in the future. Currently, more females than males are majoring in recreation programs in universities and colleges, but the number of people of color entering the profession remains low. Women and people of color gradually are taking on greater visibility in leadership in recreation services, but progress is slow.

Issues will need to be addressed concerning how work environments can be hospitable to emerging professionals from historically marginalized groups. For example, work environments will need to become more flexible for many women who still have primary child care responsibilities in their lives. In addition, issues in other professions that confront women and other marginalized people such as sexual harassment, wage discrimination, and the glass ceiling, cannot be ignored. A diverse workforce employed in recreation services also will likely result in more diverse participants.

Citizen involvement, particularly in the planning and policy aspects of recreation services, is currently and will continue to be essential, especially in the public and nonprofit sectors. All monumental social changes (e.g., civil rights, environmental, women's rights) have occurred because of citizen grassroots movements. In all sectors, political forces affect recreation services. A citizen is often in a better position than a paid professional to address political forces and advocate for the value of recreation services. Likewise, citizen involvement in program planning, facility acquisition and development, and evaluation ensures a recreation future based on grass-roots input. Recreation professionals must continue to nurture and develop opportunities for citizen participation in all sectors. Good management will be needed for the future, but so will vision and leadership.

Strategies for Action

Not only should professional leadership involve nurturing and developing opportunities in others, but professionals should view their professional status as one that requires regular continuing education. Organizations usually require continuing professional education in the form of continuing education units (CEUs) to maintain certification. However, a professional by definition should recognize that continuing education is a responsibility, regardless of what degrees an individual may have and how many continuing education units they are required to get. The conferring of a B.A. or B.S. degree is simply the brief pause before one enters a career of continual education.

Several emerging trends about continuing education may be useful to note. Since the need for learning is at an all-time high, many resources exist. E-learning, for example, includes all forms of electronically supported learning, online opportunities, and webinar training. It may be possible to be certified in different areas of expertise through online courses. Training is also available through new venues such as iTunes University and YouTube videos. New courses are continually offered through recreation organizations as well as in many other disciplines that offer training and education.

Finally, to be successful in recreation services requires that people practice what they preach. In other words, professionals must have leisure interests themselves. Finding ways to unwind, de-stress, and enjoy life is essential. Situations in one's professional life are sometimes out of one's control such as people's emotions, customer expectations, traffic, and politics. Stress relief is necessary and can be achieved by blocking off time to do something just for oneself, both in small increments of time (e.g., ½ hour a day) and in larger blocks through holidays and vacations. Similarly, a professional must learn not to fret over the things that cannot be controlled in one's job. Finding ways to laugh and have fun is essential.

Other considerations for self-care leading to personal and professional growth include eating healthy and being kind to your body. In addition, many people find that being organized and having a daily schedule is important. A helpful hint may be to get to some of the least favorite and most important jobs done immediately, rather than procrastinating. Time management is an essential aspect of stress management.

The life of any profession is filled with exciting opportunities as well as challenges. Having the skills and expertise to do the job, knowing your professional identity and why it is important, possessing leadership skills, and focusing on continued growth through education and positive daily living will make your career one that will be exciting and fulfilling.

Reflection Questions

1. What does it mean to you to be a professional?

2. What characteristics do you currently possess that you think will help you be a successful professional leader?

3. What do you envision as your preferred future as a recreation services professional? What do you aspire to?

4. How can you take care of yourself personally so that you can be an effective professional?

Epilogue

Leisure is a part of everyone's life and has great potential to contribute to people's well-being. I hope this book has shown how recreation services are instrumental in facilitating leisure experiences for people and contributing to the quality of community life. Recreation services are changing and evolving within the public, nonprofit, and private business sectors. In addition, the plethora of specialties (e.g., parks and recreation, outdoor management, sport management, event management, therapeutic recreation, tourism) that exist within recreation services offer numerous career opportunities.

The foundation of this book is on how recreation services can be sustained into the future. Sustainable recreation services are a means to optimize human development and create communities that can provide health and well-being for residents and visitors. Sustainable recreation includes activities that address social needs and interests by considering economic implications while preserving the environment and respecting people's lives. Sustainable recreation services also mean that opportunities are inclusive and just (i.e., fair) for individuals.

The foundation of sustainability considers social, economic, and environmental aspects as necessary to ensure that recreation services are supported, upheld, and enduring. Sustainability related to recreation services also means that opportunities for leisure experiences will be available for today's generations and generations to come.

Social, economic, and environmental aspects must *all* be present for sustainability to occur. All are interdependent. Some people describe this trilogy for sustainability as like a 3-legged stool. If any one of the legs is removed, the stool will be unstable and basically unusable. Without a natural environment with clean air and water, nothing would exist, including recreation services. The social implications are huge when examining the benefits of leisure experiences. Additionally, when one commits to being inclusive and fair, all individuals can claim the right to leisure and access meaningful recreation opportunities. Further, regardless of the sector, recreation services must have financial resources. The diminishing of any one of these three aspects will drastically change recreation services now and into the future.

Changes in the demographics of the population, economic conditions, and the health of the environment will continue to influence how recreation services are offered. Major changes have occurred during the past century, but many more changes are guaranteed in the future. These changes will open the door for new opportunities that have yet to be considered. In addition, cooperation and partnerships will be needed across all sectors. Further, although the specialties within recreation services have somewhat different objectives, all must be focused on facilitating enjoyable and meaningful leisure experiences for people.

The potential of leisure in people's lives on a global basis is huge. A recreation services system is needed to ensure that activities provided are socially, economically, and environmentally sustainable. The challenge exists for recreation professionals to provide inclusive and sustainable opportunities into the 21st century.

References

Adams, M., Bell, L. A., & Griffin, P. (Eds.). (1997). *Teaching for diversity and social justice*. New York: Routledge.

Alberti, L. B. (1969). *The family in renaissance Florence*. Trans. R. N. Watkins. Columbia, SC: University of South Carolina Press. (Work originally published 1443.)

American Association of Leisure and Recreation. (2003). *Leisure education in the schools: Taskforce on leisure education in the schools*. Reston, VA: American Alliance for Health, Physical Education, Recreation, and Dance.

Astin, A. W. (1993). *What matters in college? Four critical years revisited*. San Francisco: Jossey-Bass.

Austin, M. M., & Vidal-Naquet, P. (1977). *Economic and social history of ancient Greece: An introduction*. Trans. M. M. Austin. Berkeley: University of California Press.

Bailey, S. M. (1993). The current status of gender equity research in American schools. *Educational Psychologist, 28*(4), 321–339.

Barner, R. (1996). The new millennium workplace: Seven changes that will challenge managers and workers. *The Futurist, 30*(2), 14–18.

Beard, E. (2012, May). Rejuvenating the senior center. Parks & Recreation, pp. 41–45.

Begun, B. (2000, January 1). USA: The way we'll live then. *Newsweek*, 34–35.

Bialeschki, M. D. (1992). We said "Why not?": A historical perspective on women's outdoor pursuits. *Journal of Physical Education, Recreation, and Dance, 63*(2), 52–55.

Bogle, T., Havitz, M. E., & Dimanche, F. (1992). Sector biases in adults' recreation fitness facility selection. *Journal of Park and Recreation Administration, 10*(3), 49–74.

Bolino, A. C. (1998). *From depression to war: American society in transition—1939*. Westport, CT: Praeger.

Braden, D. R. (1988). *Leisure and entertainment in America*. Dearborn, MI: Henry Ford Museum and Greenfield Village.

Bronfenbrenner, U. (1979). *The ecology of human development*. Cambridge, MA: Harvard University Press.

Brooks, C. (1988). Armschair quarterbacks. *American Demographics, 10*(3), 28–31.

Brown, D. R., Heath, G. W, & Levin Martin, S. (Eds). (2006). *Promoting physical activity: A guide for community action*. Champaign, IL: Human Kinetics.

Bullaro, J., & Edginton, C. (1986). *Commercial leisure services: Managing for profit*. New York: MacMillan.

Burke, P. (1987). *The Renaissance*. Atlantic Highlands, NJ: Humanities Press International.

Campbell, A., Converse, P. E., & Rodgers, W. L. (1976). *The quality of American life: Perceptions, evaluations, and satisfactions*. New York: Sage.

Carcopino, J. (1940). *Daily life in ancient Rome: The people and the city at the height of the empire*. Trans. E. O. Lorie. New Haven, CT: Yale University Press.

Carpenter, G., & Blandy, D. (Eds.). (2008). *Arts and cultural programming: A leisure perspective*. Champaign, IL: Human Kinetics.

Ceram, C. (1971). *Gods, graves and scholars*, quoted in Kraus, R. (1971). *Recreation and leisure in modern society*. Englewood Cliffs, NJ: Prentice-Hall.

Chamoux, F. (1965). *The civilization of Greece*. Trans. W. S. Macguinness. New York: Simon and Schuster.

Chubb, M., & Chubb, H. (1981). *One third of our time*. New York: John Wiley & Sons.

Cipolla, C. (1994). *Before the Industrial Revolution: European society and economy, 1000–1700* (3rd ed.). New York: W. W. Norton.

Clawson, M., & Knetsch, J. L. (1966). *Economics of outdoor recreation*. Baltimore: The Johns Hopkins Press.

Cousins, N. (1979). *Anatomy of an illness*. New York: Norton.

Crompton, J. L. (2007). *Community benefits and repositioning: The keys to park and recreation's future viability*. Ashburn, VA: National Recreation and Park Association.

Csikzentmihalyi, M. (1975). *Beyond boredom and anxiety: The experience of play*. San Francisco: Jossey-Bass.

Csikzentmihalyi, M. (1990). *Flow: The psychology of optimal experience.* New York: Harper & Row.

Davis, J. M. (1978). Leadership in leisure service. In H. Ibrahim & F. Martin (Eds.), *Leisure: An introduction.* Los Alomitos, CA: Hwong Publishing.

de Toqueville, A. (1945). *Democracy in America.* New York: Vintage Books. (Original work published in 1835.)

de Vries, J. (1994). The Industrial Revolution and the industrious revolution. *Journal of Economic History, 54,* 249–270.

Dewey, J. (1939). *Democracy and education.* New York: McGraw-Hill.

Dickason, J. (1985). 1906: A pivotal year for the playground movement. *Parks & Recreation, 20*(8), 40–45.

Driver, B. L., Brown, P. J., & Peterson, G. L. (1991). *Benefits of leisure.* State College, PA: Venture Publishing, Inc.

Driver, B. L., Dustin, D., Baltic, T., Elsner, G., & Peterson, G. (Eds.). (1996). *Nature and the Human Spirit.* State College, PA: Venture Publishing, Inc.

Dulles, F. (1965). *Recreation in America.* New York: Appleton-Century Crofts.

Dumazedier, J. (1967). *Toward a leisure society.* New York: The Free Press.

Dustin, D. L., & Goodale, T. L. (1999). Reflections on recreation, park, and leisure studies. In E. L. Jackson & T. L. Burton (Eds.), *Leisure studies: Prospects for the twenty-first century* (pp. 477—486). State College, PA: Venture Publishing, Inc.

Dustin, D. L., & Schwab, K. (2008). Consider the Kirtland's Warbler. *Schole, 23*: 1–8.

Eccles, J., & Gootman, J. A. (Eds.) (2002). *Community programs to promote youth development.* Washington, DC: National Academy Press.

Edwards, M., & Peachey, J. (2010). Irreconcilable differences or vibrant habitat? An examination of sport management's perceived invasion of recreation's nest. *Sport Management Education Journal, 4*: 18–30.

Ellis, G., & Witt, P. (1991). Conceptualization and measurement of leisure: Making the abstract concrete. In T. Goodale & P. Witt (Eds.), *Recreation and leisure: Issues in an era of change* (pp. 377–396). State College, PA: Venture Publishing, Inc.

Erikson, E. (1968). *Identity: Youth and crisis.* New York: W.W. Norton & Company.

Fain, G. S. (1991). Moral leisure. In G. S. Fain (Ed.), *Leisure and ethics: Reflections on the philosophy of leisure* (pp. 7–30). Reston, VA: American Association for Leisure and Recreation.

Fennell, D. A. (1999). *Ecotourism.* London: Routledge.

Ferguson, W. K. (1940). *The Renaissance*. New York: Holt, Rinehart, & Winston.

Ferguson, W. K. (1968). The interpretation of the Renaissance. In P. O. Kristeller & P. P. Wiener (Eds.), *Renaissance essays* (pp. 61–73). New York: Harper Torchbooks.

Fraser, A. (1966). *A history of toys*. New York: Delacorte Press.

Freud, S. (1964). *The standard edition of the complete psychological works of Sigmund Freud*. London: Hogarth Press.

Garin, E. (1965). *Italian humanism: Philosophy and civic life in the Renaissance*. Trans. P. Munz. New York: Harper & Row.

Gibson, H. (2008). Comment on Dustin and Schwab article "Consider the Kirtland's Warbler." *Schole, 23*: 17–20.

Gittell, R., & Vidal, A. (1998). *Community organizing: Building social capital as a development strategy*. Thousand Oaks, CA: Sage.

Godbey, G. (1989). Implications of recreation and leisure research for professionals. In E. L. Jackson and T. L. Burton (Eds.), *Understanding leisure and recreation: Mapping the past, Charting the future* (pp. 613–628). State College, PA: Venture Publishing, Inc.

Godbey, G. (1997). *Leisure and leisure services in the 21st century*. State College, PA: Venture Publishing, Inc.

Goetz, H. W. (1993). *Life in the Middle Ages from the seventh to the thirteenth century.* Trans. A. Wimmer. S. Rowan, (Ed.). Notre Dame, IN: University of Notre Dame Press.

Goodale, T. L., & Godbey, G. C. (1988). *The evolution of leisure*. State College, PA: Venture Publishing, Inc.

Green, B. C. (2005). Building sport programs to optimize athlete recruitment, retention, and transition: Toward a normative theory of sport development. *Journal of Sport Management, 19*, 233–253.

Gutman, H. G. (1977). *Work, culture, and society in industrializing America*. New York: Vintage Books.

Haggard, L. M., & Williams, D. R. (1991). Self-identity benefits of leisure activities. In B. L. Driver, P. J. Brown, & G. L. Peterson (Eds.), *Benefits of leisure* (pp. 103–119). State College, PA: Venture Publishing, Inc.

Haggard, L. M., & Williams, D. R. (1992). Leisure symbols of the self. *Journal of Leisure Research, 24*(1), 1–18.

Hemingway, J. L. (1988). Leisure and civility: Reflections on a Greek ideal. *Leisure Sciences, 10*, 179–191.

Hemingway, J. L. (1999). Leisure, social capital, and democratic citizenship. *Journal of Leisure Research, 31*, 150–165.

Hendee, J., Stankey, G., & Lucas, R. (1990). *Wilderness management*. Golden, CO: North American Press.

Henderson, K. A. (1981). A converging view of leisure and education. *Lifelong Learning: The Adult Years, 5*(12), 6–8.

Henderson, K. A. (1992). Invisible pioneers? The impact of women in the Recreation Movement. *Leisure Sciences, 14*, 139–153.

Henderson, K. A. (1993). A feminist analysis of selected professional recreation literature about girls/women from 1907–1990. *Journal of Leisure Research, 25*(2), 165–181.

Henderson, K. A. (1993). Rediscovering spirituality. *Camping Magazine, 65*(4), 23–27.

Henderson, K. A. (1997). Just recreation: Ethics, gender, and equity. *Journal of Park and Recreation Administration, 15*(2), 16–31.

Henderson, K. A. (2010). The future of leisure studies: The sky is falling? *Leisure Sciences, 32*(4), 391–400.

Henderson, K. A. (2011). A continuum of leisure studies and professional specialties: What if no connections exist? *World Leisure Journal, 53*(2), 76–90.

Henderson, K. A., & Bialeschki, M. D. (2010). *Evaluating leisure services: Making enlightened decisions* (3rd ed.). State College, PA: Venture Publishing, Inc.

Henderson, K. A., Bialeschki, M. D., Hemingway, J., Hodges, J. S., Kivel, B., & Sessoms, H. D. (2001). *Introduction to recreation and leisure services* (8th ed.). State College, PA: Venture Publishing, Inc.

Henderson, K. A., & Rannells, J. S. (1988). Farm women and the meaning of work and leisure: An oral history perspective. *Leisure Sciences, 10*(1), 41–50.

Hooyman, N., & Kiyak, H. A. (1999). *Social gerontology: A multidisciplinary perspective.* (5th ed.). Boston: Allyn & Bacon.

Hoschild, A., & Machung, A. (1990). *The second shift.* New York: Viking Press.

Huizinga, J. (1949). *Homo ludens: A study of the play element in culture.* London: Routledge and Kegan Paul, Ltd.

Hunnicutt, B. K. (1985). Economic constraints on leisure. In M. G. Wade (Ed.), *Constraints on leisure* (pp. 243–286). Springfield, IL: Charles C. Thomas.

Hunnicutt, B. K. (1988). *Work without end: Abandoning shorter hours for the right to work.* Philadelphia: Temple University Press.

Ibrahim, H., & Cordes, K. (1993). *Outdoor recreation.* Madison, WI: Brown & Benchmark Publishers.

Jackson, E. L., & Scott, D. (1999). Constraints to leisure. In E. L. Jackson & T. L. Burton (Eds.), *Leisure studies: Prospects for the twenty-first century* (pp. 299–321). State College, PA: Venture Publishing, Inc.

Jackson, R. (1997). *Making special events fit in the 21st century.* Champaign, IL: Sagamore Publishing.

Jardine, L. (1996). *Worldly goods: A new history of the Renaissance.* New York: W. W. Norton.

Jensen, C. R. (1977). *Leisure and recreation: Introduction and overview.* Philadelphia, PA: Lea and Febiger.

Kaplan, S. (1995). The restorative benefits of nature: Toward an integrative framework. *Journal of Environmental Psychology, 15,* 169–182.

Kelly, J. R. (1978). Situational and social factors in leisure decisions. *Pacific Sociological Review, 21,* 313–330.

Kivel, P., & Kivel, B. (2000). Beyond cultural competence: Building allies and sharing power in recreational programs. In M. T. Allison and I. E. Schneider (Eds.), *Diversity and the recreation profession* (pp. 263–277). State College, PA: Venture Publishing, Inc.

Kleiber, D. A. (2000). The neglect of relaxation. *Journal of Leisure Research, 32,* 82–86.

Kleiber, D. A., Walker, G. J., & Mannell, R. C. (2011). *The social psychology of leisure.* State College, PA: Venture Publishing, Inc.

Knapp, R., & Hartsoe, C. (1979). *Play for America.* Arlington, VA: National Recreation and Park Association.

Kunstler, R. (1993). Serving the homeless through recreation programs. *Park and Recreation, 28*(9), 16–22.

Leffert N., Benson, P. L., Scales, P. C., Sharma, A. R., Drake, D. R., & Blyth, D. A. (2006). Developmental assets: Measurement and prediction of risk behaviors among adolescents. *Applied Developmental Science, 2*(4), 209–230.

Le Goff, J. (1980). *Time, work, and culture in the middle ages.* Trans. A. Goldhammer. Chicago: University of Chicago Press.

Leopold, A. (1949). *A Sand County almanac.* New York: Oxford University Press.

Lerner, R. M., Lerner, J. V., Almerigi, J., & Theokas, C. (2005). Positive youth development: A view of the issues. *Journal of Early Adolescence, 25*(1), 10–16.

Louv, R. (2005). *Last child in the woods: Saving our children from nature-deficit disorder.* Chapel Hill, NC: Algonquin Books.

Mahon, F., Mactavish, J., Mahon, M., & Searle, M. (1995). *Older adults with mental disabilities: Exploring the meanings of independence.* Winnipeg, MB: University of Manitoba.

Manville, P. B. (1990). *The origins of citizenship in ancient Athens.* Princeton, NJ: Princeton University Press.

Marasco, D. (n.d.). *Jackie goes to Wrigley.* (http://pubweb.acns.nwu.edu/~dmarasco/jrwrig.html).

Martin, T. R. (1996). *Ancient Greece: From prehistoric to hellenistic times.* New Haven, CT: Yale University Press.

Masteralexis, L. P., Barr, C. A., & Hums, M. A. (2011). *Principles and practice of sport management.* Sudbury, MA: Jones & Bartlett Publishers.

McDaniel, W. B. (1924). *Roman private life and its survivals.* Boston: Marshall Jones.

McLeroy, K. R., Bibeau, D., Steckler, A., & Glanz, K. (1988). An ecological perspective on health promotion programs. *Heath Education Quarterly, 15,* 351–377.

Mead, G. H. (1963). Mind, self, and society. In C. W. Morris (Ed.), *Perspectives in the social order* (pp. 139–141). New York: McGraw-Hill.

Meyer, H., & Brightbill, C. (1964). *Community recreation* (3rd ed.). Englewood Cliffs, NJ: Prentice-Hall.

Molotch, H. (1988). The rest room and equal opportunity. *Sociological Forum, 3*(1), 128–132.

Morris, D., & Walls, M. (2009). Climate change and outdoor recreation resources. Washington, DC: Resources for the Future.

National Recreation and Park Association. (1968). *Supply/demand study Professional and pre-professional recreation and park occupations.* Washington, DC: Author.

Neulinger, J. (1981). *To leisure: An introduction.* Boston, MA: Allyn & Bacon.

Owen, J. D. (1976). Workweeks and leisure: An analysis of trends, 1948–75. *Monthly Labor Review, 99*(4), 3–8.

Patterson, C. (1994). The case against Neaira and the public ideology of the Athenian family. In Boegehold, A. L., & Scafuro, A. C. (Eds.), *Athenian identity and civic ideology* (pp. 199–216). Baltimore, MD: Johns Hopkins University Press.

Payne, L. L. (2002). Progress and challenges in repositioning leisure as a core component of health. *Journal of Park and Recreation Administration, 20*(4), 1–11.

Piaget, J. (1962). *Play, dreams and imitation in childhood.* New York: W. W. Norton and Company.

Pieper, J. (1963). *Leisure: The basis of culture.* Trans. A. Dru. New York: New American Library.

Pullan, B. (1973). *A history of early Renaissance Italy: From the mid-thirteenth to the mid-fifteenth century.* London: Allen Lane/Penguin Books.

Putnam, R. (1993). *Making democracy work: Civic traditions in modern Italy.* Princeton, NJ: Princeton University Press.

Putnam, R. (2000). *Bowling alone: The collapse and revival of American community*. New York: Simon and Schuster.

Rhode, D. L. (Ed.). (1990). *Theoretical perspectives on sexual difference*. New Haven: Yale University Press.

Rioux, M. H. (1993). Rights, justice, power: An agenda for change. In M. Nagler & E. J. Kemp (Eds.), *Perspectives on disability* (2nd ed.). Palo Alto, CA: Health Markets Research, pp. 515–523.

Roberts, S. (Feb 21, 2008). Most children still live in two-parent homes, Census Bureau reports. *New York Times*. Retrieved from www.nytimes.com/2008/02/21/us/21census.html

Robinson, J. P., & Godbey, G. (1999). *Time for life: The surprising ways Americans use their time* (2nd ed.). University Park, PA: Pennsylvania State University Press.

Rose, J., & Dustin, D. (2009). The neoliberal assault on the public university: The case of recreation, park and leisure research. *Leisure Sciences, 31*, 397–402.

Salamon, L. M. (1999). *America's nonprofit sector: A primer*. New York: Foundation Center.

Sallis, J. F., Bauman, A., & Pratt, M. (1998). Environmental and policy interventions to promote physical activity. *American Journal of Preventive Medicine, 15*(4), 379–397.

Schmader, S. W., & Jackson, R. (1997). *Special events: Inside and out*. Champaign, IL: Sagamore Publishing.

Schor, J. (1991). *The overworked American: The unexpected decline of leisure*. New York: Basic Books.

Schwab, K., Timmerman, D., Wells, M., & Dustin, D. (under review). Choosing sport management as a college major. *Schole*.

Sessoms, H. D. (1990). On becoming a profession: Requirements and strategies. *Journal of Park and Recreation Administration, 8*(4), 33–42.

Sessoms, H. D. (1993). *Eight decades of leadership development. A history of programs of professional preparation in parks & recreation 1909–1989*. Arlington, VA: National Recreation and Park Association.

Sessoms, H. D., & Henderson, K. A. (2009). *The noble experiment: A history of NRPA*. Champaign, IL: Sagamore Publishing.

Sessoms, H. D., & Orthner, D. (1992). Our growing invisible populations. *Parks and Recreation, 27*(8), 62–65.

Shaw, S. (2008). Family leisure and changing ideologies of parenthood. *Sociology Compass, 2*, 688–703.

Sheffield, E. (2012, July). Five trends shaping tomorrow today. *Parks & Recreation*, pp. 16–17.

Sherlock, J. (1999). *The fifties: A brief history.* (http://www.joesherlock.com/fifties.html).

Snodgrass, A. (1980). *Archaic Greece: The age of experiment.* Berkeley: University of California Press.

Stebbins, R. A. (1982). Serious leisure: A conceptual statement. *Pacific Sociological Review, 25,* 251–272.

Stebbins, R. A. (1999). Serious leisure. In E. L. Jackson & T. L. Burton (Eds.), *Leisure studies: Prospects for the twenty-first century* (pp. 69–79). State College, PA: Venture Publishing, Inc.

Stebbins, R. A. (2011). Leisure studies: The road ahead. *World Leisure Journal, 53*(1), 3–10.

Stokols, D. (1992). Establishing and maintaining healthy environments. *American Psychologist, 47*(6), 6–22.

Storrmann, W. (1996). Recreation's role in community development. *Journal of Applied Recreation Research, 21,* 143–164.

Stubbs, R. A. (1998). A recipe for nonprofit success: Managing the linkages and key elements of successful organizations. *Fund Raising Management, 28*(11), 17–21.

Sugrue, T. J. (1996). *The origins of urban crisis: Race and inequality in postwar Detroit.* Princeton, NJ: Princeton University Press.

Tedrick, T., & Henderson, K. A. (1989). *Volunteers in leisure: A management perspective.* Reston, VA: AAHPERD.

Thompson, E. P. (1967). Time, work-discipline, and industrial capitalism. *Past and Present, 38,* 56–97.

Toner, J. P. (1995). *Leisure and ancient Rome.* Cambridge, MA: Polity Press with Basil Blackwell.

Tuan, Y. (1977). *Space and place: The perspective of experience.* Minneapolis, MN: University of Minnesota Press.

U.S. Department of Labor. (1980). *Exchanging earnings for leisure: Findings of an exploratory national survey on work time preferences.* Washington, DC: U.S. Government Printing Office.

Walvin, J. (1978). *Leisure and society 1830–1950.* London: Longman.

Warren, K. (1996). Educating for environmental justice. *Journal of Experiential Education, 19*(3), 135–140.

Weber, M. (1930). *The Protestant ethic and the spirit of capitalism.* Trans T. Parsons. London: Unwin Hyman.

Wellman, D., Dustin, D., Henderson, K. A., & Moore, R. (2008). *Service living: Building community through public parks and recreation.* State College, PA: Venture Publishing, Inc.

Whitman, T. L., Merluzzi, T. V., & White, R. D. (1999). *Life-span perspectives on health and illness.* Mahwah, NJ: Lawrence Erlbaum.

Williams, S. (1998). *Tourism geography*. London: Routledge.

Wilson, A., & Wilson, P. (1994). *Theme parks, leisure centres, zoos, and aquaria*. New York: John Wiley and Sons, Inc.

World Leisure. (2005). *Charter for Leisure*. Retrieved from: http://www. worldleisure.org

Zabriskie, R. B., & McCormick, B. P. (2001). The influences of family leisure patterns on perceptions of family functioning. *Family Relations, 50,* 281–289.

Zill, N., Morrison, D., & Coiro, M. (1993). Long-term effects of parental divorce on parent-child relationships: Adjustment and achievement in early adulthood. *Journal of Family Psychology, 7*(1), 91–103.

Zuefle, D. M. (1999, September). The spirituality of recreation. *Parks & Recreation*, pp. 28–33, 48, 197.

Index

Other Books by Venture Publishing, Inc.

Reference Manual for Writing Rehabilitation Therapy Treatment Plans
   by Penny Hogberg and Mary Johnson
Service Living: Building Community through Public Parks and Recreation
   by Doug Wellman, Dan Dustin, Karla Henderson, and Roger Moore
A Social Psychology of Leisure, Second Edition
   by Douglas A. Kleiber, Gordon J. Walker, and Roger C. Mannell
Special Events and Festivals: How to Organize, Plan, and Implement
   by Angie Prosser and Ashli Rutledge
The Sportsman's Voice: Hunting and Fishing in America
   by Mark Damian Duda, Martin F. Jones, and Andrea Criscione
Survey Research and Analysis: Applications in Parks, Recreation, and Human Dimensions
   by Jerry Vaske
Taking the Initiative: Activities to Enhance Effectiveness and Promote Fun
   by J. P. Witman
Therapeutic Recreation and the Nature of Disabilities
   by Kenneth E. Mobily and Richard D. MacNeil
Therapeutic Recreation: Cases and Exercises, Second Edition
   by Barbara C. Wilhite and M. Jean Keller
Therapeutic Recreation in Health Promotion and Rehabilitation
   by John Shank and Catherine Coyle
Therapeutic Recreation Practice: A Strengths Approach
   by Lynn Anderson and Linda Heyne